INTERSECTIONALITY IN EDUCATIONAL RESEARCH

Additional titles in the **Engaged Research and Practice for Social Justice in Education series:**

Research, Actionable Knowledge, and Social Change
Reclaiming Social Responsibility Through Research Partnerships
Edward P. St. John

Reflection in Action
A Handbook for Student Affairs Faculty and Staff
Kimberly A. Kline

Critical Action Research
A Guide for Students and Practitioners
Leticia Bustillos and Edlyn Peña
Publication date: Spring 2016

Transforming Understandings of Diversity in Higher Education
Demography, Democracy, and Discourse
Penny A. Pasque, Noe Ortega, Maria Ting, and John C. Burkhardt
Publication date: Fall 2016

Using Action Inquiry in Education Reform
A Guide
Edward P. St. John, Kim Lijana, and Glenda Musoba
Publication date: Fall 2016

Engaged Research and Practice
Higher Education and the Pursuit of the Public Good
Betty Overton-Adkins, Penny A. Pasque, and John C. Burkhardt
Publication date: Winter 2016

Intersectionality in Educational Research

Edited by Dannielle Joy Davis, Rachelle J. Brunn-Bevel, and James L. Olive

Foreword by Susan R. Jones
Series Foreword by Penny A. Pasque

STERLING, VIRGINIA

COPYRIGHT © 2015 BY
STYLUS PUBLISHING, LLC

Published by Stylus Publishing, LLC
22883 Quicksilver Drive
Sterling, Virginia 20166-2102

Library of Congress Cataloging-in-Publication Data
The CIP data for this title has been applied for.
Davis, Dannielle Joy, 1974-
  Intersectionality in educational research / Dannielle Joy Davis,
Rachelle J. Brunn Bevel & James L. Olive ; foreword by Susan
Jones.
    pages cm. -- (Actionable research for social justice in education
and society)
    Includes bibliographical references and index.
  ISBN 978-1-62036-095-8 (cloth : alk. paper)
  ISBN 978-1-62036-096-5 (pbk. : alk. paper)
  ISBN 978-1-62036-097-2 (library networkable e-edition)
  ISBN (invalid) 978-1-62036-098-9 (consumer e-edition)
  1. Education--Research.   2. Education--Research--Social aspects.
  3. Interdisciplinary research.   I. Title.
   LB1028.D28 2014
   370.72--dc23
                                                            2015005171
  ISBN 978-1-62036-095-8 (cloth)
  ISBN 978-1-62036-096-5 (paper)
  ISBN 978-1-62036-097-2 (library networkable e-edition)
  ISBN 978-1-62036-098-9 (consumer e-edition)

Printed in the United States of America

All first editions printed on acid-free paper
that meets the American National Standards Institute
Z39-48 Standard.

Bulk Purchases

Quantity discounts are available for use in workshops and for
staff development.
Call 1-800-232-0223

First Edition, 2015

10   9   8   7   6   5   4   3   2

Dannielle Joy Davis

To my amazing son, Bryce Davis, and my mother, Linda Davis: Thank you both for bringing joy and wonder to my life.

Rachelle J. Brunn-Bevel

For my parents, Albert and Celia Brunn. Thank you for always supporting and believing in me.

James L. Olive

To my husband, Dan, my son, Bryce, and my daughter, Dayja: Thank you three for your ongoing love, support, and encouragement in all my endeavors. You continue to make me a better man.

CONTENTS

Foreword

In a recent article, Patricia Hill Collins (2012) traces her own scholarly trajectory by returning to what she refers to as two social locations (e.g., her six years of involvement with the community schools movement and her 23-year career as a professor in an African American studies department). She then uses the significance of these two social locations to point the way to her current scholarly commitments. She discusses intersectionality as a "travelling theory . . . being used across disciplinary boundaries and in different national contexts, as well as across boundaries that separate scholarly knowledge from the everyday knowledge of social activists" (p. 21). Related, and perhaps as a result, she notes the rush to define *intersectionality*, which diminishes the complexity intersectionality is designed to capture. Collins (2012) writes:

> But what exactly is intersectionality? Because intersectionality constitutes the term currently applied to a diverse set of practices, interpretations, methodologies, and political orientations, we cannot assume that we are studying a fixed body of knowledge, methodological framework, or theoretical orientation. Is intersectionality a concept? Is it a paradigm, a heuristic device? Or is it a theory? (pp. 21–22)

Indeed, as Carbado, Crenshaw, Mays, and Tomlinson (2013) point out, it is not so important to define what intersectionality *is*, as "to assess what intersectionality *does*" (p. 304).

In their volume, *Intersectionality in Educational Research*, editors Dannielle Joy Davis, Rachelle J. Brunn-Bevel, and James L. Olive put intersectionality to work in and across educational contexts and a diverse array of research topics. Responding in part to McCall's (2005) observation that "there has been little discussion of *how* to study intersectionality, that is, of its methodology" (p. 1775), the chapter authors in this edited volume each discuss how they deploy intersectionality (e.g., as a research paradigm, framework, theoretical consideration, methodology, analytic lens, etc.) in relation to the empirical investigation of a particular topic. This approach provides readers with varying conceptualizations of intersectionality; applications of intersectionality to research projects and methodological strategies; and exposure to topics that span the educational spectrum from kindergarten through grade 12, higher education, and institutional contexts. This comprehensive approach, as the editors point out, is unique in its focus and scope across educational contexts.

Drawing upon the foundational work of Kimberlé Crenshaw, intersectional scholars have identified four characteristics that define *intersectional research and analysis*:

1. centering the lived experiences of individuals, and specifically those of people of color and other marginalized groups;
2. complicating identity and examining both individual and group identities;
3. exploring identity salience as influenced by systems of power and privilege and unveiling power in interconnected structures of inequality; and
4. advancing a larger goal of promoting social justice and social change (Collins, 2007; Dill & Zambrana, 2009; Jones, 2009).

Research informed by intersectionality, or intersectional research, ought to look different from research conducted without this analytic lens. That is, researchers interested in conducting intersectional research need to consider what it means to do intersectional research. For example, how do epistemological assumptions undergirding intersectionality differ from other worldviews (e.g., postpositivism or constructivism)? What difference does this make in a research design? What constitutes intersectional interview questions? Or survey items? What data analysis strategies lend themselves to intersectionality? How do researchers study multiple variables at the same time rather than controlling for or holding them constant? In an article discussing the application of intersectionality to research in psychology, Cole (2009) identified three questions researchers might ask to address intersectional questions: "Who is included within this category?" "What role does inequality play?" and "Where are the similarities [across social categories]?" (p. 3). These are the important questions and considerations, among others, researchers using intersectionality need to think through as they embark upon, and claim, intersectional research. In other words, scholarship that is good, complex, and nuanced is not necessarily intersectional research (Nash, personal communication, January 29, 2015).

It is important to point out that as interest in intersectionality has exploded in educational contexts (e.g., recently published text edited by Mitchell, Simmons, and Greyerbiehl, 2014), running the risk of its becoming so popular as to become a "buzzword" (Davis, 2008, p. 75) in educational lexicon, and critiques point to the appropriation of intersectionality by those with little investment in its historical origins and commitments (e.g., Black feminists and social change). Indeed, as Nash (2008) poignantly suggests,

> While intersectionality has worked to disrupt cumulative approaches to identity (i.e., race + gender + sexuality + class = complex identity), and to problematize social processes of categorization through strategic deployments of marginalized subjects' experiences, intersectional projects often replicate precisely the approaches that they critique. (p. 6)

Nash goes on to raise a provocative question, one that I think plagues educational research claiming to be intersectional, and that is, "Who is intersectional?" She suggests that an "unresolved theoretical dispute makes it unclear whether intersectionality is a theory of marginalized subjectivity or a generalized theory of identity" (p. 10).

Readers will see reflected in the chapters in *Intersectionality in Educational Research* both the core characteristics of intersectionality and the tensions that necessarily emerge when either conducting intersectional research or applying the tenets of intersectionality to empirical investigations. This is not a critique of the volume, but more an acknowledgment that intersectional work is hard and comes with no formulaic or universal strategies to follow. In these chapters it is clear what draws researchers to intersectionality as an analytic that animates work that enables, in fact insists upon, both micro and macro analyses; that interrogates structures of inequality and power; and that advances social change. The breadth of topics covered also demonstrates how attention to intersectionality illuminates the experiences of those individuals and groups previously underrepresented in educational research. Educational contexts are as entangled in these institutional structures as in others, so a specific focus on educational experiences and outcomes is both warranted and critical to the success of the educational enterprise as well as the lives within it. *Intersectionality in Educational Research* contributes much to these efforts and to advancing an understanding of the applications of intersectionality to educational inquiry.

Susan R. Jones
The Ohio State University
Columbus, Ohio

References

Carbado, D. W., Crenshaw, K. W., Mays, V. M., & Tomlinson, B. (2013). Intersectionality: Mapping the movements of a theory. *Du Bois Review, 10*(2), 303–312.

Cole, E. R. (2009). Intersectionality and research in psychology. *American Psychologist, 64*(3), 170–180.

Collins, P. H. (2007). Pushing the boundaries or business as usual? Race, class, and gender studies and sociological inquiry. In C. J. Calhoun (Ed.), *Sociology in America: A history* (pp. 572–604). Chicago: University of Chicago Press.

Collins, P. H. (2012). Looking back, moving ahead: Scholarship in service to social justice. *Gender & Society, 26*(1), 14–22.

Davis, K. (2008). Intersectionality as buzzword: A sociology of science perspective on what makes a feminist theory successful. *Feminist Theory, 9,* 67–85.

Dill, B. T., & Zambrana, R. E. (2009). Critical thinking about inequality: An emerging lens. In B. T. Dill & R. E. Zambrana (Eds.), *Emerging intersections: Race, class, and gender in theory, policy, and practice* (pp. 1–21). New Brunswick, NJ: Rutgers University Press.

Jones, S. R. (2009). Constructing identities at the intersections: An autoethnographic exploration of multiple dimensions of identity. *Journal of College Student Development, 50,* 287–304.

McCall, L. (2005). The complexity of intersectionality. *Signs: Journal of Women in Culture and Society, 30,* 1771–1800.

Mitchell, D., Jr., Simmons, C. Y., & Greyerbiehl, L. A. (Eds.). (2014). *Intersectionality & higher education: Theory, research, and praxis.* New York: Peter Lang.

Nash, J. C. (2008). Re-thinking intersectionality. *Feminist Review, 89,* 1–15.

Series Foreword

In *Intersectionality in Educational Research*, the editors Dannielle Joy Davis, Rachelle J. Brunn-Bevel, and James L. Olive—together with the chapter authors—reflect on the existing literature on intersectionality across an array of fields and disciplines as well as advance conceptualizations of intersectionality in educational research toward social change. To be sure, educational research is situated to play an instrumental role in addressing injustices, yet it often reifies current inequities and fails to foster needed social change. The editors and contributors directly confront these issues by defining and addressing intersectionality in educational research through various theoretical, methodological and topical arenas.

As Hardiman, Jackson, and Griffin (2013) point out, "intersectionality suggests that markers of difference do not act independent of one another. Instead, our various social identities interrelate to negate the possibility of a unitary or universal experience of any one manifestation of oppression" (p. 30). However, the interdisciplinary term *intersectionality* is used in various contexts, yet often without theoretical, historical, methodological, and reflexive understandings of the complexities of the term. As such, this book is of paramount importance to educational research across fields and disciplines as it provides in-depth historical and contemporary insights into the term as well as contributes to content knowledge and methodological approaches in this critical area of inquiry.

Importantly, this volume incorporates qualitative, quantitative, and mixed methods approaches in order to explore the multiple manifestations of intersectionality. To use one example, the qualitative methodologies offered throughout this book include grounded theory, phenomenology, case study, autoethnography, discourse analysis, scholarly personal narrative, and so on. As Hardiman et al. (2013) and many chapter authors within this book discuss as a foundational principle, intersectionality is nonadditive; one cannot simply add one identity on top of another and name it intersectionality. It "requires us to examine all social locations simultaneously—and that degree of complexity is daunting and frequently impractical" (Stewart & McDermott, 2004, p. 537), particularly when many methodologies were not intentionally crafted to explore the intersections of social groups and social structures, including the individual and systemic oppressions that permeate society. As such, this book offers relevant intersectionality definitions and findings as it explores often "daunting" innovations in methodologies; an important and timely contribution to the field of education.

This is the third book in the Engaged Research and Practice for Social Justice in Education book series (St. John, Pasque, Bensimon, & Harper, Eds.), which focuses on informing policies, practices, and methodologies aimed at reducing inequalities within education and society. Books in this series advance the understanding of strategies for promoting social justice, including:

- *actionable research* generated by practitioners engaged in assessing causes of and experimenting with remedies to inequalities in opportunity (e.g., projects using the Equity Scorecard);
- *research informing reform*, including assessment and evaluation studies by researchers working in partnerships with educational and community organizations (e.g., projects using action inquiry);
- *methods and methodologies,* including works reconstructing theory, methodology and methods for advancing social justice through education reform; and
- *guidebooks* that inform the development of partnerships between researchers and practitioners engaged in problem-solving.

Intersectionality in Educational Research will be useful for scholars, instructors, graduate students, and practitioners who seek to explore intersectionality in educational theory, research, policy, and practice. Readers will benefit from the reflexive questions at the end of the book as they are designed to deepen thinking around intersectionality. These thoughtful questions help readers extend understandings regarding the complexities within the chapters and how they relate to systemic, institutional and individual oppression; research approaches; and lived experiences. This volume concludes on an invitational note—one that encourages readers to address educational inequities as we craft liberatory research designs, policies, and practices that center intersectionality in order to foster a new era of educational equity and social justice that directly impacts people's daily lives.

Penny A. Pasque, PhD
Brian E. and Sandra O'Brien Presidential Professor
University of Oklahoma

References

Hardiman, R., Jackson, B. W., & Griffin, P. (2013). Conceptual foundations. In M. Adams, W. J. Blumenfeld, C. Castañeda, H. W. Hackman, M. L. Peters & X. Zúñiga (Eds.), *Readings for diversity and social justice, (3rd ed., pp. 26–35).* New York, NY: Routledge.

Stewart, A. J., & McDermott, C. (2004). Gender in psychology. *Annual Review of Psychology, 55,* 519–544.

INTRODUCTION

Rachelle J. Brunn-Bevel, Dannielle Joy Davis, and James L. Olive

In March 2014, the U.S. Department of Education, Office for Civil Rights released four issue briefs using data from the 2011–2012 Civil Rights Data Collection (CRDC) surveys that highlight the continued racial inequality that American public school children face daily. The issue briefs focused on school discipline, early learning, college readiness, and teacher equity (Hsieh, 2014). First, let us turn to the school discipline findings, which seem to garner the most popular media attention. The school discipline issue brief documents widespread racial inequality at the very beginning of children's educational careers. Black children comprise 18% of preschool enrollment, but account for 48% of preschool children receiving more than one out-of-school suspension (U.S. Department of Education, Office for Civil Rights, 2014b). The early learning issue brief illustrates that Native Hawaiian, other Pacific Islander, American Indian, and Native Alaskan kindergarten students are held back or retained at almost twice the rate of White kindergarten students (U.S. Department of Education, Office for Civil Rights, 2014a).

Second, gender disparities are also readily apparent in these documents, and if one looks closer, inequality at the intersections of race, ethnicity, and gender is quite visible. For example, boys account for 61% of kindergartners retained for one year (U.S. Department of Education, Office for Civil Rights, 2014b). Additionally, boys, who comprise 54% of overall preschool enrollment, represent 79% of preschool children who have been suspended at least once (U.S. Department of Education, Office for Civil Rights, 2014b). However, Black girls have higher suspension rates than girls of any other race or ethnicity and most boys. Similarly, American Indian and Native Alaskan girls are suspended at higher rates than White girls or boys (U.S. Department of Education, Office for Civil Rights, 2014b).

Third, educational inequality is also evident at the collegiate level. Contemporary higher education serves a diverse global population, where the intersection of race, ethnicity, gender, sexual orientation, socioeconomic status, and ability levels shape the lenses of individuals within a campus community and their interactions with each other in that environment. For instance, when completing college, Black men graduate 22 percentage points below their White male peers, while Black women graduate 24 points below their White female counterparts (Bowen, Chingos, & McPherson, 2009). In sum, these disparities lead us to question how the intersecting elements of race, class, and gender—from preschool through the postsecondary experience—interact in shaping educational access, experiences, and outcomes.

This book seeks to advance understanding of intersectional theory and its application to research in education. This book will prove useful for policymakers and scholars and for training students. It will be particularly useful for those interested in intersectionality's theoretical contributions who are seeking practical research methods to advance certain lines of inquiry. Research using intersectional theory enhances critical thinking skills and decision-making practices related to the intersections of race, class, gender, sexual orientation, religious background, ability, and other identities.

The scholars whose work appears in this volume use intersectional theory and research methods to work in fields and disciplines such as education, sociology, women's studies, ethnic studies, Africana studies, human development, higher education administration, leadership studies, and justice studies. This book illustrates how intersectional theory can be used in both quantitative and qualitative education research projects on college student access and success, faculty satisfaction and professional development, and K–12 educational issues, such as teachers' attitudes and behaviors about race and schools' influences on students' gender identity and expression. Our work is unique in that few books to date explicitly focus on how intersectionality theory can be applied to educational experiences and outcomes using appropriate research methods. The volume will be especially useful in research methods courses; sociology courses, such as the sociology of education and sociology of gender; women's studies courses, such as race, class, and gender; and education courses, such as contemporary issues in higher education, diversity and higher education, gender and education, and multicultural issues in education.

We hope that readers of this volume will complete three learning objectives. First, readers will learn the basic tenets of intersectionality and how it can be useful in education research. Second, readers will learn how intersectionality theory can be used to analyze both quantitative (large-scale survey) and qualitative (interview, participant observation, and ethnographic) data. Finally, readers will learn how intersectionality theory can be particularly useful for examining the experiences of diverse groups of students attending elementary schools, high schools, and colleges and universities, and faculty working at postsecondary institutions.

What Is Intersectionality?

Although they did not use the term *intersectionality*, the Combahee River Collective (1995) was the first to write about a particular brand of Black feminism that articulated how Black women were affected simultaneously by their race, gender, and class. However, the origins of intersectionality appeared much earlier (Bowleg, 2008; Cole, 2009). For example, Sojourner Truth's (1851) "Ain't I a Woman" speech, delivered at the Women's Convention in Akron, Ohio, exposed the limited application of the "cult of true womanhood" (Cott, 1977). Essentially the ideology didn't apply to her as a Black woman (Truth, 1851). The term *intersectionality*, and its theoretical framework, is most often credited to Crenshaw (1991, 1993) and was further expounded upon by Collins (2000) in her seminal work *Black Feminist Thought*. Since its inception in the early 1990s, intersectionality has been theorized in legal studies, ethnic studies, women's studies, and feminist literature, as well as in literature in sociology, psychology, education, and political science.

Crenshaw (1993) discusses three types of intersectionality—structural, political, and representational. Structural intersectionality "refer(s) to the way in which women of color are situated within overlapping structures of subordination" (p. 114). Political intersectionality highlights the tendency to ignore women of color in discussions about race or gender inequality (1993). As a result, women of color are either negatively affected or underserved by public policies. Representational intersectionality entails using both race and gender stereotypes to frame images of women of color (1993).

Collins (2000) and Andersen and Collins (2012) use a matrix of domination framework to understand the influence of race, class, and gender in people's lives. The matrix of domination emphasizes the importance of social structure and history (e.g., U.S. laws about what groups were allowed to intermarry in the early 1900s) for understanding how the intersection of race, class, and gender manifests differently in individual lives (Andersen & Collins, 2012). In explicating the concept of intersectionality, Andersen and Collins (2012) argue that structural arrangements in society result in different systems of privilege and advantage. In addition, they remind us that race, class, and gender affect the experiences of all groups, including those on the "top" and "bottom" of the social hierarchy. Browne and Misra (2003) also contend that studies of intersectionality need to move past an exclusive focus on women of color to examine the experiences of all groups. The contributors to this volume answer this call.

As Crenshaw (1991) notes, race and gender are not the only factors that are important in shaping people's identity and life outcomes. Class, sexuality, ethnicity, nationality, and age are also important aspects of identity that shape individuals' lives (Andersen & Collins, 2012; Collins, 2000; Crenshaw, 1991, 1993). Andersen and Collins (2012) emphasize that neither race, class, nor gender is universally more important than the others and warn against "ranking oppressions." The impact of each identity is situational and depends on each of the other categories.

In the *Emerging Intersections* anthology, Dill and Zambrana (2009) assert that intersectionality has four "theoretical interventions" (p. 1). These are drawing on the experiences of racial-ethnic minorities and other marginalized groups to create theory; highlighting both individual identities and within-group differences; demonstrating how the structural, disciplinary, hegemonic, and interpersonal domains of power work together to support inequality; and linking theory and practice to promote social change (pp. 5–13).

Choo and Ferree (2010) argue that sociologists should be "clear about which specific style of intersectional analysis they prefer" (p. 130). The authors discuss three styles (intersectionality as inclusion, as process, and as a complex system) that progress in their level of complexity. First, and likely the most familiar, style focuses on telling the stories of groups that have historically been marginalized in multiple ways (Choo & Ferree, 2010). Choo and Ferree (2010) remind researchers to interrogate the experiences of "unmarked" normative groups such as Whites, men, and members of the middle class. Second, the scholars underscore the importance of the interactional component (multiplication, not addition) of intersectionality at both the structural and individual levels. Last, they remind us to resist ranking inequalities and to focus instead on how race, class, and gender inequality mutually constitute each other and affect all institutions (Choo & Ferree, 2010).

Davis (2008) refers to intersectionality as "the interaction of multiple identities and experiences of exclusion and subordination" (p. 67). The theory calls for acknowledging the complexity and interaction of marginalized differences in the review, analysis, and interpretation of research. Similarly, Cole (2009) discusses implications for thinking about intersectionality at each stage of the research process. In her article, which focuses on psychological research, Cole emphasizes examining diversity within categories, interrogating structural inequality, and "seeking sites of commonality across difference" throughout the research process (2009, p. 175).

In a special issue of *Signs*, edited by Cho, Crenshaw, and McCall (2013), the editors contend that the "field of intersectional studies" has "three loosely defined sets of engagements" (p. 785). The first is to use intersectionality to frame a variety of different research projects and teaching endeavors (2013,

p. 785). The second interrogates "intersectionality as theory and methodology" (p. 785). Some scholars who adhere to this approach study how intersectionality has "traveled" within the academic disciplines. The third applies intersectionality to remedy social problems and advance the cause of social justice in our society (p. 786).

In 2013, the *Du Bois Review* also published a special issue dedicated to intersectionality, edited by Carbado, Crenshaw, Mays, and Tomlinson. In the editorial introduction, the scholars write, "Rooted in Black feminism and Critical Race Theory, intersectionality is a method and a disposition, a heuristic and analytic tool" (2013, p. 303). The editors outline themes that address the various movements of intersectionality. These themes include that intersectionality is not constrained to one particular set of issues, and that it does not belong exclusively to one discipline or apply only to the U.S. context (2013). The editors also discuss the critique that intersectionality has focused too much attention on Black women and highlight "the social movement dimensions of intersectionality" (p. 305).

Some scholars have focused more explicitly on intersectionality's methodological challenges. Hancock (2007) holds that in research, intersectionality includes six assumptions. The first assumption involves examining more than one axis of inequality (such as gender, class, or race). This is necessary to understand and eradicate complex social problems such as discrimination. The second assumption is that scholars should investigate the influence of race, class, and gender in their research projects. However, the association among race, class, and gender in any particular context must be tested empirically. The third assumption Hancock puts forth is that race, class, and gender are influential at both the personal and structural levels: "Such categories are simultaneously contested and enforced at the individual and institutional levels of analysis" (Hancock, 2007, p. 251). The fourth assumption states that "each category of difference has within-group diversity that sheds light on the way we think of groups as actors in politics and on the potential outcomes of any particular political intervention" (p. 251). The fifth assumption asserts that intersectional research must investigate complex race, class, and gender interactions at the micro and macro levels of analysis. Hancock's sixth and final assumption is that the utility of the intersectional framework necessitates a focus on the theory, methods, and practical application of a research project (Hancock, 2007).

In a more condensed explanation, Landry (2007) argues that the intersectional framework rests on two assumptions. The first, called simultaneity, states that race, class, and gender cannot be separated. Although these characteristics of individual identity are always present, all of them may not be relevant in every situation. The second assumption, called multiplicity, asserts that the relationship among race, class, and gender is interactive and not simply additive. In other words, the impact of the three categories is more than the sum of its parts. Landry (2007) concludes that both of these assumptions must be tested empirically. Indeed, Bowleg (2008) contends that adequately reflecting the interactive nature of race, class, and gender is particularly difficult methodologically. She argues that most qualitative and quantitative research tends to rely on an additive assumption—at least in the beginning stages of data collection and analysis (Bowleg, 2008).

Clarke and McCall (2013) argue that "it seems just as appropriate to define *intersectionality* by the process of doing research as it does to define it by whether or not it uses a definition of categories as mutually constituted, or some other traditional marker of an intersectional project" (p. 350). The authors note that researchers sometimes encounter and employ intersectionality later in a research project that begins by attempting to better understand and remedy a social problem (2013). At its roots, intersectional theory is about promoting social justice and social change (Carbado et al., 2013; Cho et al., 2013; Dill & Zambrana, 2009; Jones & Abes, 2013). "It [intersectionality] also provides an analytical framework for combining the different kinds of work that need to be included in the pursuit of social justice: advocacy, analysis, policy development, theorizing, and education" (Dill & Zambrana, 2009, p. 12). Thus, it is particularly fitting that our volume, *Intersectionality in Educational Research*, is included in the Engaged Research and Practice for Social Justice in Education book series.

Research on Intersectionality

Several books on intersectionality have been published in recent years. Strayhorn's (2013) *Living at the Intersections: Social Identities and Black Collegians* uses an intersectional lens to focus on Black students' college experiences. This volume makes a significant contribution to intersectional literature within the field of education. Bhopal and Preston's (2012) *Intersectionality and "Race" in Education* focuses on the United Kingdom and is primarily concerned with making theoretical advances in relation to racial identities through the use of qualitative methodologies such as ethnography and case studies. Dill and Zambrana's (2009) *Emerging Intersections: Race, Class, and Gender in Theory, Policy, and Practice* places emphasis on linking intersectional theory to social policy and practice. Five of the 10 essays in this text focus on education, while the remaining examine topics related to the labor market, poverty, and political participation. Landry's (2007) *Race, Gender, and Class: Theory and Methods of Analysis* is divided into three parts examining intersectional theory, qualitative approaches to intersectional analysis, and quantitative approaches to intersectional analysis. Five of the chapters in

Landry's book are specifically related to educational experiences and, of those five, only one, "Generalized Expectancies for Control Among High-School Students at the Intersection of Race, Class, and Gender" by Brett A. Magill (2007), explicitly applies intersection theory.

Lutz, Vivar, and Supik's (2011) *Framing Intersectionality: Debates on a Multi-Faceted Concept in Gender Studies* explores the use of intersectionality in Europe; however, none of the contributors discusses educational outcomes and experiences. Similarly, Berger and Guidroz's (2009) *The Intersectional Approach: Transforming the Academy Through Race, Class, and Gender* consists of four parts—two of which center on the foundations of intersectionality and theoretical contributions but do not explicitly focus on educational outcomes. In addition to these texts, several anthologies have been introduced that highlight and discuss the theory of intersectionality. However, similar to the texts, no collections specifically target educational outcomes (Andersen & Collins, 2012; Rothenberg, 2009). Our volume seeks to build on the work of Strayhorn (2013) by interrogating the intersectional experiences of Black college students as well as those from other racial-ethnic backgrounds and by examining the educational experiences of collegiate faculty and K–12 students. This text, therefore, endeavors to address a gap within the preexisting literature on intersectionality by focusing specifically on the theory's application to educational contexts.

Intersectionality in Educational Research

Education scholars have documented the importance of attending to issues of race, class, and gender in schools (Weis & Fine, 1993). Subsequently, intersectionality is increasingly being used in educational research (Bettie, 2000; Bhopal & Preston, 2012; Cassidy & Jackson, 2005; Dill & Zambrana, 2009; Griffin & Reddick, 2011; Jones & Abes, 2013; Strayhorn, 2013). Tate (1997) asserts, "The three variants on the intersectional theme (as discussed in Crenshaw [1993])—structural, political, and representational—provide a conceptual framework for analyzing the interplay of race, class, and gender in educational contexts" (p. 233). In 2000, 2001, and 2004, the journal *Race, Gender, & Class* published special issues on education. The 2004 issue focused on postsecondary education. Intersectional theory holds great promise for exploring access to educational opportunities, students' in-school experiences, and educational attainment for marginalized groups. In essence, application of the theory promotes critical complex thinking regarding the intersectionality of race, class, and gender for both student and faculty outcomes.

Until recently, few researchers explored the intersection of race, class, and gender among students in educational institutions. Instead, the influence of race, class, or gender was analyzed separately (Grant & Sleeter, 1986). "A failure to consider the integration of race, social class, and gender leads at times to an oversimplification or inaccurate understanding of what occurs in schools, and therefore to inappropriate or simplistic prescriptions for educational equity" (p. 197). Grant and Sleeter (1986) found that only three of the 71 total articles that explored K–12 educational issues published in the *American Educational Research Journal, Harvard Educational Review*, the *Review of Educational Research*, and the *Teachers College Record* between 1973 and 1983 focused equally on race and class and gender. Moreover, only one of the three articles (Rumberger, 1983) integrated race, class, and gender.

The scarcity of research is due, in part, to the fact that the study of intersectionality is inherently complex and little attention (in any research area) has been paid to its methodology (McCall, 2005). This gap in the literature is unfortunate, especially given that K–12 and postsecondary education is becoming increasingly diverse as a result of demographic changes in the U.S. population. This volume seeks to bridge that gap. Intersectionality theory is especially ripe for helping researchers understand the educational experiences of an increasingly diverse student populace.

Research has begun to focus on student populations that have previously been ignored, such as lesbian, gay, bisexual, transgender, and queer college students (Marine, 2011). The study of racial/ethnic minority and female undergraduates is especially important because their enrollment as a percentage of all undergraduates in institutions of higher education has grown steadily in recent years. In addition, these groups make up the majority of nontraditional students. Baker and Velez (1996) argue that in the 1990s, "in many undergraduate institutions, the average student [was] a woman, older than 22, working and perhaps supporting her own family, and possibly attending classes only on a part-time basis; in short, the average undergraduate student is a 'nontraditional' student'" (p. 82). Paulsen and St. John (2002) find that low-income students are also more likely to be of nontraditional age, married, working, and financially independent. However, Baker and Velez (1996) assert that the proportion of nontraditional students also depends on the type of postsecondary institution.

Some scholars (Alexander, Entwisle, & Bedinger, 1994; Kohr, Masters, Coldiron, Blust, & Skiffington, 1989; May & Dunaway, 2000; Solorzano, 1992) do study students' race, class, and gender identities. However, they do not draw explicitly on intersectionality theory. Cho and colleagues (2013) view intersectionality as an "analytic sensibility." They write,

> Then what makes an analysis intersectional is not its use of the term "intersectionality," nor its being situated in a familiar genealogy, nor its drawing on lists of standard citations. Rather, what makes an analysis intersectional

. . . is its adoption of an intersectional way of thinking about the problem
of sameness and difference and its relation to power. (p. 795)

The contributors to this volume use intersectionality as an analytic tool to
tackle educational problems.

This book is divided into four sections. This introduction highlights
the history and basic tenets of intersectionality theory, its use in education
research, and its importance in exploring students' experiences in K–12 education; college access, success, and outcomes; and diverse faculty issues. The
following is a brief outline of each subsequent chapter.

Part One: Intersectionality and Methodologies

In chapter 1, Olive discusses how intersectionality can be used in conjunction with other theoretical approaches and discusses one such union in which
the lens of intersectionality is used with that of queer theory. He presents
a conceptual model of this process and walks through an example analysis
using narratives from a previous study.

In chapter 2, Vaccaro describes how core elements of qualitative inquiry
can be used in the construction of rich intersectionality studies in education. Endeavoring to bring these core concepts to life, she shares select findings from a qualitative research project about the experiences of six college
students who navigated multiple intersecting identities. Vaccaro's findings
exemplify how elements of qualitative design can be used to delve deeply into
complex issues of intersectionality in education and other settings.

In chapter 3, Ruiz Alvarado and Hurtado use intersectionality as a frame
through which to first examine how the salience of race, gender, class, and
sexual orientation differ among Latina/o college students through a comparison of intersecting identities. The authors then use their preliminary analysis
to examine whether particular intersections of identity are more salient than
others depending upon an individual's context.

Part Two: Intersectionality and K–12 Education

In chapter 4, Stoll's institutional ethnography of three elementary schools in
the Chicago suburbs employs strategic intersectionality, which suggests that
persons who have marked identities may under certain circumstances exhibit
a "multiple identity advantage" that may situate them as particularly effective
advocates for others who are disadvantaged (Fraga, Martinez-Ebers, Lopez,
& Ramirez, 2006). While this research finds some support for the influence
of social location on the extent to which teachers recognize racial inequality

in schooling, it also finds three types of privilege that generally work against teachers' addressing contemporary, institutional racism: privilege associated with individual teachers' social location, privilege associated with White students and their families, and privilege associated with the community surrounding the school.

In chapter 5, Prior uses qualitative methodology, including participant observation, focus groups, interviews, and content analysis of high school ephemera, to analyze how youth attending a charter arts school "do" gender (West & Zimmerman, 1987) in a variety of implicit and explicit ways. The chapter also examines how schools challenge and reinforce normative notions of gender (particularly as they relate to race, class, and sexuality). Prior's research indicates that sexuality, race, and religion are three of the identities that heavily influence how young people navigate their gender identity construction and how they interpret the gender identities of others.

Part Three: Intersectionality and Postsecondary Education

Chapter 6 explores the academic success and multiple identities of high-achieving Latina students. Fujimoto holds that generalizations related to race limit our understanding of various factors within a given group's outcomes, including the use of English in the home and gender. Intersectionality serves as the lens in working toward serving this important student population.

In chapter 7, Guillermo-Wann unconventionally applies intersectionality to look at multiple oppressions within the category of race for multiracial college students. The research draws from a larger study of semistructured interviews with 14 undergraduates attending a public university in the western United States. The author develops a new Integrative Model of Multiraciality (IMM) for campus climate, which helps examine how different forms of racism intersect to create nuances in multiracial experiences of campus climate.

In chapter 8, Wong uses a combination of intersectionality and critical theory as a tool by which to reconceptualize how race and racial identities are constructed in the United States. While her analysis focuses primarily on Chinese American and Filipino postsecondary students, Wong puts forth a broader argument against the addition to or combination of various models of identity development.

In chapter 9, Tillapaugh uses intersectionality as a lens through which to explore the multiple identities of three gay college men and to gain a deeper understanding of how identity is constructed and negotiated depending upon one's context. The author also uses intersectionality to analyze how instances of inclusion and exclusion can affect one's sense of self.

Myers, Laker, and Minneman examine the intersectional identities of men with disabilities in the media in chapter 10, which considers stereotypes and irony related to both masculinity and disability. These authors prompt readers as consumers of entertainment to consider the complex portrayal of gender and ability.

Part Four: Intersectionality and Academe

In chapter 11, Iverson considers how multiple identities converge to play roles in various forms of oppression. Her work explores how the concept of intersectionality can potentially reconstruct our understanding of diversity in postsecondary diversity action plans. This application of the theory includes reconsideration and expansion of the concepts of community and inclusion.

In chapter 12, Manohar and Bullen use intersectionality in their analysis as Black and Asian Indian women faculty members. They consider how race, ethnicity, class, nationality, and gender influence their experiences as members of academe, including their professional mobility. Following an overview of scholarship on minority female faculty, they share how their ethnic and cultural backgrounds played roles in how they are perceived and the challenges they face as they seek tenure and promotion in their academic spaces.

Bertrand Jones uses scholarly personal narrative (SPN) in chapter 13 to understand her own experiences as a Black woman in academe. Via the analysis of journaling, she highlights her own voice as a researcher and how these experiences inform work with and research on other Black women. She holds that the intersectionality of race and gender calls for academic socialization models rooted in the validation of difference.

In chapter 14, Davis uses Helms's Racial Identity Model for Whites as a framework to understand professional interactions in higher education. Her work considers the intersectionality of both race and gender as a Black female in academe. This scholarship notes the importance of considering racial identity development in the learning processes of White students and its potential influences upon the teaching evaluations of minority academics.

The concluding chapter summarizes the major aims of each section of the book. Olive highlights intersectionality's theoretical implications and methodological implications and its utility for promoting issues of social justice. He also discusses the future of intersectional research in the field of education and beyond.

Conclusion

The work herein illustrates the utility and importance of intersectionality in understanding personal experiences and outcomes in education, as well as institutional inequality and social structures. Specifically, using it as a framework holds the potential for providing insight to leaders, such as presidents, deans, provosts, student affairs administrators, and faculty, in addressing race, class, and gender disparities in higher education. However, it is also important to note that intersectionality's usefulness extends far beyond educational spaces.

Intersectionality has the potential to contribute to efforts to train those in the helping professions (teachers, school counselors, nurses, social workers, police officers, emergency personnel, etc.) in communicating and working with individuals of different races, genders, sexual orientations, class backgrounds, and ability levels. When diversity training is offered, whether it is in the form of university graduate education or a police academy, it usually centers on cultivating communication across race. Intersectionality holds the potential to take such training one step further, toward creating greater compassion, social justice, and critical decision making within the helping professions via its incorporation within curricula. For example, how might the outcome of the 2014 slaying of unarmed 18-year-old Michael Brown in Ferguson, Missouri, have been changed if intersectionality had been a component of the training of the officer involved?

Acknowledging the complexity of intersecting identities and implementing practices addressing the varied components of individuals' lives promises to yield outcomes reflecting parity, fairness, and maximized personal and social potential. When applied, intersectionality highlights the marginalized voices of others. At its root, this theory prompts the connection needed for true global discourse across racial, ethnic, and gender lines. This theory further holds the potential to prompt compassion throughout the research process, thereby promoting inclusion of traditionally invisible segments of the research community.

References

Alexander, K. L., Entwisle, D. R., & Bedinger, S. D. (1994). When expectations work: Race and socioeconomic differences in school performance. *Social Psychology Quarterly, 57*(4), 283–299.

Andersen, M. L., & Collins, P. H. (Eds.). (2012). *Race, class & gender: An anthology gender & sexism* (8th ed.) Belmont, CA: Wadsworth.

Baker, T. L., & Velez, W. (1996). Access to and opportunity in postsecondary education in the United States: A review. *Sociology of Education, 69*, 82–101.

Berger, M. T., & Guidroz, K. (Eds.). (2009). *The intersectional approach: Transforming the academy through race, class, and gender.* Chapel Hill, NC: University of North Carolina Press.

Bettie, J. (2000). Women without class: Chicas, cholas, trash and the presence/absence of class identity. *Signs, 26*(1), 1–35.

Bhopal, K., & Preston, J. (Eds.). (2012). *Intersectionality and "race" in education.* New York: Routledge.

Bowen, W. G., Chingos, M. M., & McPherson, M. S. (2009). *Crossing the finish line: Completing college in America's public universities.* Princeton, NJ: Princeton University Press.

Bowleg, L. (2008). When Black + lesbian + woman ≠ Black lesbian woman: The methodological challenges of qualitative and quantitative intersectional research. *Sex Roles, 59,* 312–325.

Browne, I., & Misra, J. (2003). The intersection of gender and race in the labor market. *Annual Review of Sociology, 29,* 487–513.

Carbado, D. W., Crenshaw, K. W., Mays, V. M., & Tomlinson, B. (2013). Intersectionality: Mapping the movements of a theory. *Du Bois Review: Social Science Research on Race, 10*(2), 303–312.

Cassidy, W., & Jackson, M. (2005). The need for equality in education: An intersectionality examination of labeling and zero tolerance practices. *McGill Journal of Education, 40*(3), 435–456.

Cho, S., Crenshaw, K. W., & McCall L. (2013). Toward a field of intersectionality studies: Theory, applications, and praxis. *Signs, 38*(4), 785–810.

Choo, H. Y., & Ferree, M. M. (2010). Practicing intersectionality in sociological research: A critical analysis of inclusions, interactions, and institutions in the study of inequalities. *Sociological Theory, 28*(2), 129–149.

Clarke, A. Y., & McCall, L. (2013). Intersectionality and social explanation in social science research. *Du Bois Review: Social Science Research on Race, 10*(2), 349–363.

Cole, E. R. (2009). Intersectionality and research in psychology. *American Psychologist, 64*(3), 170–180.

Collins, P. H. (2000). *Black feminist thought: Knowledge, consciousness, and the politics of empowerment* (2nd ed.). New York: Routledge.

Combahee River Collective. (1995). A Black feminist statement. In B. Guy-Sheftall (Ed.), *Words of fire: An anthology of African American feminist thought* (pp. 232–240). New York: New Press.

Cott, N. (1977). *The bonds of womanhood.* New Haven, CT: Yale University Press.

Crenshaw, K. (1991). Mapping the margins: Intersectionality, identity politics, and violence against women of color. *Stanford Law Review, 43*(6), 1241–1299.

Crenshaw, K. (1993). Beyond racism and misogyny: Black feminism and 2 Live Crew. In M. J. Matsuda, C. R. Lawrence III, R. Delgado, & K. W. Crenshaw (Eds.), *Words that wound: Critical race theory, assaultive speech, and the First Amendment* (pp. 111–132). Boulder, CO: Westview Press.

Davis, K. (2008). Intersectionality as buzzword: A sociology of science perspective on what makes a feminist theory successful. *Feminist Theory, 9*(1), 67–85.

Dill, B. T., & Zambrana, R. E. (Eds.). (2009). *Emerging intersections: Race, class, and gender in theory, policy, and practice.* New Brunswick, NJ: Rutgers University Press.

Fraga, L., Martinez-Ebers, V., Lopez, L., & Ramirez, R. (2006). *Strategic intersectionality: Gender, ethnicity, political incorporation.* Berkeley, CA: Institute of Governmental Studies.

Grant, C. A., & Sleeter, C. E. (1986). Race, class, and gender in education research: An argument for integrative analysis. *Review of Educational Research, 56*(2), 195–211.

Griffin, K. A., & Reddick, R. J. (2011). Surveillance and sacrifice: Gender differences in the mentoring patterns of Black professors at predominantly White research universities. *American Educational Research Journal, 48*(5), 1032–1057.

Hancock, A. (2007). Intersectionality as a normative and empirical paradigm. *Politics & Gender, 3*(2), 248–254.

Hsieh, S. (2014, March 21). 14 Disturbing stats about racial inequality in American public schools. *The Nation.* Retrieved from http://m.thenation.com/blog/178958-14-disturbing-stats-about-racial-inequality-american-public-schools

Jones, S. R., & Abes, E. S. (2013). *Identity development of college students: Advancing frameworks for multiple dimensions of identity.* San Francisco: Jossey-Bass.

Kohr, R. L., Masters, J. R., Coldiron, J. R., Blust, R. S., & Skiffington, E. W. (1989). The relationship of race, class, and gender with mathematics achievement for fifth, eighth, and eleventh grade students in Pennsylvania schools. *Peabody Journal of Education, 66*(2), 147–171.

Landry, B. (2007). *Race, gender, and class: Theory and methods of analysis.* Upper Saddle River, NJ: Prentice Hall.

Lutz, H., Vivar, M. T. H., & Supik L. (Eds.). (2011). *Framing intersectionality: Debates on a multi-faceted concept in gender studies.* Burlington, VT: Ashgate.

Magill, B. A. (2007). Generalized expectancies for control among high-school students at the intersection of race, class, and gender. In B. Landry (Ed.), *Race, gender, and class: Theory and methods of analysis* (pp. 410–422). Upper Saddle River, NJ: Pearson Prentice Hall.

Marine, S. B. (2011). Stonewall's legacy: Bisexual, gay, lesbian, and transgender students in higher education. In Kelly Ward & Lisa E. Wolf-Wendel (Eds.), *ASHE Higher Education Report, 37*(4). Hoboken, NJ: Wiley Periodicals.

May, D. C., & Dunaway, R. G. (2000). Predictors of fear of criminal victimization at school among adolescents. *Sociological Spectrum, 20*, 149–168.

McCall, L. (2005). The complexity of intersectionality. *Signs: Journal of Women in Culture and Society, 30*(3), 1771–1800.

Paulsen, M. B., & St. John, E. P. (2002). Social class and college costs: Examining the financial nexus between college choice and persistence. *The Journal of Higher Education, 73*(2), 189–236.

Rothenberg, P. S. (2009). *Race, class, and gender in the United States: An integrated study* (8th ed.). New York: Worth.

Rumberger, R. W. (1983). Dropping out of high school: The influence of race, sex, and family background. *American Educational Research Journal, 20*(2), 199–220.

Solorzano, D. G. (1992). An exploratory analysis of the effects of race, class, and gender on student and parent mobility aspirations. *Journal of Negro Education, 61*(1), 30–44.

Strayhorn, T. (Ed.). (2013). *Living at the intersections: Social identities and Black collegians.* Charlotte, NC: Information Age Publishing.

Tate, W. F., IV (1997). Critical race theory and education: History, theory, and implications. *Review of Research in Education, 22*, 195–247.

Truth, S. (1851). Ain't I a woman? [Electronic Version]. Retrieved June 2, 2014, from http://www.fordham.edu/halsall/mod/sojtruth-woman.asp

U.S. Department of Education, Office for Civil Rights, Civil Rights Data Collection. (2014a, March 21). *Data snapshot: Early childhood education, Issue Brief No. 2.*

U.S. Department of Education, Office for Civil Rights, Civil Rights Data Collection. (2014b, March 21). *Data snapshot: School discipline, Issue Brief No. 1.*

Weis, L., & Fine, M. (1993). *Beyond silenced voices: Class, race, and gender in United States schools.* Albany, NY: State University of New York Press.

West, C., & Zimmerman, D. (1987). Doing gender. *Gender & Society, 1*(2), 125–151.

PART ONE

INTERSECTIONALITY AND METHODOLOGIES

1

QUEERING THE INTERSECTIONAL LENS

A Conceptual Model for the Use of Queer Theory in Intersectional Research

James L. Olive

s can be seen from the other chapters in this book, intersectionality
provides a framework that facilitates analyses across multiple identity
structures. Another strength of intersectionality is its complementary
nature and the ease with which it can be used in conjunction with other
theoretical approaches. In this chapter, I discuss one such union in which
the lens of intersectionality is used with that of queer theory. I begin with a
brief history of intersectionality, which leads to a discussion of two paradigms
that have emerged since its introduction via Crenshaw's (1989) seminal piece
regarding the challenges women of color face. The next section is a historical
account of queer theory and an explanation of its underpinnings. Following
the overviews of these theoretical frameworks, I present a conceptual model to
demonstrate the ways in which queer theory and intersectionality can be used
in tandem. Using this model and portions from an earlier ethnographic study,
I conclude the chapter with a guided analysis of one participant's experiences.

The Paradigms of Intersectionality

Intersectionality provides a systematic means by which to critically analyze
and deconstruct the interrelations among gender, sex, race, class, ethnicity,
and sexuality. Crenshaw first introduced the concept of intersectionality due
to her perceived need to address the experiences and struggles that women of
color faced that were not being addressed by feminist and antiracist literature.
Since that time, the applications of an intersectional framework have become
just as diverse as the topics it seeks to address. At this point, "it is not at all
clear whether intersectionality should be limited to understanding individual

experiences, to theorizing identity, or whether it should be taken as a property of social structures and cultural discourse" (Davis, 2008, p. 68). As such, two paradigms (or strands) have emerged within intersectional research.

The first intersectional paradigm has focused primarily on exclusion. Duong (2012) refers to this line of intersectional research as "descriptive representation" (p. 372), as its focus is on the multiple dimensions of identity. Studies conducted within this paradigm address exclusion in one of two ways. The first approach calls attention to circumstances or situations in which certain identities are being excluded. Examples of such research can be found in the work produced by Black feminist theory scholars who have addressed the exclusion of women of color in White, feminist literature (see Anthias, 1998; Collins, 2000; hooks, 1981). The second approach taken within this paradigm analyzes contexts in which one identity is marginalized in favor of another—for instance, when an individual privileges gender at the expense of sexual orientation.

The second intersectional paradigm endeavors to show how social structures such as racism, poverty, and classism reify essentialized identities and, in doing so, marginalize the inherent diversity within a select group. Research conducted within this paradigm critically analyzes intersecting, hegemonic structures of power rather than human characteristics. As Duong (2012) explains, "rather than responding with inclusion via attention to exclusion, the response from the critical approach is to attend to structures and processes that render the world resistant to fundamental emancipation" (p. 374). Though the primary focus of the previous paradigms may differ, the underlying purpose of intersectional research remains the same—to increase understanding of how certain identities intersect, to illuminate the various ways in which people navigate their identities, and to advocate for recognition and inclusion of all identities.

Queer Theory

Since a comprehensive account of queer theory is beyond the scope of this chapter, what I provide in this section is a brief overview of its history as well as a working definition. Originally used as a title for a conference held in February 1990, the term *queer theory* was coined by Professor Teresa de Lauretis of the University of California, Santa Cruz (1991). Halperin (2003) explains that, from the very beginning, de Lauretis fashioned the term *queer theory* as a tool whose intention was to upset the complacency perceived to exist within lesbian and gay studies at that time. While de Lauretis may have created the term *queer theory*, much of what serves as its theoretical foundation rests upon Michel Foucault's earlier work on the interplay between knowledge and power (Foucault, 1979, 1990).

de Lauretis's (1991) research focused primarily upon the perpetuation of gender hierarchies since the scholar viewed the terms *lesbian, gay,* and *homosexual* as intrinsically chauvinistic. de Lauretis posited that queer theory would provide a tool to critically analyze and circumnavigate the predominantly male hegemonic structures prevalent throughout society. She believed that "the term queer allowed for the possibility of keeping open to question and context the element of race—or class, age or anything else—and its often complicated, unpredictable relationship to sexuality" (Turner, 2000, p. 133).

Foucault's work related to queer theory focused on the concept of power. One of the scholar's central tenets was that power is not a tangible item that can be wielded by a dominant group or majority (Foucault, 1979, 1990; Spargo, 1999; Turner, 2000; Watson, 2005). Rather, power is the result of relationships and interactions that occur between individuals or groups, assumes many forms, and is in a state of continuous flux. Foucault theorized that knowledge plays a fundamental role in the distribution of power when it resides on only one side of a conversation. In reflecting on society's past, Foucault scrutinized the means by which religion, science, and dominant groups made use of their superior knowledge to oppress those perceived to be morally, ethically, mentally, or physically inept. Discourses of the past, or the various cultural "messages" passed down through history, have served as the medium through which new, oppressive identities have emerged for groups looked upon by the majority as deviant. That is to say, rather than actions or behaviors being labeled as abnormal, the oppressed individual is assigned a completely new identity—one society views collectively as inherently inferior and subject to corrective action by those perceived as most knowledgeable or powerful (i.e., police, doctors, etc.) (Watson, 2005).

Though coined by de Lauretis and subsequently built upon Foucault's theoretical structure, what serves as the crux of queer theory originates from two seminal texts: Eve Sedgwick's (1990) *Epistemology of the Closet* and Judith Butler's (1990) *Gender Trouble: Feminism and the Subversion of Identity.* The impetus for Sedgwick's text stemmed from her desire to address an ongoing debate taking place around the same time between gay and lesbian scholars. This debate involved differing views of sexual identity development, with one side favoring essentialism and the other finding value in social constructionism. Queer theory provided Sedgwick with a much-needed alternate view on human sexuality and desire. Central to this new perspective was the belief that each person's lived experience is distinctive, so no two individuals share the exact same sexual identity. Judith Butler (1990) expanded the purview of queer theory by asserting that a basic understanding of biology is based on a flawed culture, which considers one gender as superior to the other. In *Gender Trouble,* Butler used queer theory to argue that the heteronormative nature of society is best challenged through the use of reverse discourses conveyed via forms of satirical actions (i.e., drag). An additional outcome of Butler's *Gender Trouble* was the idea that gender, sex, and sexuality are inherently performative and established through repeated acts within society's discourse.

By its very nature, the term *queer* resists defining. However, Jagose (1996) provides the following succinct and useful working definition:

> Queer [theory] defines those gestures or analytical models which dramatise incoherencies in the allegedly stable relations between chromosomal sex, gender and sexual desire. Resisting that model of stability—which claims heterosexuality as its origin, when it is more properly its effect—queer focuses on the mismatches between sex, gender, and desire. (p. 3)

Those who conduct queer research maintain "an interrogative and, frequently, interventionist position taken on the basis of a skepticism toward the supposedly 'natural' undergirdings of human society such as sexuality, race, class, and gender" (Holmes, 1994, p. 53).

Queer Intersectional Analysis

Both queer theory and intersectionality seek to address marginalization in its various forms. When used in tandem, the combination of frameworks offers an enhanced analytic and methodological approach to research focused on exclusion. Rahman (2010) argues that "queer intersectionality is simply the necessary tautology: intersectionality is inevitably disruptively queer, and queer must be analytically intersectional" (p. 956). Similarly, Carlin (2011) maintains that since queer theory's central goal is to deconstruct essentialized identities and eliminate hierarchies it is "both an appropriate and constructive tool in any intersectional analysis that examines how multiple and interconnected strands of social categories and power relations shape human experience and create systemic oppressions" (p. 56). When endeavoring to synthesize multiple theoretical frameworks, conceptual models are useful tools as they can provide visual representations of the complementary relationships that exist between frameworks (Shields & Rangarajan, 2013). To that end, Figure 1.1 presents a conceptual model that I created to show how queer theory and intersectionality can be used together to analyze an experience or situation. It should be noted that, while multiple dimensions of identity are represented in my Queer Intersectional Analysis (QIA) model, what is shown is not a conclusive list. Additionally, these dimensions should not be viewed as possessing greater value or more prominence in the total composition of an individual's identity.

Figure 1.1 Model of Queer Intersectional Analysis

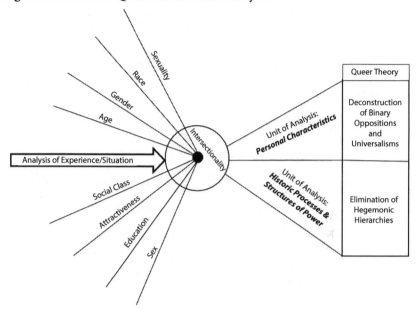

As I discussed earlier, the fundamental issue or concern that intersectionality seeks to address is exclusion. However, the research conducted within intersectionality approaches this topic in two distinct ways: exclusion on the basis of personal characteristics or exclusion as a function of historic processes or structure. This distinction is shown in the QIA model as two paths through which an analysis may traverse. The units of analysis in the top path are *personal characteristics* wherein a study focuses on (a) a person or group of people who are excluded on the basis of one or more dimensions of identity, or (b) the exclusion of one identity dimension in favor of another. Conversely, studies conducted along the bottom path use *historic processes* and *structures of power* as their units of analysis.

Since the primary goals of queer theory are the deconstruction of binary oppositions in any form and the elimination of hegemonic systems of power, the supplemental application of its theoretical framework enhances the overall analysis. This logical progression is depicted on the right of the QIA model wherein intersectional research conducted on the basis of personal characteristics can make use of queer theory's approach to binary deconstruction. Similarly, intersectional studies related to exclusionary processes and structures of power can benefit from queer theory's techniques of critically analyzing and eliminating hierarchies. The QIA model provides a means to envision how queer theory and intersectionality complement each other analytically.

What follows are details and portions from a previous study involving one participant who self-identified as queer and experienced marginalization across multiple identity spectrums. Following a brief description of the study and the participant, I use select narratives from the interview sessions to show how the QIA model can facilitate a queer intersectional analysis.

Methodology of the Study

The information presented in this chapter stems from a previous ethnographic case study involving six postsecondary students who self-identified as nonheterosexual. One of the initial purposes of my earlier study was to identify the personal, familial, and contextual characteristics that facilitate the academic success of sexually marginalized individuals. Additional information on the study and its initial findings can be found elsewhere (Olive, 2010, 2012). What follows are select portions from that study that exemplify the use of queer theory in intersectional research.

Participant

The analysis in this chapter centers on one self-identified queer participant from my original study who was chosen purposefully from the undergraduate student population of a large Midwestern public institution. Additionally, this individual was also chosen due to her status as a leader within the lesbian, gay, bisexual, transgender, and queer (LGBTQ) student organizations on campus.

Data Collection and Analysis

I conducted three semistructured interviews over the course of one academic school year with the participant. The interview sessions took place in different locations based on her preferences. One benefit of allowing her to choose the interview locations was that it often afforded me numerous opportunities to obtain unique and/or sensitive types of data such as photographs, memorabilia, and personal documents. A majority of the interviews were conducted in the participant's home, which allowed me to see not only where and how she lived but also what she considered to be valuable in terms of personal belongings and family photos. Each digitally recorded interview lasted between 60 and 90 minutes and was transcribed verbatim. To increase the trustworthiness of the study, I shared all notes and transcripts from the interviews with the participant.

From the data obtained during our interview sessions, I constructed a life history narrative of the participant, portions of which are provided in the following section. Data were analyzed and themes identified through a constant comparative process during which I categorized key words and phrases while simultaneously resorting the information as new data were obtained. To further increase the trustworthiness of my findings, each time a new theme or thematic connection was uncovered, I discussed it with the participant to ensure that what I saw in the data was authentic.

Raven

Raven (a pseudonym) was a White 24-year-old majoring in women's studies who was born into a lower-middle-class family and self-identified as a queer lesbian. During one of our interview sessions, Raven recounted an experience she had while using one of the restrooms on campus. Her experience provides an excellent example in which queer theory can be used as an effective tool in an intersectional analysis. What follows are portions of the life history narrative that we co-constructed as well as the details of one situation in which Raven's gender, sexual, and queer identities intersected.

Background

Raven's appearance is what would stereotypically be classified as "masculine" (dark-colored sports T-shirts, jeans, etc.), and she has a number of facial piercings. Consequently, Raven stated during our first interview that most people consider her style "alternative or rough" due to her outward appearance, and they sometimes mistake her for a male. Raven's personality, however, was not dark or rough. In fact, Raven proved to be quite timid and conveyed a warmth and gentleness in most of our interactions. During our initial meeting, Raven's mannerisms and body language conveyed nervousness, which I initially attributed to our just having met. However, over time, I came to realize that Raven's level of anxiety is constant and is due in part to what she has experienced as a queer person.

As Raven was growing up, she considered her family middle class and stated that she was raised in a "typical" suburban neighborhood. Raven was raised primarily by her mother and stepfather. Since her biological parents divorced when she was two years old, she had a very strained relationship with her father. Raven described her mother as a strong, "go-getter" sort of person who is interested in "bettering things for women" and runs a professional women's organization. In subsequent conversations, Raven recognized the influence of her mother on many of her decisions regarding schooling and her current area of study.

Raven attended small elementary, middle, and high schools that were primarily White and said that in middle school and high school she was a member of the *inbetweeners*, a term that she went on to explain as "people who were in between, like, the popular people and the nerds and the geeks. We never fit into one specific stereotype." Being different was and continues to be important to Raven. When she was 18, Raven got her first facial piercing. She explains, "I wanted to stand out. Different was better for me, because, when you grow up with the same people all your life, it gets boring." This same desire to be different may partially explain Raven's preference to identify as queer. Raven explains, "I consider and identify myself as queer to those who know what queer is. So sometimes I consider myself queer and sometimes I consider myself a lesbian." When I asked Raven to define what *queer* means to her, she explained, "Queer is an umbrella term that describes a person or group of people who choose to identify with the nonheteronormative ideals of what sexuality is." From this definition and subsequent conversations with Raven, I came to understand that she perceived *lesbian* as a term that deals primarily with sexuality, whereas *queer* deals with sexuality and anything related to one's existence or day-to-day activities, feelings, or decisions as a nonheterosexual. Raven's self-acceptance as a lesbian occurred around the age of 14, and when she reached that point, there was no turning back. "I was just basically like 'Wow. This is it. This is what I am. This is what I've always been. And this is what I will be and I'm 100% sure.'" Though she stated that she was initially "okay" with the term *lesbian*, Raven explained that her preference now is to self-identify as queer whenever possible. When I asked her to explain, she answered, "That's just me. I'm not really a lesbian. I'm more queer than I am a lesbian because lesbian just doesn't fit my identity."

Raven's refusal to abide by society's widely accepted stereotypes regarding how males and females should dress has led to some hostile reactions and feelings of alienation. However, her nonconformity also facilitated her growth as an activist on campus. Raven explained,

> Because I look so different and because I don't fit the norms, I find myself speaking out more in class. I feel more free to express my opinions on the topics I care about, and now I have people asking me different questions about what it means to be queer. That feels awesome.

Queer Experiences

Unfortunately, the same qualities that enabled Raven's activism on campus also produced frequent feelings of pain and discomfort. One example that Raven gave related to her choice when using restroom facilities on campus. When prompted for more on this topic, she explained,

> Because I am queer, I have to be cautious about which bathrooms I use around campus. I mean, I'm queer, but not everyone knows that by looking

at me or even what the term means. They just see, like, someone tall, someone broad shouldered—they see a male from the back. So, in bathrooms
around campus, I've gotten a lot of mean comments.

When I asked Raven whether she heard those types of comments from the
males or females on campus, she answered,

> Well, at first, I thought about trying to use the men's room just like I would
> the women's room because I do look more like a guy, but that was a dis-
> aster. Like, the first time I went into one, this guy was washing his hands
> and said, "Um, are you sure you're supposed to be in here?" When I said,
> "Yeah, I'm supposed to be in here," he said, "No you're not—freak. Now
> get the [expletive] out of here or I'm going to call campus police." So I, like,
> backed out and took off out of the building—it was horrible. So, I don't
> ever use the men's rooms.

I asked whether this type of experience had ever happened to her in a wom-
en's restroom on campus and she stated that it did:

> I guess I kind of expected that from the male population, but not the
> female population. But, oh yeah, I get comments all the time from women
> on campus, too. I've had a few say, like, the same sort of thing—"Are you
> supposed to be in here?" So I just try to talk or say something when I first
> walk in so they can hear my voice. I'll say, like, "Hi," or something.

When asked about the frequency of these types of experiences, Raven
answered,

> It used to happen a lot—like almost every day. But not so much anymore
> now that my hair's grown out a little bit. When I had, like, a crew cut, it
> would happen a lot. People would come in, look at me, go back out, like,
> to look at the bathroom sign, and come back in. I mean, I know that, like,
> part of it's just ignorance, but it gets old. So, like, sometimes I don't use the
> restroom in places because I'm worried that somebody will come in and I
> wash my hands really fast. Sometimes, I don't wash my hands at all. I try to
> get in and get out as fast as possible.

Application of the QIA Model

Raven's experiences depict an individual situated at an intersectional location
who is, in effect, challenging the dominant identities associated with gender,
sex, and sexuality. As I discussed earlier, research using the framework of

intersectionality is conducted within one of two paradigms. To illustrate this process and the potential application of queer theory in both paradigms, I provide an analysis of Raven's experiences using the QIA model.

Intersectional research conducted along the top path shown in Figure 1.1, in which the units of analysis relate to personal characteristics, analyzes various contexts as a means of addressing situations and circumstances in which exclusion occurs in one of the following ways: (a) when an identity group is omitted due to marginalization, or (b) when one or more identities of a person are privileged at the expense of others as a result of exclusionary practices or procedures. In Raven's example, she was excluded from using the men's restroom because of society's insistence on labeling her sex. When she entered the men's room, the male student called her a "freak"—a verbal attack that made it painfully clear she was not welcome. Additionally, the student threatened to call the authorities since he believed that she was attempting to do something wrong. Consequently, Raven was forced to choose between identification as a male or female whenever she needed to use a campus restroom. What is more, each time Raven did so, she was left with no other alternative than to privilege her sexual identity at the expense of her gender identity. Similarly, when Raven used the women's restroom, the critical looks and derogatory comments she received were due to her transgressions against what society deems appropriate "female" attire. Questions like, "Are you supposed to be in here?" again communicated to Raven that she was not welcome. In these types of situations, however, it was her gender identity that was being excluded.

Along the bottom path of the QIA model, intersectional research uses historic processes and structures of power as its units of analysis—lending itself to more of a macro-level approach. From this standpoint, an intersectional framework calls into question the various components that led up to Raven's experiences in the men's and women's restrooms. For example, why was Raven forced to choose between restrooms in the first place? The answer resides in past practices and procedures. Historically, building construction has been conducted within a heteronormative framework in which only males and females require consideration. Consequently, Raven and those like her who identify as queer are often overlooked in the design of new buildings and restroom facilities—the same being true for people who identify as transgender or transsexual. Similar exclusions can also be seen in the design of residence halls, locker rooms, health care facilities, and certain types of institutional documents and records. In each of these examples, those who do not comply with society's heteronormative standards are absent from the equation. A number of scholars have recognized this continued oversight on the part of today's campus administrators, building planners, and architects and work to address such inequities (see Beemyn, 2005; Beemyn, Domingue, Pettitt, & Smith, 2005; Messinger, 2009; Schmidt, 2013).

As the QIA model shows, whether a study is situated within the first or second intersectional paradigm, queer theory offers additional benefits. That is, while purely intersectional research endeavors to resolve exclusion by promoting inclusivity, queer theory provides an additional means of addressing such inequities by challenging the basic ontological and epistemological foundations upon which the actions are built. Intersectional studies that focus on exclusion based on personal characteristics can avail themselves of queer theory's approach to deconstructing binary oppositions and universalisms. Similarly, research conducted within the second intersectional paradigm can use queer theory's tools for eliminating hierarchies. As such, queer theory advances the previous analysis of Raven's experiences to include a deeper examination of how restrooms categorized by sex perpetuate a heteronormative standard that is predicated upon performative, socially constructed labels attached to gender and sex. Queer theory further calls into question how reinforcing the heteronormative standard reifies the historic view of what is deemed "normal."

References

Anthias, F. (1998). Rethinking social divisions: Some notes towards a theoretical framework. *Sociological Review, 46*(3), 557–580.

Beemyn, B. (2005). Making campuses more inclusive of transgender students. *Journal of Gay & Lesbian Issues in Education, 3*(1), 77–87.

Beemyn, B., Domingue, A., Pettitt, J., & Smith, T. (2005). Suggested steps to make campuses more trans-inclusive. *Journal of Gay & Lesbian Issues in Education, 3*(1), 89–94.

Butler, J. (1990). *Gender trouble: feminism and the subversion of identity.* New York: Routledge.

Carlin, D. (2011). The intersectional potential of queer theory: An example from a general education course in English. *New Directions for Teaching and Learning, 125,* 55–64.

Collins, P. H. (2000). *Black feminist thought: Knowledge, conciousness, and the politics of empowerment* (2nd ed.). New York: Routledge.

Crenshaw, K. (1989). Mapping the margins: Intersectionality, identity politics, and violence against women of color. *Stanford Law Review, 43*(6), 1241–1279.

Davis, K. (2008). Intersectionality as buzzword: A sociology of science perspective on what makes a feminist theory successful. *Feminist Theory, 9*(1), 67–85.

de Lauretis, T. (1991). Queer theory: Lesbian and gay sexualities. *Differences, 3*(2), iii–xviii.

Duong, K. (2012). What does queer theory teach us about intersectionality? *Politics & Gender, 8*(3), 370–386.

Foucault, M. (1979). *Discipline and punish: The birth of the prison.* New York: Random House.

Foucault, M. (1990). *The history of sexuality: An introduction.* New York: Vintage Books.

Halperin, D. M. (2003). The normalization of queer theory. *Journal of Homosexuality, 45*, 339–343.

Holmes, M. M. (1994). Chalkdusting. In L. Berlant et al. (Eds.), Forum: On the political implications of using the term "queer," as in "queer politics," "queer studies," and "queer pedagogy." *Radical Teacher, 45*, 52–57.

hooks, b. (1981). *Ain't I a woman? Black women and feminism.* Boston: South End Press.

Jagose, A. (1996). *Queer theory: An introduction.* New York: New York University Press.

Messinger, L. (2009). Creating LGBTQ-friendly campuses. *Academe, 95*(5), 39–42.

Olive, J. (2010). Relating developmental theories to postsecondary persistence: A multiple case study of gay, lesbian, and bisexual college students. *Journal of Ethnographic & Qualitative Research, 4*(4), 197–212.

Olive, J. (2012). Reflections on the life histories of today's LGBQ postsecondary students: Potential ramifications of a friendlier world. *Journal of LGBT Youth, 9*(3), 247–265.

Rahman, M. (2010). Queer as intersectionality: Theorizing gay Muslim identities. *Sociology, 44*(5), 944–961.

Schmidt, D. A. (2013). Bathroom bias: Making the case for trans rights under disability law. *Michigan Journal of Gender & Law, 20*(1), 155–186.

Sedgwick, E. K. (1990). *Epistemology of the closet.* Berkeley, CA: University of California Press.

Shields, P. M., & Rangarajan, N. (2013). *A playbook for research methods: Integrating conceptual frameworks and project management.* Stillwater, OK: New Forums Press.

Spargo, T. (1999). *Foucault and queer theory.* New York: Totem Books.

Turner, W. B. (2000). *A genealogy of queer theory.* Philadelphia: Temple University Press.

Watson, K. (2005). Queer theory. *Group Analysis, 38*(1), 67–81.

2

A CASE FOR USING QUALITATIVE INQUIRY TO STUDY INTERSECTIONALITY IN COLLEGE STUDENTS

Annemarie Vaccaro

Qualitative inquiry, with its emphasis on deep understandings, holistic accounts, emergent themes, inductive reasoning, and rich description, provides an effective vehicle for educational researchers to study complex phenomena such as identity development and intersectionality. In this chapter, I describe how core elements of qualitative inquiry can meet the need for intersectionality studies in education. In an attempt to bring qualitative concepts to life, I share select findings from a research project about the experiences of six college students who navigated multiple intersecting identities in a variety of school, family, and community settings.

Characteristics of Qualitative Inquiry

Qualitative researchers use various methodologies (e.g., case study, ethnography, narrative inquiry, phenomenology, grounded theory) to understand people's experiences. While each methodology is unique, they all share common characteristics, such as naturalistic settings, researcher as instrument, inductive data analysis, participants' meanings, emergent design, interpretive inquiry, and holistic accounts (Creswell, 2007, pp. 37–39). Feminist and critical scholars also argue that an essential component of qualitative research is affording voice to participants (Jones, Torres, & Arminio, 2006; Reinharz, 1992). By emphasizing depth, complexity, and holistic accounts; emergent and flexible design; naturalistic settings; and voice and agency, qualitative researchers are in an ideal position to study complexities of the human experience, including how individuals make meaning of their identities and intersectionality over time.

Depth, Complexity, and Holistic Accounts

Qualitative inquiry affords researchers an in-depth understanding of an issue or phenomenon (Creswell, 2007; Merriam, 2009). Through interviews, focus groups, observations, and other data collection techniques, qualitative researchers strive to deeply understand multifaceted social and educational issues. Qualitative methodology

> allows the researcher to approach the inherent complexity of social inter-
> action and to honor the complexity, to respect it in its own right. To do
> justice to complexity, researchers avoid simplifying social phenomenon and
> instead explore the range of behavior. (Glesne, 1999, p. 6)

All individuals possess a variety of social identities, and the intersection of those identities is often abstruse. By honoring depth and complexity, qualitative researchers are best poised to offer comprehensive and holistic accounts of participant experiences and their meaning-making processes.

Emergent and Flexible Design

Because qualitative researchers study intricate and often very involved phenomena, research design is most effective when it is flexible. Qualitative scholars sometimes take a constructivist perspective, which suggests "meanings are constructed by human beings as they engage with the world they are interpreting" (Crotty, 1998, p. 43). In effect, they seek to understand an event or phenomenon as participants perceived and experienced it. Once participants begin to share their interpretations or meanings, a researcher might need to exhibit flexibility by rethinking the focus or design of a study. Merriam (2009) argues that, ideally, "the design of a qualitative study is *emergent and flexible* [emphasis in the original], responsive to changing conditions of the study in progress" (p. 16). For instance, researchers may begin a study in hopes of understanding a particular phenomenon, but participant narratives may lead scholars to see that they began the study with incomplete understandings or inaccurate assumptions about the topic. Or the initial method, timing, or venue for data collection may prove to be inadequate for capturing the intricacy of an issue, event, or experience.

Naturalistic Settings

In their quest to obtain a deep understanding of a topic, qualitative researchers study participants in naturalistic settings. Individuals are shaped by the environments in which they live, learn, play, and work, *and* by the individuals and institutions they interact with in those domains. By studying participants in the context of their familial, cultural, educational, and work settings, researchers more fully understand the "whole" of the human experience.

In addition to being in the setting with participants, qualitative researchers often interact with participants over time. Creswell (2007) argues that "extensive time spent in the field . . . add[s] to the value or accuracy of a study" (p. 207). Developmental meaning making is an ongoing process; to understand how people make sense of their intersecting identities, researchers may need to engage with participants for an extended period.

Voice and Agency

Merriam (2009) argues, "Qualitative researchers are interested in understanding how people interpret their experiences, how they construct their worlds, and what meaning they attribute to their experiences" (p. 5). Such research processes allow participants agency over sharing their life experiences. Indeed, scholars often use qualitative research when they want to empower people to share their narratives so that others may learn from their experiences (Creswell, 2007; Jones et al., 2006). A perspective of empowerment is especially important when studying members of marginalized groups. Many scholars argue that the experiences of underrepresented groups are largely missing from research studies and these omissions reinforce the needs, perspectives, and experiences of privileged groups (Delgado, 1989; Reinharz, 1992). By focusing specifically on the experiences of marginalized people, new and more inclusive social realities can be created. While feminist and critical race scholars have focused on voice and agency of women and people of color, few qualitative studies (Jones, 2009; Patton, 2011; Stewart, 2008, 2009) highlight the empowered voices of individuals navigating the intersections of multiple identities (e.g., race, gender, class, sexual orientation, religion, ability, age).

The Study

Intersectionality data included in this chapter represent a portion of findings from an ethnographic study of 49 LGBT individuals involved in queer university organizations at one midsize higher education institution. Findings from the complete study are described elsewhere (Vaccaro, 2009, 2012). An initial focus of the ethnographic study was to understand how diverse LGBT individuals made meaning of their identities as members of queer affinity groups on campus. However, narratives from a subset of students (i.e., queer students of color) revealed complicated images of identity, intersectionality, and environmental influences that warranted further analysis. Hence, the initial ethnographic study design was altered to accommodate emergent themes and additional data collection efforts.

Ethnographic fieldwork often includes a variety of data collection techniques, such as observation, document analysis, and interviews (Creswell, 2007; Wolcott, 1999). I engaged in observation of queer campus groups for two years and reviewed their archival materials. "At the root of in-depth interviewing is an interest in understanding the experience of other people and the meaning they make of that experience" (Seidman, 1998, p. 3). Two semistructured interviews were the vehicle through which diverse college students shared how they made meaning of their intersecting identities. The initial research plan included a single interview but was altered to include a two-interview sequence with queer students of color. Five of the six students of color participated in a second interview.

Interviews were conducted over the course of one calendar year. Each lasted between 60 and 120 minutes. Open-ended questions included, "Tell me a little bit about how you self-identify"; "What is it like being a queer person of color on campus?"; "Tell me about your experiences on campus and in the Queer Student Group." Probes such as, "Tell me more about that" and "Can you explain that to me?" were used to delve more deeply into the student experience.

Qualitative researchers often use purposive sampling (Creswell, 2007; Merriam, 2009) to identify participants who have experienced, and can illuminate, the phenomenon being studied. Since an initial emphasis of the study was on the identities of individuals in queer campus groups, participants were invited via e-mail lists and announcements at group meetings. The Queer Student Group (QSG) was a university club for undergraduate gay, lesbian, bisexual, and transgender activists and their allies. All of the students described in this chapter were members of the QSG.

Rich Description of Student Identity Journeys

The following pages offer a glimpse into the multifarious intersectionality experiences of six diverse college students. The narratives explicate how students navigated the intersections of their multiple identities over time in a variety of familial, educational, and community settings.

Roberto

During both interviews, Roberto talked at length about how he managed his multiple identities in different environments at different points in his life. He grew up in a predominantly Latino neighborhood and attended elementary and high schools with a mostly Latino population. He recognized his sexual feelings in middle school, and by high school Roberto was known as "the gay kid."

Although he grew up in an environment surrounded by Latinos, Roberto never self-identified as Latino. He told a painful story of his first attempt to claim his Latino heritage and identity. It began when he started pronouncing the Spanish version of his name with the appropriate accent. The first time he referred to himself as Roberto instead of Robert was at the podium in a high school assembly. Roberto explained,

> It was very difficult, because . . . a lot of people didn't even recognize me as someone whose grandmother was from Mexico. . . . It was . . . a student assembly, and the Latino kids just started laughing hysterically. "You're not Latino! You're White."

He hoped that the other Latino students would welcome him into their community, but they merely laughed at him. Despite this hurdle, Roberto began to explore what it meant to be Latino. During his later high school years, Roberto founded a tolerance club, which became a safe environment to concurrently explore his intersecting ethnic and sexual identities. The club existed in stark contrast to most familial and educational settings where he felt forced to pick between these two important identities. He described the pressure as follows: "There's that thing . . . like, you can't be gay and Latino."

Roberto's family life had a significant influence on how he made meaning of his intersecting identities. As a child of divorced parents, he experienced very different levels of acceptance from his mother and father. While both parents struggled with his sexual orientation and gender identity, his mother learned to accept and affirm Roberto much more quickly than his father did.

As early as elementary school, Roberto noticed the ways his father tried to influence him to be more "manly" and "less gay." One of his most memorable and painful experiences was when he realized his father was ashamed of his gender expression and afraid that he would influence his younger brothers to act too feminine and become gay. It was early experiences like these that prompted Roberto's thinking about the intersections of his gender and sexual identities. He explained,

> There were all . . . these issues around my femininity. I remember [it] well. . . . We were playing putt-putt golf. He said, "Do you have to act like that? Do you have to do things like that sort of thing?" I was . . . being too gay. . . . He [said], "You're going to influence them to be like [you]." . . . I was really hurt by it.

Despite rejection by his father, Roberto continued to explore his sexual orientation and gender identity. During his sophomore year in high school, he decided to dress in drag. His mother feared for his safety, yet she supported his decision. Roberto felt a sense of strength in his drag identity, which was a visible embodiment of his intersecting racial, ethnic, gender, and sexual identities. Roberto shared,

> I didn't really have a wig, I . . . borrowed clothes from my friend. [I] got a lot of, like, crap. . . . People were just, like, "Who is this kid? He's crazy!" But it didn't stop me. . . . My drag identity . . . is just fierce! I did it and it was really transforming for me. Actually, I graduated in drag, which was really interesting because I also had to give a speech. A lot of people were not very happy with me, particularly the student body vice president!

Roberto exhibited incredible resilience and confidence as he weathered rejection from peers and family. Despite obstacles on his journey, he continued to navigate his intersecting multiple identities in search of a holistic sense of self.

When Roberto arrived at an expensive, predominantly White university, his identity consciousness shifted yet again. While he still focused on his intersecting gender and sexual identities, the locus of those intersections became even more sophisticated. He explained:

> Initially when I got to campus, there were these . . . identities that I was just, like, hit with all at once. All of a sudden these . . . identities were very salient . . . my socioeconomic status, my race, and then my sexual orientation, and my gender. . . . A lot of them I never had to deal with, my class, like my socioeconomic status . . . especially when it came to paying to go to [this university] . . . I wanted to buy, like, Abercrombie and all this stuff. Frankly, I couldn't afford that stuff. I was, like, "I don't fit in." . . . And *then* there's all these things related to being a Chicano [in] this very White gay world! (Vaccaro, 2009)

Whereas Roberto struggled to validate his ethnic, gender, and sexual identities in high school, additional identities crept into his consciousness when he arrived at college. Roberto was now faced with a predominantly White, wealthy university environment, giving new meaning to his race, ethnicity, and class. He became the campus queer kid, a working-class student in a wealthy environment, and a representative of his race, ethnicity, and social class to wealthy, White peers. His switch from using the term *Latino* to *Chicano* between interviews and also speaks to the evolving nature of his identity between college and high school.

Throughout his interviews, Roberto talked about a desire to integrate his identities into a cohesive whole. Being a working-class, queer Chicano was more than the sum of his parts. Yet, he admitted, there was a constant pressure to pick one salient identity. He explained the pressure to "choose one or the other." But, Roberto did not want to choose; he wanted to live at the intersections of these different identities.

Jackson

Jackson grew up as the only African American male in a predominantly White community. He described a back-and-forth motion between his White peers in high school and his African American relatives. As a young person, he learned that particular attitudes and behaviors were expected in these two very different environments. He had done much internal reflection on his sexual identity during his high school years but was not out to most of his friends or family. He said, "We didn't really have a [gay-straight] alliance . . . and I wasn't really comfortable at that point." Jackson also described how his single parent was not very supportive of LGBT issues. In fact, he described coming out to his father (after he left for college) as "one of the scariest things possible."

Upon arrival at the university, Jackson became active in both the queer and Black student groups. In the QSG he was able to explore more deeply what it meant to be gay. As a sophomore he described himself as "a definitely new person who . . . is comfortable with being gay . . . and comfortable with being African American." Through further conversation, it was apparent that although Jackson was "comfortable," he still struggled with managing what sometimes felt like competing identities. Jackson felt pressures to pick a single salient identity. For instance, in the Black Student Group he was pushed to identify as an African American with no acknowledgment of his sexual orientation. The QSG foregrounded his sexual orientation often at the expense of his race. He described how identities sometimes "pulled" him in opposite directions, especially when it came to participating in these clubs. Jackson, however, talked about his attempts to center all of his identities. He shared,

> I'm kind of struggling along two fronts. I'm . . . struggling on being LGBT and being African American. And so I feel not necessarily torn, but I know that both of these are my passions and they both lead separate directions sometimes. . . . Right now my passion is more on diversity at this university and especially the Black Student Alliance. . . . I'd almost say there's more LGBT people on this campus than there are Black people. . . . . That's an issue for me. . . . Getting our name out there and raising awareness for African Americans is . . . where I'm being led right now. (Vaccaro, 2009)

During his first interview, he said he was "led" to activism by his African American identity. He even mentioned not wanting to run for an officer position in the QSG so he could focus on Black issues on campus. A year later, Jackson described how homophobia in the Black Student Group and a racist incident in the QSG reminded him of the importance of his identity intersections. He wasn't just Black or gay. He was a gay, Black man. For Jackson, the idea of coming full circle meant focusing holistically on the complicated nature of his multiple identities. He explained, "Sometimes [race] kind of takes precedent over being LGBT. I think . . . it all comes full circle. I mean, eventually you'll get back around to [focusing on all your identities]." For Jackson, "coming full circle" meant finding the space to focus on the complicated intersections of his multiple identities. Jackson hoped someday to live and work in environments where he could come full circle.

Jun

Jun struggled to find a sense of self that encompassed her gender, sexual, and ethnic identities. When she was in middle school, Jun's family moved to a new state. As a first-generation Chinese American, she was socialized into a predominantly White community that contained many ethnic subcultures, but no Chinese. At the same time, Jun was trying to understand her same-sex feelings. She did not have anyone to help her navigate her identity journey. She shared,

> [In this state] there's lots of Latinos and . . . White people. I'm not the only Asian, but the Asians around me are like Hmong and Vietnamese and they grew up here. That's why it's hard for me to integrate into that culture. I really didn't have anyone I could talk to. I didn't know what was going on [with my sexual orientation].

As an adolescent, Jun felt cultural and familial pressure to be heterosexual and she tried to ignore her same-sex feelings. Jun talked about the pain of being closeted around her family and Asian friends. Coming out to kin was something she hoped to do soon, but she struggled with "how." She said,

> [Being gay is] something hush-hush that our culture doesn't do. . . . How do I . . . tell my parents? "Mom and Dad, I'm LGBT." But in Asian culture I can't just do it like every other gay movie says! I just come out and they are all right? It doesn't work that way! There's a lot to be confronted.

For Jun, cultural values and expectations seemed an ill match for her sexual identity, but they were central to her Chinese American identity. Nonetheless, she expressed hope to reconcile these identities someday.

By the time she arrived at college, Jun had done some exploring of her sexual identity. During her sophomore through senior years in high school, she participated in a diversity club that provided a safe environment where she could explore her emerging bisexual identity. When she reached college, she began to identify as queer. She expressed an expectation (or hope) that the college environment would be more inclusive of her intersecting identities. Sadly, she found that while there were many single-identity clubs such as the Chinese Student Association (CSA) and QSG, no university organizations validated her multiple identities. She explained,

> [As an] LGBT woman of color... we're not really being seen. We're not recognized. . . . [We do] not exist in the LGBT group or in the people of color group. So that's really challenging.... How do I deal with that?

At college, the QSG offered a safe space for her as a queer person, but it was not a comfortable environment for her as a feminist or Chinese American woman. Her predominantly White LGBT peers made her Chinese identity invisible—a painful form of racial oppression. Conversely, the CSA exhibited homophobia in her presence. Neither environment welcomed her as a whole human being comprising intersecting multiple identities. Jun also talked about the lack of role models. She longed to meet well-adjusted adults who lived happily at the intersections of their complicated identities. She explained,

> I'm LGBT, I'm Asian. How do I deal with that? If I [had] LGBT people of color . . . as my mentor[s], I think I wouldn't struggle so much with my identities. . . . Knowing their personal experience would help me a lot. I wouldn't be so lost.

During the interviews, Jun explained how familial socialization and cultural expectations shaped her identity as a queer, Chinese American woman. She explained, "I just feel such injustice, especially because I'm a woman and I'm supposed to be quiet, and that just really bothers me." She was conscious of both U.S. and Chinese expectations for women and behaved in radically different ways on campus and at family gatherings. Two months after her interview, Jun took a leave of absence from college to care for her ill father. It was her duty as the oldest daughter.

Fernando

Fernando described coming out to his mother "by accident" when he was in tenth grade. He explained,

> My mom found a note . . . and she asked me about it. I couldn't lie to my own mom. She already knew, but she decided to ask me a few questions

and I had to answer them honestly. My mom is . . . a traditional Latina woman and in the Latino culture it's not good for men to be gay. . . . You have to be tough. You have to be manly. For a male to be LGBT is a big issue. My mom's dealing with it. She still has a lot of issues with it, but I'll always be her baby.

Clearly, this mother's love for her son overrode any negative stereotypes she had regarding gay men. Despite her support, Fernando sometimes struggled to navigate the local Latino community. Fernando described how, as an adolescent, cultural pressures of hegemonic masculinity and heterosexuality negatively affected his sense of self. He said, "I see, like, that misogynistic image of a male. I can't stand those traditional guys who think they're tough. [But for a long time] . . . some of those issues . . . made me not like my own gender."

When he arrived at college, Fernando made an effort to join the Latino and queer student groups. Unlike Roberto, Jackson, and Jun, he described a relatively positive experience in both student associations. He felt welcome in both places and did not describe a pressure to pick or focus on one identity over another. He did, however, have a less than ideal experience in a Latino fraternity where antigay sentiments abounded.

By the time of his second interview, Fernando seemed to be at peace with his intersecting identities. He described himself as "confident" being an out, gay Latino at home and school and in his fraternity. In the second interview, he also described his intersecting identities in a matter-of-fact fashion. He described himself: "Like every person I have, like . . . different identities. I'm a Latino male . . . identifying as Roman Catholic . . . who is in the LGBT community."

Essence

In contrast to Fernando, who was eager to talk about his multiple intersecting identities, Essence was in the early stages of navigating her identity intersections. Essence came out as a lesbian while attending an arts high school in the Midwest. Before she came to terms with her lesbian identity, she acted as an ally to her LGBT peers. During her first year in high school she became a student advocate for a nonprofit LGBT youth center in her community. She described that organization as a validating "community" and "family" offering "support." Affirming experiences in that community organization inspired Essence to begin to identify as a lesbian instead of an ally during her junior year in high school.

While the community organization was supportive, her high school was a much less affirming environment. She and her LGBT peers faced many obstacles when they tried to create a Gay-Straight Alliance (GSA). By protesting, including at a school board meeting, Essence and her friends eventually succeeded in creating a high school GSA.

While Essence spent much time exploring her sexual orientation in high school, intersections with her race did not come until college. During her interview, Essence struggled to find words for her racial experiences. Being adopted by a wealthy, White, Jewish family who lived in a predominantly White community gave her little opportunity to interact with other people of color. She said, "I can't say that I've had too many experiences [with people of color]. I'm just recently realizing that I'm African American." While Essence was quite aware of her dark brown skin, she only recently associated her skin color with a racial identity. In fact, she explained how her race was rarely acknowledged in her home or K–12 school settings. She shared, "I never experienced anything within the community where people . . . acknowledge my race, really." When she arrived at the predominantly White university, she began to explore the intersections of her race and sexual orientation. Her quest to focus on intersectionality led her to seek an officer position in the QSG. Unfortunately, Essence left the institution before her second interview, so it was impossible to document if, and how, her perspectives and identity intersections changed over the course of the year.

James

James was raised in a deeply religious home where he[1] learned that gays "go to hell." But he knew from a very young age that he was gay. He often "pray[ed] not to be gay." Because James did not find safety at home, he desperately longed for the support of a GSA in high school. Unfortunately, such a club did not exist. He explored his identity away from the view of his family, dating boys and experimenting sexually.

Prior to college, James did not think about his race. Even though James was the child of an interracial couple (Black father and White mother), his racial heritage was never discussed in family settings. Only after meeting Roberto, Jackson, and Jun did James begin to identify as biracial. Throughout high school, he identified as White. During his first interview, James described this identity progression as follows:

> For me it's really hard because I didn't realize that I was colored until I came to college, and I thought of myself always as White. But now I'm . . . embracing it. I'm three-quarters French and a quarter African American. I don't look it, and that's what's really hard for me. . . . I was always raised in upper-class White communities.

One year later, James had a different perspective on his racial identity. He said, "Since our last interview, I now identify as a person of color—all the way."

While James was never very close to his "homophobic" family, he became even less connected to them as he developed his identity as a person of color. He shared: "I never related to my family and I'm getting farther and farther out from them. . . . It's just really hard for my mom. She's White and she doesn't understand. . . . I don't know how to relate to [her]."

James also explained how his gender and sexual identities transformed over the course of the study. He shared, "I now identify as 'queer' instead of 'gay,' and I'm also now working on identifying as 'gender queer' instead of 'male.'" He explained the transition in his gender identity by saying,

> I am still a biological male, and I'm not changing it anytime soon, and most people will perceive me as bio male. [But] I realize I'm not necessarily male any more. . . . I want to go out and buy a skirt, and just wear it. I'm gender queer, I don't fit gender norms.

The transition to queer and gender queer was prompted by James's desire to honor the integration of his gender, sexual, and racial identities. Yet, there were many environments where living at these intersections was problematic. During his second interview, James explained how he was turned off by local gay organizations because they failed to recognize the complexity of his multiple and intersecting identities. He said:

> The gay community, to me, is *just* gay. Most of them are White and kind of wealthy. For me, the queer community [is more accepting of] queer people of color, and is very trans heavy . . . and way more accepting than the gay community.

Like the other students in this study, James wished for environments where he could live at the intersections of his multiple identities and be appreciated and welcomed for all of who he was.

Applying Qualitative Fundamentals

In this section, I return to the key elements of qualitative research and show how honoring depth, complexity, and holistic accounts; emergent and flexible design; naturalistic settings; and voice and agency afforded me an opportunity to document rich and complicated intersectionality narratives from six college students.

Depth, Complexity, and Holistic Accounts

In the previous section, participants' narratives offered a glimpse into their deep and complex identity intersectionality journeys. Students in this study discussed how they were often pressured to reject or hide particular identities in campus groups, in community settings, and sometimes at home. Some students also felt familial and cultural pressures to deny their gender or sexual identity or to suppress their desired gender expression. For instance, Fernando felt cultural pressures to be a "tough" Latino. Roberto was scolded by his father for being too "girly" and was met with equally negative responses from peers when he went to school dressed in drag. Students in the study described a "pull" to compartmentalize their identities in different environments. In effect, they were pressured not to be "whole."

By examining student experiences through a holistic lens, an intricate picture of intersectionality emerged. In fact, findings suggested students desired a holistic sense of identity where they could comfortably live at the intersections of their multiple identities. They were not merely conscious of their intersecting identities, but they actively sought integrated or fused identities (Jones, 2009; Stewart, 2008). A holistic lens also allowed me to see the significance of identity intersections across time and space. Two years of data collection, including interviews two years apart, enabled a holistic and nonstatic image of intersectionality to emerge. Such a view would not have been possible from data collected at one point in time.

Emergent and Flexible Design

If this study had not been flexible, and had not honored emergent topics, I could not have written this chapter. As the larger ethnographic study progressed, it became clear that queer students of color had rich and complex intersectionality experiences. A single interview combined with group observation seemed insufficient for exploring their identity realities. Thus, a second interview was conducted with this subgroup of students. When the second interviews were planned, the scope of the research was still shaded by the researcher's assumptions, paradigms, and the limited identity and intersectionality literature. My assumptions led me to focus narrowly on the ways queer students of color made meaning of their experiences in the QSG. Yet, student narratives painted a far more complicated image of identity, intersectionality, and environments. These emergent concepts far overshadowed my narrow emphasis on two intersecting identities (race and sexual orientation) and my focus on a single student setting (QSG). Participants did *not* describe their identities *only* as the intersection of their race or ethnicity and sexual orientation, nor was the campus group the only environment that influenced their identity journeys. Honoring emergent themes through flexibility of design and expanding foci allowed rich and complex intersectionality narratives to emerge. Roberto's quote about his intersecting socioeconomic status, race, gender, and sexual orientation highlights how crucial it is for qualitative researchers to listen for and honor emergent themes that push the bounds of a research project beyond the anticipated scope.

Naturalistic Inquiry

Qualitative researchers study individuals in their natural settings as opposed to laboratories or neutral environments. An initial focus of this study was the queer university groups on campus. However, as the study progressed, it became apparent that a narrow focus on group settings did not do justice to the complicated environments that shaped the identity journeys of students. Through interview narratives, I came to understand how students navigated their multiple identity journeys in a variety of environments, both on and off campus. Many settings influenced their journey toward a holistic identity. Jun's struggle in familial and school environments is just one example. If I had limited my focus to her experiences in the QSG, I would have missed the richness and complexity of her intersectionality journey. By honoring emergent themes, I learned that Jun navigated complicated family and cultural dynamics as a queer feminist and was often forced to hide those identities when she interacted with her Chinese and Chinese American kin. I also learned about the homophobia she faced in the CSA and the racial exclusion she felt in the QSG. Neither group welcomed her as a whole person. All participants in this study also described how they were forced to navigate home, school, and community settings where they had to highlight or hide parts of their identities. In short, I learned that many different naturalistic settings influenced the identity development processes for these college students.

Length of time in naturalistic settings is an important aspect of qualitative studies (Creswell, 2007). Through two years of observations, I collected a wealth of rich data. Moreover, by conducting the interviews a year apart, I was able to explore how students made meaning of their intersecting identities at two different moments in time. As James described so eloquently, his racial, gender, and sexual identities transformed quite significantly in the year between interviews. Had I limited data collection to a single interview, I would have missed many powerful details of his identity journey. The same is true for Roberto, who, in the first interview, described high school reflections on what it meant to be gay and Latino. In the second interview, he boldly claimed a working-class, Chicano, and queer identity. A single interview, or two interviews conducted less than a year apart, may not have yielded such rich information about these identity transformations.

Voice and Agency

Higher education literature often emphasizes the challenges and struggles of students of color and LGBT students (Evans & Broido, 1999; Feagin, Vera, & Imani, 1996; Patton, 2011; Rankin, Weber, Blumenfeld, & Frazer, 2010; Wall & Evans, 2000; Watson, Terrell, & Wright, 2002). While these students experienced trials in a variety of environments, they also exhibited strength, resilience, and agency. Through two in-depth interviews, students were given the space to describe their resilience and agency. I also witnessed their strength during group observations. Roberto weathered genderism and homophobia in high school. Yet, he described his drag identity as "fierce" and the process of dressing in drag as "transforming." Roberto was not merely a survivor of marginalization, he was an empowered young person who exhibited agency in the face of oppression.

A common way that students exemplified agency was by rejecting the notion that they had to pick one salient identity. All of the students actively worked to find an integrated identity that encompassed their complex and intersecting social locations. Students in this study were searching for what Du Bois (1903) called "the truer self" and what Stewart (2008) referred to as "all of me" (p. 183). They also exhibited queer authorship (Abes & Kasch, 2007) as they navigated friendly and unfriendly environments. They shared a desire to achieve *and* have others recognize their holistic sense of self. They wanted educational, familial, and community environments where all aspects of their "self" would be validated. Participants spoke up in meetings, challenged family members, and assumed leadership roles in their quest to transform their environments into more inclusive spaces (see Vaccaro, 2009; Vaccaro & Mena, 2011). In sum, these six students exhibited agency and resilience in their quest to locate (and/or transform environments into) settings where they could be recognized and affirmed for living at the intersections of their multiple identities.

Conclusion

In this chapter, I described the essential elements of qualitative research: (a) depth, complexity, and holistic accounts; (b) emergent themes and flexible design; (c) naturalistic settings; and (d) voice and agency. To bring these qualitative elements to life, I shared snapshots of the rich identity narratives of six students. In the final section of the chapter, I argued that qualitative research can be an excellent match for studying complicated phenomena such as evolving intersectionality journeys.

Note

1. Since James used masculine instead of gender-neutral pronouns at the time of the study, I use masculine pronouns here.

References

Abes, E. S., & Kasch, D. (2007). Using queer theory to explore lesbian college students' multiple dimensions of identity. *Journal of College Student Development, 48*(6), 619–636.

Creswell, J. W. (2007). *Qualitative inquiry and research design: Choosing among five traditions* (2nd ed.). Thousand Oaks, CA: Sage.

Crotty, M. (1998). *The foundations of social research: Meaning and perspective in the research process.* Thousand Oaks, CA: Sage.

Delgado, R. (1989). Storytelling for oppositionists and others: A plea for narrative. *Michigan Law Review, 87*(8), 2411–2441. Retrieved from http://www.jstor.org/stable/1289308

Du Bois, W. E. B. (1903). *The souls of black folk.* New York: W. W. Norton.

Evans, N. J., & Broido, E. M. (1999). Coming out in college: Negotiation, meaning making, challenges, supports. *Journal of College Student Development, 40*(6), 658–668.

Feagin, J. R., Vera, H., & Imani, N. (1996). *The agony of education: Black students at white colleges and universities.* New York: Routledge.

Glesne, C. (1999). *Becoming qualitative researchers: An introduction* (2nd ed.). New York: Longman.

Jones, S. R. (2009). Constructing identities at the intersections: An autoethnographic exploration of multiple dimensions of identity. *Journal of College Student Development, 50*(3), 287–304.

Jones, S. R., Torres, V., & Arminio, J. (2006). *Negotiating the complexities of qualitative research in higher education: Fundamental elements and issues.* New York: Routledge.

Merriam, S. B. (2009). *Qualitative research: A guide to design and implementation.* San Francisco: Jossey-Bass.

Patton, L. D. (2011). Perspectives on identity, disclosure, and the campus environment among African American gay and bisexual college men at one historically black college. *Journal of College Student Development, 52*(1), 77–100.

Rankin, S., Weber, G., Blumenfeld, W., & Frazer, S. (2010). *The state of higher education for lesbian, gay, bisexual and transgender people.* Charlotte, NC: Campus Pride.

Reinharz, S. (1992). *Feminist methods in social research.* New York: Oxford University Press.

Seidman, I. (1998). *Interviewing as qualitative research: A guide for researchers in education and the social sciences* (2nd ed.). New York: Teachers College Press.

Stewart, D. L. (2008). Being all of me: Black students negotiating multiple identities. *The Journal of Higher Education, 79*(2), 183–207.

Stewart, D. L. (2009). Perceptions of multiple identities among Black college students. *Journal of College Student Development, 50*(3), 253–270.

Vaccaro, A. (2009). Intergenerational perceptions, similarities and differences: A comparative analysis of lesbian, gay, and bisexual millennial youth with generation X and baby boomers. *Journal of LGBT Youth: Special Edition on Millennial Teens, 6*(2–3), 113–134.

Vaccaro, A. (2012). Campus microclimates for LGBT faculty, staff, and students: An exploration of the intersections of social identity and campus roles. *Journal of Student Affairs Research and Practice, 49*(4), 429–446.

Vaccaro, A., & Mena, J. (2011). It's not burnout, *it's more*: Queer college activists of color and mental health. *Journal of Gay and Lesbian Mental Health, 15*(4), 1–29.

Wall, V., & Evans, N. (Eds.). (2000). *Toward acceptance: Sexual orientation issues on campus.* Lanham, MD: University Press of America.

Watson, L., Terrell, M. C., & Wright, D. (2002). *How minority students experience college: Implications for planning and policy.* Sterling, VA: Stylus.

Wolcott, H. F. (1999). *Ethnography: A way of seeing.* Walnut Creek, CA: Alta Mira.

3

SALIENCE AT THE INTERSECTION

Latina/o Identities Across Different Campus Contexts

Adriana Ruiz Alvarado and Sylvia Hurtado

In 2012, Latinas/os for the first time became the largest racial minority group on the nation's four-year college and university campuses, representing 16.5% of college enrollments overall (Fry & Lopez, 2012). Though this milestone is no surprise, as the population has been growing consistently for years, it has not been accompanied by the more profound understanding of Latina/o identity that is necessary to ensure that these students are successful in their pursuit of degrees. Although more Latinas/os entering college come from middle-class backgrounds than in years past, nearly 40% are the first generation in their families to step onto a college campus (Hurtado, Saenz, Santos, & Cabrera, 2008). There is considerable heterogeneity among the Latina/o racial group in terms of not only ethnic origin but also race, class, gender, and sexual orientation.

The intersections of these multiple social identities uniquely position Latinas/os within educational contexts and may determine college outcomes. For example, researchers now describe Latino males as "vanishing" and less likely to complete their degrees than Latinas in higher education (Saenz & Ponjuan, 2009). Researchers have not asked if Latinas/os strongly identify with their race and gender or if the salience of this combination of identities is a source of strength or vulnerability. Racial salience can be a source of strength in college and is associated with higher scores on important outcomes such as critical consciousness and willingness to take action, integrating learning across courses and contexts, taking civic action, and acquiring skills and dispositions to participate in a diverse workforce (Hurtado, Ruiz, & Guillermo-Wann, 2011). It seems we need to begin to understand how intersections of identity work to inform our understanding of college student experiences and outcomes.

Even within the single-identity dimension of race, there are stark differences in how Latinas/os perceive themselves. For instance, data from the 2010 U.S. Census demonstrate the variability of racial identification among Latinas/os, with the percentage of those identifying as "White" ranging from 30% for Dominicans to 85% for Cubans (U.S. Census Bureau, 2011). The variability might be smaller if Latina/o itself was an option on the U.S. Census' race question, but the differences here nonetheless suggest that there is likely even greater variability in how Latinas/os view themselves when taking into account a broader range of identity dimensions. To better understand the experiences of and necessary support for Latina/o college students, it is important to get insight into how they think about their own identities, because how they view themselves in relation to a world marked by inequality shapes their college experiences.

The purpose of this chapter is to examine the salience of different social identities among Latina/o college students, across a variety of campus contexts, to create a more nuanced understanding of Latina/o identity. We first use an intersectionality frame to examine how the salience of race, gender, class, and sexual orientation differs among the students in our sample, comparing students' intersecting identities. This creates a general portrait of identity that will serve as a baseline for comparison in the second part of our analysis, where we examine whether particular intersections are more or less salient in different college contexts.

Relevant Literature

Along with the intersectionality frame, research on Latina/o identity, identity salience, and the role of context guide the design of the study.

Intersectionality

Originating in feminist theory and women's studies, the intersectionality paradigm (Crenshaw, 1989) quickly crossed disciplinary boundaries to areas such as psychology, law, and sociology, and its use in higher education research has also been growing in recent years (Covarrubias, 2011; Griffin & Museus, 2011; Jones, 2009; Schwartz, Donovan, & Guido-DiBrito, 2009; Strayhorn, 2010). Unlike "additive" analyses where individuals' social identities are each treated separately and oppression is viewed as increasing with the addition of each stigmatized identity (Bowleg, 2008), intersectionality is the examination of the unique experiences created by the integration of multiple social identities. It suggests that no one social identity can be understood without examining how it interacts with each of the other social identities of an individual. Embedded in an intersectionality lens is an understanding that intersections exist within structures of inequality and that they can create both privilege and oppression (Bowleg, 2008; Shields, 2008; Thornton Dill, McLaughlin, & Nieves, 2012). Reay (2007) offers another consideration: "Different aspects of self become more prominent in some contexts than in others" (p. 607). Therefore, in some cases, one identity is foregrounded and the other muted, whereas in specific situations or contexts, the reverse may be true. The theoretical and empirical challenge for researchers is how to hold together conceptions of difference and structural inequalities that exist in different contexts.

McCall (2005) delineates three approaches for intersectionality research: anticategorical, intracategorical, and intercategorical. The *anticategorical* approach deconstructs master analytical categories, such as work that has taken the identity of gender from having two categories to countless ones. The *intracategorical* approach examines dimensions across categories, identifying social groups at "neglected points of intersection" (p. 1774) such as comparing middle-class Arab women to middle-class Arab men. The *intercategorical* approach uses all dimensions of each social identity in the analysis. For instance, if gender and class are included, then the total number of groups in the analysis is six (two gender × three class). This can quickly become very complex, and McCall urges researchers to limit the identity dimensions in an analysis for the sake of comprehension.

In terms of method, there is little agreement about "best methods" for conducting intersectionality research. Quantitative techniques have been critiqued as inappropriate for studying the complexity that intersectional identities entail (Stewart & McDermott, 2004). At the same time, others argue that restricting methodologies also restricts the scope of knowledge that can be produced (McCall, 2005). Quantitative work can present a macro-level view of patterns (Bowleg, 2008; Shields, 2008), and it has been argued that it can help to provide a complete account of simultaneous impact (Covarrubias, 2011).

Latina/o Identity

Whereas the racial identity development models of most racial groups have traditionally consisted of fluid developmental stages (Cross, 1995; Helms, 1995; Kim, 2001), the racial identity of Latinas/os has been examined in terms of orientations due to the diversity within the population (Ferdman & Gallegos, 2001). In the latest update to their six Latina/o identity orientations, Gallegos and Ferdman (2012) describe both the value and challenge of each of the orientations as adaptive strategies, stating that some are better suited for some contexts than others. For example, in environments where homogeneity is valued, an undifferentiated orientation that views race as invisible might be most adaptive, while a Latino-integrated orientation that views race as dynamic might be most adaptive in a highly diverse environment. We highlight this difference between undifferentiated and Latino-integrated identity orientations to demonstrate the complexity of Latina/o identity and the need to examine intersections of identity in different contexts, given that context influences how Latinas/os identify racially and also how they likely view their other social identities.

Identity Salience and the Role of Context

In their Model of Multiple Dimensions of Identity (MMDI), Jones and McEwen (2000) portray three components that influence an individual's identity. The first is the "core sense of self," which rests in the middle of the model. The second is a set of intersecting rings around the core, that represent the individuals' multiple social identities and the idea that they cannot be viewed singularly. The third, and surrounding the first two components, are the contextual influences that determine the salience of each of the social identity dimensions. According to the MMDI, when social identities are merely prescribed by others, they are not part of an individual's core sense of self; only the social identities that are salient are integrated into the core.

Though contextual influences are believed to shape identity salience, research has found conflicting results about the extent to which these influences uniformly shape all dimensions within a particular identity (Cota & Dion, 1986; Sanders-Thompson, 1999; Steck, Heckert, & Heckert, 2003). According to distinctiveness theory (McGuire, McGuire, Child, & Fujioka, 1978), an individual's distinctive traits in relation to other people in a particular context will be more salient than their more common traits. Research in experimental psychology using open-ended probes of self-concept ("Tell me what you are") to examine ethnic and gender salience has found support for the theory in both school classrooms for children and manipulation of demographic representation conditions for university students (Cota & Dion, 1986; McGuire et al., 1978; McGuire, McGuire, & Winton, 1979). Using three test conditions (minority sex, uniform sex, and majority sex), Cota and Dion (1986) found that the salience of gender decreased from 34% in the minority sex context to 16% in the majority sex context for both males and females at one college.

In contrast, White students at a historically Black college and university (HBCU) were found to think about race less than Black students, despite being a numerical minority in that setting (Steck et al., 2003). The same study found that White students at the HBCU did not exhibit higher racial identity salience than White students at a predominantly White institution.

Likewise, Sanders-Thompson (1999) found that race was salient for African American adults even in communities where they are the majority and where most socializing takes place with other African Americans. Both of these studies suggest that privilege and subordination transcend context to a certain degree and that subordinated identities are more salient across situations.

We examine the salience of several social identities for Latina/o college students across various intersecting dimensions of ethnicity, gender, income, sexual orientation, generation, and citizenship to test the interplay of distinctiveness theory with the idea that privilege and subordination transcend context. The theory that an identity will become more salient as it becomes more distinctive in an individual's proximal context, and the idea that identities that are underrepresented in general are consistently more salient, are not necessarily in conflict with one another, but have not been tested together. In short, we explore how the phenomenon of societal underrepresentation works among the Latina/o racial group by examining the salience of different identities in varied contexts.

Methods

In order to create a more nuanced understanding of Latina/o identity, a two-part analysis is employed using a diverse population of Latina/o college students across a variety of campus contexts.

Data and Sample

Student-level data for this study came from the 2010 pilot and the 2011 national administrations of the Higher Education Research Institute's (HERI) Diverse Learning Environments (DLE) survey. Institutional-level data came from the Integrated Postsecondary Education Data System (IPEDS). A total of 34 institutions participated in the survey, including 3 community colleges, 13 public four-year, and 18 private four-year institutions across the United States. The full sample of 29,547 was filtered to include only those who identified as Latina/o, resulting in a final sample of 4,200 students. The ethnic composition of the final sample comprised 61% Mexican Americans, 2.6% Puerto Ricans, 8.4% Central Americans, and 28% other Latina/o. Females accounted for 67.4% of the sample and 46.1% were first-generation college students. In terms of class standing, the sample included 16.3% freshmen, 27.1% sophomores, 30.9% juniors, and 25.7% seniors. Over one fourth of the students in the study entered their institutions as transfer students, and 16% of the sample was older than age 24. See Table 3.1 for a description of the identities represented in the sample.

TABLE 3.1

SOCIAL IDENTITIES OF SAMPLE (*N* = 4,200)

	Percentage of Total Sample	
Social Identity	*Male* n = *1,369*	*Female* n = *2,831*
Ethnicity		
Mexican American	20.0	41.0
Puerto Rican	0.8*	1.8
Central American	2.8	5.6
Other Latina/o	9.0	19.0
Income		
Quartile 1—Less than $50,000	19.7	42.3
Quartile 2—$50,000–$74,999	5.6	11.4
Quartile 3—$75,000–$149,999	5.6	10.1
Quartile 4—$150,000+	1.8	3.5
Sexual Orientation		
Heterosexual	27.9	59.5
LGBT and Other	4.7	7.9

*Indicates cell count is *n* < 50.

Measures

Research has operationalized identity salience and examined intersecting identities in various ways. As such, it is necessary to describe how these are measured in this study and the contexts in which they are compared.

Salience. Hancock (2007) recommends creating new ways of quantitative data collection that captures individual-level perceptions of identity. Prior research suggests that social identity can be thought of as consisting of three dimensions: cognitive centrality, ingroup affect, and ingroup ties (Cameron, 2004). In this representation of identity, *cognitive centrality* is defined as the amount of time that one spends thinking about being a member of the social identity group, and this dimension most closely resembles the concept of salience that is used in this study. Although data limitations prevent us from tapping into all three social identity dimensions, our measure of salience is a more nuanced way of understanding the individual-level perceptions of identity than simply relying on demographic categories.

This study included five individual items asking students to select how often they think about their different social identities on a five-point Likert scale (1 = never to 5 = very often). For reporting purposes, students who indicated that they "often" or "very often" think about a social identity will be referred to as having "high salience" for that particular identity. Race, class, gender, and sexuality, the identities most often examined in intersectionality research (Weber, 1998), constitute the salience items in our study.

Intersectionality. One of the critiques of intersectionality research using quantitative methods is its reliance on preexisting data because most surveys have limited demographic categories that can be used to create meaningful intersections (Hancock, 2007). The DLE, however, was intentionally created for use in analyses that place diverse students and their multiple social identities at the center, following the Multicontextual Model for Diverse Learning Environments (Hurtado, Alvarez, Guillermo-Wann, Cuellar, & Arellano, 2012). Dubrow (2008) suggests that gender, class, and race should be the variables used first in quantitative intersectionality work, but also recommends expanding on these identity groups whenever possible because using categories aside from the master ones can "give way to undiscovered salient social cleavages" (p. 87). For this study, we examine intersections between Latina/o students' gender and their ethnicity, income, and sexual orientation. Our chosen analytical technique follows the intercategorical approach in that all dimensions of all the aforementioned social identity groups are included in the descriptive analysis.

Context. IPEDS data were used to create measures representing the percentage of full-time-equivalent undergraduate students at each campus who were Latina/o, underrepresented minorities (URM), female, Latina, and federal Pell Grant recipients.

Results

More than two thirds of our sample (67.8%) indicated high salience for at least one of the four social identities examined. Just under half (48.4%) of the Latina/o students in the sample reported high salience on at least two of the identities, and almost one third (30.2%) designated three of the social identities as being highly salient to them.

Salience Across Intersecting Identities

The first part of the analysis examined how the salience of different identities varies among Latina/o students. In particular, the amount of time students spend thinking about their race, class, gender, and sexual orientation based on particular intersections of their identity sets a backdrop for understanding the role that context may play in this process.

Race. Prior research (Hurtado et al., 2011) has found that Latinas/os think about their race significantly more than do their White peers. Our analysis shows that, as a whole, 47.3% of Latinas/os "often" or "very often" think about the fact that they are Latinas/os. Disaggregating the sample by different social identities, we see that among two genders and four Latina/o ethnic groups, Central American females think about race the most, with 57.5% having high racial identity salience. Though all four ethnic groups are part of the larger Latina/o group, it could be that the minority status of Central Americans within the Latina/o population in the United States and on college campuses contributes to higher racial identity salience. The three largest Central American communities—El Salvador, Guatemala, and Honduras—combined comprise only 7.2% of the Latina/o population in the country, while Mexicans make up 64.9% and Puerto Ricans 9.2% of that population (Motel & Patten, 2012). With regard to gender, Hurtado et al. (2011) found that being female was a positive predictor for racial identity salience for all students, and our findings confirm that this holds true when disaggregating for a Latina/o-only sample, as Latinas report having higher salience than Latinos across all social identity dimensions examined.

Class. Of the four social identities examined for salience, socioeconomic class is the most frequently thought about by the full sample, with almost half (49.3%) of all Latina/o students indicating high salience. When looking at particular intersections of identity we see that, as with race, Central American females have higher social class salience (59.6%) than all other ethnic group dimensions. However, while both Central American men and women have higher racial identity salience than their Mexican American, Puerto Rican, and other Latina/o counterparts, Puerto Rican women (54.8%), Mexican American men (47.3%), and Mexican American women (53.9%) all report higher social class salience than do Central American men (46.2%). This finding highlights the importance of examining intersections, since looking at the aggregate for Central Americans (53.8%), it would appear that males and females think about their class identity in a similar fashion.

With regard to income, a decreasing pattern of social class salience as income quartile increases is evident for both males and females, with the exception of males from the highest income quartile (more than $150,000), for whom class salience increases from that of males in the third income quartile (42.4% compared to 30.5%), countering the idea that the more privileged the identity, the less salient it is to an individual (see Figure 3.1). The income quartiles are based on reported combined parental income, with incomes less than $50,000 constituting the lowest quartile, incomes between $50,000 and $74,999 constituting the second quartile, incomes between $75,000 and $149,999 constituting the third quartile, and incomes above $150,000 constituting the highest quartile.

Gender. As a whole, 34.9% of the students report high salience of gender identity, but disaggregating demonstrates that Latinas think about gender much more than do Latinos (40.9% compared to 22.4%). Females have higher levels of gender identity salience across all social identity intersections, supporting the idea that they think more about disparaged or politicized social identities than privileged ones (Hurtado, Gurin, & Peng, 1994). With only one exception, no striking differences appear in the level of gender salience

Figure 3.1 Percentage of Students Indicating High Racial Salience, by Percentage Latina/o at Their College and by Ethnicity

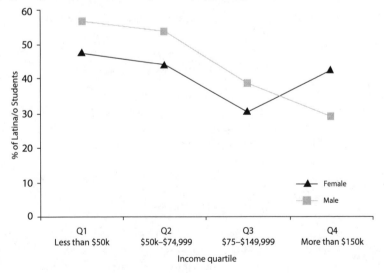

reported across the different dimensions of all the social identity groups, as both male and female gender salience rates are fairly stable throughout all examined intersections. The only exception is that more than half (51.6%) of all females and 40.6% of all males who identify as LGBT or other sexual orientation report thinking about gender "often" or "very often." Gender might be more salient for both males and females who identify as LGBT because their sexual orientation highlights intragroup differences within their gender group. This finding highlights the interdependence of gender and sexual orientation and the importance of considering that intersection in research.

Sexual Orientation. Only 11% of the entire sample has high salience of sexual orientation identity, but this is the only one of the social identities where males for the most part report higher salience than females. As with gender, the rates are fairly stable across all dimensions of the different social identities examined, with males a little higher than average and females a little lower. Latino males who identified as LGBT or other sexual orientation, however, had remarkably higher salience than heterosexual males and females as well as LGBT females. Almost a full three quarters (72.5%) of all Latino LGBT males often or very often think about their sexual orientation, compared to 11.7% of heterosexual males, 12.3% of heterosexual females, and 58.3% of LGBT females. As the salience of gender analysis demonstrated, the intersection between gender and sexual orientation warrants attention. It appears that gender is a more prominent identity for LGBT females than for males and that sexual orientation is more salient for LGBT males than for females (see Figure 3.2). For this particular identity, high salience could indicate a lengthy questioning process or difficulty disclosing (Rosario, Schrimshaw, & Hunter, 2004). Prior research has also linked high salience of sexual orientation to stigma awareness (Pachankis & Goldfried, 2006). Though this study does not provide insight about whether high sexual identity salience for this population is due to positive or negative experiences, the fact that salience is higher for males than for females does call to mind the challenge that some Latino men may face in reconciling a gay sexual identity with cultural expectations of machismo (Almaguer, 1993).

General Patterns. In sum, our first set of findings demonstrates that, indeed, the pattern of less privileged identities being more salient than privileged ones exists for Latinas/os across all social identities, regardless of gender. Class salience decreases as income increases; sexual orientation salience is higher for LGBT students; gender is more salient for females; and Central Americans, who are a minority within the Latina/o population, have

Figure 3.2 Percentage of Students Indicating High Salience of Gender and Sexual Orientation, by Gender

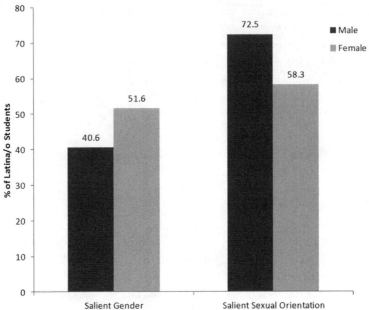

higher racial identity salience. The next section discusses whether this pattern changes in different contexts where underrepresentation is associated with a particular identity.

Salience Across Different Contexts

Intersectionality scholars (Dubrow, 2008; Warner, 2008) have recommended using social contexts to aid in the selection of the demographics and intersections to be used in an analysis. For this study, we selected several contexts that might individually influence one of the identity salience measures, and then we selected the demographic categories to test the theory of distinctiveness based on what we hypothesized would best correspond with the context of interest. For instance, to test whether changes in the percentage of a student body that is female would influence the salience of gender, we examined how it separately influenced males and females. Due to a lack of available measures representing the percentage of students who identify as LGBT, we were unable to examine the relationship between increasing distinctiveness in a context and the salience of sexual orientation. See Table 3.2 for a list of context variables and their values.

TABLE 3.2

MEASURES USED IN ANALYSIS TO TEST FOR EFFECT OF CONTEXT ON IDENTITY SALIENCE

Context Measures	Context Values	Salience Measure	Identity Dimensions Tested
Percentage URM	1 = Less than 20% 2 = 20–35% 3 = More than 35%	Race	Ethnicity (Mexican American, Puerto Rican, Central American, Other Latina/o)
Percentage Latina/o	1 = Less than 20% 2 = 20–35% 3 = More than 35%	Race	Ethnicity (Mexican American, Puerto Rican, Central American, Other Latina/o)
Percentage Receiving Pell Grants	1 = Less than 20% 2 = 20–35% 3 = More than 35%	Class	Income Quartile (Q1 = Less than $50,000; Q2 = $50,000–$74,999; Q3 = $75,000–$149,999; Q4 = $150,000+
Percentage Female	1 = 0–45% 2 = 46–55% 3 = More than 55%	Gender	Gender (Male, Female)
Percentage Latina	1 = Less than 10% 2 = 10–20% 3 = More than 20%	Gender	Gender (Male, Female)

Racial Identity Salience, Latina/o Ethnic Groups, and URM Context. Two different context variables, percentage of Latinas/os and percentage of URM, were used to compare ethnic groups and test whether racial identity salience changed as the Latina/o racial group became less distinctive (increased representation) in its college environment. As the percentage of the student body that is Latina/o increases, the salience of race decreases for both Mexican Americans and Puerto Ricans. The opposite occurs, however, for Central Americans and other Latinas/os (see Figure 3.3). Since Mexican Americans constitute the largest of the Latina/o ethnic groups, an increase in the percentage of Latinas/os on campus almost necessarily translates to an increase in Mexican Americans on campus, which can possibly explain the decrease in racial identity salience. Conversely, Central Americans and other Latinas/os might begin to feel more distinct when the Latina/o population is larger because it allows for more identification of intragroup differences within the Latina/o student population.

Similar patterns and similar salience levels are present as the proportion of URM increases for Mexican Americans, Puerto Ricans, and other Latina/o. For instance, for Mexican Americans, Puerto Ricans, and other Latinas/os,

Figure 3.3 Percentage of Students Indicating Racial Identity Salience, by Latina/o Ethnic Groups

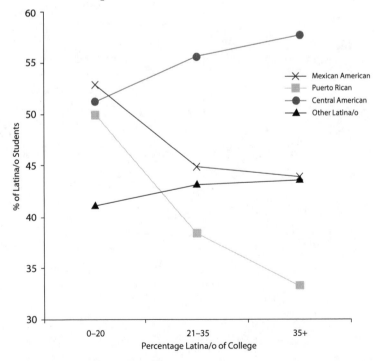

there is less than a 1% difference between the levels of high salience reported on a campus with less than 20% Latinas/os and those at a campus with less than 20% URM. There is also a less than 1% difference between the levels of high salience reported on a campus with more than 35% Latina/o enrollment and those at a campus with more than 35% URM enrollment. This could mean that the frequency of thinking about race for Mexican Americans, Puerto Ricans, and other Latinas/os is most related to feeling distinct around White students rather than around other non-Latinas/os. Central Americans had no clear pattern as percentage of URM context changed.

Social Class Salience, Income Groups, and Pell Recipient Context. Pell Grants are grants offered by the federal government to students who demonstrate financial need, so a higher percentage of Pell Grant recipients on a campus also indicates a larger low-income student population. The percentage of students receiving Pell Grants at an institution was used to examine the influence of context on the salience of social class, comparing across Latina/o students in each of the income quartile groups. Confirming that as individuals become less of a minority for a particular social identity group the salience corresponding to that identity begins to decrease, the level of high class salience for Latina/o students in the lowest income quartile decreases from 65.7% at institutions where the proportion of Pell Grant recipients is less than 20% to 53.7% at institutions where the proportion of recipients is more than 35%. The salience of class identity also decreases for students in the second and third income quartiles. Though having more peers of the same income group does not financially help low-income students, their larger presence in the student body might indicate an environment that feels more supportive of financial difficulties or concerns.

For students in the highest income quartile, there is a drop in class salience between colleges with the lowest percentage of Pell Grant recipients and those institutions in the second level of Pell Grant recipients (21–35%), but then there is an increase in salience as Pell Grant recipients reach the third level of representation (at least 35%) in the student body (see Figure 3.4). Though high-income students are a privileged group in society with typically lower class identity salience (Hurtado et al., 1994), being around peers who cannot always engage in the same lifestyle can create a heightened awareness of their own social class identity.

Gender Salience and Gender Context. Two context measures were used to test the distinctiveness effect on students by gender, and they appear to have opposite effects on the salience of gender for Latino men. At institutions with less than 45% full-time undergraduate females, where males are

Figure 3.4 Percentage of Students Indicating High Salience of Class, by Percentage of Pell Grant Recipients at Their College and Income Quartile

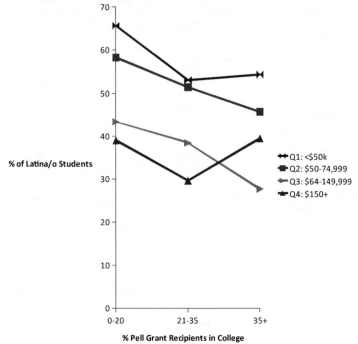

the numerical majority, 25% of Latino males report high salience of gender. The rate of high gender salience decreases to 20.8% when female enrollment exceeds 55%. This downward pattern seems to contradict the hypothesis of distinctiveness theory because gender is seemingly less salient to men when they are in the minority than when they are the majority.

The Latina female context, however, does lend support to distinctiveness theory as the salience of gender increases for males when the percentage of Latina women on campus increases. When the student body is less than one-tenth Latinas, 20.5% of Latino males often or very often think about their gender. When the proportion of Latinas increases beyond one fifth of students, 26.4% of Latino males have high salience of gender (see Figure 3.5). The conflicting patterns for Latino men can be attributed to the unique intersection of race and gender and can possibly reflect the composition of social circles. For instance, if Latinos socialize mostly with other Latinas/os, their male gender salience might not necessarily be affected as much by an increase in females overall but more so by an increase in Latina females on campus. These conflicting patterns may also reflect increased competition among men of various races when there are fewer women in the student body in general.

Figure 3.5 Percentage of Males Indicating High Gender Salience, by Level of an Institution's Percentage Female and Percentage Latina

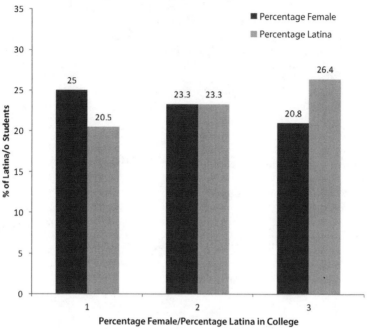

General Patterns. A larger presence of low-income students at an institution, as represented by the proportion of Pell Grant recipients on the campus, is related to lower class identity salience for students from the lower income quartiles. The same increase in percentage of low-income students at an institution is associated with higher class salience for Latina/o students from the highest income quartile. These patterns, upward for some students and downward for others, support the premise of distinctiveness theory in which a larger presence of a contrasting identity in a context creates identity salience. Changes in the racial identity salience of Mexican Americans, the largest of the Latino ethnic groups, as Latina/o or other URM students become a larger presence on campus also support the theory. Yet, although distinctiveness theory does help us to interpret most of our contextual results, it does not fully explain every single pattern. One contradictory finding is that the percentage of males who have high salience of gender identity actually decreases as females become a greater presence at an institution, unless the females are Latina, in which case their gender identity salience does increase. It appears that there is an effect related to the intersection of race and gender that is driving these patterns, but they are nonetheless not explained by sheer distinction of identity.

Conclusion

Among the myriad implications that Latina/o demographic changes have had and will continue to have on higher education research and practice is that it is increasingly important to avoid viewing heterogeneous populations with a homogeneous lens. This study begins to create an understanding of how Latina/o college students think about their multiple social identities, deconstructing static social categories that are typically used for analysis. Moreover, we illustrate the relationship between contexts of unequal representation and identity salience, which helps us to better identify patterns of intersectionality that reveal more vulnerability among certain Latina/o groups. For instance, Latina/o students from the lower income quartiles think about their social class more frequently at institutions where there are fewer Pell Grant recipients than at institutions where there are higher numbers, a finding that suggests a certain degree of feeling different, which might lead to difficulty in achieving a sense of belonging in higher-income contexts. Practitioners who work directly with students should consider intersecting identities when creating structures of support, because, to use the same example, low-income Latina/o students will have different needs than high-income Latina/o students.

One of the challenges facing intersectionality work is that identity is complex and it is hard to capture the interrelatedness of different dimensions (Gallegos & Ferdman, 2012). In our study, not all of our social identity groups could be disaggregated across all of the dimensions of each social identity for lack of a sufficient sample size for each of those breakdowns. However, we were able to identify patterns evident in the data that suggest there are power dynamics at play—even though we only capture a moment in time for a given set of intersections. Future research should investigate the multiple social identities of the same individuals in different contexts across time.

The general patterns across our data that are apparent both with and without contexts demonstrate that those with less privileged identities think about those identities considerably more than do those with privileged identities. In the first part of our analysis, we see that females, low-income students, LGBT students, and students of smaller Latina/o ethnic groups compared to Mexican Americans all think about their gender, class, sexual orientation, and race more often than do their peers. In our analysis across contexts, we see that this applies even in environments where the less privileged identities have a larger representation—where they are less distinct. On a campus where more than 35% of the student body are Pell Grant recipients, for instance, students in the highest income quartile think about class more than do those on a campus with less than 20% Pell Grant recipients. Yet, in both contexts, those in the lowest income quartile still have higher class salience. This prevalence of salience for students who hold these less privileged identities indicates that distinctiveness theory is not capturing what might be better explained as a phenomenon of societal underrepresentation in which the salience of particular identities and intersection of identities transcends contexts.

It is critical to keep in mind that there are other factors at play in understanding the salience of Latina/o college students' various identities, including phenotype, language, citizenship, and so on. Future research should continue examining intragroup differences and similarities to better understand the types of support structures needed to ensure success for Latinas/os who are not just continuously growing in numbers but also in complexity. Intersections of identity among Latinas/os can be explored further to identify those who are most vulnerable and assist them in their journey through college.

References

Almaguer, T. (1993). Chicano men: A cartography of sexual identity and behavior. In H. Abelove, M. A. Balare, & D. M. Halperin (Eds.), *The lesbian and gay studies reader*, (pp. 255–273) New York: Routledge.

Bowleg, L. (2008). When Black + lesbian + woman ≠ Black lesbian woman: The methodological challenges of qualitative and quantitative intersectionality research. *Sex Roles, 59*, 312–325.

Cameron, J. E. (2004). A three-factor model of social identity. *Self and Identity, 3*(3), 239–262.

Cota, A. A., & Dion, K. L. (1986). Salience of gender and sex composition of ad hoc groups: An experimental test of distinctiveness theory. *Journal of Personality and Social Psychology, 50*(4), 770–776.

Covarrubias, A. (2011). Quantitative intersectionality: A critical race analysis of the Chicana/o education pipeline. *Journal of Latinos and Education, 10*(2), 86–105.

Crenshaw, K. (1989). Demarginalizing the intersection of race and sex: A black feminist critique of antidiscrimination doctrine, feminist theory, and antiracist politics. *University of Chicago Legal Forum, 140*, 139–167.

Cross, W. E., Jr. (1995). The psychology of nigrescence: Revising the Cross model. In J. G. Ponterotto, J. M. Cases, L. A. Susuki, & C. M. Alexander (Eds.), *Handbook for multicultural counseling* (pp. 93–122). Thousand Oaks, CA: Sage.

Dubrow, J. K. (2008). How can we account for intersectionality in quantitative analysis of survey data? Empirical illustration of Central and Eastern Europe. *ASK: Society, Research, Methods, 17*, 85–102.

Ferdman, B. M., & Gallegos, P. I. (2001). Racial identity development and Latinos in the United States. In C. L. Wijeyesinghe & B. W. Jackson III (Eds.), *New perspectives on racial identity development: A theoretical and practical anthology* (pp. 32–66). New York: New York University Press.

Fry, R., & Lopez, M. H. (2012). *Now largest minority group on four-year college campuses: Hispanic student enrollments reach new highs in 2011.* Washington, DC: Pew Research Center.

Gallegos, P. V., & Ferdman, B. M. (2012). Latina and Latino ethnoracial identity orientations: A dynamic and developmental perspective. In C. L. Wijeyesinghe & B. W. Jackson III (Eds.), *New perspectives on racial identity development: Integration emerging frameworks.* New York: New York University Press.

Griffin, K. A., & Museus, S. M. (2011). Application of mixed-methods approaches to higher education and intersectional analyses. *New Directions for Institutional Research, 151,* 15–26.

Hancock, A. (2007). When multiplication doesn't equal quick addition: Examining intersectionality as a research paradigm. *Perspectives on Politics, 5*(1), 63–79.

Helms, J. E. (1995). An update of Helms's White and People of Color racial identity models. In J. G. Ponterotto, J. M. Casas, L. A. Suzuki, & C. M. Alexander (Eds.), *Handbook of multicultural counseling* (pp. 181–198). Thousand Oaks, CA: Sage.

Hurtado, A., Gurin, P., & Peng, T. (1994). Social identities—A framework for studying the adaptations of immigrants and ethnics: The adaptations of Mexicans in the United States. *Social Problems, 41*(1), 129–151.

Hurtado, S., Alvarez, C. L., Guillermo-Wann, C., Cuellar, M., & Arellano, L. (2012). A conceptual framework for diverse learning environments: The scholarship on creating and assessing conditions for student success. In J. C. Smart & M. B. Paulsen (Eds.), *Higher education: Handbook of theory and research* (Vol. 27, pp. 41–122). New York: Springer.

Hurtado, S., Ruiz, A., & Guillermo-Wann, C. (2011). *Thinking about race: The salience of racial and ethnic identity and its relationship to perceptions of campus climate.* Paper presented at the Association of Institutional Research Annual Forum, Toronto, ON, Canada

Hurtado, S., Saenz, V. B., Santos, J. L., & Cabrera, N. L. (2008). *Advancing in higher education: A portrait of Latina/o college freshmen at four-year institutions, 1975–2006.* Los Angeles, CA: Higher Education Research Institute.

Jones, S. R. (2009). Constructing identities at the intersections: An autoethnographic exploration of multiple dimensions of identity. *Journal of College Student Development, 50*(3), 287–304.

Jones, S. R., & McEwen, M. K. (2000). A conceptual model of multiple dimensions of identity. *Journal of College Student Development, 41*(4), 405–415.

Kim, J. (2001). Asian American identity development theory. In C. L. Wijeyesinghe & B. W. Jackson III (Eds.), *New perspectives on racial identity development: A theoretical and practical anthology* (pp. 67–90). New York: New York University Press.

McCall, L. (2005). The complexity of intersectionality. *Signs, 30*(3), 1771–1800.

McGuire, W. J., McGuire, C. V., Child, P., & Fujioka, T. (1978). Salience of ethnicity in the spontaneous self-concept as a function of one's ethnic distinctiveness in the social environment. *Journal of Personality and Social Psychology, 36,* 511–520.

McGuire, W. J., McGuire, C. V., & Winton, W. (1979). Effects of household sex composition on the salience of one's gender in the spontaneous self-concept. *Journal of Experimental Social Psychology, 15,* 77–90.

Motel, S., & Patten, E. (2012). *Hispanic origin profiles, 2010*. Retrieved from http://www.pewhispanic.org/2012/06/27/country-of-origin-profiles/

Pachankis, J. E., & Goldfried, M. R. (2006). Social anxiety in young gay men. *Journal of Anxiety Disorders, 20*, 996–1015.

Reay, D. (2007). Future directions in difference research: Recognizing and responding to difference in the research process. In S. N. Hesse-Biber (Ed.), *The handbook of feminist research: Theory and praxis* (pp. 605–612). London: Sage.

Rosario, M., Schrimshaw, E. W., & Hunter, J. (2004). Ethnic/racial differences in the coming-out process of lesbian, gay, and bisexual youths: A comparison of sexual identity development over time. *Cultural Diversity and Ethnic Minority Psychology, 10*(3), 215–228.

Saenz, V. B., & Ponjuan, L. (2009). The vanishing Latino male in higher education. *Journal of Hispanic Higher Education, 8*(1), 54–89.

Sanders-Thompson, V. L. (1999). Variables affecting racial-identity salience among African Americans. *The Journal of Social Psychology, 139*(6), 748–761.

Schwartz, J. L., Donovan, J., & Guido-DiBrito, F. (2009). Stories of social class: Self-identified Mexican male college students crack the silence. *Journal of College Student Development, 50*(1), 50–66.

Shields, S. (2008). Gender: An intersectionality perspective. *Sex Roles, 59*, 301–311.

Steck, L. W., Heckert, D. M., & Heckert, D. A. (2003). The salience of racial identity among African American and White students. *Race and Society, 6*, 57–73.

Stewart, A. J., & McDermott, C. (2004). Gender in psychology. *Annual Review of Psychology, 55*, 519–544.

Strayhorn, T. L. (2010). When race and gender collide: Social and cultural capital's influence on the academic achievement of African American and Latino males. *The Review of Higher Education, 33*(3), 307–322.

Thornton Dill, B., McLaughlin, A. E., & Nieves, A. D. (2012). Future directions of feminist research: Intersectionality. In S. N. Hesse-Biber (Ed.), *Handbook of feminist research: Theory and praxis*. Thousand Oaks, CA: Sage.

U.S. Census Bureau. (2011). *The Hispanic population: 2010. 2010 Census brief.* Retrieved from www.census.gov/prod/cen2010/briefs/c2010br-04.pdf

Warner, L. R. (2008). A best practices guide to intersectional approaches in psychological research. *Sex Roles, 59*, 454–463.

Weber, L. (1998). A conceptual framework for understanding, race, class, gender, and sexuality. *Psychology of Women Quarterly, 22*, 13–32.

PART TWO

INTERSECTIONALITY AND K–12 EDUCATION

4

TEACHERS' PERSPECTIVES ON RACE AND RACIAL INEQUALITY

Strategic Intersectionality and the Countervailing Effects of Privilege

Laurie Cooper Stoll

As a policy solution, education is often considered a panacea for racism. This argument is predicated on several fundamental assumptions: (a) racism is primarily if not entirely an individual-level problem, (b) the U.S. education system is structured for equality, (c) teachers and administrators are race neutral, (d) racism is irrational, and (e) education necessarily mitigates ignorance. Yet, empirical evidence clearly demonstrates that racism is structural in nature (Bonilla-Silva, 2006); grave disparities exist within the institution of education in the United States (Delpit, 2006; Kozol, 1991; Oakes, 1985; Valenzuela, 1999); teachers and administrators are not only influenced by cultural assumptions regarding race but also often perpetuate these assumptions whether deliberate or not (Ferguson, 2001; Foster, 1990); dominant group members have a rational interest in maintaining social inequalities (Lipsitz, 2006); and, finally, education actually may provide more effective strategies for masking racism as opposed to challenging it (Kane & Kyyrö, 2001).

Even so, education remains a common answer to the question of what can be done to address race-based prejudice, and multiculturalism is assumed to be the most common palliative. However, I believe this approach holds far less promise of alleviating individual and institutional racism than does an increase in antiracist teachers who structure the learning environment in such a way that unearned privilege, whether White, male, and/or heterosexual, is not only proscribed but also fundamentally problematized. This is a solution that can only be effective, however, if teachers are indeed sensitive to these types of privileges and systems of inequality.

Strategic intersectionality suggests that persons who have marked identities, especially those who are identified with more than one, may exhibit under certain circumstances a "multiple identity advantage" (Fraga, Martinez-Ebers, Lopez, & Ramirez, 2006) that may situate them as particularly effective advocates for others who are disadvantaged. The logic implied here supposes, for example, that women teachers of color from working-class backgrounds are more likely to be sensitive to privileges and inequalities related to race, class, and gender, and therefore may be uniquely positioned to structure the learning environment in ways that challenge racism and sexism at both the micro and macro level. What about teachers, however, whose social location includes membership in one or more dominant groups? Are they less sensitive to social inequality, and, if so, is this primarily a factor of their Whiteness, their masculinity, their heterosexuality, or their economic advantage, for example? In this chapter I use data from my book, *Race and Gender in the Classroom* (Stoll, 2013), to explore the parameters of strategic intersectionality by examining the extent to which teachers' social locations influence their attitudes about race and racial inequality, and the countervailing forces of privilege that undermine teachers' efforts to address racism in schooling and beyond.

Intersectional Approaches to Understanding Social Inequalities

Underlying intersectionality theory is a fundamental problematizing of privilege. A basic premise on which intersectionality theory is predicated is that oppressions related to race, class, gender, and sexuality, for example, cannot be understood in isolation from one another; each of these types of inequalities is in fact "interconnected" or "interlocking." Intersectionality theorizing assumes that to elucidate the consequences of sexism, for example, one must take into account its relationship to racism and socioeconomic status, since everyday experiences in the larger social structure will vary for White, affluent women as opposed to non-White, poor women (Frankenberg, 1993; Hurtado, 1996). A significant contribution of intersectionality theory, therefore, is its conceptual approach to understanding inequality. According to Collins (2000), "Intersectional paradigms remind us that oppression cannot be reduced to one fundamental type, and that oppressions work together in producing injustice" (p. 18; see also Frisby, Maguire, & Reid, 2009).

Intersectionality theory has its roots in Black feminist thought (Collins, 2000) and multiracial feminism (Zinn & Dill, 1996; see also Belkhir & Barnett, 2001). Indeed, a major catalyst for the rise of intersectionality theory was the marginalization of Black women both within and outside the academy (Branch, 2007; King, 1988; Simien & Clawson, 2004). Research by intersectionality scholars has documented multiple ways that public policy, the legal system, and academic scholarship concerned with "women" and "minorities" generally render Black women "invisible" by treating these categories as mutually exclusive (Crenshaw, 1991; Hurtado, 1996; Marchetti, 2008).

It is important to note that intersectionality scholars do not discount the complexities associated with elucidating numerous intersecting social identities (Collins, 2008). In fact, according to Collins, few theorists can grasp the nuances of scholarship surrounding systems of power related to race, class, gender, sexuality, ability, and age, for example, and therefore intersectional work is typically partial, generally focusing on specific intersections (p. 71). In fact, while recognizing the significance of myriad intersecting oppressions is fundamental to intersectionality theorizing, in everyday life certain intersecting oppressions are more relevant under certain circumstances than others (Acker, 2006; Battle, 2006; McCall, 2005; Warner 2008). As Collins points out, "All systems of power are always in every situation, but the *salience* of any given system of power will vary across time and space" (2008, p. 74; emphasis in original).

While intersectionality theory fundamentally seeks to illuminate the consequences of interlocking oppressions, *strategic* intersectionality suggests that persons who are part of more than one subordinate group may, under certain circumstances, experience a "multiple identity advantage" (Fraga et al., 2006) that can uniquely position them, for example, to address social inequalities. Indeed, as Hunt and Zajicek (2008) point out, intersectionality supposes that one's social location shapes not only his or her identity and position within a power structure, but also the individual's perspectives on social reality as well. Empirical evidence suggests, for example, that young, working-class women, compared to other demographic groups, are perhaps the most likely to be racially progressive (Bonilla-Silva, 2006; see also Schuman, Steeh, Bobo, & Krysan, 1997).

With the basic tenets of strategic intersectionality in mind, I was particularly interested in this study to identify the extent to which teachers' social locations shaped their attitudes about race and racial inequality. At the most fundamental level this included whether teachers even acknowledged the existence of institutional racism. It also included whether teachers understood racial inequality to be structural in nature, not merely an individual-level problem. Further, I wanted to explore how teachers' perspectives on race and racial inequality influenced how they addressed (or avoided) race-related issues in the learning environment and beyond. Therefore, it was important for me to not only interview teachers but also observe how they do "race" (West & Fenstermaker, 1995) in their everyday interactions with students, teachers, and administrators.

Methodology

Over the course of the 2010–2011 school year, I interviewed, observed, and then interviewed a second time 18 teachers who work at three different elementary schools within the same school district in a suburb north of Chicago: Morgan Elementary, Mason Elementary, and Helis Elementary, all of which offer instruction in kindergarten through fifth grade. Semistructured initial interviews allowed me to gather background information on each teacher before observation. In these interviews, teachers were asked about their unique educational and career trajectory, teaching philosophy and pedagogy, as well as their subjective understanding of their social location. Several questions from the initial interview schedule were adapted from Lortie's (1975) influential study of schoolteachers.

My observation of teachers spanned a period of eight months during which I spent four to five hours in elementary classrooms daily, and included approximately 15 hours of formal observation with each individual teacher. In this phase of the research, I also incorporated the analysis of texts that included the curricular materials that were used during periods of observation, rules regarding classroom etiquette and activities, and physical aspects of the classrooms and the schools. After the observation period was concluded, I conducted a second semistructured interview that asked about teachers' attitudes toward educational policy in general and race- and gender-based policies specifically. This final interview also allowed me to ask questions about specific events that I observed while in the teachers' classrooms and for teachers' feedback regarding the data collected during this period. To protect teachers' anonymity, all of their names as well as the names of administrators and students, the names of the schools in which they work, the name of the school district in which these schools are located, and the name of the town have been changed.

The schools in which the teachers in this study work are located in the District 21 public school system in Lakeview, Illinois, a suburb north of Chicago. Lakeview's population of approximately 75,000 residents is racially diverse and politically liberal; compared with national averages, residents, for example, have a much higher level of formal education, and the town prides itself on an ethos of social justice. One might reasonably expect that a city with these demographic features would house a public school system structured for equality. Yet, like most cities, Lakeview is very racially segregated and this segregation is, of course, reflected in the populations and student test scores of most of its 10 public elementary schools.

While similarities in curricula, teacher quality, and use of best practices can be found across all three schools, Morgan, Mason, and Helis differ in important ways, including racial composition (see Table 4.1). Morgan is a

TABLE 4.1

RACIAL COMPOSITION OF MORGAN ELEMENTARY, MASON ELEMENTARY, AND HELIS ELEMENTARY

School	*White*	*Black*	*Hispanic*	*Other*
Morgan Elementary	65%	14%	12%	9%
Mason Elementary	20%	45%	27%	8%
Helis Elementary	37%	21%	34%	8%

Source: Stoll, 2013.

predominantly White school where White students comprise 65% of the student body. Indeed, to increase racial diversity, Morgan is the only school in District 21 that includes in its attendance area a predominantly Black and Hispanic neighborhood that does not border the immediate area of the school, which is almost all White. Mason, on the other hand, is a predominantly Black school with 45% of students identifying as Black or African American. The next largest demographic group at Mason is Hispanic students, who account for approximately 27% of the student body. In addition, Mason enrolls the smallest percentage of White students in District 21, approximately 20% of the student body. Finally, Helis has the largest population of Hispanic students in the district, accounting for approximately 35% of the student body; Black students comprise one fifth and White students comprise just over one third.

After gaining permission from the principal of each school in this study to conduct my research, teachers were contacted by e-mail and telephone to ask for their participation. In the end, eight teachers volunteered to take part at Morgan, four at Mason, and six at Helis. Like the schools in which they work, the teachers in this study are diverse on several important measures (see Table 4.2). First, the teachers vary in terms of gender and age. Of the 18 teachers in this study, 12 are women and 6 are men. The youngest teacher is 25, while the oldest is 61; the average teacher age is 50. Second, the teachers identify with several racial and ethnic groups, including White, Black, Hispanic, Middle Eastern, Asian, and biracial. Third, teachers also vary in terms of their social class background. Based on the level of education and the occupation of their father and mother, their family of origin household composition, and other pertinent information teachers provided about their upbringing, eight teachers grew up in upper-middle-class households, four in middle-class households, and six in working-class households. Fourth,

TABLE 4.2

TEACHERS' GENDER, RACE, SCHOOL, GRADE LEVEL, AND CURRICULAR PROGRAM

Teacher	Gender	Race/Ethnicity	School	Grade Level	Curricular Program
Chang	Female	Asian	Helis	3	General Education
Foy	Male	White	Morgan	4	General Education
Gira	Male	White	Morgan	5	General Education
Gold	Male	Middle Eastern	Morgan	3	General Education
Hamilton	Male	White	Morgan	3	General Education
Hurley	Female	White	Mason	3	General Education
Jackson	Female	White	Helis	5	General Education
Lee	Female	Biracial	Helis	2	Inclusion
Lopez	Female	Hispanic	Morgan	3	Dual Language
Martin	Female	Black	Helis	2	General Education
Mendez	Female	White	Morgan	1	Dual Language
Norman	Female	White	Helis	5	General Education
Parker	Female	White	Morgan	2	General Education
Roberts	Female	White	Morgan	1	General Education
Smith	Female	White	Mason	5	Dual Language
Stevens	Female	White	Helis	2	Dual Language
Swain	Male	Black	Mason	3	General Education
Williams	Male	Biracial	Mason	K	General Education

Source: Stoll, 2013.

teachers have different years of experience in the classroom. The shortest time spent teaching is 4 years, and the longest is 31; the average number of years teaching is 22. Fifth, teachers work with children of different grade levels; one teaches kindergarten, two teach first grade, three teach second grade, six teach third grade, one teaches fourth grade, four teach fifth grade, and one teaches part-time in a second-grade classroom and part-time in a third-grade classroom. Finally, teachers work in different District 21 curricular programs; 13 teach in the general education curriculum, 4 teach in the dual language program, and 1 is a special education/inclusion teacher.

Teachers' Attitudes About Race and Racial Inequality: Multiculturalism in the Color-Blind Classroom

> I've just found that I try not to see gender, you know, race, that stuff—you just can't even look at that. They're [students] just people. I think that's the smartest way to approach it. (*Mr. Gira*, fifth-grade teacher, Morgan Elementary School)

In the United States, race is pervasive yet "invisible," invisible yet "obvious." The institutions in which the teachers work, the ethos of the Lakeview community itself, and the teachers' personal beliefs and experiences converge in myriad ways to reflect and reproduce these paradoxes. On the one hand, in District 21 "race" does not exist; the maxim is every student can learn and be successful regardless of social location—the foundation of the contemporary color-blind classroom. On the other hand, teachers are forced to acknowledge race because the No Child Left Behind Act of 2001 requires educators to address inequalities among students or face mandated sanctions, and disparities in test scores clearly manifest along racial lines. Further, because Lakeview takes pride in billing itself as a racially progressive community, teachers are encouraged and expected to celebrate racial diversity. The result is that anything negative associated with race, such as acknowledging the existence of institutional discrimination that calls into question the basic tenets of what I came to refer to as the *social equality maxim*, is off-limits; anything positive associated with race such as the recognition of Hispanic Heritage Month is embraced and heralded as an example of the social progressiveness of District 21 and the Lakeview community. The contradictions teachers face in having to deny the material consequences of race while also confronting them are perhaps best illustrated in their perspectives on multiculturalism (see also Lewis, 2005). As I show in the following, it is these perspectives on multiculturalism that provide important insights into teachers' attitudes about race and racial inequality and influence how they approach both in their classrooms.

The Korean Fan Dance: Embracing Multiculturalism

District 21 takes great pride in considering itself a racially progressive school system. In the 1960s the district voluntarily instated a formal desegregation plan in an attempt to racially balance the population of all its schools. Then, in the mid-1980s, District 21 adopted a policy that no defined racial group should comprise more than 60% of any one school's population. To remain in compliance with this policy, the district has occasionally redrawn school attendance boundaries, located magnet programs in certain schools to attract particular racial groups, and bussed students to schools outside of their neighborhoods, as is the case at Morgan Elementary. Despite these efforts, two schools in the last few years, including Morgan, have exceeded the 60% racial threshold, with more than 60% of enrolled students being White.

District 21 also takes great pride in considering itself a multicultural school system. In the following, Mr. Hamilton, a White, openly gay, third-grade teacher at Morgan, expresses the overwhelming sentiment shared by the teachers I worked with regarding multiculturalism in District 21:

> *LCS*: Do you feel supported in your efforts to incorporate multicultural curricula in your classroom?
>
> *Mr. Hamilton*: Oh, absolutely! I think, uh, the one thing I love about teaching in Lakeview is that we are self-consciously oriented toward equity and justice—multiculturalism. I mean, the more obscure the culture, the better it seems sometimes! You know, I, if I were teaching children how to do a Korean fan dance, I'll bet you I would have very little resistance from, uh, from administration or faculty on how to do it. They would want to know what standards I was teaching, how to do it, curriculum, they would want to know those things. But they would have no objection to me doing that, um, so, yeah, certainly there's a huge support for those kinds of things.

At the same time that Mr. Hamilton acknowledges the overwhelming support that teachers receive for bringing multicultural curricula into the classroom, his juxtaposition of the "obscurity" of other cultures with what is perhaps assumed to be the "normal" (White) culture of everyday schooling points to teachers' obliviousness of privilege, if not inequality. Also note that support for multiculturalism, according to Mr. Hamilton, is contingent upon teachers' justifying its legitimacy to their principals and to parents.

After spending several months talking with and observing teachers and students, attending field trips and assemblies, even just walking the school halls, it was clear to me that multiculturalism in District 21 was expressed in the following ways: (a) celebrating racial and ethnic holidays and special accomplishments by people of color; (b) placing pictures of notable people of color on school walls as well as posters with catchy slogans extolling the virtues of diversity like "The Hand of Friendship Has No Color"; (c) incorporating literature about people of color and/or written by people of color; and (d) providing enrichment opportunities including field trips and school assemblies. Multiculturalism did not include any systematic critique of White privilege and inequality. Indeed, if there was any discussion of racial injustice with students, it was generally introduced through the lens of history in the context of a social studies lesson.

Further, because there was no required, explicitly defined multicultural curricular program in place within District 21, principals and teachers generally had the autonomy to determine how much of any of the four elements of multiculturalism they wanted to integrate into their schools and classrooms. In the following, two White general education teachers at Morgan discuss the nature of multiculturalism incorporated in their classes. The examples of multiculturalism they provide are typical of the classrooms I observed.

> *Mr. Foy*: We see it [multicultural curriculum] mostly in social studies when we study a particular topic. I think it's [the social studies curriculum] pretty good about including African and, um, Hispanic, um, elements of the culture, Native American elements. We're going to start a unit on Illinois history pretty soon and, um, and there's a focus on, um, both the experiences of Native Americans' history and the experience of African American history and Illinois history. Some of the books we read, uh, many of the books that we read, that are part of the curriculum are by African American authors about the African American experience. Um, I just finished reading aloud to my class, um, *The Watsons Go to Birmingham 1963*. We talk a lot about that. We talk a lot about the Civil Rights Movement. So it's there. Does it need to be more? I suppose. I'm sure I could do more. But I'm fairly confident that I include as much as I should.

While multiculturalism in Mr. Foy's class occurred primarily in the context of social studies lessons, once again reinforcing the idea that racial inequality was an unfortunate consequence of history that was rectified by the Civil Rights Movement, multiculturalism in Mr. Hamilton's class was expressed through the selection of certain texts. In the following, Mr. Hamilton responds to a question I posed about how he incorporates multiculturalism in his classroom:

> *Mr. Hamilton*: Um, I, I would say being very, just cognizant of the characters that, that I'm choosing to read, you know, very cognizant of who the characters in my story are and, I'll do that where, okay, this particular, um, theme of this story happens in Mexico. The theme of this story, um, is the African American family . . . um, and so I am very conscious about choosing those things . . . and that's the attitude I tend to take when it comes to, comes to that [multicultural] curriculum.

While Mr. Hamilton's strategy for incorporating multiculturalism in his classroom may be pedagogically different from Mr. Foy's, the result is the same. Just as Mr. Foy fails to acknowledge contemporary racial injustice by situating institutional racism as historically contingent, Mr. Hamilton's attempts to celebrate racial diversity through his selection of literature, while perhaps noble, glosses over enduring racial inequalities. Mr. Hamilton's words and pedagogy express the notion that race does not matter, yet in reality there remain material consequences attached to race in the United States.

In the end, while all teachers expressed the importance of multiculturalism and felt there was ample support from the district and their school communities to incorporate multicultural curricula in their classrooms, there were limits even within the narrow scope of "acceptable" multiculturalism. It was perfectly defensible to read books by authors of color, to celebrate Black History Month, to teach students how to do a Korean fan dance. It was not permissible, however, to have an entire African-centered curriculum, at least not according to the majority of teachers in this study.

Where Is the Program for Polish Students? The Limits of Multiculturalism

African-Centered Curriculum (ACC) is a magnet program offered at only one school in District 21, Mason Elementary, where the population of Black students is approximately 45% of the total population. The ACC program was instituted in 2006 amid controversy within the school system and the community at large. The main objection to instituting ACC was that it would reinstate formal segregation within a school district that had a long history of supporting integration. Although the program would be open to applications from all District 21 students, the assumption (and later reality) was that it would be primarily, if not entirely, African American students who would enroll. The main endorsement for instituting ACC was that a program built on smaller class sizes, strong family involvement, and increasing the self-esteem and confidence of racial minority children through an emphasis on "culturally relevant" curricula would decrease the disparities in test scores between White and Black students that had long plagued the district as measured by scores on the Illinois Standard Achievement Test (ISAT).

Very few teachers in this study, including general education teachers at Mason, knew anything substantive about ACC, including its philosophical, pedagogical, and curricular foundation; however, everyone had an opinion about the program. My intention was to build rapport with the teachers before specifically asking for their perspectives on the program, but in the case of Ms. Stevens, a White dual-language teacher at Helis, it came up in our first meeting as we discussed the potential emphasis on Hispanic culture in the dual-language program, which she strongly supported (in theory if not practice). ACC was another story:

Well, I don't know. I just, I don't know anyone [associated with ACC], and I honestly don't know that much about it. I just think . . . it's like they don't have, like, a program for, you know, for, like, all the kids who are Polish, to learn together about Poland. They're not learning Polish, they're just learning about Poland. It's, like, why do we need a whole program just to learn about Africa? When, like, I don't know. I just, I get that it's a big cultural group, but I just think if you're going to offer one for African Americans, you should also offer one for kids who are Polish or Czechoslovakian or whatever. I don't know. That's just my opinion.

According to the 2000 census, persons of Polish ancestry accounted for less than 6% of the population of Lakeview while African Americans made up one fourth. Indeed, no other racial minority group comprises more than 7% of the population, making Whites and African Americans the two largest racial demographic groups in Lakeview, a combined 91.5% of the population. I did not, however, intuit Ms. Stevens's argument as one that could be assuaged by demographic data. Indeed, Ms. Stevens's comments reflected what most teachers expressed as their overarching concern with ACC: the self-segregation of Black students within a curricular program focused on Africa and African Americans. After all, if the social equality maxim viewed all students as equal (which was interpreted by teachers as "the same"), then why should District 21 offer the option of enrolling in a race-specific curricular program? Further, if District 21 was going to provide such a program, why was it geared toward *those* (Black) students as opposed to students of Polish ancestry (White students), for example?

Indeed, as Ms. Jackson, a White, fifth-grade general education teacher at Helis, asked me, with no critical reflection of the dominance of Eurocentric curricula in the district, "Can you imagine them [District 21] saying, 'We need to have a special program for White kids because they're not getting enough [attention]'?" In fact, Ms. Jackson questioned the need for the ACC program given her personal experiences with "reverse racism." In the following exchange, Ms. Jackson advances the notion that the racial pendulum, at least in District 21, has swung too far in the opposite direction (toward people of color and away from Whites). Further, while Ms. Jackson claims she is empathetic to race matters because she "gets" the history of racial inequality, she uses the argument that younger generations (who are among the most likely to be influenced by the contemporary color-blind classroom) do not "get it" to justify the commonsense wisdom that so many of the teachers in this study expressed, that racial equality is essentially a zero sum game.

Ms. Jackson: You know, in some ways in Lakeview it's, I mean, I've, my children have experienced reverse racism, of being called bad names for being White, so—

LCS: Can you give me an example?

Ms. Jackson: Of reverse racism? Well, I came from California, where I grew up in a totally diverse setting. Then I came to Chicago and I'm, like, oh, there's, I feel like there's this big separation and I felt like when I worked at schools in Chicago and some African American people treated me very poorly. And were very angry at me [laughs]. And I was like, oh, they're pissed [laughs]. They don't like me because I'm White. So that felt like reverse racism. Then they got, I mean, I had a woman come up to me my first year at a school in Chicago and said, "You know, I usually, I don't like White people, but you're pretty good." You know, that kind of stuff. And then also my sons go to King Elementary and they have this big, huge African American celebration, which is fabulous.

LCS: For Black History Month or . . . ?

Ms. Jackson: Yeah, for Dr. King Day because it's King Elementary. So they have this two-hour assembly every year. It's like this big fanfare. And I think that is wonderful. But at some point I felt like here's my child, who is at a school that's pretty much 50-50. And he doesn't know the history, he has no concept of what people fought for, nothing. He's a blank slate, right? And when he looks up on stage and all he sees is a representation of, like—they had two African Americans win awards at that ceremony. No White kids.

LCS: Is it always African American children who receive the awards?

Ms. Jackson: Uh-huh. So for him, I'm thinking, you know, from my perspective, I'm, like, I get where it comes from. But he's five, and he's looking up there going, "Oh, where am I in that picture?" Just like every kid should feel represented in their school. Um, so I think that, that kind of balance needs to be brought back a little bit.

Note that Ms. Jackson's concerns about "racial balance" do not take into account the gross underrepresentation of role models of color for minority students in District 21. Indeed, "racial balance" as used in this exchange is simply another way of expressing that Whites should not lose out on the educational privileges they have historically accrued to advance racial equality; it is acceptable to provide opportunities to minority groups that have historically been denied as long as White students do not lose out on any opportunities. This is the context in which concerns about "racial balance" were most often expressed in this study. Therefore, it is not surprising that racial balance was something most of the teachers saw as antithetical to ACC. In fact, almost every teacher whom I asked about ACC was strongly opposed on the grounds that it was essentially a segregated program. In the following, two White general education teachers at Morgan and a biracial dual-language teacher at Helis share their perspectives of ACC.

Mr. Foy: I'm not, I'm not very supportive of it. I think it promotes, um, I think it promotes segregation. I think it promotes different, you know, kids are different. I'm not exactly sure what Afrocentric education means. What are you—how are those kids that much different? How is the education that much different? Um, I think it's important to promote in our curriculum, um, models of African American achievement, and, um, teach African American history and to, um, celebrate cultural achievements of Africans and African Americans, um, maybe, maybe even slightly more so than European. But, in general, we need to celebrate in the limited time we have, celebrate the cultures and achievements of everybody.

In this excerpt, Mr. Foy goes so far as to suggest that maybe it is okay to focus on the cultural achievements of African Americans even more so than those of Whites, but in the next breath dismisses this claim by arguing that teachers do not have much time to devote to celebrating various cultures anyway, and when they do, every racial group should get "their fair share." Once again, the use of color-blind logic assumes there are no significant differences among racial groups (e.g., Mr. Foy's question about whether Black students in ACC are that *different* from their non-ACC counterparts and his dismissive tone that asserts they are not), and therefore no group should be singled out for "special treatment," all while ignoring the pervasiveness of White privilege.

As yet another example of the obliviousness of privilege, Mr. Gira expresses his skepticism of the need for ACC given the scope of multiculturalism in District 21 and teachers' *cultural sensitivities*. Cultural sensitivities did not dictate, however, that Mr. Gira educate himself about the ACC program before dismissing its legitimacy.

You know, I, I don't—I know very little about it [ACC]. I remember when it was initiated, um, I, I think it's more important that kids just—it's nice to provide them with interesting materials, but I think we're [teachers] really aware of that now [the importance of multiculturalism]. I think, you know, we provide a mix of all types of literature, you know, we go out of our way to make sure that we cover, you know, the holidays and the special events and the people that are important to our history. That's not a problem in this district. And, um, if those [Black] kids get the right training [the standard general education curriculum] up front, it won't be an issue.

When I asked Ms. Lee for her perspective, she attempted to juxtapose ACC with dual language, a magnet program that she was instrumental in bringing to Lakeview:

Well, I, I don't see it [ACC] as an inclusive model. Um, I see it as an exclusive model, and I don't personally, I don't believe in that. The dual-language model, which I was, I was one of the hugest, uh, biggest, most prominent, you know, pioneers, you know, for that. We gave a lot of presentations and I was the chair of many committees to get dual language into Lakeview, um, and that is an all-inclusive model. I mean, any child can participate.

To be fair, not *any* child could participate in dual language. Students who were not English-language learners could apply for the magnet program (just as they could the ACC program) and were selected by lottery with preference given to students who had siblings already in the dual-language program and students whose neighborhood school offered dual language. Even so, I did not take Ms. Lee's point about the inclusive nature of the dual-language program as an invitation to quibble over the eligibility guidelines, but to appeal once again to the social equality maxim. In sum, the general attitude expressed by teachers when it came to multiculturalism was that while it was acceptable to *add* culturally relevant materials to the existing (White) curriculum, particularly the literacy and social studies curriculum, it was not acceptable to offer an entire curricular program focused on a specific racial (minority) group. Ms. Mendez, a White, first-grade, dual-language teacher at Morgan, encapsulates this sentiment in the following excerpt:

> I think that's [ACC] going against what you want, what you want to teach because I mean, I'm not—I don't know 100% about the program, but I know it's, you know, centered on African curriculum and, you know, teaching all about that and, I, I just don't, I don't think it's necessary to do that. I think you probably have a class, you know, about that or have, you know, have—and we do stuff with, you know, African American history month and things like that, and I just don't know—I mean, I don't even know if people who are African would want their kids to be only learning African because my understanding, and I'm not sure, but my understanding of the program is it's just, it's every, like math, everything is just taught with African culture, in a kind of African culture setting and that. I mean, I don't even know if I was even from Africa, I don't know that I'd want my kid in a program where that's like the main things since there are so many other cultures and they don't really talk about them, um, and so I think what I heard from other teachers, too, like, a lot of people don't want to put their kids in it because it's so dominated by one particular culture.

Ms. Mendez overlooks the fact that District 21's standard general education curriculum is dominated by one particular culture: White Europeans.

Given the overwhelmingly negative attitudes expressed about ACC, I found the following dialogue with a White, second-grade teacher at Morgan particularly insightful.

LCS: What do you think about ACC as a strategy for addressing racial inequalities in schooling?

Ms. Parker: Um . . . I think that . . . it's hard to say because they [the district] keep it under wraps a lot.

LCS: How so?

Ms. Parker: We don't hear anything about it. They don't share stories of it. Um, it's not talked about ever.

This exchange, of course, begs the question of why ACC "is kept under wraps." But perhaps a more important question is whether teachers' attitudes about ACC might change if teachers throughout the district received regular, substantive information about the program. It seems that teachers who taught in curricular programs other than ACC at Mason were more likely to identify positive aspects of the program. However, their concerns also mirrored those of teachers in other schools. In the following a Black general education teacher offers his insights regarding ACC:

LCS: Since you mentioned an early desire to work with African American males, I'm curious to know if you have ever worked in the ACC program here at Mason.

Mr. Swain: No, I haven't.

LCS: You wanted to teach gen ed?

Mr. Swain: Yes, I wanted to do that because, yeah, I feel like for me and just my experience it's—I don't want the kids to feel segregated and I don't think—

LCS: So it is sort of a segregated program in that there is not a lot of interaction between the ACC classes and other classes?

Mr. Swain: There are. Well, um, we do a lot because we have the dual-language program, and then we have ACC and we have two gen ed teachers at our grade level, myself, and there's another teacher on the other side of me who also does gen ed, and most of the grade levels work that way, and we do interact, you know. The kids get a chance to do different activities and things together throughout the year, not so much early in the year, but as the year goes on.

LCS: So it's not like you've got these different tracks and there's no interaction?

Mr. Swain: No, they interact. I just like the diversity. I guess that's the easiest way to say it. I like the diversity of the gen ed classroom. I like to, um, the kids sort of get to see different races and backgrounds and I think that, to me, is the strongest way to teach because it's more reflective of what they see in real life, you know?

In this exchange, Mr. Swain expresses his preference for teaching in the general education curriculum due to the lack of diversity in the ACC program, a concern shared by most of the teachers in this study, including those who considered themselves racially progressive. Yet, in their concerns about the "segregation" of the ACC program, none of these teachers raised the fundamental question of *why* there were no White students interested in enrolling in ACC. Inevitably the assumption was that "diversity" was achieved by integrating students of color into general education classes, as opposed to integrating White students into ACC classes. The implication about which curricular program is viewed as more important and therefore desirable is clear.

Despite a number of attempts to solicit participation, no teacher in the ACC program volunteered to participate in this research. This was particularly unfortunate given the widespread criticisms of the program by the teachers who did take part. While this study benefited from the differences across general education classes and through working with several dual-language classes, I believe observations in the ACC program would have further enriched the findings and perhaps allowed important counterclaims about the program.

In the end, teachers' attitudes about multiculturalism in general and the ACC program in particular provided valuable insights into how they think about race and racial inequality and their beliefs about the role that education should play in alleviating discrimination. In general, teachers' attitudes reflected what Bonilla-Silva (2006) refers to as the new form of racism in the post–civil rights era: color-blind racism. Through adoption of the social equality maxim and the construction of color-blind classrooms, teachers reinforced the message that race no longer matters. Yet, to what extent did teachers' social location influence whether they fully supported this logic or whether they acknowledged that institutional racism was still a major problem in society and should be addressed?

Discussion and Conclusion

Strategic intersectionality suggests that because of their marked identities within systems of privilege, teachers of color, gay and lesbian teachers, and women teachers, particularly if they are from working-class backgrounds, should be the most likely to recognize the pervasiveness of racial inequality in schooling and uniquely positioned to work toward its alleviation (Hunt & Zajicek, 2008). I spent several months observing teachers "do race" (West & Fenstermaker, 1995) in their use of curricula, and in their everyday interactions with students, teachers, and administrators. Through my conversations with teachers and both formal and informal observations, I attempted to uncover whether these behaviors, as well as teachers' attitudes, varied by race, class, and gender.

Keeping in mind the basic tenets of strategic intersectionality, in the course of this research I tried to identify antiracist teachers with the expectation they would be the most inclined to not only acknowledge racial inequalities as enduring problems within education but also employ strategies for addressing racism at both the individual and institutional level. However, simply relying on teachers to self-identify as antiracists or to reject this label is clearly not sufficient for exploring the parameters of strategic intersectionality. Indeed, practically every teacher in this study wanted to be thought of as an antiracist teacher. However, after months of observing teachers in classrooms, it was apparent that a number of self-described antiracist teachers rarely if ever broached the topic of racial inequality with their students and at times engaged in behaviors that appeared antithetical to the basic premises of antiracism. Therefore, to fully explore the parameters of strategic intersectionality requires not only an understanding of how teachers see themselves in relation to antiracism, but also an examination of teacher attitudes and behaviors to identify whether teachers (a) believe racial inequality remains a significant problem in schooling today; (b) understand racial inequality to be structural in nature, not merely an individual-level problem; and (c) actively seek to address racism inside and outside their classrooms.

Who are the teachers in this study who believe racial inequality is still a significant problem in schooling? Every teacher except for two stated that racial inequality remains a problem in education to some degree. However, of the five White teachers who spoke the most passionately about racial inequality, they include a gay man (Mr. Hamilton), two women who are interracially married and who voluntarily attended an antibias curriculum training series (Ms. Roberts and Ms. Parker), a woman from a working-class background with advanced degrees in inner-city studies and English as a second language (Ms. Smith), and a visibly obese teacher who described herself as feeling marginalized while growing up (Ms. Hurley). (While Ms. Hurley did not refer to herself as "obese," she did share with me her inability to engage in certain activities such as sitting comfortably on the floor with her students because of her weight.) Every teacher of color believed racism was still a major problem in schooling. In sum, as strategic intersectionality suggests, the teachers in this study who are themselves part of marginalized groups or who are intimately connected to marginalized groups are the most likely to acknowledge the existence of racism in schooling and beyond.

Additional considerations imperative for exploring the parameters of strategic intersectionality are whether the teachers who believe racial disparities exist in schooling also understand these to be institutional-level problems, and, if so, whether they actively challenge racial inequality and White privilege. Of the teachers who believe that racial inequality is still a problem in schooling, all expressed the belief that racism went beyond individual-level discrimination to some extent. Yet, in the classrooms, these teachers rarely framed racial inequalities as contemporary, institutional problems.

These findings offer an interesting caveat to the basic suppositions of strategic intersectionality. As this theoretical strand suggests, the teachers in this study with marked identities, including every teacher of color, women teachers from working-class backgrounds and/or who interracially married, and the sole gay teacher in this study, acknowledged the pervasiveness of racial inequality in schooling and believed it was a problem that extended beyond the school halls. These teachers were uniquely positioned as potential advocates for social justice in education. Unlike other teachers in this study who were also concerned about inequalities in schooling, they had personal connections to minority communities and firsthand experiences of discrimination. Yet, I found several examples of privilege that subverted this potential "multiple identity advantage" (Fraga et al., 2006) in the same ways it possibly prevented other teachers from even acknowledging the prevalence of racism in schooling.

In general, I found three types of privilege that worked against teachers addressing contemporary, institutional racism: privilege associated with individual teachers' social location, privilege associated with White students and their families, and privilege associated with the community of Lakeview. It is important to note that each type of privilege, while interrelated, is not similar in construct; indeed, privilege can take the form of both conferred dominance in which one group is given power over another group, and unearned entitlements in which one group is given access to resources or things of value that are systematically denied to other groups (McIntosh, 1992). Individual privilege among teachers, for example, primarily takes the form of conferred dominance, while student privilege and community privilege typically manifest as unearned entitlements.

One underlying factor in teachers' resistance to acknowledging *and* addressing institutional racism is their own privilege. At times this privilege may be a result of their Whiteness, their masculinity, their social class, and/ or their heterosexuality. The interaction of these many identities of course creates a unique social location for each teacher in this study; the privilege shared by all the teachers, however, is that associated with their advanced teacher training and socialization into the U.S. education system. Teachers are essentially highly trained "experts" who are granted significant authority as agents of the institution to promote and sanction what they believe is the proper family-school relationship (Lareau, 1987). The privilege afforded to teachers as a result of occupying this role is particularly evident in their definitions of what constitutes *good* parents and *bad* parents, and their construction and enforcement of a dominant classroom culture.

A second type of privilege that undermines teachers' efforts to raise and address concerns about inequality is associated with the White privilege of many of their students and their students' families. In this instance, the overarching problem is that unearned privilege is simply not problematized. While poverty places many students at an obvious disadvantage in terms of mastering the mandated curricula, students who have access to cultural capital, accentuated by their access to social capital via their parent-advocates (e.g., Bourdieu, 1986), are consistently at an advantage. These students are generally the better-prepared students in class, the students whom teachers do not worry about compromising their standardized test score averages. Therefore, even though the majority of the privileged students are White, illuminating a clear racial disparity between subgroups, because they exhibit the traits teachers value and seek to cultivate (Lareau, 2003) in their classrooms, to problematize students' unearned privilege is tantamount to problematizing the foundation of teachers' educational philosophies (see also Hurtado, 1996). In the end, as long as unearned privilege is understood to be inherently beneficial (McIntosh, 1992), there is no space for teachers to critique systems of power like White privilege, patriarchy, heteronormativity, and ableism.

A third type of privilege that undermines teachers' efforts to acknowledge and address institutional racism concerns the community itself. While Lakeview has a reputation for being progressive, enlightened, and concerned with matters of social justice, the privilege associated with certain (White) residents also creates parameters around defining "acceptable" means to address race-related issues. For example, the brand of multiculturalism in District 21 that receives community support is not critical in nature, challenging systems of privilege and institutional discrimination, but a palatable way to attend to the needs and desires of students of color while increasing the "cultural competence" or cultural capital of White students (see also Darder & Torres, 1998; Lewis, 2005; Perry, 2001). The paradox is that it is Lakeview's reputation for social progressiveness, I believe, that shields many privileged residents from being forced to acknowledge the pervasiveness of racial inequality. Living in Lakeview as a White person allows one to claim an identity marked by racial, gender, and sexual progressiveness, without necessarily having to confront and attend to racial, gender, and sexual inequality. This same phenomenon occurs when Whites believe they can reject the label of racism and claim insider status on racial matters because they have a "Black friend" (Bonilla-Silva, 2006): White residents of Lakeview need not prove their commitment to diversity, equity, and justice; they are residents of *Lakeview*, after all.

In the end, education is *not* a panacea for racism. Yet, I do believe that recruiting antiracist teachers can increase the probability of greater social justice advocacy in education than is currently the case. Noncritical multicultural add-ons that remain peripheral to the dominant Eurocentric curricula endemic to contemporary schooling (Darder & Torres, 1998; Lewis, 2005; Perry, 2001), for example, do not seem nearly as effective as a means of addressing micro- and macro-level racism as students interacting daily with educators who are committed to antiracism and structure the entire learning environment to reflect this commitment. My call for specifically "antiracist" teachers as opposed to simply more teachers of color is not because I disagree with the notion that we need more teachers of color in a profession that continues to be dominated by White women from middle-class backgrounds, but because my research shows (Stoll, 2013) and as other scholars have also pointed out, people of color can rely on the frames of color-blind racism (Bonilla-Silva, 2006) and the tools of Whiteness (Picower, 2009), too. Regardless of race, therefore, we need *antiracist teachers* in an institution and society that remains highly racialized. In the interim, scholars must continue to both listen to and challenge teachers' perspectives on race, recognizing that as long as systems of power are not problematized, the countervailing effects of privilege, along with the increasing demands placed on teachers and their decreasing control over the profession, are likely to impede any consistent efforts to address institutional racism.

References

Acker, J. (2006). Inequality regimes: Gender, class, and race in organizations. *Gender & Society, 20*, 441–464.

Battle, J. (2006). Race, sexuality and schools: A quantitative assessment of intersectionality. *Race, Gender & Class, 13*, 180–199.

Belkhir, J. A., & Barnett, B. M. (2001). Race, gender and class intersectionality. *Race, Gender & Class, 8*, 157–174.

Bonilla-Silva, E. (2006). *Racism without racists: Color-blind racism and the persistence of racial inequality in the United States* (2nd ed.). Lanham, MD: Rowman & Littlefield.

Bourdieu, P. (1986). The forms of capital. In J. G. Richardson (Ed.), *Handbook of theory and research for the sociology of education* (pp. 241–258). New York: Greenwood.

Branch, E. H. (2007). The creation of restricted opportunity due to the intersection of race and sex: Black women in the bottom class. *Race, Gender & Class, 14*, 247–264.

Collins, P. H. (2000). *Black feminist thought: Knowledge, consciousness, and the politics of empowerment* (2nd ed.). New York: Routledge.

Collins, P. H. (2008). Reply to commentaries: Black sexual politics revisited. *Studies in Gender and Sexuality, 9,* 68–85.

Crenshaw, K. W. (1991). Mapping the margins: Intersectionality, identity politics, and violence against women of color. *Stanford Law Review, 43,* 1241–1299.

Darder, A., & Torres, R. D. (1998). Social theory and the "race" fixation: A critique of multicultural education discourse. *Cultural Circles, 2,* 17–32.

Delpit, L. (2006). *Other people's children: Cultural conflict in the classroom* (2nd ed., text rev.). New York: The New Press.

Ferguson, A. A. (2001). *Bad boys: Public schools in the making of black masculinity.* Ann Arbor, MI: University of Michigan Press.

Foster, M. (1990). The politics of race: Through the eyes of African-American teachers. *Journal of Education, 172,* 123–141.

Fraga, L., Martinez-Ebers, V., Lopez, L., & Ramirez, R. (2006). *Strategic intersectionality: Gender, ethnicity, political incorporation.* Berkeley, CA: Institute of Governmental Studies.

Frankenberg, R. (1993). *The social construction of whiteness: White women, race matters.* Minneapolis, MN: University of Minnesota Press.

Frisby, W., Maguire, P., & Reid, C. (2009). The "f" word has everything to do with it: How feminist theories inform action research. *Action Research, 7,* 13–29.

Hunt, V. H., & Zajicek, A. M. (2008). Strategic intersectionality and the needs of disadvantaged populations: An intersectional analysis of organizational inclusion and participation. *Race, Gender & Class, 15,* 162–179.

Hurtado, A. (1996). *The color of privilege: Three blasphemies on race and feminism.* Ann Arbor, MI: University of Michigan Press.

Kane, E. W., & Kyyrö, E. K. (2001). For whom does education enlighten? Race, gender, education, and beliefs about social inequality. *Gender & Society, 15,* 710–733.

King, D. K. (1988). Multiple jeopardy, multiple consciousness: The context of a black feminist ideology. *Signs, 14,* 42–72.

Kozol, J. (1991). *Savage inequalities: Children in America's schools.* New York: Harper Perennial.

Lareau, A. (1987). Social class differences in family-school relationships: The importance of cultural capital. *Sociology of Education, 60,* 73–85.

Lareau, A. (2003). *Unequal childhoods: Class, race, and family life.* Berkeley, CA: University of California Press.

Lewis, A. E. (2005). *Race in the schoolyard: Negotiating the color line in classrooms and communities.* New Brunswick, NJ: Rutgers University Press.

Lipsitz, G. (2006). *The possessive investment in whiteness: How white people profit from identity politics.* Philadelphia: Temple University Press.

Lortie, D. C. (1975). *Schoolteacher: A sociological study.* Chicago: University of Chicago Press.

Marchetti, E. (2008). Intersectional race and gender analyses: Why legal processes just don't get it. *Social & Legal Studies, 17,* 155–174.

McCall, L. (2005). The complexity of intersectionality. *Signs, 30,* 1771–1800.

McIntosh, P. (1992). White privilege and male privilege: A personal account of coming to see correspondences through work in women's studies. In M. L. Anderson & P. H. Collins (Eds.), *Race, class, and gender: An anthology* (pp. 70–81). Belmont, CA: Wadsworth.

Oakes, J. (1985). *Keeping track: How schools structure inequality.* New Haven, CT: Yale University Press.

Perry, P. (2001). White means never having to say you're ethnic: White youth and the construction of "cultureless" identities. *Journal of Contemporary Ethnography, 30,* 56–91.

Picower, B. (2009). The unexamined whiteness of teaching: How white teachers maintain and enact dominant racial ideologies. *Race Ethnicity and Education, 12,* 197–215.

Schuman, H., Steeh, C., Bobo, L., & Krysan, M. (1997). *Racial attitudes in America: Trends and interpretations.* Cambridge, MA: Harvard University Press.

Simien, E. M., & Clawson, R. (2004). The intersection of race and gender: An examination of black feminist consciousness, race consciousness, and policy attitudes. *Social Science Quarterly, 85,* 793–810.

Stoll, L. C. (2013). *Race and gender in the classroom: Teachers, privilege, and enduring social inequalities.* Lanham, MD: Lexington Books.

Valenzuela, A. (1999). *Subtractive schooling: U.S-Mexican youth and the politics of caring.* Albany, NY: State University of New York Press.

Warner, L. R. (2008). A best practices guide to intersectional approaches in psychological research. *Sex Roles, 59,* 454–463.

West, C., & Fenstermaker, S. (1995). Doing difference. *Gender & Society, 9,* 8–37.

Zinn, M. B., & Dill, B. T. (1996). Theorizing difference from multiracial feminism. *Feminist Studies, 22,* 321–333.

5

GENDER IN SCHOOLS

Constructing Identity in High School

Sarah Prior

For many adolescents, high school is a critical period of self-awareness, peer influence, and identity construction. During this volatile period, young people explore how to express themselves in ways that range from conformity to nonconformity and transgression. This is particularly true when it comes to young people's understanding and expression of gender identity. For some youth, personal form(s) of gender expression aligns neatly with social expectations; for others, it does not. When gender expression does not align with social expectations, students may be vulnerable to bullying, harassment, and/or violence from peers and adults. Often, youth who are policed and regulated by their classmates through bullying or harassment are targeted based on their perceived identity, be that racial/ethnic, citizenship, or, frequently, gender and sexuality (Ferguson, 2001; Garcia, 2009; Pollock, 2001). Because gender expression (and gender nonconformity) is frequently tied to other forms of identity, it is often policed most severely, particularly for students of color (Pascoe, 2007).

Gender nonconformity among students who embody multiple "other" identities are punished or regulated more harshly because they express multiple overlapping and intersecting identities, each of which carries its own kind of stigma (McCready, 2010). Because bullying and harassment have significant implications for school achievement and success (Hutzell & Payne, 2012), this chapter analyzes how high school students attending a charter arts school navigate and construct gender identity amid their many intersecting identities.

Data in this chapter are both timely and relevant in terms of assessing the needs of youth as they navigate the social aspects of gender identity construction in high school.

This research builds upon previous literature on the range in gender expression among youth (Best, 2007) and provides insight into what is at stake for youth within their peer cohort and their everyday lives at school when they express their gender identity. Though this project took place within a specific setting and group of students, it highlights the ways charter school staff and administration respond to youth identity expression more broadly and youth gender identity more specifically (Prior, 2012). Because of its autonomy from school district rules and regulations, this school (and many like it) provides a particularly interesting setting for students to navigate gender identity. This project advances the need for research done from a critical youth studies perspective and provides new insight into the types of language and practices youth use to express, perform, and "do" gender (West & Zimmerman, 1987).

Based on an intersectional framework and analysis, research findings contribute to a more nuanced understanding of gender identity construction in high school settings and how it intersects with other identities (e.g., race, religion, sexuality). Research findings also add to an interdisciplinary understanding of identity and youth culture, building on the sociology of education and gender literature as well as critical youth studies (Carter, 2005).

Despite the wide range of inquiry on youth, much of the literature on young people has traditionally been adultist (Fields, 2008) in its theoretical orientation, methodological stance, and ethical perspectives. By *adultist*, I mean that the design, implementation, and analysis of the research, as well as the theoretical and ideological questions, have been largely from adult perspectives—frequently neglecting the wants, needs, and desires of the youth participants. With recent exceptions, research on youth has reproduced understandings of youth as unidimensionally bound by their age, as vulnerable, and as unable to speak for themselves. Building on youth studies literature, this project was youth centered (Best, 2007); that is, youth were part of the design, data collection, and analysis. As such, youth provide their voice to describe and demonstrate how they "do" gender in schools, amid a variety of intersecting identities.

This study[1] examined how youth "do" gender (West & Zimmerman, 1987); that is, the way they describe and enact gender and the ways gender is policed in and through schools. It also examined the variety of external factors at play in creating students' gendered identities. This research highlights not only the ways gender and other identities are used to enact social control, but also the ways youth develop and embrace alternative interactions and ways of being. It is essential that both educators and scholars understand how youth make sense of identity through localized cultural practices because these practices "infiltrate and mediate other important processes, appearing in schools, for instance, as distractions and sometimes as components of lesson plans, and deeply influencing students' social and personal identities" (Wortham, 2011, p. vii). By understanding the way youth navigate their gender, racial, and sexual identities in schools, we can understand the hierarchies and the maintenance and reproduction of inequalities that shape young people's experiences.

As Stritikus and Nguyen (2007) point out, differences can be lost, or never even discovered, when gender and sexuality are not thought of as being constantly produced, (re)produced, and changing within specific contexts and social relations. Gender and sexuality interact with organizational discourses and practices of race and social class across such contexts as family, peers, school, and religious and ethnic communities.

Review of the Literature

Research has long been conducted on youth in a variety of settings and from a variety of disciplinary perspectives. Youth have been analyzed as participants in and creators of culture (Austin & Willard, 1998; Hebdige, 1979; Skelton & Valentine, 1998), as victims and instigators of violence (Ferguson, 2001; Grossman et al., 2009; Messerschmidt, 2004; Miller, 2008), and as sexual and sexualized beings (Ashcraft, 2006; Carpenter, 2005; Tolman, 2005). Further, young people have been researched as being part of, rejecting, or being neglected by school curriculum (Fisher, 2009; Irvine, 2004; Weis & Fine, 2001), and as receptors and creators of media (Brown & Cantor, 2000; Gray, 2009). However, rather than focusing on the particular ways gender identity is influenced by other intersecting identities, previous research has often focused on specific aspects of gender as it relates to other things (e.g., gender and violence, schooling, and/or media).

Gender Expression and Identity

Gender expression among youth can be understood from several broad interdisciplinary arenas. Youth navigate their identity construction amid multiple identities, so scholars have begun to be attentive to not only one aspect of their identities (i.e., race or gender or sexuality) but also the way these many identities intersect and inform one another.

Schools are frequently sites where notions about gender are both solidified and regulated and are often spaces where gender transgressions are policed and controlled (Herdt, Russell, Sweat, & Marcullo, 2007). Schools operate as central institutions for social reproduction, which makes them important sites for analyzing the ways youth interact with gender ideologies at both the personal and organizational levels.

Though adolescence is often still closely linked to biology (some would call this biological determinism), many scholars now understand adolescence as a socially constructed category (Corsaro, 2005). Adolescence has emerged as a useful way of explaining youth behavior, while simultaneously contributing to how we define and control that same behavior. The definition of *adolescence* involves an understanding of young people in a specific stage of development between childhood and adulthood. Young people who inhabit this stage are usually seen as "becomings" rather than "beings and becomings" (Best, 2007) and are frequently not taken seriously by a society that "negate[s] their personhood" (Myers & Raymond, 2010, p. 169).

Regardless of its universal, timeless, localized, or temporal features, U.S. adolescence is currently constructed as a time when young people create identity and make the transition from childhood to adulthood. Adolescence is a "subject position heavily laden with normative assumptions and social meaning" (Raby, 2007, p. 48). The concept of adolescence is shaped by a variety of cultural practices, values, and definitions where multiple meanings have been constructed (Campbell, 2000). Much is taken for granted about the construction of adolescence, particularly in the United States. Not all young people experience adolescence in this way. There are cultural variations in the distinctions between child and adult, and in the characteristic features of what it means to "grow up," so, therefore, it is important to understand that the construction of adolescence as previously outlined is a Western notion.

Competing images of the "adolescent" infuse contemporary culture. We are presented with the image of the overworked, high-performing teen, depicted by a student who is scheduled from morning till night in sports, academics, and extracurricular activities, contrasted with the idea of the dangerous "at-risk" teen, depicted through images of violence, school shootings, and teen pregnancy (Males, 1999). These images are perpetuated and reinforced in academic discussions as well as through the media and are particularly racialized, classed, and gendered. For example, the exhausted, overscheduled teen is depicted as a White middle- to upper-class teen, whereas the pregnant teen is depicted often as a young woman of color, or, if White, a poor, young woman who herself is often the child of an uneducated single mother. While these are just two of the many stereotypical notions of adolescents, the construction of youth in this way has supported the need for policies and interventions that alternately "protect" or penalize youth, depending on their background (Males, 1999; Weis & Fine, 2001).

Similarly, the concept of "youth" is a social construction, one that is frequently conflated with adolescence. For some, however, "youth" can carry different meanings. The term *youth* tends to indicate recognition of agency among young people (Best, 2007; Bucholtz, 2002). The definition is based in part on "explicit efforts to classify young people as either acceptable or dangerous[;] to fashion White, middle-class norms for youth- and gender-appropriate behavior[;] and to identify and control youth who resisted these processes" (Adelman & Yalda, 2000, p. 40). Youth participate in a variety of adolescent cultures and have a wide range of hybrid identities (Corsaro, 2005; Hebdige, 1979). Youth culture, which is linked to the way adolescents live their lives, refers to the shared norms, values, activities, and practices that connect young people. This socially constructed category is "located in liminal social spaces, at the blurred boundaries between 'childhood' and 'adulthood'" (Morrill, Yalda, Adelman, Musheno, & Bejarano, 2000, p. 526).

Young people lack citizenship (legal and social)—and therefore lack what it means to be taken seriously as human beings with rights and responsibilities. As Glenn (2004) articulates, citizenship "refers to full membership in the community in which one lives. Membership in turn implies certain rights in and reciprocal duties toward the community" (p. 19). Young people lack this citizenship in both a legal and social sense. They do not meet the qualifications of citizenry; therefore, it can be argued that they are not treated as fully human. This is important when understanding the rights and responsibilities of young people and their ability to express themselves and their identity "freely." Decisions that affect youth are frequently not made by youth, but by adults.

Intersectionality

Young people construct a sense of identity in relation to others and have multiple layered identities that are derived from social relations, history, and power structures. Moreover, identities are fluid and changing over time and across situations and audiences; they are never static. Youth occupy multiple identities, are part of multiple communities simultaneously, and navigate experiences of oppression and privilege through and in relation to these institutions and identities. The concept of intersectionality (Crenshaw, 1991) is used to grasp the many identities people have and seeks to bring to light the multiple contesting frames and situations of young people's everyday lives. According to Nash (2008), intersectionality has three main purposes. Intersectionality:

1. "Helps to underscore the 'multidimensionality' of the lived experiences of marginalized subjects."
2. "Aspires to provide a vocabulary to respond to critiques of identity politics."

3. "Invites scholars to come to terms with the legacy of exclusions of multiple marginalized subjects from feminist and antiracist work, and the impact of those absences on both theory and practice" (pp. 2–3).

Since theories of justice are particularly concerned with whether, how, and why some people are treated differently from others, there is a need to account for overlapping, intersecting, dynamic, and converging identities of youth. This means addressing issues of gender, race, socioeconomic class, power, and sexual orientation, not just as separate identities added up, but in terms of how the embodiment of each of these identities collectively constructs youth identity (Collins, 2000; Johnson, Flett Prior, Abbott, & Ableser, 2011). The intersectional analysis of youth identity is at the heart of this chapter and has been threaded throughout this literature review. It is important to note that "students do not merely come to school with neatly packaged and predetermined identities that can be sorted along ethnic, class, or gender lines. Instead, identities are constantly under co-construction and respond to images created by self and others within particular school sites" (Rolon-Dow, 2004, pp. 25–26).

Sexuality, gender, race, and class (among others) cannot be understood "apart from the context in which they are accomplished" (McCready, 2010, p. 120). This is useful in understanding that identity categories cannot be "fully understood through seemingly fixed attributes such as skin color, sexual anatomy, or sexual orientation" (p. 120). Further, certain aspects of young people's identity "become more salient during face-to-face interactions in certain contexts" (p. 120). The young people whose voices provide the rich data presented herein navigated these dynamics within our focus groups and interviews.

The construction of youth gender identity is about more than just gender. Instead, the way young people construct and define themselves, as well as the way their identity is defined by others, is based on many intersecting identities. Significant research has been done on how young people navigate these multiple identities. For example, several recent authors have investigated how young people construct their own sexual identities within schools and within the classroom (Fields, 2008; Garcia, 2009), how young people construct their gender identity in relation to class (Bettie, 2003; Brown, 1997), and how youth navigate race and gender identity (Carter, 2005; Ferguson, 2001).

As this literature review has shown, young people are forced to navigate treacherous territory (high school), which can be even more precarious for youth who occupy multiple marginalized identities. The data in this chapter describe how sexuality, race, and religion influence the way students at "Academy" navigate and describe their own identity construction, particularly in relation to their gender identity.

Methodology

This research, which took place in 2011–2012, began with the following research questions:

- How do youth describe and make sense of gender?
- How do youth enact and navigate gender in various school settings?
- How do the official and hidden curricula shape youth ideas and enactments of gender? How do peers shape each other's ideas and enactment of gender?
- How do youth navigate their many intersecting identities (race, class, citizenship, religion, and sexuality) in relation to gender?

This project used a mixed-method approach to data collection, including (a) participant observation, (b) formal and informal interviews, (c) focus group interviews, (d) collection of survey data, and (e) collection and content analysis of school ephemera. The findings and thematic issues presented in this chapter emerged largely from the qualitative aspects of this mixed-method approach.[2] The data presented are largely drawn from the focus group and interview data.

Research Setting

Arizona Academy for Creative Minds (Academy)[3] is a charter art school located in the greater Phoenix metropolitan area. Academy serves grades 7–12. The middle school–aged youth are in their own separate wing of the school, separated from the high school students (this is ostensibly for their own "protection"). A total of 268 students attended Academy when I conducted my research, including—85 males and 183 females. There is a somewhat diverse racial makeup, which includes 7 Asian students, 29 Black students, 59 Hispanic students, 9 Indian students, and 164 White[4] students. The 25 staff and teachers from varying backgrounds and degrees of experience at Academy are less racially diverse than the student body and consist largely of White teachers ranging from mid-20s to late 50s. The demographic breakdown by sex mirrors that of the student body, with more than 70% of the school staff being female.

The racial diversity of the school mirrors its location. Though Academy is not bound by specific districting policies like many other public schools in school districts, its location in an urban metropolitan city center provides additional racial/ethnic and class diversity. Students range in socioeconomic status (again this can be attributed partially to the lack of specific districting policies), with some students coming from the very poor areas near downtown and others commuting in from wealthier neighborhoods around the city.

Two focus group sessions were conducted with 16 students. These students were part of the Student Advisory Club (SAC). Focus groups included a pregroup questionnaire where students were asked to self-select/identify demographic questions; choose a pseudonym/alias; and report on matters such as how much media they consume on a daily basis, how they define their gender, and so on. The SAC comprised students ranging in grade level, interests, racial demographics, and backgrounds. They provide a nice representation of the school across all demographic areas. There were 13 girls and 3 boys in the focus groups. Given Academy's gender breakdown, the group demographic was representative of the student body. Additionally, the SAC included Caucasian, African American, Latino, and students who identified as biracial. Students also described having a variety of sexual orientations (e.g., straight, homosexual/gay/lesbian, pansexual, bisexual) and gender representations, including being cisgender, or gender-conforming, and gender-nonconforming. Students ranged in age from 14 to 18 and in grade level from freshman to senior.

In addition to conducting focus group sessions, I conducted 10 formal[5] and several informal interviews with students, teachers, and staff throughout the data collection process. While this research project was youth centered, it was important to talk with the people the youth interacted with every day and to understand how teachers/staff framed gender because this can influence how the young people I worked with frame and understand gender (Prior, 2012).

There is significant disparity between the number of male and female students. Academy reported approximately 70% female students in attendance when data were collected. When I asked about this, faculty indicated that as long as they had been working with charter schools, this gender breakdown was "normal." Additionally, administrators discussed the constraints of having only two gender categories: Students are only able to be classified as male or female, regardless of whether either of those matched their identity presentation. For example, while administrators spoke of students "cross-dressing" and "transitioning," they are bound by policies that only reflect students in binary terms. In addition to the dichotomous way gender was "officially" described, students were categorized by rigid racial categories that do not reflect the overlapping categories students described.

Intersectionality of Identities

At the beginning of the project I was worried about how to ask youth about intersecting identities without running the risk of having them prioritize any one of their many intersecting identities over others. Often, intersecting identities are viewed as simply additive rather than synergistic (Nash, 2008), or one identity is seen to take priority over others. Without even having to ask students about their many other identities, they described many different aspects of their identity (e.g., religion, race, and sexual orientation) that clearly influenced how they understood, interpreted, and articulated their gender identity. I use Glenn's (2004) integrated framework to discuss how these identities overlap and intersect with one another. As Glenn discusses, identity categories are defined as mutually constituted systems of relationships—including norms, symbols, and practices—organized around perceived differences (p. 12); they are "relational concepts whose constitution involves . . . representation and material relations . . . in which power is a constitutive element" (pp. 12–13).

One of the most important identities when it comes to how students understand their own gender identity is sexuality. For many of these youth, sexuality was the aspect of their identity that most influenced how they navigated their own gender identity and expression. Sexuality influenced the way they made meaning around gender, the way they expressed their own gender, and the way they understood gender as expressed in others. Following are a few of the many examples that emerged during focus group sessions and interviews. In addition to sexuality, race/ethnic identity and religion thoroughly influenced identity construction for some students.

Gender = Sexual Orientation?

One important aspect of our discussions about gender was the conflation of gender with sexual orientation/sexuality. Sexual orientation "is based on the gender of one's erotic object of choice; sexual orientation and gender are often confused" (Grossman & D'Augelli, 2006, p. 112). Sexual identity is one of many overlapping and converging identities that influence how young people make sense of and navigate gender expectations in their everyday lives.

My interview protocol did not specifically address sexuality for several reasons. First, given that many school districts and administrators, especially in parts of Arizona, are uncomfortable about the idea of researchers inquiring about sexuality with youth, I was hesitant to include any questions about sexuality for fear of being denied access to schools. I also did not want to build questions into my interview protocol that would make parents hesitant to give permission to participate. Second, I was primarily interested in how youth talk about gender, not just sexuality, as other research has looked more closely at sexuality (Fields, 2008; Gray, 2009; Pascoe, 2007). As that literature points out, there is often a conflation between gender and sexuality, and

I wanted to avoid making any indirect links with my own questions. So I asked questions specifically about gender and masculinities/femininities and did not ask any specific questions about sexuality, sexual orientation, or sexual identity. Last, because I was seeking to understand what other identities were important to youth when they think about gender identity construction, I did not want to create those identities for them, but rather, I wanted students to tell me what was important to them. For example, I did not want to ask explicitly about race, religion, class, or sexuality. Instead, I let students tell me which of their identities were important in their construction of gender identity, and then I asked probing questions.

In the focus groups, several students linked (and conflated) gender and sexuality, often referring to them as one and the same:

> *Katy Perry*[6]: It's like everybody has their own opinion as to what gender is and what it means to be gay, what it means to be lesbian, and what it means to be straight.
>
> *Darth Vader:* Expanding upon her idea, I think she's meaning, like, metrosexual to, like, I don't know—being straight or lesbian, or bisexual, like that does have a big impact on how I think of gender.
>
> *Lilly Jade*: [B]ut I personally feel like with Amber that personally, because it goes along with my sexuality. . . .

Further, when I asked what images and ideas popped into their heads when I said, "femininity," Lilly Jade provided the following response, which clearly shows her linkage between gender and sexuality and how she conflates her ideas about femininity with sexuality. This excerpt also exemplifies how gender expression is read as sexual orientation.

> *Lilly Jade:* With femininity, honestly, this is something that I've had to deal with on my own. . . . In my upbringing, first and foremost, you don't date somebody out of your race. . . . When I went to . . . LGBT National last year, before I came out to my family, they said, "Oh, they're trying to convert you," and this and that. I had to lie my whole way to get to . . . National and say that I was *straight*. . . . With femininity, though, there is that issue, because in sexuality there is the lipstick lesbians and then there is the butch. I just had a conversation . . . with my mother and saying, "Oh, I don't want you to be going all butch on me." I said to her, "Mom, I'm not going all butch on you, for God's sakes."

The previous quote provides a look into the many different things that influence how Lilly Jade understands femininity. She implicates race, family/upbringing, and sexuality as intersecting identities that overlap in her life.

Additionally, she provides an important example of the negative classification of lesbian women (either as lipstick lesbians or butch) and the ideas about what appropriate/proper femininity looks like.

When asked about where they get their ideas about their own gender, Amber again clearly shows how blurred the line is between gender and sexual orientation. For Amber, her peers have great influence over her understanding of masculinity and femininity, but so does her sexuality.

> *Amber*: I'd have to say definitely my peers . . . I mean, *I'm bisexual, I guess you could call it,* and I used to have really long hair. I remember when I chopped it off I felt like more people were starting to—I felt even myself, I started dressing more masculine. I started feeling like I had to be more masculine, because I cut my hair off. That kinda seemed weird to me, because the reason I cut it off was because I felt like long hair was making me feel like I had to be more feminine.

When making reference to her ideas about masculinity and femininity, she frames it within her discussion of her own sexual orientation, though the question did not make reference to sexual identity. Amber, like Lilly Jade, also paints a picture of what appropriate femininity is supposed to look like (i.e., Connell, 1987).

Part of the link between gender and sexuality was the fact that for several students, gender depended on sexuality—that is, their gender expression was about who they wanted to attract.

> *Charlotte*: Gender is just kind of—I don't know. I think you choose your gender. I think it's whatever you want to be. It's, to me, *what you want to attract*, I guess, and I think you are the opposite of that.

In her individual interview, Charlotte also described how she reads gender in others. She discussed how feminine boys are thought of as less of a man because they will not be able to attract women—she believes that women and girls are taught to look for strong, dominant men when seeking a partner.

Students had a difficult time discussing gender detached from sexuality unless specifically asked to pull them apart, and, even then, they seemed unable to articulate the difference other than to say that personally they viewed them as two separate things. Throughout our discussions, these youth continually conflated sexual orientation (their own and others'). It was almost unconscious, but when it was brought to their attention, students were hesitant to articulate what they thought the link between gender and sexuality was. Part of this has to do with the intersecting and overlapping of particular identities for these young people.

The students were not the only ones to conflate gender and sexuality. When I spoke with several teachers about my project, their immediate response was that Academy was a good place to be conducting research because they had a lot of students who identified as gay, lesbian, or bisexual. Additionally, in their online survey, two teachers expressly linked gender and sexuality. When asked what gender means to them, one teacher said, "Sexual identity, all types" and another said, "Gender is the way a person perceives themselves in regard to his or her sexual identity."

One of the first teachers I spoke with upon arriving at Academy for participant observation clearly conflated sexual orientation and gender. When I observed a dance class, the instructor was very interested in what I was researching. When I told her that I was attempting to learn how high school students at Academy understand gender, she said, "What a great place to study; we have lots of students here who are gay and lesbian." She claimed that Academy staff and students are "more open," and she also described the parents as not as "open" as the students, but they seemed to be able to be swayed given where they chose to send their students to school. She described how she thinks Academy allows students the chance to solidify identity before going to college. She also thought that since students who go to Academy are encouraged to "be themselves" and are free to express themselves (and their sexual orientation), this leads to less sexual risk taking in college. Only one teacher did not make this connection of gender with sexuality. When I explained my project to the theatre teacher, his first response was, "How interesting. We have a variety of gender roles here. There is a lack of traditional gender roles, so you should find some very interesting things."

The conflation of sexuality and gender is not new and it is not confined to those I worked with. Often, within the literature, sexuality is conflated with gender identity. This is an especially important discussion given that the regulation of gender identity is frequently based on perceived sexual expression. For example, youth who are regulated and policed because of their gender expression are more commonly being regulated based on their perceived sexuality; a very feminine young man is commonly not being policed because he is feminine but, rather, because that femininity is being read as sexual orientation. To be more specific, that young man is being bullied/regulated because he is seen as gay based on his gender expression, not necessarily because his gender expression matches his orientation.

The conflation of gender and sexuality has significant implications for how we understand both gender and sexuality because it reinforces a heteronormative binary framework. If gender expression continues to be read as sexual expression, then young people will continue to be bullied and harassed based on their *assumed* sexual orientation. Additionally, because of this dichotomous thinking, gender is not understood as fluid and stereotypes are continually reinforced.

Race, Ethnicity, and Gender

In addition to sexuality, race and cultural heritage played a role for these students in terms of how they understood gender, gender roles, and the appropriate presentation of self. As one can see from the following excerpt, Lilly Jade grapples with the standards and expectations she was raised with and how *masculinity* and *femininity* were defined. She cannot disengage her own understanding of gender from the identity and expectations that her family and heritage have instilled in her, even though they do not agree with or condone her sexual "preferences." She describes the way her Hispanic/Mexican heritage has heavily influenced not only how she understands herself, but also how she relates to her family. She is constantly grappling with creating her own identity and attitudes, while balancing how she was raised.

> *Lilly Jade*: With the upbringing I was raised . . . was very Mexican, very Hispanic, very black and white, women are supposed to do this, men are supposed to [do] this. *If a women speaks up, that means she's being masculine.* That means you're not supposed to talk back if a male speaks to you in Mexican society. . . . I was raised around a bunch of strong females, so those females affected me almost to a point where I've been considered very dominant and manly, and dominance is connected to masculinity because of that upbringing. Sometimes I do honestly question whether that upbringing and the constant question of masculinity dominance has kinda altered my sexual orientation. Also, as well with society and how females are brought up, and what I see [as] masculine, immediately the first name that came to my head was Brad Pitt. Okay, then I started thinking, and then I'm thinking of all the males.

Lilly Jade points out several interesting contradictions. While she says that she was raised by a "bunch of strong females" and that sometimes she is thought of as "manly," she also talks about the dominance of masculinity (what Lilly Jade refers to as machismo) in her heritage and the fact that dominance is masculine and girls are never to be masculine. Previous scholars have investigated the impact of culture and heritage on the meaning making of gender identity, particularly looking at the hegemonic notions surrounding machismo (Lancaster, 1994). For example, building on Lancaster's (1994) investigation into machismo and masculinity in Guatemala, Gutmann

(2006) critiques the common correlation of machismo with dominance and stereotypes of male culture in Mexico City. As both of these authors show, race and national identity significantly influence gender and sexuality, because, as Weeks (1995) argues, sexuality is the "magnetic core that lies at the heart of the national and political agenda" (p. 4).

Later in Lilly Jade's discussion, she also references that she is very "girly" and has worn makeup and her mother's heels for as long as she could remember, and this connects her previous statement about assuring her mother that she would not be "butch." For Lilly Jade, her heritage and cultural experience came up several times in our discussions. Ethnicity, for her, seemed to be a dominant identity that influenced how she understood her gender (and her sexuality). Few other students discussed race as openly and continuously as Lilly Jade.

In another interview, I asked Kay if her ideas about who she is change based on who she is with. For Kay, again, identity is clearly linked to sexuality.

> *Kay*: I surprise myself, but I'm still the same person. I surprise myself because I hadn't thought that broad before. I hadn't thought, "Oh, one day you're going to be dating a White girl." If I would have told that to myself, I'd be like, "Oh, okay." . . . I'm just used to growing up and dating guys or supposed to be dating guys anyway. There's no real difference. I'm just happy with my outside life.
>
> *Sarah:* Is it dating a girl or dating a White girl that's most surprising to you?
>
> *Kay:* Oh, . . . I think it's just a girl because—you're good. No, I'm pretty sure it's just a girl because, like, I've learned to adapt to, like, the whole race thing. I went to charter schools back where I'm from and even though the population of the whole state was, like—or the Black percentage was higher, but I went to schools where I was in school with a whole bunch of, like, rich White kids, rich Indian kids, rich Asian kids. Not necessarily the race card that surprised me [cause] I'm learning to adapt to each and every race and not really—I mean, how can you say that you can't see race because you do see it. I'm used to that part, not necessarily dating a girl part.

Kay (an African American) provides interesting commentary on how some identities outweigh others and how she thinks of some identities as mattering more than others. In the second focus group, Kay also said:

> I'm confused. I feel a lot of the time, all of the time, I'm not sure how to act, as far as feminine goes. My mom, she never taught me, like, to put on makeup or wear heels. . . . I have one brother, so, of course, he made me tough and had this kind of attitude toward that. Then I did ballet. . . .

Then it's just like then I grew up in a society where okay, you're gonna marry this. I asked my mom one time, "How would you feel if I married somebody of a different race?" She was like, "Well, I guess I'll just have to get used to it." Now, it's like, okay, well, not just a different race, but now I'm in a relationship with somebody who is of a different sex. I don't know how to act. I just find myself acting as if I made up my own gender, as if I made up my own rules. I think it's better than acting like a girl or like a guy. That's just me.

Here again, Kay clearly connects her gender with her sexuality, but also with her race. She worries that her family would not accept a partner who is of a different race and whether they will accept someone of the same sex. In response to her own confusion about how to act, Kay states that she has created her own gender, which, to her, is better "than acting like a girl or like a guy." Like Kay, Lilly Jade also made reference to dating someone outside her race and believing that, unlike Kay, it would be both race and gender that would cause her family to react negatively.

The students in the focus groups comprised a variety of different racial identities. Similar to the school's racial makeup, I had two students who identified as Black, three who identified as biracial, two who identified as Hispanic/Mexican, and nine who identified as White. As described, for some students, their racial/ethnic identity was a stronger influence than for others. It is interesting that none of the White students made reference to his or her own racialized identity. While some of the students of color commented on how race influences their conceptions of gender and identity, not a single White student made the same claim. This is not to say that their racialized identity does not play a role in the way they define their gender identity, or the way others define and understand their gender identity and gender presentation, just that they did not make reference to it during either the focus groups or the interviews.[7] While sexual identity seemed to play the largest role in how these youth defined and navigated gender identity, race and religion also seemed to heavily influence how they understand themselves.

The Bible Tells Me So

In addition to sexuality and race, religion is a very strong aspect of many people's identity. Religion, like ethnicity/culture, has historically framed understandings of gender and sexuality (Avishai, 2008; Erzen, 2006; Stoler, 1995). And religion, like media, circulates messages that shape young people's identities. Many religions have specific teachings on appropriate gender and sexuality, and religion remains one of the defining forces in how we frame gender. For many of the students I worked with, religion played a large role in how they understood gender (and sexuality). Coming from various different religious perspectives (Mormon, Christian, and Catholic[8]), several students indicated that religion dictated how they should understand gender, and for many of them, their identities conflicted with their religion.

In response to where these students got their ideas about masculinity and femininity, Ryan, a senior girl, offered the following during one of the focus groups:

> *Ryan:* To me, a lot of it has to do with religion, at least in my family. Most religions don't think it's right for a man and a man to be together or a woman and a woman to be together. It's really hard for me, because I like men and women. Even since I was a child, I always was taught that it was—at least with my dad, because he's from Texas and his family are strong Christians. They just don't think that's right. I used to always think it was weird that I would find certain girls pretty and I would have crushes on some of my friends. I was like, "Oh, my God, I'm a freak. What's wrong with me?" I would pray and be like, "Please, God, don't let me be like this." This was when I was nine, eight. I never really talked about this, but just this past two weeks, my parents found out that I do like girls as well, and they just don't talk about it. They kind of ignored it and act like nothing happened, because they don't want to accept it. They think that it's a phase. It's just hard not being able to be open about it with my family. It's hard, because I am Christian and a lot of people don't know that, because so many Christians are really judgmental towards other people and I'm not like that whatsoever. I'm very open with everyone and it just sucks that my family can't accept that. They just ignore it.

For Ryan, her faith and her family have a lot to do with the way she understands herself and the world. She worries that her religious identity conflicts with her sexual identity, and she is concerned about the many complications that causes. She fears being herself at home because of her sexuality and about being her Christian self at school because of the negative connotations. Religion influences the way Ryan understands sexuality as well, as can be seen in the way she describes being brought up in a religious home. What is interesting about this quote is that she never mentioned gender—rather, she interpreted the questions as inquiring about her sexuality. Here, again, is an example of how the students talk about their own sexuality when discussing questions of gender.

Like Ryan, Katy Perry was strongly influenced by her religion, which has been difficult, given the fact that after her parent's divorce, her mother came out as a lesbian and is now married to a woman. For Katy, the way she lives at home often contradicts the way she was religiously raised. Katy shared the following:

> *Katy Perry*: When I was growing up, I grew up in a Christian home. It was just me and my mom actually living in the house, but my aunt was really close to us as well, probably over every day, practically my second parent. Growing up, I was always taught what femininity and masculinity were based on the fact that we were really Christian. It was all about how our religion pretty much told us what was right and what was wrong. If we veered to the right or the left at all, it was considered wrong. I just remember it was pretty much yes or no, black or white. There was no gray area at all. Then, when I was about 15, my mom came out to me . . . and we no longer lived a Christian lifestyle, I suppose. Now, my eyes are a little more open to the fact that there's kind of a bigger world than just the black and white. I suppose, because I was living around a bunch of women when I was little, I've always just been the girlie-girl-type person. I just think that so many different things came into play when I was little that made me believe what I believe today. I guess I can't really pinpoint if it's my mom or if it's my religion. It's just I think that it's definitely not a black or white question. There's a whole bunch of gray.

Katy provides an interesting discussion of her religion's conflict with her mother's sexual identity. She thinks that they no longer live a Christian "lifestyle" because her mother came out as a lesbian. Because of this, she does not believe that they are "really Christian" anymore. Here again is an example of how religious identity influences how some students understand gender and how gender and sexual identity can influence the way some students understand their religious identity.

In her interview, Francesca provided a different perspective on religion. Religion and family are a very big influence in Francesca's life. Her Christian identity is the first thing she talks about. Her religion has a powerful influence on how she makes sense of herself, and she talks about how her religion has taught her to always love everyone and it has also structured the way she understands gender and sexuality.

> *Francesca*: It's just how you look on it is how you get influenced by it. If I went to church, . . . and the church said, "Oh, we don't like gays." You can say, "Okay, I don't agree with that," or you can say, "Okay. I do agree with that." You have to really analyze what you're being influenced by and you have to analyze what they're telling you. The church that I go to, . . . I don't think anybody would necessarily look upon you any different. I believe that you're supposed to be loving to everybody. Every single person that's out

there, you have to love them, and you have to accept them for who they are. Hate the sin, not the sinner. Because if a person feels that they're being discriminated against because of what they feel or what they think, then you're never gonna get anybody to—not necessarily be that religion, but to look at it in a positive light, because I mean—I don't know. It's just I've always learned to love every single person you meet, no matter who they are.

Francesca provides a unique perspective here. While Lilly Jade's and Ryan's religion conflicts with their identity and Katy Perry's religion conflicts with her mom's identity, Francesca identifies as heterosexual and her religion does not conflict with the way she identifies herself. She discusses how her religion has influenced her in that it has taught her to be loving toward everyone and to accept people for who they are. But her religion has also influenced the way she understands both gender and sexuality. As the previous excerpts describe, for Francesca, sexuality is a choice.

In a different discussion about religion, during my observations of the theatre class one day I heard the following conversation between a young girl and a few of her friends in class:

> While waiting for the class to be dismissed, several of the students mill around by the door . . . talking over each other. One girl is talking to two other girls and one boy student and she says, "This guy that I like might be super gay but he's Mormon, which means he will never come out of the closet, right? But he's super gay so I don't know. I wonder if we would date even though he's probably gay." Her friends seem to laugh it off, but one responds, "Well, if he's Mormon, he will probably never come out, so you should be good."

In this excerpt, one can see clearly how sexuality and religion influence one another. This young woman's ideas about Mormonism influence the way she thinks another student will respond to his assumed sexuality. This is an example of how students not only understand (and self-describe) their own identities, but also how they discuss others' identities and the assumptions that go along with how these students navigate the many identities of their peers. As one can see from the previous examples, students are grappling with many overlapping and intersecting identities as they create and sustain their own gender identity. They are not only traversing through their own identity construction and how many identities influence and often challenge each other, but also navigating their assumptions about identity and how they understand each other.

Conclusion

Young people have a variety of different identities that influence, intersect, and overlap with one another. Sometimes, these intersecting and overlapping identities compete with each other, as was the case for both Katy Perry and Ryan. Their religious identity conflicted with their gender identity and, in Ryan's case, sexual identity. For Lilly Jade, her racial/ethnic identity conflicted with her gender and sexual identity as well as with her religion (which for her was tied to her Hispanic/Mexican heritage). These examples highlight the fact that it is impossible to look at gender alone. Instead, we must look at the many identities young people have and how those identities influence the way they make sense of their own (and others') gender identity.

Many of these identities influenced how they navigated, made sense of, and described gender. Sexuality, race, and religion were three of the identities that heavily influenced how young people navigated their gender identity construction and how they interpreted the gender identities of others. For almost all of the students, sexuality was a prevalent identity category that heavily influenced the way they make sense of gender. Sexual orientation and identity dictate appropriate gender presentation, and gender and sexuality are often conflated as being one and the same. Race and cultural heritage were particularly important for Kay and Lilly Jade. Many of their comments explored the ways that race influences how they not only make sense of their own identity, but also read gender and sexuality in others and how others (particularly their parents and families) read their gender presentation. For others, religious identity played a strong role in defining what gender means in their everyday lives. Particularly for Ryan, Katy Perry, and Francesca, religion dictates how they make sense of their own identity. Multiple identities influence the way these young people are able to understand gender. As such, analyzing gender both theoretically through Glenn's (2004) framework and methodologically through an intersectional lens provides alternate ways to understand how young people act and describe their identity and situations.

Notes

1. Data for this chapter come from dissertation research (Prior, 2012).
2. For additional discussion of the findings, see Prior (2012).
3. All names are pseudonyms.
4. Racial demographic language is based on information provided by school administration. By "Indian," Academy is referring to American Indian populations.
5. Formal interviews were voluntary. While all but three students volunteered to participate, due to time constraints, I was able to schedule interviews with only 10 female students.
6. Students chose their own pseudonyms. Many students chose names that blurred gender binaries—for example, Darth Vader is a girl.

7. This reinforces the normalization of Whiteness in schools and White privilege (Castagno, 2008; Pollock, 2001, 2004), and this neglect is common in research on racial/ethnic identity.

8. While students may identify with other religions, Christianity, Mormonism, and Catholicism were the only ones mentioned.

References

Adelman, M., & Yalda, C. (2000). Seen but not heard: The legal lives of young people. *Political and Legal Anthropology Review, 23*(2), 37–58.

Ashcraft, C. (2006). Ready or not . . . ? Teen sexuality and the troubling discourse of readiness. *Anthropology and Education Quarterly, 37*(4), 328–346.

Austin, J., & Willard, M. N. (1998). *Generations of youth: Youth cultures and history in twentieth-century America.* New York: New York University Press.

Avishai, O. (2008). "Doing religion" in a secular world: Women in conservative religions and the question of agency. *Gender & Society, 22*(4), 409–433.

Best, A. (Ed.). (2007). *Representing youth: Methodological issues in critical youth studies.* New York: New York University Press.

Bettie, J. (2003). *Women without class: Girls, peace and identity.* Berkeley, CA: University of California Press.

Brown, J., & Cantor, J. (2000). An agenda for research on youth and the media. *Journal of Adolescent Health, 27*(2), 2–7.

Brown, L. M. (1997). Performing femininities: Listening to white working-class girls in rural Maine. *Journal of Social Issues, 53*(4), 683–701.

Bucholtz, M. (2002). Youth and cultural practice. *Annual Review of Anthropology, 31*, 525–552.

Campbell, N. (Ed.). (2000). *American youth cultures.* New York: Routledge.

Carpenter, L. (2005). *Virginity lost: An intimate portrait of first sexual experience.* New York: New York University Press.

Carter, P. (2005). *Keepin' it real: School success beyond Black and White.* New York: Oxford University Press.

Castagno, A. (2008). I don't want to hear that: Legitimating whiteness through silence in schools. *Anthropology and Education Quarterly, 39*(3), 314–333.

Collins, P. H. (2000). *Black feminist thought: Knowledge, consciousness, and the politics of empowerment* (2nd ed.). New York: Routledge.

Connell, R. W. (1987). *Gender and power: Society, the person and sexual politics.* Stanford, CA: Stanford University Press.

Corsaro, W. (2005). *The sociology of childhood* (2nd ed.). Thousand Oaks, CA: Pine Forge.

Crenshaw, K. (1991). Mapping the margins: Intersectionality, identity politics, and violence against women of color. *Stanford Law Journal, 43*(6), 1241–1299.

Erzen, T. (2006). *Straight to Jesus: Sexual and Christian conversions in the ex-gay movement.* Berkeley, CA: University of California Press.

Ferguson, A. (2001). *Bad boys: Public schools in the making of Black masculinity.* Ann Arbor, MI: University of Michigan Press.

Fields, J. (2008). *Risky lessons: Sex education and social inequality.* New Brunswick, NJ: Rutgers University Press.

Fisher, C. (2009). Queer youth experiences with abstinence-only-until-marriage sexuality education: "I can't get married so where does that leave me?" *Journal of LGBT Youth, 6*(1), 61–79.

Garcia, L. (2009). Now why do you want to talk about that? Heteronormativity, sexism and racism in the sexual (mis)education of Latina youth. *Gender & Society, 23*(4), 520–541.

Glenn, E. N. (2004). *Unequal freedom: How race and gender shaped American citizenship and labor.* Cambridge, MA: Harvard University Press.

Gray, M. (2009). *Out in the country: Youth, media and queer visibility in rural America.* New York: New York University Press.

Grossman, A., & D'Augelli, A. R. (2006). Transgender youth. *Journal of Homosexuality, 51*(1), 111–128.

Grossman, A., Haney, A. P., Edwards, P., Alessi, E. J., Ardon, M., & Howell, T. J. (2009). Lesbian, gay, bisexual and transgender youth talk about experiences and coping with school violence: A qualitative study. *Journal of LGBT Youth, 6*(1), 24–60.

Gutmann, M. (2006). *The meanings of macho: Being a man in Mexico City.* Berkeley, CA: University of California Press.

Hebdige, D. (1979). *Subculture: The meaning of style.* New York: Routledge.

Herdt, G., Russell, S., Sweat, J., & Marcullo, M. (2007). Sexual inequality, youth empowerment and the GSA. In N. Teunis & G. Herdt (Eds.), *Sexual inequalities and social justice* (pp. 233–252). Berkeley, CA: University of California Press.

Hutzell, K., & Payne, A. (2012). The impact of bullying victimization on school avoidance. *Youth Violence and Juvenile Justice, 10*(4), 370–385.

Irvine, J. (2004). *Talk about sex: The battles over sex education in the United States.* Berkeley, CA: University of California Press.

Johnson, J., Flett Prior, S., Abbott, K., & Ableser, E. (2011). *Theories on justice.* Dubuque, IA: Kendall Hunt.

Lancaster, R. (1994). *Life is hard: Machismo, danger, and the intimacy of power in Nicaragua.* Berkeley, CA: University of California Press.

Males, M. (1999). *Framing youth: 10 myths about the next generation.* New York: Common Courage Press.

McCready, L. (2010). *Making space for diverse masculinities: Difference, intersectionality, and engagement in an urban high school.* New York: Peter Lang.

Messerschmidt, J. (2004). *Flesh and blood: Adolescent gender diversity and violence.* Lanham, MD: Rowman & Littlefield.

Miller, J. (2008). *Getting played: African American girls, urban inequality and gendered violence.* New York: New York University Press.

Morrill, C., Yalda, C., Adelman, M., Musheno, M., & Bejarano, C. (2000). Telling tales in school: Youth culture and conflict narratives. *Law & Society Review, 34*(3), 521–565.

Myers, K., & Raymond, L. (2010). Elementary school girls and heteronormativity: The girl project. *Gender & Society, 24*(2), 167–188.

Nash, J. (2008). Re-thinking intersectionality. *Feminist Review, 89*, 1–15.

Pascoe, C. J. (2007). *Dude you're a fag: Masculinity and sexuality in high school.* Berkeley, CA: University of California Press.

Pollock, M. (2001). How the question we ask most about race in education is the very question we most suppress. *Educational Researcher, 30*(9), 2–12.

Pollock, M. (2004). Race bending: "Mixed" youth, practicing strategic racialization in California. *Anthropology and Education Quarterly, 35*(1), 30–52.

Prior, S. (2012). Schooling gender: Identity construction in high school (Doctoral dissertation). Available from ProQuest Dissertations and Theses data base. (UMI No. 3547689)

Raby, R. (2007). Across a great gulf? Conducting research with adolescents. In A. Best (Ed.), *Representing youth: Methodological issues in critical youth studies* (pp. 39–60). New York: New York University Press.

Rolon-Dow, R. (2004). Seduced by images: Identity and schooling in the lives of Puerto Rican girls. *Anthropology & Education Quarterly, 35*(1), 8–29.

Skelton, T., & Valentine, G. (Eds.). (1998). *Cool places: Geographies of youth culture.* New York: Routledge.

Stoler, L. (1995). *Race and the education of desire: Foucault's history of sexuality and the colonial order of things.* Durham, NC: Duke University Press.

Stritikus, T., & Nguyen, D. (2007). Strategic transformation: Cultural and gender identity negotiations in first-generation Vietnamese youth. *American Education Research Journal, 44*(4), 853–895.

Tolman, D. (2005). *Dilemmas of desire: Teenage girls talk about sexuality.* Cambridge, MA: Harvard University Press.

Weeks, J. (1995). *Invented moralities: Sexual values in an age of uncertainty.* Cambridge, MA: Polity.

Weis, L., & Fine, M. (2001). Extraordinary conversations in public schools. *Qualitative Studies in Education, 14*(4), 497–523.

West, C., & Zimmerman, D. (1987). Doing gender. *Gender & Society, 1*(2), 125–151.

Wortham, S. (2011). Introduction: Youth cultures and education. *Review of Research in Education, 35*, vii–xi.

PART THREE

INTERSECTIONALITY AND POSTSECONDARY EDUCATION

6

UNDERSTANDING THE ACADEMIC ACHIEVEMENT OF LATINA COLLEGE GRADUATES

A Call for Intersectionality as a Methodological Framework

María Oropeza Fujimoto

Latinas/os continue to comprise an increasingly larger proportion of college-age populations. Reports and policy memos in higher education consistently reiterate racial gaps among students in enrollment, retention, and graduation (Aud, Hussar, Johnson, et al., 2012; Carey, 2008; Hussar & Bailey, 2009). For example, in a recent report by the U.S. Department of Education, "the gap in the attainment of a bachelor's degree or higher between Whites and Hispanics widened from 17 to 26 percentage points" from 1980 to 2011 (Aud et al., 2012).

A vexing problem in research is the tendency toward oversimplification and unidimensional explanations of entire populations (Braxton, 2005). For example, the potential for Latinas/os to make educational progress is typically characterized in terms of risk factors (Swail, Cabrera, Lee, & Williams, 2005). The underlying assumption is that academic failure is related to Latina/o students' possessing several of these risk factors. Apart from the question of whether the data actually support the view of Latina/o students as particularly at risk, this type of research emphasizes the individual student characteristics, and its methodology presumes that something is lacking in the participants.

Latinas occupy multiple social and demographic positions. Most studies do not "offer a concomitant analysis of how the participants' social class or gender locations interface with their racial locations" (O'Connor, Lewis, & Mueller, 2007). Moreover, most research tends to group Latinas and Latinos together despite gender differences in college enrollment (National Center for Education Statistics [NCES], 2010) and graduation rates (Snyder & Dillow, 2012a, 2012b). While researchers might suspect that both Latinas and Latinos would have similar cultural norms, educational opportunities, and family backgrounds, and perhaps face similar institutional barriers, Latinas are denigrated through differences in dimensions of their social identities, which are often understood in terms of inferiority. Villalpando (2004) explains:

> When a Latina student experiences cultural alienation and isolation in college this experience is not only based on her ethnicity as Latina but is also influenced by how she is treated as a woman, as a member of a certain socioeconomic class and in relation to her English language proficiency . . . and her perceived immigrant generation status. (p. 43)

The everyday nature of "cultural alienation and isolation" through multiple aspects of a student's identity deserves close scrutiny. This is particularly true in light of a student's capacity to succeed within these seemingly oppressive confines. Recognizing how these multiple aspects of a student's identity intersect, interrelate, and hold in place socially oppressive and life-limiting conditions is key to understanding the overcoming of such barriers.

Intersectionality provides an approach to move beyond deterministic models and examine how inequities are maintained through structures, ideology, and everyday practices (Dill & Zambrana, 2009). Intersectionality "is rooted in illuminating the complexities of race and ethnicity as it intersects with other dimensions of difference" to examine inequality (Dill & Zambrana, 2009, p. 5). In this chapter, an intersectional methodology is used to make visible how research methodologies limit what can be known about Latinas, challenge the (over)emphasis of research that draws on risk factors, and present a more nuanced understanding of Latina student experiences and their academic success.

Methodological Issues

The conventional methodological approach to research on race as a variable in college student achievement is problematic. Race/ethnicity is used to make broad generalizations about who goes to college, who stays in college, and who graduates. Such research is inadequate to address the needs of Latina/o students for the following reasons: (a) its failure to recognize the specific ways in which ethnicity is racialized; (b) its tendency to focus on a specific social identity category while ignoring others; and (c) the limitations of using racial groups in comparison with each other. Each of these is explained next.

First, a "commonsense" understanding of race and its influence on research methodology has contributed to the failure to recognize the particular ways that ethnicity is racialized to subordinate Latinas/os. This "commonsense" understanding of race is based on Blacks and Whites and excludes other racial/ethnic groups (Latinas/os, Asian Americans, Indigenous peoples) and their particular issues (e.g., immigration, language, sovereignty) (Delgado & Stefancic, 2012). This understanding also leads to an underexamination of the background and experiences of nontraditional, but growing, populations in higher education, such as Latinas.

Second, a factor that can restrict our understanding of the Latina student experience is the tendency to focus on a specific social identity. This may take the form of an essentialized version of a particular "race/ethnicity," gender, social class, disability, and so on. Our capacity to understand the more complex nature of student identities and experience can depend on our ability to grasp how multiple social identities simultaneously affect student's lives. Making a methodological shift and focusing on the multiple, complex identities in a more selective population (i.e., Latina college graduates) can contribute to our understanding of the limits of overgeneralizing.

Third, a methodological issue entails using comparison groups in which White, middle-class students are used as a reference group to which people and groups of color are judged. The typical explanation for the achievement gaps in terms of risk factors is presented as race- and gender-neutral; that is, it assumes that enrollment and retention factors in college will be the same for members of racial/ethnic minorities and women of color as they are for Whites and women generally. Yet, research suggests that minority students experience academic achievement processes in a different manner from Whites (Carter & Hurtado, 2007). The difference between White students' experiences and those of other groups suggests questions of validity. Shilling and Shilling further argue that using group comparisons to assess progress "often leads us to concentrate more on where [a group] stands in relation to others and less in examining how to enhance or diminish the quality of students' learning experiences" (as cited in Haworth & Conrad, 1997, p. 165). Further, a group-comparison approach is methodologically limited in its ability to create equity among racial groups because it assumes deficits. This is not simply an abstract theoretical issue; it is also a significant methodological problem. Comparison research often results in a "one-size-fits-all" approach to addressing students' needs, thereby limiting the types of needs that are addressed.

These ideas of a more nuanced definition and use of social identities, the limitations of focusing on a single identity, and the potential for "intersectionality" to unravel the complexities of multiple identities are examples of how intersectionality can help to better explain the growing number and proportion of Latinas completing postsecondary education and how this may inform the research and practice regarding those who are not succeeding as well.

Intersectionality as a Guiding Framework

Intersectionality holds that no one can be fully understood in terms of a singular identity such as race or gender; nor can any individual be understood as simply the sum total of these identities. Intersectionality posits that "we are the interdependent intersections of our race, gender, color, ethnicity, nationality, ancestry, culture and language" (Hernández-Truyol, 1997, p. 883; see also Anzaldúa, 1987; Crenshaw, 2003; Zavella, 1997). While many Latinas/os share a common experience of a racialized identity, Latinas' gender and other social identities also play a part in their academic achievement (López, 2002; Morales, 2000, 2008). Reasons given for academic failure often obscure the role of gender and generation in the United States[1] in Latinas' academic successes. Latinas' academic success represents an opportunity to understand intersectionality as an analytical tool.

Intersectionality: Informing Purpose, Research Questions, and Design of the Study

This section provides information about the purpose, research questions, and design of the study. The present study centralizes the multiple identities of Latinas to reveal underlying assumptions of academic failure as related to Latina/o students' possessing several risk factors.

Purpose. Crucial to alleviating barriers Latinas face is the use of a research methodology that moves beyond singular definitions of *social identity*. In the context of studying Latina graduates, such a methodological framework can reduce the gap between what we know about the relatively few Latina students who enter and finish higher education and the dominant, deficit-focused assumptions prevalent among higher education practitioners, theorists, and policymakers.

This study sought to examine academic success through Latinas' different social identities (race/ethnicity, gender, generation living in the United States, linguistic background, and social class). Without recognition of

Latinas' multiple social identities, inequities in their educational experiences may be overshadowed by the statistical probability and potential of academic failure leading to oversimplified explanations of individual exceptionalism. Moreover, a methodological focus of the intersections of these identities would enable us to examine how Latinas' social identities can interact in ways to prevent them from accessing resources that could help them, highlight how social identities influenced their agency, and present different ways of understanding the phenomena of student academic success.

Research Questions. This study sought to better understand academically successful Latinas. These women are often generalized as the "cream of the crop"—middle/upper class with strong academic backgrounds. However, such an assumption implies that Latina college graduates are exceptions to the rule and emphasizes an essentialized notion of Latinas that overlooks their gender, linguistic background, generation in the United States, and other relevant social identities. Equally important is to explore the experiences of difference and disadvantage among Latinas in college through the lenses of these identities and their intersections, and how these women acquire and deploy the knowledge, skills, and resources that enable them to achieve academically. Finally, after learning *who* advances academically and *how* they succeed, it is important to consider *how* research on intersectionality can be used to study Latinas in higher education to improve their college experience and help them attain a college degree. One of the questions this study examined was:

> *RQ:* How do academically successful Latinas respond to experiences of difference and disadvantage in college? How does intersectionality help us to understand the experiences of academically successful Latinas?

Study Design. This chapter is part of a larger sequential multimethod study with a qualitative emphasis (Oropeza, 2011). It consisted of the following data sets: (a) a qualitative pilot study, (b) a quantitative survey, (c) a qualitative collective interpretation, and (d) qualitative in-depth interviews. The decision to use multimethods stemmed from an interest in gaining a more thorough understanding of college-educated Latinas (Creswell & Plano, 2011). As a result, qualitative or quantitative data collection and analysis were used to answer specific research questions. Survey data identified Latinas' structural positionalities, and interview data increased awareness of Latinas' sense of selves or their process of identification. The former has implications for language use and cultural and educational backgrounds, and the latter guides behaviors and decisions and reveals how Latinas struggled against inequities.

For purposes of this chapter, a section of the quantitative survey portion of the research is highlighted.

Survey. Data for this study came from a quantitative survey. A new instrument was developed that was based on a conceptual meta-analysis model developed by Padilla (2007). The survey objectives were to (a) identify the demographic characteristics of college-educated Latinas, (b) describe their college experiences, and (c) identify the resources and barriers that influenced attainment of their educational goals.

Measures. The questionnaire consisted of 67 items of yes/no dichotomous and 4- or 5-point Likert scale questions. The demographic section of the survey included 27 items about respondents' generational status; family characteristics (mother's level of education, use of public assistance); and demographics of respondents' school and community, including size, race, and class.

Survey Procedures and Description. A purposive snowball sampling method was used to recruit respondents for the Latina College Graduate Survey. A total of 264 Latina college graduates completed the survey, resulting in 262 usable surveys.

The demographics of the survey sample were similar to those of the national population of Latinas/os. Seventy-five percent (*n* = 198) of respondents reported speaking another language at home, compared to 71% of the overall Hispanic population (Llagas, Snyder, & NCES, 2003). The geographic location of the sample was also similar to national data (U.S. Bureau of the Census, 2002), with respondents growing up in the Northeast (12.2%, compared with 13.3% nationally) and the West (43.9%, compared with 44.2%). The Midwest region was overrepresented, with 23.3% of survey respondents, compared with 7.7% of the national population. The sample's underrepresentation from southern states reflects the actual underrepresentation of Latinas from Florida and Texas. The Latina/o public school population in the South falls primarily in those two states (Fry & Gonzales, 2008). Only 16% of this sample grew up in the South, while 34% of the nation's total Hispanic population resides there (U.S. Bureau of the Census, 2002).

The survey sample also demonstrated some socioeconomic heterogeneity. Latina college graduates had mothers whose educations were similar to those of the overall female Latina population. Respondents were less likely to report that their mothers had no formal or only some formal schooling (35%), compared with 42% of the Hispanic population (U.S. Bureau of the Census, 2006). Both groups were similar in terms of having mothers who completed a high school education, at 53% and 51%, respectively. There were also no significant differences in college degree attainment. Almost 13% of respondents had mothers who had attained a college degree or above, in comparison to 13.1% of the overall female Latina population (U.S. Bureau of the Census, 2006).

With regard to poverty, 36% of respondents self-reported that their families received public assistance while growing up, compared to about 30% of all Hispanic children living below the poverty line (Llagas et al., 2003). Public assistance used as a proxy for poverty in the Latina College Graduate Survey may lead to a conservative estimate, given the extent to which public assistance excludes immigrants. However, because it was not my goal to estimate the percentage of Latina college graduates who grew up in poverty, I focused on how socioeconomic status is positioned solely as a risk factor. Survey respondents graduated from more than 122 different institutions of higher education. The majority of respondents were the only ones from their institution, and no one institution accounted for more than 4.6% of the entire sample. The survey sample represents a segment of college graduates that the literature has largely ignored—Latina females who are mostly bilingual, immigrants or children of immigrants, and first-generation college students. By focusing on the particularity of this group, loaded assumptions in the research on racial minorities, and Latinas specifically, can be revealed and new frameworks developed. The extent to which findings contradict previous research about college graduates should suggest new directions for study regarding Latinas and other marginalized groups based on larger, more generalizable samples, using a success-based perspective.[2]

Credibility. Through the multimethods approach of this study, I attempted to establish "credibility" by articulating the research design, identifying the procedures used, and noting the limited extent of generalizability. The goal is not to establish "truth" or objectivity as much as it is to strive for legitimacy and trustworthiness (Angen, 2000). Ultimately, this study attempts to establish "credibility" through the inferences drawn from the data and not the data themselves (Hammersley & Atkinson, 1983).

Overall, the methods and samples presented in this study provided an ideal starting point for examining the characteristics of Latina college graduates, examining their experiences of difference and disadvantage in college, and drawing on intersectionality to better understand and ultimately serve Latinas and other diverse populations.

Intersectionality Informed Analysis

The descriptions of Latina identity in this study help us understand how students' school experiences are influenced by their individual choice (agency), interactions with others, and social structures. Additionally, risk factors determine how Latinas are seen, constructed, and exist, and they emphasize Latina students' deficiencies or barriers. This leaves the power to define *Latinas* in singular (and inferior) terms unchallenged. It "does not tell *their* stories or describe *their* needs, interests and concerns" (Hernández-Truyol, 1997, p. 895; emphasis in original). The present study draws on intersectionality to complicate risk factors as a unidimensional explanation of Latina success. Intersectionality incorporates the multidimensionality of Latina gender, culture, and language and recognizes that improving our understanding about Latinas/os can lead to improvements in education and society (Valdés, 1998). One of the ways that intersectionality does this is through scholarship that examines social and educational conditions. Using intersectionality to respond to risk factors increases higher education's understanding of Latinas and allows for alternative interpretations of risk factors and the likelihood of future academic success. This broader understanding is essential for higher education policymakers and practitioners to develop educational policies and practices that foster academic success. While scholars committed to traditional quantitative research might see the use of intersectionality as specious (Hernández-Truyol, 1997), such use allows us to see how multiple social identities uniquely contribute to the experiences of Latina college students.

Findings: Latina College Graduate Survey

The findings from the Latina College Graduate Survey present a descriptive analysis of two nonacademic risk factors (language use and low educational attainment of mothers). The left-hand column in Table 6.1 illustrates these findings.

Nonacademic Risk Factors

Identification of nonacademic risk factors has been used to contribute to the understanding of broader societal issues influencing student success. However, focusing on such risk factors can lead to unintended consequences of reinforcing academic failure (i.e., the idea that failure is normal for students who possess these risk factors), by blaming the subjects for their lack of success as the focus on risk factors fails to adequately explain students' success, as illustrated in the following examples.

Language Use. Speaking a language other than English at home is considered a risk factor for academic achievement. Over 75% reported speaking a language other than English at home (41.9% English and Spanish, 34.2%

Spanish only). A relatively high percentage of the Latina college graduate respondents (44.4%) attended a linguistically segregated high school in which 50% of the students came from families that spoke a language other than English at home. Yet, only about 5% of the college graduate respondents in this study reported participating in English as a Second Language (ESL) instruction in high school. Additionally, almost two thirds of respondents reported speaking Spanish as part of their job after graduating from college.

Low Educational Attainment of Mothers. Having a mother who attained little education is also identified as a risk factor in the literature for educational achievement. Over one third of respondents' mothers completed less than a high school education (35.4%). A slightly larger percentage of respondents' mothers had some college education (37.6%), suggesting significant variability in mothers' educational attainment.

Discussion: Intersectionality Provides More Nuanced Understanding of Latinas and Achievement

> Intersectional analysis, as knowledge generated from and about oppressed groups, unveil[s] . . . domains of power and reveal[s] how oppression is constructed and maintained through multiple aspects of identity simultaneously. (Dill & Zambrana, 2009, p. 7)

On the right side of Table 6.1, I draw on intersectionality to propose alternative ways of interpreting risk factors as a source of strength or resource rather than a deficit.[3] In doing so, I challenge and critique specific risk factors associated with Latinas/os' educational achievements and attainments.

Language

As mentioned, speaking a language other than English at home is considered a risk factor for academic achievement, but the respondents to the Latina College Graduate Survey contradict previous studies. Given the large percentage of Latina graduates speaking Spanish in their work lives, bilingualism appears to be far from a risk factor. Rather, speaking both English and Spanish seems to be an essential aspect of their daily and professional lives. This supports Delgado Bernal's (2001) findings of Chicana college students who perceived that they would have additional professional opportunities in the future because of their bilingualism.

TABLE 6.1

NONACADEMIC RISK FACTORS: A REINTERPRETATION

Risk	%	(n)	(Re)interpretation of risk	%	(n)
Language					
Language spoken at home			Speak Spanish as part of job		
Both English and Spanish	41.9%	(109)	Yes	63.6%	(154)
Spanish	34.2%	(89)	No	36.4%	(88)
English	23.8%	(62)			
Linguistically segregated H.S.			Language instruction		
Yes	44.4%	(115)	Yes	5.3%	(249)
No	55.6%	(144)	No	95.0%	(14)
Educational Attainment/Generational Differences					
Mother's level of education			College-educated family		
No formal or less than H.S.	35.4%	(93)	Yes	52%	(137)
H.S. degree	26.6%	(70)	No/don't know	47.5%	(124)
Some college	37.6%	(99)			
Bachelor's degree or higher	12.9%	(34)			
			Education leads to more opportunities for me than my mother		
			Describes me well/very well	83.2%	(218)
			Does not describe me/describes me a little	16.8%	(44)

Recent studies also show that students who attend racially segregated (Fry, 2005) and linguistically segregated (Olsen, 1997; Valenzuela, 1999) high schools have less favorable educational outcomes. Findings in this study complicate this research in two areas. First, a relatively high percentage of the Latina college graduate respondents (44.4%) attended a linguistically segregated high school in which 50% of students came from families that spoke a language other than English at home. This high percentage appears to belie any notions of individual exceptionalism on the part of these students. If not exceptionalism, what might explain their subsequent success?

A second finding on second-language instruction may provide a possible alternative explanation for the success of these students from racially and linguistically segregated schools. Only about 5% of the college graduate respondents in this study reported participating in ESL instruction in high school. Given the high percentage of respondents who spoke Spanish at home (over 75%), and the high percentage of immigrants and children of immigrants among the respondents (69.3%), we might expect a higher number of respondents participating in ESL instruction. Why would only 5% of these students have participated in such instruction? One might assume the sample includes a disproportionately large number of private high school graduates (suggesting either less access to ESL or higher socioeconomic status), yet only 15.8% of respondents fall into this group. Another possible explanation for the respondents' low participation in ESL instruction may be that the respondents in this study were high achieving and did not need additional language instruction. This would suggest that respondents successfully acquired English proficiency, and that they maintained their home language outside the school.

This finding on second-language instruction appears to reinforce the findings of earlier studies showing that those who do participate in second-language instruction may have a more difficult time accessing a college-bound curriculum (Callahan, 2005; Harklau, 1994; Suárez-Orozco & Suárez-Orozco, 2001). The literature on culturally and linguistically diverse students shows that those who participate in English-language acquisition instruction are thus negatively influencing their learning and educational progress. In sum, speaking a different language at home may not be a major obstacle for academically successful Latinas. Rather, it may be that structuring school curriculum that disadvantages language learners is a major obstacle for Latinas/os enrolling in and graduating from college.

Educational Attainment and Generational Differences

When mothers' educational attainment is seen solely as a risk factor, it obscures the influence of social support from the extended family. For example, 52% of Latina college graduates reported having a family member who earned a college degree. It appears that the nuclear and extended family level of education beyond the respondents' mothers also influenced Latinas' educational progress and attainment.

Also challenging this notion of mothers' educational attainment as a risk factor is the generational difference that emerges in these findings. Latina college graduates may be generationally different from their mothers in maintaining a close connection with their extended family, receiving support for college, and expecting to achieve more academically than their mothers did. Respondents viewed education as a vehicle for opportunities beyond their mothers' attainment level. Related findings in this study showed 98.9% of respondents reporting that "in spite of obstacles I usually accomplish what I set out to do," and 96.6% agreeing that "education is so important that it is worth putting up with the things I don't like." These results would appear to confirm earlier findings on Latina student resiliency in accessing college (Morales, 2000, 2008).

Under a success-based framework the strengths of the student, family, and community would be considered important. New questions are needed that acknowledge differences, systematic barriers, and individual agency. Furthermore, we can better understand what students are capable of when we interpret data from an intersectional framework. For example, Kuh and Love (2000) ask that we consider identifying experiences and values that would be beneficial for college students to possess, such as having a strong work ethic, being able to negotiate different contexts (as cited in Kuh et al., 2006), resiliency (Morales, 2000, 2008), and cultural identity (Torres, 1999; Torres, Howard-Hamilton, & Cooper, 2003). Initial data from the Latina College Graduate Survey show that many respondents indicated possessing these qualities. Further study is needed to better understand these generational differences in terms of both the generation going to college and the generation growing up in the United States.

National data from the survey of Latina college graduates suggest that traditional explanations of differences based on language and parents' education levels are insufficient for predicting academic success. The findings drew on Latinas' backgrounds and identities to allow us to gain a better understanding of high-achieving Latinas as a group rather than "exceptions to the rule." The reinterpretations of the risk factors were grounded in Latinas' experiences and individual identities.

To date, few studies have questioned mainstream notions of student success in higher education (e.g., Why do students drop out? What places students at risk for not completing their education?). The lack of questioning and theorizing about race/ethnicity in higher education has left the field with incomplete and inaccurate models for considering Latina students.

Conclusion

This chapter illuminates how using intersectionality in higher education to investigate the college experiences of academically successful Latinas leads to a reinterpretation of risk factors. Research currently equips practitioners with a framework for understanding the experiences of Latinas/os in terms of risk factors and marginality. Less is known about how Latinas' backgrounds and experiences empower them. Moreover, to date, few studies have considered Latinas' academic achievement. The prevailing theory suggests that these Latina students succeed by adjusting (or conforming) to the norms of college. This ignores the current and historical realities of Latina/o college students and leaves the social institutions and power structures unexamined. By examining various social contexts and intersections of social identities, our ability to understand who academically successful Latina students are and how to develop effective programs and policies to serve their needs is expanded.

In theoretical terms, this chapter contributes to how postsecondary education studies Latinas by focusing on race and ethnicity; challenging research approaches that rely on widespread comparisons and generalizations across racial groups; and illustrating Latina graduates' experiences of oppression, resistance, and liberation. In doing so, this chapter seeks to (a) broaden the role and meaning of race/ethnicity in education by drawing on intersectionality, (b) contest how Latinas/os are defined and present alternative interpretations of their background and experiences, and (c) give voice to and spotlight experiences of academically successful Latinas. Additionally, it shifts the research approach to measuring student success from the markers of access and retention to those of graduation.

Notes

1. Generation in the United States affects Latinos differently from Latinas, with levels of assimilation significantly higher for the former (Suárez-Orozco & Suárez-Orozco, 2001).

2. Generalizability can help us gain a better understanding of groups. Unfortunately, generalizability can also be used to essentialize a group, emphasizing how it deviates from the norm rather than how it contributes to understanding (Cole, 2009).

3. This is not to suggest that there is no association between risk factors and educational achievement and progress; it is more to suggest that different interpretations or measures might help to explain the experiences of academically successful Latinas. I attempt to resist essentialist assumptions of who Latina college graduates are by drawing on intersectionality to examine the backgrounds (demographics, immigration, and community) and connection to a group, resiliency, experience of oppression, and differentiation of Latina college graduates.

References

Angen, M. J. (2000). Evaluating interpretive inquiry: Reviewing the validity debate and opening the dialogue. *Qualitative Health Research, 10*(3), 378–395.

Anzaldúa, G. (1987). *Borderlands: The new mestiza = La frontera.* San Francisco: Spinsters/Aunt Lute.

Aud, S., Hussar, W., Johnson, F., Kena, G., Roth, E., Manning, E., Wang, X., & Zhang, J. (2012). *The condition of education 2012 (NCES 2012-045).* U.S. Department of Education, National Center for Education Statistics. Washington, DC. Retrieved from http://nces.ed.gov/pubsearch

Braxton, J. (Ed.). (2005). *Reworking the student departure puzzle.* Nashville, TN: Vanderbilt University Press.

Callahan, R. M. (2005). Tracking and high school English learners: Limiting opportunity to learn. *American Educational Research Journal, 42*(2), 305–328.

Carey, K. (2008). *Graduation rate watch: Making minority student success a priority.* Washington, DC: The Education Sector.

Carter, D. F., & Hurtado, S. (2007). Bridging key research dilemmas: Quantitative research using a critical eye. *New Directions for Institutional Research, 133*, 25–35.

Cole, E. R. (2009). Intersectionality and research in psychology. *American Psychologist, 64*(3), 170–180.

Crenshaw, K. (2003). Demarginalizing the intersection of race and sex: A Black feminist critique of antidiscrimination doctrine, feminist theory, and antiracist politics. In A. K. Wing (Ed.), *Critical race feminism: A reader* (pp. 357–383). Critical America. New York: New York University Press.

Creswell, J. W., & Plano Clark, V. L. (2011). *Designing and conducting mixed methods research.* Thousand Oaks, CA: Sage.

Delgado Bernal, D. (2001). Learning and living pedagogies of the home: The Mestiza consciousness of Chicana students. *Qualitative Studies in Education, 14*(5), 623–639.

Delgado, R., & Stefancic, J. (2012). *Critical race theory: An introduction.* Critical America. New York: New York University Press.

Dill, B. T., & Zambrana, R. E. (2009). *Emerging intersections: Race, class, and gender in theory, policy, and practice.* New Brunswick, NJ: Rutgers University Press.

Fry, R. (2005). *The high schools Hispanics attend: Size and other key characteristics.* Washington, DC: Pew Hispanic Center.

Fry, R., & Gonzales, F. (2008). *One-in-five and growing fast: A profile of Hispanic public school students.* Washington, DC: Pew Hispanic Center.

Hammersley, M., & Atkinson, P. (1983). *Ethnography: Principles in practice.* London, UK: Tavistock.

Harklau, L. (1994). Jumping tracks: How language-minority students negotiate evaluations of ability. *Anthropology & Education Quarterly, 25*(3), 347–363.

Haworth, J. G., & Conrad, C. (1997). *Emblems of quality in higher education: Developing and sustaining high-quality programs.* Boston: Allyn & Bacon.

Hernández-Truyol, B. E. (1997). Borders (en)gendered: Normativities, Latinas, and a LatCrit paradigm. *New York University Law Review, 72*(4), 882–927.

Hussar, W. J., & Bailey, W. J. (2009). *Projections of education statistics to 2018* (37th ed.) (Report No. NCES 2009-062). Retrieved from http://nces.ed.gov/pubs2009/2009062_1.pdf

Kuh, G., Kinzie, J., Buckley, J., Bridges, B., & Hayek, J. (2006). *What matters to student success: A review of the literature.* Washington, DC: National Postsecondary Education Cooperative.

Kuh. G. D., & Love, P.G. (2000). A cultural perspective on student departure. In J. M. Braxton (Ed.), *Reworking the Student Departure Puzzle* (196–212). Nashville, TN: Vanderbilt University Press.

Llagas, C., Snyder, T. D., & National Center for Education Statistics. (2003). *Status and trends in the education of Hispanics.* Washington, DC: National Center for Education Statistics, U.S. Department of Education, Institute of Education Sciences.

López, N. (2002). Rewriting race and gender high school lessons: Second-generation Dominicans in New York City. *Teachers College Record, 104*(6), 1187–1203.

Morales, E. E. (2000). A contextual understanding of the process of educational resilience: High achieving Dominican American students and the resilience cycle. *Innovative Higher Education, 25*(1), 7–22.

Morales, E. E. (2008). Exceptional female student resilience and gender in higher education. *Innovative Higher Education, 33,* 197–213.

National Center for Education Statistics (NCES). (2010). *Total fall enrollment in degree-granting institutions, by race/ethnicity, sex, attendance status, and level of student: Selected years, 1976 through 2009.* Washington, DC: U.S. Department of Education.

O'Connor, C., Lewis, A., & Mueller, J. (2007). Researching "Black" educational experiences and outcomes: Theoretical and methodological considerations. *Educational Researcher, 36*(9), 541–552.

Olsen, L. (1997). *Made in America: Immigrant students in our public schools.* New York: The New Press.

Oropeza, M. (2011). *Academically successful: Latina college graduates: A multi-methods study.* (Doctoral dissertation). Available from ProQuest Dissertations and Theses: Database. (UMI No. 3485596)

Padilla, R. (2007). *Camino a la universidad: The road to college: What we know about Latino student access and success in postsecondary education.* Indianapolis, IN: Lumina Foundation.

Snyder, T. D., & Dillow, S. A. (2012a). Bachelor's degrees conferred by degree-granting institutions, by sex, race/ethnicity, and field of study: 2009–10. *Digest of Education Statistics 2011* (NCES 2012-001). Washington, DC: National Center for Education Statistics, Institute of Education Sciences, U.S. Department of Education.

Snyder, T. D., & Dillow, S. A. (2012b). Graduation rates of first-time postsecondary students who started as full-time degree/certificate-seeking students, by sex, race/ethnicity, time to completion, and level and control of institution where student started: Selected cohort entry years, 1996 through 2007. *Digest of Education Sta-*

tistics 2011 (NCES 2012-001). Washington, DC: National Center for Education Statistics, Institute of Education Sciences, U.S. Department of Education.

Suárez-Orozco, C., & Suárez-Orozco, M. M. (2001). *Children of immigration.* Cambridge, MA: Harvard University Press.

Swail, W. S., Cabrera, A. F., Lee, C., & Williams A. (2005). *Latino students and the educational pipeline from middle school to workforce: Latino students in the educational pipeline.* Arlington, VA: Educational Policy Institute.

Torres, V. (1999). Validation of a bicultural orientation model for Hispanic college students. *Journal of College Student Development, 40*(3), 285–298.

Torres, V., Howard-Hamilton, M. F., & Cooper, D. L. (2003). Identity development of diverse populations: Implications for teaching and administration in higher education. *ASHE-ERIC Higher Education Reports, 29*(6), 1–117.

U.S. Bureau of the Census. (2002). Table 18.1. Population by region, sex, Hispanic origin, and race with percent distributions. *Current Population Survey, March 2002, Ethnic and Hispanic Statistics Branch Population Division.* Washington, DC: U.S. Government Printing Office. Retrieved from http://www.census.gov/population/www/socdemo/hispanic/ppl-165.html

U.S. Bureau of the Census. (2006). *Hispanics in the U.S. census: American community survey.* Washington, DC: Government Printing Office. Retrieved from http://www.census.gov/population/www/socdemo/hispanic/files/Internet_Hispanic_in_US_2006.pdf

Valdés, G. (1998). The world outside and inside schools: Language and immigrant children. *Educational Researcher, 27*(6), 4–18.

Valenzuela, A. (1999). *Subtractive schooling: U.S.-Mexican youth and the politics of caring.* Albany, NY: State University of New York Press.

Villalpando, O. (2004). Practical considerations of critical race theory and Latino critical theory for Latino college students. *New Directions for Student Services, 105*(5), 41–50.

Zavella, P. (1997). Reflections on diversity among Chicanas. In M. Romero, P. Hondagneu-Sotelo, & V. Ortiz, (Eds.), *Challenging fronteras: Structuring Latina and Latino lives in the U.S.: An anthology of readings* (187–194). New York: Routledge.

7

INTERSECTIONALITY OF MULTIPLE RACISMS

A Case Study of Campus Climate for Three Mixed Race Undergraduate Women

Chelsea Guillermo-Wann

Intersectionality typically exposes important intersections of oppressions corresponding to multiple social identities such as race, class, and gender (Crenshaw, 1991; McCall, 2005). However, as mixed race identities become more prominent and politicized in the post–civil rights era, the possibility of intersectionality *within* the category of race of mixed racial identities with multiple racisms emerges. That is, multiracial individuals may experience multiple forms of racial oppression and/or privilege based on respective racial backgrounds as well as mixed race statuses, given the norm of singular and monoracial constructions of race (Johnston & Nadal, 2010). This is particularly intriguing given that mixed race identities can also be situational based on context (Renn, 2004a), much like an individual's various social identities may become more or less salient in a given setting (e.g., Reay, 2007). Although multiraciality may have been less fruitful to examine in earlier eras (Crenshaw, 1991), doing so now can counter public discourse that misuses the perceived growth of the post–civil rights multiracial population to suggest the declining significance of race (Brunsma, 2006; Daniel & Castañeda-Liles, 2006; Morning, 2005).

Such politicized issues around multiraciality frame and influence the campus climate for diversity in college (Hurtado, Milem, Clayton-Pedersen, & Allen, 1998, 1999) at the same time that this generationally increasing population is likely to transform student demographics (Renn, 2009). Campus climate for diversity is a site in higher education where critical issues around race arise, which in turn shape key conditions for learning and success (Harper & Hurtado, 2007; Hurtado, Alvarez, Guillermo-Wann, Cuellar, &

Arellano, 2012; Hurtado, Dey, Gurin, & Gurin, 2003). Campus climate affects vital transitions for underrepresented students, such as adjustment to college (Cabrera, Nora, Terenzini, Pascarella, & Hagedorn, 1999; Hurtado et al., 1999; Hurtado et al., 2007), student retention (Rhee, 2008), and degree completion (Museus, Nichols, & Lambert, 2008). It is also linked to key learning outcomes for the twenty-first century such as habits of mind for lifelong learning, multicultural competencies, and retention and achievement (Hurtado et al., 2012). For example, as Harper and Hurtado (2007) note, when students engage across racial groups, some positive outcomes include decreased interracial anxiety (Levin, van Laar, & Sidanius, 2003) and less balkanization (Sáenz, Ngai, & Hurtado, 2007), which may decrease racial segregation trends after college (Milem, Umbach, & Liang, 2004). However, although campus climate research on monoracially constructed groups in college is flourishing (Hurtado et al., 2012), as is research on intersectionality (Davis, 2008), both research areas are relatively scant regarding mixed race, with campus climate studies (e.g., Guillermo-Wann, 2010, 2013b, 2013c; Guillermo-Wann & Johnston, 2012) and theories (e.g., Guillermo-Wann & Johnston, 2012; Hurtado et al., 2012) only recently accounting for mixed racial identities that have been well studied in the literature (e.g., Renn, 2004a).

If higher education is to truly educate for a more just and equitable society, campus climate for diversity must be made inclusive for all students (Hurtado, 2007), and must increase understanding of multiracially identifying students who may be located within, between, and/or at the margins of monoracially constructed groups on campus. Therefore, the purpose of this study is to illustrate how different forms of racism intersect in multiracial students' experiences in college, creating within-group nuances in their quality of campus climate. The nexus of understanding mixed race through intersectionality and, in turn, improving campus climate is but one arena in which to address the "so what" of intersectionality research in terms of practical interventions (Nash, 2008).

Clarifying Concepts

Multiracial scholarship raises the question of whom to consider as part of a multiracial population, given that most racial groups in the United States have mixed racial ancestry (Daniel, 2001; Davis, 1991; Feagin, 2006; Gomez, 2007; Morning, 2000, 2005; Nadal, 2009; Smith, 1999). To clarify whom this study examines, *race* is first presented as

> *a concept which signifies and symbolizes social conflicts and interests by refer-*
> *ring to different types of human bodies.* Although the concept of race invokes

biologically based human characteristics (so-called "phenotypes"), the selection of these particular human features for purposes of racial signification is always and necessarily a social and historical process. . . . Race is a matter of both social structure and cultural representation. (Omi & Winant, 1994, pp. 55–56)

Racial formation processes have typically created racial groups as separate and monoracially defined, despite the fact that the social groups classified as different "races" are difficult to define because of the pervasiveness of mixed ancestry within groups (Omi & Winant, 1994).

Therefore, to avoid reifying race in an essentialist sense (see Renn, 2004b), *multiracial* is defined here as the combination of two or more monoracially constructed groups "understood in [one's] day as . . . distinct races regardless of whether this intermixture stemmed from their parents' generation or farther back" (Morning, 2005, p. 42). For study participants, I operationalize multiracial as acknowledging any combination of two or more of these groups in one's ancestry: Arab American, Asian American, black, Latina/o, Native American, and white.[1] Some of these groups are not federally recognized as "races," but in social relations, all are racialized in that meaning is attached to each group, which informs social interaction, power, and privilege (Omi & Winant, 1994). The terms *multiracial* and *mixed race* are used interchangeably, whereas *biracial* refers to only two racial groups. Recognizing the limitations of these terms in light of the socially constructed nature of race, phrases such as *multiracially identifying* are used to disrupt static notions of race as biologically essential or discrete (see also Guillermo-Wann & Johnston, 2012; Osei-Kofi, 2011). I use the term *multiraciality* as an all-encompassing phenomenon of multiracial identity, persons, groups, and so on, in a broader sense.

Multiracial "Experiences" and Campus Climate Literature

A growing body of literature details negative experiences around multiraciality in college despite common assumptions that multiracially identifying students may be exempt from race-based marginalization. For example, when analyzed as a group, some mixed race students do not feel that monoracially constructed peer groups accept them (King, 2008; Nishimura, 1998; Renn, 2000, 2003, 2004a; Sands & Schuh, 2004), report more experience with prejudice compared to their black and white peers at one southern institution (Brackett et al., 2006), and may struggle with social integration in informal peer interactions (Sands & Schuh, 2004). In particular, these students can find navigating campus spaces challenging due to others' perceptions of them based on their physical appearance, cultural knowledge, and how they act, as these are measured against monoracially constructed norms (King, 2008). Mixed race students may find that institutional practices such as monoracially dominant student affairs programs create limiting spaces (Sands & Schuh, 2004), and that the lack of private and public space that is both psychological and physical may even lead students to consider leaving the institution (Renn, 2000). In a national study, multiracially identifying students indicate the lowest perceptions of institutional support, even after controlling for interactions across difference, and report the second-lowest levels of supportive relationships on campus of all racial groups (Laird & Niskodé-Dossett, 2010). However, this research fails to link multiracial experiences to theories of racism, campus climate frameworks, and a broader fight against all forms of oppression, leaving such scholarship and activism vulnerable to sending mixed messages about its interests and the state of racial relations in society (Guillermo-Wann & Johnston, 2012).

On the other hand, research on the campus climate for diversity tends to operationalize race using singular racial categories and, until recently, has generally overlooked college students who identify multiracially (Guillermo-Wann, 2013b; Hurtado et al., 2012). The campus climate for diversity is a multidimensional framework for assessing historical, compositional, psychological, behavioral (Hurtado et al., 1998, 1999), and organizational aspects of higher education (Milem, Chang, & Antonio, 2005) to advance equitable learning environments for diverse student success (Hurtado et al., 2012). As expected from the multiracial "experiences" literature, known campus climate studies on multiraciality in college find that students acknowledging mixed racial ancestry can experience a negative climate across various dimensions (Guillermo-Wann, 2010, 2013b), although variation clearly exists within this group as well (Guillermo-Wann, 2013b). Specifically, multiracially identifying undergraduates detail *multiracial microaggressions*, which target multiraciality across racial backgrounds and phenotypes (Johnston & Nadal, 2010) as well as across the behavioral, psychological, compositional, and organizational dimensions of campus climate (Guillermo-Wann, 2010). Negative perceptions of the organizational dimension of campus climate are heightened for mixed race students with lower socioeconomic status, less white cultural knowledge, and greater participation in monoracially based student organizations; the inverse is evident among positive perceptions of climate (Guillermo-Wann, 2013c). Additionally, when multiracial quantitative data are aggregated as a group, students indicate higher mean levels of discrimination and bias as an aspect of the behavioral dimension than do monoracially classified Latina/o or white students (Guillermo-Wann, 2013a; Hurtado, Ruiz, & Guillermo-Wann, in revision), and double-minority multiracial students indicate higher levels than their peers indicating minority/white multiracial backgrounds

(Guillermo-Wann, 2013a). These emerging studies on multiraciality link racialized experiences to campus climate and racism using the Integrative Model of Multiraciality (IMM; Guillermo-Wann & Johnston, 2012).

The Integrative Model of Multiraciality

The IMM addresses race and racism in higher education contexts (Guillermo-Wann & Johnston, 2012). It builds upon perspectives from racial formation theory (Omi & Winant, 1994), critical race theory (e.g., Bell, 1980; Ladson-Billings & Tate, 1995; Solórzano, Ceja, & Yosso, 2000), multiracial identity theory (e.g., Renn, 2004a), and campus climate (Hurtado et al., 1998, 1999, 2012; Milem et al., 2005). In augmenting and connecting these theories, the model integrates concepts of *traditional racisms* targeting monoracially constructed groups with *monoracism* targeting multiraciality through the maintenance of monoracial norms (Guillermo-Wann & Johnston, 2012; Johnston & Nadal, 2010). The IMM draws on an understanding of *racism* as:

> a multi-faceted social phenomenon, with different levels and overlapping forms. It involves attitudes, actions, processes, and unequal power relations. It is based on the interpretations of the idea of "race," hierarchical social relations and the forms of discrimination that flow from this. Racism is not confined to extreme cases, but is present in a whole continuum of social relations. (Garner, 2010, p. 18)

This understanding of racism allows for multiple racisms, including racisms that are gendered, classed, and so on (Garner, 2010; Phoenix, 1999), which can encompass monoracism, and thus expose the intersectionality of multiple racial oppressions within the social category of race. The concept of monoracism modestly suggests that there is relative privilege in belonging to a monoracially constructed group, even if that is a category of color (Johnston & Nadal, 2010). This disorienting form of privilege illuminates how multiraciality disrupts normalized monoracial notions of race, racism, and racial privilege. Consequently, monoracism challenges racial theory on power, privilege, and oppression and specifies that dominant white racial privilege is maintained through the intersectionality of monoracism with other racisms (Guillermo-Wann & Johnston, 2012; Johnston & Nadal, 2010). Monoracism often plays out around students' racial identities through multiracial microaggressions, which may occur at an interpersonal and/or systemic level and may be invisible to the perpetrator or recipient (Johnston & Nadal, 2010). Such microaggressions can have cumulative negative effects on mental health (Pierce, 1995; Solórzano et al., 2000) and are a focus of this study. In connecting multiple racisms to campus climate, the IMM aims to strengthen alliances with monoracially constructed communities to work toward the eradication of traditional racisms, monoracism, and their intersectionality with other oppressions (Guillermo-Wann & Johnston, 2012).

The IMM contextualizes campus climate within broader sociohistorical, policy, and local community contexts, and specifies that the external contexts are where racial formation takes place in which traditional racism and monoracism intertwine, and that multiple racisms manifest in the campus climate (Guillermo-Wann & Johnston, 2012). Specifically, the IMM details processes hypothesized to inform the quality of racial climate for students in light of multiraciality. Key individual-level factors that influence the quality of campus climate through their role in students' racial classification include racial ancestry, physical appearance, cultural knowledge, and socioeconomic status—four components that play a crucial role in multiracial identity (Korgen, 2010; Renn, 2004a, 2008). Two additional factors can influence the level of importance of the individual factors in racial classification: interest convergence (Bell, 1980) and the fluidity of peer culture (Renn, 2004a, 2008), or group boundaries. To varying degrees, these components then inform racial classification, which acknowledges that the subsequent meaning attached to the ascribed race of one student may vary from another and across contexts (Guillermo-Wann & Johnston, 2012). Students may thus experience multiple and contradictory racial classifications in various circumstances, triggering multiracial microaggressions, monoracially based microaggressions, monoracially based privilege, and/or white privilege. Hence, the IMM can expose how multiple racisms can intersect through the campus racial climate for college students with various mixed racial ancestries and racial identities.

Methodology

Data for this analysis were collected in 2010 at a public university in the western United States at which no racial group comprises a numerical majority, and were drawn from a larger study (Guillermo-Wann, 2010, 2013a). The data consist of semistructured interviews with three undergraduate women who affirmed they could "check" two or more of the categories Asian American, Arab American, black, Latina/o, Native American, and white. Collectively, the women span all these backgrounds except Native American and also include Persian American. These women were selected out of the larger sample because they offer differing perceptions of the quality of campus climate and have different racial ancestries. All participants featured in this study exhibit situational racial identities, and two evidence situational racial identities in which they switch among a single monoracial identity, multiple monoracial identities, a multiracial identity, and/or opt out of racial identification in various situations (Renn, 2004a). Given the wide variation of possible multiracial backgrounds and racial identity patterns, I used a unique case study to define each student as a single, unique case (Yin, 2009). Data analysis followed a constant comparative method of inductive and deductive coding.

This study has various limitations. The extent to which mixed race individuals even constitute a group can be questioned. However, given the rising visibility and politicization of mixed race identities, particularly around postracial claims in public discourse, the social identification and location of this group in the public sphere warrants examination. Similarly, mixed race individuals are commonly excluded as "authentic" members of monoracially constructed groups (Johnston & Nadal, 2010), so this study correspondingly highlights their multiple marginalities. However, it does not focus on privilege within racial groups that may simultaneously elevate a mixed race status. Foremost, I limit this analysis to the social identity category of race, while intersectionality research traditionally includes at least one more social identity. However, given the complexity of mixed race, I withhold such an analysis of additional social identities to highlight intersectionality within race. All other aspects of the study clearly exhibit an intersectional approach in that the racial categories matter equally, there is dynamic interaction between individual and institutional factors, the group members are diverse, the analysis integrates the individual with the institution, and the study is both empirical and theoretical (Hancock, 2007). Thus, this study might be considered an intracategorical study (McCall, 2005) in that it examines the intersections of multiple racial categories, identities, oppressions, and privileges within individuals.

Last, I assume there is a campus racial climate for multiracial students because I identify as multiracial, having Filipina, Mexican, and white backgrounds. My positionality could have influenced data analysis, as I was interested in documenting aspects of a negative racial climate to challenge neoconservative claims about the declining significance of race buoyed by multiraciality. In light of this, I additionally sought disconfirming evidence (Patton, 2002), through which the intersectionality of multiple racisms surfaced (see Guillermo-Wann, 2013a).

Findings and Discussion

This section shares stories from three undergraduate women who indicate having mixed racial ancestry and who identify in a variety of racial and ethnic manners to understand how they experience intersections of multiple racisms and racial privilege in college. Looking at each student de-essentializes mixed race as a category and brings to life the heterogeneity within this group as well as within the respective monoracially constructed groups to which they may belong. Each of the women selected for this analysis portrays a different perception of the campus climate; one states it is negative, another positive, with the last student balancing both perspectives. The first and last stories focus on aspects of the organizational dimension of campus climate, while the second story highlights the importance of compositional diversity. The three contrasting accounts of campus climate highlight differences in these women's mixed race identities and intersections of multiple racisms as they play out in college. Each section first summarizes each woman's family background and racial identities, and then recounts their stories of marginalization based on mixed and monoracial identities or ascriptions.

Theresa: "Latina" and "Biracial" Identities

Theresa's stories focus attention on the importance of college curriculum as an aspect of the organizational dimension of campus climate, and how she experiences marginalization both as a person of mixed heritage and as a Latina. Theresa has Mexican and white ancestry and exhibits a situational identity shifting between one singular monoracial identity, "Latina," and a multiracial identity, "biracial." She does not identify as white, but rather identifies more broadly as a student of color, as she feels that her experience reflects that of a "more light-skinned" person of color, recognizing relative privilege based on skin color. Theresa grew up with her single white mother, who is Irish Catholic and Jewish, and biracial brother of the same Mexican Catholic father in a predominantly black working-class neighborhood; like much of the community, they rented their home. They were the only whites and Latinas/os in the area, so Theresa's early socialization was mostly in the black community and with her white mother. She feels that her cultural knowledge is more black than white due to her peers and community, and that she had little opportunity to be socialized into Latina/o communities until college, which she has since pursued. Her father was not involved in her life or cultural socialization, and her mom raised her and her brother in a nonreligious but spiritual home. Theresa's mother attended some college and her father graduated from high school, so she also proudly attends the university as a low-income student who will be of the first generation in her family to graduate.

Theresa details monoracism that marginalizes mixed race students as well as traditional racism targeting Latinas/os. Reflecting on such experiences in college, she states, "I've felt marginalized as a Latina person, or woman, before, but literally the past few months I've felt more marginalized as a multiracial person." A vivid example of monoracism from her campus climate perceptions details the multiracial microaggression of *exclusion or isolation via endorsement of a monoracial society and norms* (Johnston & Nadal, 2010). While endorsement of monoracial norms can be intentional, it is often unconscious and reflects the broader social assumption of races as distinct categories of people and the relative invisibility of multiraciality. Theresa illustrates the endorsement of monoracial norms through curriculum, recalling,

> In interracial dynamics class if we're talking about race or something, I'll make a comment about how the course reader has nothing about biracial/multiracial people or history or just, like, experience or anything. . . . I couldn't find it, that . . . again, it's not recognized and I just felt uncomfortable with the fact that, like, . . . you know, everyone gets a blurb in the history book, right. Sadly it might be only a paragraph on the Civil Rights Movement, but it is there, right, or, like, the Chicano/Chicana Movement is there, but, like, the fact that it's just . . . it's absent, it's not talked about . . . and just I would say lived experience is just how I get my information because there's no . . . I feel like there's no other way to get it, it doesn't really exist formalized, right. There's no multiracial studies at [this university], studies program, right. . . . I was like, "Wait a minute. We don't have our own, like, . . . yeah, we come from these different communities, but we don't have our own study or department or center or something. That's not okay."

That multiraciality is overlooked or excluded from curriculum intended to address racial matters bothers Theresa greatly, as she says she knows that mixed race people have played critical roles in social movements and have been subjected to racism and mistreatment. She knows monoracially constructed communities of color have fought and are necessarily fighting to include those histories and scholars in the curriculum "canon." However, in attempts to educate and examine race, multiracial histories are often excluded from the knowledge base that is part of the organizational dimension of campus climate that can structurally privilege or marginalize groups of people. The exclusion of multiraciality from curriculum in this case has the effect of endorsing a monoracial society and monoracial norms, even in potentially inclusive spaces.

With regard to racism targeting monoracially constructed groups that relies on a white/nonwhite binary, Theresa recalls an exchange with a white male friend regarding ethnic studies in which he both expresses bias typical of white privilege and doubts the validity of such departments. She reflects on a conversation they had walking to their dorms, saying,

We definitely disagree on things, though, and I was talking about my classes and I told him I was taking Chicano/Chicana Studies, an intro class, and he was like, "okay, how do you like it?" And I was like, "It's pretty cool. I learn a lot about myself and how to question things and just, like . . . it's been very interesting," and then he goes, . . . "You know, my problem with Ethnic Studies, it's just so biased. It's only taking one perspective and it's only, like, it's very negative," and I just stopped and I laughed and laughed and I was like, "Are you serious?!" He was like, "What?" I was like, "This whole system is biased!" I was like, "We are living in a Western European Judeo Christian world. Like, where have you been?" I got so heated . . . it was one of those moments of astonishment, of just, like, "No way! You really think that?!" . . . He didn't take well to it and he shut me down and probably cut me off, I think as a lot of people tend to do when you try and defend something that they're not comfortable with. . . . I think he thinks that if you recognize histories of people of color or of not the average history of whatever, that's somehow attacking him as a white male and I was like, "Welcome to my world."

Theresa highlights curriculum as an aspect of the organizational dimension of campus climate through which group-based racial oppression and privilege are embedded in the institution (Milem et al., 2005). She finds herself as a Latina defending ethnic studies as a valid and critical field of study to a white male peer, and simultaneously critiquing an interracial dynamics class for excluding multiracial histories within racial groups' histories. Such marginalizations show how traditional racisms and monoracism can intersect within one's racial identities.

Courtney: "Half-Chinese, Half-Persian" Identity

Courtney's narrative highlights the importance of compositional diversity of campus contexts in the shifting salience of her racial identities as it generates various forms of racial microaggressions and privilege. Courtney, who has Taiwanese and Jewish Iranian heritage, primarily exhibits Renn's (2004a) mixed racial identity, as seen in her "half-Chinese, half-Persian" identity, which she infers is easier than specifying Taiwanese and Iranian backgrounds due to the politics surrounding each of those ethnonational identities. The daughter of college-educated immigrant parents, she details the cultural practices in her home and on each side of her family who lived in close proximity. Although there were not large corresponding ethnic communities where she was raised, she says she is "very in tune with the culture on both sides" from her early family socialization. Courtney's family attended a temple that is racially diverse, opting for that over a Jewish Persian temple because, in her words, it was more "family friendly." Even so,

Courtney says, "I seem to identify more with being Persian maybe because I spend more time with that side of the family or that side of the family is bigger or more dominant. I'm not sure, but sometimes when I think about it, I feel a little bit more Persian than I do Chinese." However, in regard to her early socialization and cultural knowledge, Courtney also says, "But we're pretty Americanized, me and my sister. I don't feel very ethnic," which draws attention to the invisibility of whiteness as a cultural norm. In addition, she says she doesn't racially "look Asian," which could be affirmed by her facial features, which seem to have more Persian qualities. Courtney also has light skin, medium brown hair and eyes, is slender, and dresses in an "Americanized" fashion, as she states. In fact, of her high school friends who were mostly white, she says,

> [They] are always like, "Courtney, you act so white. You always think you're white." I'm like, "Yeah, I kind of forget that I'm really not white." It's just a little joke we have. I don't know, I think maybe because I have such a different blend of two things that I don't really identify with Asian, full Asian people, and I don't really identify with full Persian people.

So although Courtney evidences high levels of Taiwanese and Jewish Persian culture within her family setting, these identities are more private compared to the extensive white cultural knowledge she developed in her high school peer circles. In fact, she often conflates race with culture. Despite being a multiracial "double-minority," her high levels of white cultural knowledge and socioeconomic background play out in her perception of campus climate, which she says is positive, revealing a lack of critical consciousness regarding the racial microaggressions she enumerates, viewing them as isolated incidents rather than symptoms of a more pervasive hostile climate (Guillermo-Wann, 2013a).

Courtney details multiracial microaggressions pertaining to the compositional diversity of different spaces on campus. Context is a key component in intersectionality as multiple social identities move from the foreground to the background (e.g., Valentine, 2008), and as mixed race college students exhibit situational racial identities (Renn, 2004a). Despite that, Courtney feels the campus is "a very safe space to express your culture" *because she perceives it to be compositionally diverse.* She feels uneasy about joining the Chinese American hip-hop dance team, which is racially and ethnically homogeneous and has a "vibe" that makes her apprehensive about checking it out because she doesn't want to stick out in terms of physical appearance and isn't sure she would feel "comfortable" there. Instead, she joins a Filipino one because she feels it is very welcoming and racially diverse in comparison. Similarly, Courtney also chooses to be part of a sorority, which upon reflection, she realizes comprises many multiracial Asian American women, saying, "Maybe I just felt comfortable at that house because I felt like not only personality wise, but appearance wise, I fit in. I think it's very subconscious, though." Courtney avoids multiracial microaggressions that target the authenticity of her "Asianness" (see Johnston & Nadal, 2010) by seeking more compositionally diverse spaces in which her mixed race status is less visible based on her physical appearance and, therefore, less salient. In her case, homogeneous Chinese American and Persian American spaces foreground a marginalized mixed race status through normative monoracial constructions of race.

Also in contrast to Courtney's perception of a positive campus climate, she details an infuriating experience in class that can be understood as both a monoracial and a multiracial microaggression, demonstrating how multiple oppressions can occur within the category of race in a single incident. She experiences the *assumption of a monoracial or mistaken racial identity*, which often takes the form of racial jokes being made in one's presence because the person is assumed not to be part of that group (Johnston & Nadal, 2010). Similarly, a faculty member insensitively lectures about name changing among Iranian Americans, not realizing that Courtney, or possibly anyone else in class, belongs to that group. Courtney vents,

> It kind of bothered me the way he said it. . . . He was like, "This name, ASS-l. Who wants to come here and be named ASS-l? That's going to suck," and I really wanted to raise my hand and say, "Actually you know, that name's not pronounced ASS-l, it's Ah-SAHL. . . ." That really bothered me that day. . . . I probably should have said something, thinking back, because it actually does make me very upset the way . . . he said it so lightly and almost jokingly. . . . That really bothered me because he's almost playing into the whole thing, "So you're saying people should change their name because you're making fun of the name yourself," you know. So that day, oh, that day really bothered me.

Courtney also talks about how other students in class have been tokenized because of their perceived race. That she was not singled out grants her the racial privilege of not being targeted by that type of racial discrimination, but she is also invisible to him as a Persian American; he assumes a mistaken racial identity, possibly white, given the contextual clues.

The issue of context emerges in Courtney's reflections, showing that as she moves between spaces, her racial identities situationally shift to the foreground and background. The desire not to stand out physically is so strong that she avoids homogeneous spaces reflecting her two racial backgrounds, as such environments feel hostile to her as a multiracially identifying person. Rather, Courtney seeks compositionally diverse environments in college that put her at ease to go about her life and not deal with the mental and emotional tax of defending her racial authenticity. Through compositional diversity and pedagogical offense, the intersectionality of multiple racisms in Courtney's experience becomes visible through multiple marginalizations.

Nadia: "Latina," "Black," "Latina and Black," and "Biracial" Identities

Nadia brings attention back to the organizational dimension of campus climate through her reflections on equity issues for underrepresented students of color, and how those intersect with her mixed race identities. Nadia has Guatemalan and Egyptian ethnic backgrounds. Her situational racial identity shifts among Renn's (2004a) singular monoracial identity ("Latina" or "black"), two monoracial identities ("Latina and black"), and multiracial ("biracial") identity patterns. Nadia's biological parents divorced when she was 12, and she has two other sisters from their marriage. Nadia's mother is Guatemalan and remarried Nadia's stepfather, who is Mexican, soon after her divorce. Nadia grew up in a predominantly Latina/o community in a home owned by her grandmother. But for all other purposes, she was raised in a lower-income household. Nadia's mother attended some college, Nadia's father completed a college degree, and Nadia attends the university, proudly considering herself in some ways the first generation of her family to complete college, given that her mother played a much more prominent role in her life. Nadia's father's side of the family is Egyptian and identifies as Arab more so than as African or black. Nadia participates in cultural events with her Egyptian side and feels that she understands what it means to be Egyptian but says, "We were never really accepted into my dad's family to the extent that everyone else is, because one, my mom never converted to Islam, and two, we were mixed, and we were, like, mixed with Mexican, according to them, so that wasn't, like, necessarily a good thing." In addition, Nadia does not express positive feelings toward her father, saying, "He's, like, a womanizer and has a lot of different girlfriends." She also says that her dad's family's preference to avoid a black identity has made her racial identification a bit more complicated than it would already be as biracial. Even so, Nadia remains keenly aware of her Arab identity and traditional forms of racism targeting Arab Americans, sharing,

> After 9/11 that was, like, kind of a big deal because our last name's Arabic, and so that was always a thing my mom was kinda worried about for us, like, she didn't want us to be perceived in a certain way, and so I learned, like, based on that, like, just to be careful, like, because people might think certain things about us and things like that.

Nadia understands the Arab identification as a label intended to compara-tively whiten Africans from Egypt, and claims the black identity to inten-tionally critique and resist whiteness. But she recognizes as well that as a biracial African American she may also benefit from relative privilege.

Nadia balances a predominantly negative account of campus climate with a few positive stories, demonstrating an awareness of monoracial norms alongside a keen critical consciousness of racisms targeting monoracially con-structed groups. For example, she notices institutional negligence, a marker of a hostile climate (Harper & Hurtado, 2007), regarding equity issues for students of color, such as low admissions rates, subsequent underrepresenta-tion, and racial incidents and bias that are overlooked until students raise concerns to the administration. She is part of several racial organizations, including a Latina sorority; the black student union; and an academic sup-port program for low-income and first-generation college students, which she says is mostly black and Latina/o in racial composition. In Nadia's case, she says the racial organizations work together to address institutional negli-gence, expressing, "It's kind of like, 'Well, we have to work together because there are so few of us. We have to work together because if we don't do it, who's going to do it for us?'" In this way, traditional racism targeting stu-dents of color in general is visible through institutional neglect. Through the organizations Nadia belongs to, she has been able to address climate and equity issues for monoracially constructed groups of color.

But when it comes to multiple racial identities, Nadia indicates that the graduation ceremony for black students has been held at the same time as the Latina/o graduation. This presents a multiracial microaggression in which mixed race persons are forced to choose one racial identity, denying them a multiracial reality (Johnston & Nadal, 2010). She comments:

> So one of the biggest things that I'm kind of thinking about right now is graduation. I'm thinking, I guess, the African grad, but [literally] at the same time there's [the Latina/o cultural] grad, and so hopefully they don't do that this year, but even thinking about something as small as that, which one do I attend or do I attend both or can I attend both, and which is more impor-tant? . . . I felt in situations especially like the graduation thing or where the [Latina] sorority took up so much time, I pretty much pulled away from the black community where I was a lot more involved before, so, yeah . . . for me, I think I'm the super-involved type. . . . I think when it comes to actually having to choose between two different things makes me feel like I, I don't know, not, I don't know if the word is betrayed, I don't know if that's too strong of a word, but maybe I'm betraying one versus the other and I'm not doing enough to identify with both. . . . It's always like, "Am I trying to choose one?" Or it's just part of the fact that there's too much to kind of try to consider, so it's easier to go this way or . . . you know what I mean?

Although Nadia likes to be very involved, she indicates that it can be very hard to have to choose between being involved in her Latina sorority and the black student community. This is particularly visible in her conundrum about which graduation ceremony to attend, as both have been held at the same time in the past. Organizationally, these important community-oriented graduation ceremonies are scheduled at the same time, and are separate, which denies Nadia her multiracial reality and forces her to choose one over the other, especially given that she is involved in both. This also shows that racial attitudes (possibly among peers and/or staff) assume that members of the Latina/o and black communities would be separate and would not participate in or support each other's achievement, let alone that students might be both black and Latina/o. In addition, holding the separate ceremonies at the same time restricts interaction across racial groups on campus overall, an indicator of the behavioral dimension of climate. The psychological, behavioral, and organizational dimensions likely mutually reinforce one another in this instance, effectively denying Nadia a multiracial reality. In this and similar situations, staff and faculty involved in ethnic organizations may support biracial students simply by checking scheduling, which may help facilitate increased interaction among communities of color.

Implications and Conclusion

The call for research on intersectionality to yield practical interventions (Nash, 2008) seems particularly useful when paired with frameworks for assessing and improving the campus climate for diversity (e.g., Hurtado et al., 1998, 1999, 2012). Precisely because campus climate is multidimensional in nature, research can focus on specific dimensions to yield specific interventions in educational practice and policy. For example, this study focuses primarily on two institutional-level dimensions of campus climate—an institution's compositional diversity and aspects of the organizational dimension (e.g., curriculum, student affairs, and student organizations)—to show how the individual is integrated with the institution, and how racial categories demonstrate a dynamic interaction between the individual and the institution (Hancock, 2007). From the stories of these multiracially identifying women, higher education institutions might be prompted to examine their curriculum designed to be inclusive to see whether it actually is, and the extent to which it engages members of dominant social categories to address unquestioned bias and privilege. Similarly, student affairs professionals might evaluate the extent to which they create limiting or fluid spaces for multiracially identifying students that can simultaneously facilitate increased interactions across racial groups. Faculty and staff development may be natural avenues to pursue as well. With regard to compositional diversity, institutions might be prompted to consider not only their admissions yields for different groups, but also the extent to which niches on campus may or may not be welcoming to multiracially identifying group members, and how to engage such groups in difficult conversations about racial intermixture in groups' histories, relative racial privileges, and group membership. Future educational practice and research will benefit from assessment, implementation of interventions, and evaluations of their effectiveness as well as from intercategorical research (McCall, 2005) on mixed race intersections with additional social identities such as gender, class, and sexuality.

Through the narratives of these three college women, this study highlights the heterogeneity within multiracially and monoracially constructed groups, and how these women experience intersecting racisms along their mixed race identities. We begin to see in greater detail how their racialized experiences extracted from a larger study (Guillermo-Wann, 2013c), start to converge around monoracism and multiracial microaggressions. Their interpersonal- and institutional-level experiences of multiracial exclusion, questioning authenticity, and denial of multiracial realities (Johnston & Nadal, 2010) illuminate similarities in racialized experience among these mixed race women. We also see that their experiences diverge as they experience specific racisms targeting their particular racial backgrounds and identities, and experience white privilege only as far as white cultural knowledge and possible passing seems to afford. Each woman depicts a varying degree of acceptance into her respective racial groups, and yet demonstrates how multiracially identifying students can play a vital role in race-based student interests in justice as legitimate members of monoracially constructed communities. In these ways, this study begins to show an intersectionality of multiple racisms through multiracially identifying women's accounts of the campus racial climate in college, which helps realign mixed race studies and multiraciality with the advancement of social justice for all students.

Note

1. I follow Renn's (2000) suggestion to capitalize racial terms only if they pertain to a nation or continent of origin to "minimize the notion of racial categories as immutable entities" (p. 399).

References

Bell, D. (1980). *Brown v. Board of Education* and the interest convergence dilemma. *Harvard Law Review, 93*, 518–533.

Brackett, K. P., Marcus, A., McKenzie, N. J., Mullins, L. C., Tang, Z., & Allen, A. M. (2006). The effects of multiracial identification on students' perceptions of racism. *The Social Science Journal, 43*, 437–444.

Brunsma, D. L. (Ed.). (2006). Mixed messages: Doing race in the color-blind era. In D. L. Brunsma (Ed.), *Mixed messages: Multiracial identities in the "color-blind" era* (pp. 1–11). Boulder, CO: Lynne Rienner.

Cabrera, A. F., Nora, A., Terenzini, P. T., Pascarella, E. T., & Hagedorn, L. S. (1999). Campus racial climate and the adjustment of students to college: A comparison between white students and African-American students. *The Journal of Higher Education, 70*(2), 134–160.

Crenshaw, K. (1991). Mapping the margins: Intersectionality, identity politics, and violence against women. *Stanford Law Review, 43*(6), 1241–1299.

Daniel, G. R. (2001). *More than black? Multiracial identity and the new racial order.* Philadelphia: Temple University Press.

Daniel, G. R., & Castañeda-Liles, J. M. (2006). Race, multiraciality, and the neo-conservative agenda. In D. L. Brunsma (Ed.), *Mixed messages: Multiracial identities in the "color-blind" era* (pp. 125–146). Boulder, CO: Lynne Rienner.

Davis, F. J. (1991). *Who is black? One nation's definition.* University Park, PA: Pennsylvania State University Press.

Davis, K. (2008). Intersectionality as buzzword: A sociology of science perspective on what makes a feminist theory successful. *Feminist Theory, 9*(1), 67–85.

Feagin, J. R. (2006). *Systemic racism: A theory of oppression.* New York: Routledge.

Garner, S. (2010). *Racisms: An introduction.* Thousand Oaks, CA: Sage.

Gomez, L. E. (2007). *Manifest destinies: The making of the Mexican American race.* New York: New York University Press.

Guillermo-Wann, C. (2010, November). *A post-racial era? Multiracial microaggressions in the campus racial climate.* Paper presented at the 35th annual meeting of the Association for the Study of Higher Education, Indianapolis, IN.

Guillermo-Wann, C. (2013a). How you count matters: Using multiracial student data to examine discrimination and bias in college, Chapter 3. In C. Guillermo-Wann, *(Mixed) race matters: Racial theory, campus climate, and classification* (pp. 79–126). (Unpublished doctoral dissertation). University of California, Los Angeles.

Guillermo-Wann, C. (2013b). *(Mixed) race matters: Racial theory, campus climate, and classification.* (Unpublished doctoral dissertation). University of California, Los Angeles.

Guillermo-Wann, C. (2013c). Mixed race, multiple racisms: Student perceptions of the organizational dimension of campus climate, Chapter 4. In C. Guillermo-Wann, *(Mixed) race matters: Racial theory, campus climate, and classification* (pp. 127–166). (Unpublished doctoral dissertation). University of California, Los Angeles.

Guillermo-Wann, C., & Johnston, M. P. (2012). *Rethinking research of mixed race college students: Towards an integrative model of multiraciality for campus climate.* Paper presented at the 2nd Bi-Annual Critical Mixed Race Studies Conference, Chicago, IL.

Hancock, A. (2007). When multiplication doesn't equal quick addition: Examining intersectionality as a research paradigm. *Perspectives on Politics*, 5(1), 63–79.

Harper, S. R., & Hurtado, S. (2007). Nine themes in campus racial climates and implications for institutional transformation. *New Directions for Student Services*, *2007*(120), 7–24.

Hurtado, S. (2007). Linking diversity with the educational and civic missions of higher education. ASHE Presidential Address. *The Review of Higher Education*, *30*(2), 185–196.

Hurtado, S., Alvarez, C., Guillermo-Wann, C., Cuellar, M., & Arellano, L. (2012). A model for diverse learning environments: The scholarship on creating and assessing conditions for student success. In M. B. Paulsen (Ed.), *Higher education: Handbook of theory and research, 27* (pp. 41–122). New York: Springer.

Hurtado, S., Dey, E. L., Gurin, P., & Gurin, G. (2003). The college environment, diversity, and student learning. In J. Smart (Ed.), *Higher education: Handbook of theory and research, Vol. XVIII* (pp. 145–189). Amsterdam: Kluwer Academic Press.

Hurtado, S., Han, J. C., Sáenz, V. B., Espinosa, L., Cabrera, N., & Cerna, O. (2007). Predicting transition and adjustment to college: Biomedical and behavioral science aspirants' and minority students' first year of college. *Research in Higher Education*, *48*(7), 841–887.

Hurtado, S., Milem, J. F., Clayton-Pedersen, A. R., & Allen, W. R. (1998). Enhancing campus climates for racial/ethnic diversity: Educational policy and practice. *The Review of Higher Education*, *21*(3), 279–302.

Hurtado, S., Milem, J. F., Clayton-Pedersen, A. R., & Allen, W. R. (1999). *Enacting diverse learning environments: Improving the climate for racial/ethnic diversity in higher education institutions.* Washington, DC: ASHE-ERIC Higher Education Report Series, George Washington University Graduate School of Education.

Hurtado, S., Ruiz, A., & Guillermo-Wann, C. (in revision). Thinking about race: The salience of racial and ethnic identity in college and the climate for diversity. *The Journal of Higher Education*.

Johnston, M. P., & Nadal, K. L. (2010). Multiracial microaggressions: Exposing monoracism in everyday life and clinical practice. In D. W. Sue (Ed.), *Microaggressions and marginality: Manifestation, dynamics and impact*. New York: Wiley & Sons.

King, A. R. (2008). Student perspectives on multiracial identity. *New Directions for Student Services*, *2008*(123), 33–41.

Korgen, K. O. (Ed.). (2010). *Multiracial Americans and social class: The influence of social class on racial identity*. New York: Routledge.

Ladson-Billings, G., & Tate, W. F. (1995). Toward a critical race theory of education. *Teachers College Record*, *97*(1), 47–68.

Laird, T. L. N., & Niskodé-Dossett, A. S. (2010). How gender and race moderate the effect of interactions across difference on student perceptions of the campus environment. *The Review of Higher Education*, *33*(3), 333–356.

Levin, S., van Laar, C., & Sidanius, J. (2003). The effects of ingroup and outgroup friendships on ethnic attitudes in college: A longitudinal study. *Group Processes and Intergroup Relations*, *6*(1), 76–92.

McCall, L. (2005). The complexity of intersectionality. *Signs: Journal of Women in Culture and Society, 30*(3), 1771–1800.

Milem, J. F., Chang, M. J., & Antonio, A. L. (2005). *Making diversity work on campus: A research-based perspective*. Washington, DC: Association of American Colleges and Universities.

Milem, J. F., Umbach, P. D., & Liang, C. T. H. (2004). Exploring the perpetuation hypothesis: The role of colleges and universities in desegregating society. *Journal of College Student Development, 45*(6), 688–700.

Morning, A. (2000). Who is multiracial? Definitions and decisions. *Sociological Imagination, 37*, 209–229.

Morning, A. (2005). Multiracial classification on the United States census: Myth, reality, and future impact. *Revue Européenne des Migrations Internationales, 21*(2), 111–134.

Museus, S. D., Nichols, A. H., & Lambert, A. D. (2008). Racial differences in the effects of campus racial climate on degree completion: A structural equation model. *The Review of Higher Education, 32*(1), 107–134.

Nadal, K. L. (2009). *Filipino American psychology: A handbook of theory, research, and clinical practice*. Bloomington, IN: Author House.

Nash, J. C. (2008). Re-thinking intersectionality. *Feminist Review, 89*, 1–15.

Nishimura, N. J. (1998). Assessing the issues of multiracial students on college campuses. *Journal of College Counseling, 1*(1), 45–53.

Omi, M. A., & Winant, H. (1994). *Racial formation in the United States: From the 1960s to the 1990s*. New York: Routledge.

Osei-Kofi, N. (2011). Multiracialization, "mixing," and media pedagogy. In F. A. Bonner, A. F. Marbley, & M. F. Howard-Hamilton (Eds.), *Diverse millennial students in college: Implications for faculty and student affairs*. Sterling, VA: Stylus.

Patton, M. Q. (2002). *Qualitative research and evaluation methods* (3rd ed.). Thousand Oaks, CA: Sage.

Phoenix, A. (1999). Multiple racisms. *The Psychologist, 12*, 134–135.

Pierce, C. (1995). Stress analogs of racism and sexism: Terrorism, torture, and disaster. In C. Willie, P. Rieker, B. Kramer, & B. Brown (Eds.), *Mental health, racism, and sexism* (pp. 227–293). Pittsburgh, PA: University of Pittsburgh Press.

Reay, D. (2007). Future directions in difference research: Recognizing and responding to difference in the research process. In S. N. Hesse-Biber (Ed.), *The handbook of feminist research: Theory and praxis* (pp. 605–612). London, UK: Sage.

Renn, K. A. (2000). Patterns of situational identity among biracial and multiracial college students. *The Review of Higher Education, 23*, 399–420.

Renn, K. A. (2003). Understanding the identities of mixed-race college students through a developmental lens. *Journal of College Student Development, 44*, 383–403.

Renn, K. A. (2004a). *Mixed race students in college: The ecology of race, identity, and community*. Albany, NY: SUNY Press.

Renn, K. A. (2004b). Tilting at windmills: The paradox and promise of researching mixed race, with strategies for scholars. In K. R. Wallace (Ed.), *Working with mixed heritage students: Critical perspectives on research and practice* (pp. 3–24). Westport, CT: Greenwood.

Renn, K. A. (2008). Research on bi- and multiracial identity development: Overview and synthesis [Special issue]. *New Directions for Student Services, 123*, 13–21.

Renn, K. A. (2009). Education policy, politics, and mixed heritage students in the United States. *Journal of Social Issues, 65*(1), 165–183.

Rhee, B. (2008). Institutional climate and student departure: A multinomial multilevel modeling approach. *The Review of Higher Education, 31*(2), 161–183.

Sáenz, V. B., Ngai, H. N., & Hurtado, S. (2007). Factors influencing positive interactions across race for African American, Asian American, Latino, and White college students. *Research in Higher Education, 48*(1), 1–38.

Sands, N., & Schuh, J. H. (2004). Identifying interventions to improve the retention of biracial students: A case study. *Journal of College Student Retention, 5*, 349–363.

Smith, L. T. (1999). *Decolonizing methodologies: Research and indigenous peoples.* London, UK: Zed Books.

Solórzano, D. G., Ceja, M., & Yosso, T. J. (2000). Critical race theory, racial microaggressions, and campus racial climate: The experiences of African American college students. *The Journal of Negro Education, 69*(1/2), 60–73.

Valentine, G. (2008). Theorizing and researching intersectionality: A challenge for feminist geography. *The Professional Geographer, 59*(1), 10–21.

Yin, R. K. (2009). *Case study research: design and methods* (4th ed.). Thousand Oaks, CA: Sage.

8

INTERSECTIONALITY IN AND OF RACE

Identity Construction Re/Considered

Alina S. Wong

Within academic discourse, race is widely understood as a social construction through which racial categories were created as a tool of racism (Apple, 1993; Goldberg, 1993; Hall, 1992; McCarthy & Crichlow, 1993; Omi & Winant, 1994; Werbner, 1997). Racial categorizations in the United States (historically coded as White, Black, Asian, Hispanic, and Native) were created to uphold a system of White privilege such that White Americans—including White American ethnicities, values, religions, skin color, and so on—were considered ideal and normative, whereas other racialized Americans were deemed lacking at best and dehumanized at worst (Alexander, 2010; Omi & Winant, 1994). "Race" as a divisive category contributed to notions of superiority and inferiority, and as rationalizations for colonization, enslavement, discrimination, and criminalization (Apple, 1993; Spade, 2010).

Over time, these racial categories were codified into racial identities, with both positive and detrimental consequences. As the biological foundations for race were eroded, cultural justifications replaced them. This shift occurred partly because of powerful movements fought by communities of color to claim agency in defining their own identities, and to refuse negative portrayals and stereotypes. However, this move from racial categorization to racial identity also allowed dominant ideology to continue to place responsibility for discrimination, unequal access, and exclusion on the individual. If race was not biological, then behaviors and outcomes were choices. Portrayals of Mexicans as lazy, Black youth as drug dealers and gang members, or Asian Americans as irrevocably foreign created such strong stereotypes that mainstream society attributed inequity as a consequence of culture. Oppressed communities have been active in response, creating resistance movements, studying our own histories, and refusing dominant White narratives. This is the sociopolitical context in which racial identities are constructed, contested, and claimed.

I use intersectionality and critical theory to reconsider how race and racial identities are constructed in the United States, particularly by Chinese American and American college students. Research on identity and student development indicates that late adolescence is a crucial time for individuals to garner a sense of self, especially with regard to racial and ethnic identities (Torres, Jones, & Renn, 2009). With concerns about students' well-being and academic performance, scholars have studied the collegiate experiences of students of color, including Asian Americans.[1] This work provided insight into the experiences of students of color and how their college realities differed from dominant White narratives (Morrison, 2010). Yet, there has been little consideration of *being* raced and racialized. What is it to be Asian American? How do you know if you are, and what does it mean to have or claim such an identity? And what choice, if any, does one have in the matter?

In this chapter, I discuss the multiple constructions of Asian American identities and communities as well as how intersectionality and critical theory allow for more holistic understandings of racial identities than do traditional identity development models—such as Phinney's Multi-Ethnic Identity Model (MEIM) (Phinney, 1992, 1996a, 1996b; Phinney & Alpuria, 1997), Helms's racial identity schema (Alvarez, 2002; Alvarez & Helms 2001; Alvarez & Yeh, 1999), and Kim's Asian American Identity Development (AAID) (Kim 1981, 2001). Considering colleges and universities as spaces infused with and reflective of dominant racial discourses, I explored the processes of racial identity construction—how students define and construct their sense of self—in a qualitative study using in-depth interviews with Chinese American and Filipin@ American college students. Students' narratives demonstrated how identities are constantly in flux and under construction, and how identities are internally formed through personal experiences while simultaneously influenced by social relationships and politics. What it means to be Asian American (and Chinese American and Filipin@ American) was a dynamic and iterative process of negotiation and renegotiation, of definition and redefinition. As the participants discussed, racial identity is in the lived experiences of being raced and living as racialized beings. As Hall (1992) noted,

> Thus, identity is actually something formed through unconscious processes over time, rather than being innate in consciousness at birth. . . . Thus, rather than speaking of identity as a finished thing, we should speak of *identification*, and see it as an on-going process. (p. 288)

The theoretical frameworks and interventions used in this study are significant departures from the traditional ways that racial identity has been studied in higher education. Using intersectionality and critical theory is helpful to better understand students' lived realities, and to recognize the ways that discourse around race and racial identities is part of systemic oppression and institutionalized racism. Such an approach challenges the dominant racial discourse in higher education research and practice. I hope to offer space for a radical reimagining of how racial identities are conceived, studied, and liberated.

Theoretical Considerations: Intersectionality

Building on critical theory, critical race theory, and feminist theory, intersectionality (Dill & Zambrana, 2009) offers a framework to understand identity in context, to examine power structures and social contexts in research on identity. Intersectionality suggested that to understand how identities are formed, research must take into account how an individual sense of self interacts with power and social status (Jones, 2009), reminding us that we live in hegemonic power structures that place our bodies and minds in raced, gendered, classed, and sexualized hierarchies. Intersectionality is characterized by four "theoretical interventions": centering the experiences of people of color; exploring individual and group identities; interrogating power, inequality, and oppression; and working in praxis to connect research and practice toward social justice (Dill & Zambrana).

Using intersectionality as an analytic lens also broadens conversations about identity to include both race and racism. Because intersectionality considers how individual and collective identities are formed within and by systems of power, conversations about race necessarily involve an examination of racism as part of one's identity. Intersectionality provides a unique approach to understanding Asian American identities, and the processes through which students construct and make meaning of them. "The point is not to deny the importance—both material and discursive—of categories but to focus on the process by which they are produced, experienced, reproduced, and resisted in everyday life" (Weber, 1998, p. 1783). Students understood the racist policies and discourses that had created the category of "Asian American," yet also claimed it as a holistic identity of empowerment and transgression. Asian American students lived in one and several racial and cultural spaces simultaneously; not fragments of Asian and American but rather something unique and whole.

Cultural Hybridity, Transversal Politics, and Subaltern Spaces

Critical theory is concerned with "why social agents accept or consent to systems of collective representations that do not serve their objective interests but legitimate the existing power structure" (Macey, 2000, p. 75). Postcolonial studies, in particular, considered how identities were constructed by, about, and for both colonizers and the colonized. Western European constructions of the "primitive" and the "exotic" helped to justify and inspire interest in colonial projects. Such projects were also the source of postcolonial subjects and hybrid identities. As colonized peoples negotiated systems of governance, power, and identity pre- and postcolonization, what often resulted were new identities that reflected both the agency and self-determination of the oppressed people *and* the imaginations of (the supposedly departed) colonizers (Macey, 2000), also known as cultural hybridity or the subaltern (Werbner, 1997).

> The figure of hybridity is one in which the border is itself a place inhabited by the subaltern; it is literally an "in-between" place or, in Habra's terms, a "third space." Here the subaltern are different from the identities on either side of the border, but they are not simply fragments of both. (Grossberg, 1993, p. 97)

Furthermore, cultural hybridity also challenged notions of culture as fixed, biological, or inherent. These "new" identities reflected sociopolitical contexts and adapted—and were strategically created in response—to political and economic realities. Such dynamic and political maneuverings of identity eroded the static explanations of colonial power relations and were thus read as dangerous and radical. Cultural hybridity and subaltern spaces have also been used in discussions of identities in systems of dominance in inequity in what Werbner (1997) calls transversal politics:

> Transversal politics start from a denial of essentialist, fixed constructions of cultures, nations and their boundaries, and the reduction of ethnicity to "culture." Such politics also reject any universal essentialising. . . . They must learn to live with a multiple sense of self. (Werbner, p. 9)

Transversal politics resonates with intersectionality and a dialectic approach in considerations of identity and power. What is vexing is that even as communities claim the agency to define themselves, this has frequently resulted in the simple replacement of one fixed narrative with another. Critical theorists challenge communities to move from understanding race as identity to race as process and, in so doing, shift the focus back to exposing racism in its multiple forms (Brah, 2000; Mohanty, 1989–1990).

"[R]ace" must be challenged as a stable category of cultural or ideological meaning on any grounds—whether biodeterminist or socially constructivist—in order to provide an alternative to its reified conceptualization. To ask how "race" operates in daily practice as a set of complex and changeable meanings is to take one modest step away from the essentialist discourse of race and toward a focus on the *unequal effects of racism* for different groups of people. (Roman, 1993, p. 73; emphasis in original)

Praxis: Intersections of Theory, Research, and Lived Experience

I endeavored to understand how Asian America is constructed and what it means to be Asian American—that is, Asian American *as* and *in* process. This discussion is part of a larger study that also looked at the salient college experiences and relationships that influence students' sense of self. Here I focus on how students expressed themselves as racial beings.

I conducted a qualitative study using in-depth interviews of third- and fourth-year Chinese American and Filipin@ American students at two selective, public universities. I included 20 participants: 5 Filipin@ American and 5 Chinese American students from Michigan University (MU) and California University (CU).[2] They are similar in size and selectivity, but both institution and location vary greatly in the representation of Asian Americans. California has one of the largest populations of Asian Americans in the United States. At the time of the interviews, CU included 44% Asian Americans. I chose MU because it has similar institutional characteristics, but is dissimilar in student racial diversity, state demographics, and geographic location. Asian American students accounted for 12% of MU students at the time the interviews were conducted.

I chose Chinese American and Filipin@ American students because they are the two largest Asian American communities. According to the 2000 census, Asian Americans comprised 4.3% of the U.S. population, with 22.6% Chinese and 18.3% Filipin@ (U.S. Bureau of the Census, 2002). Their immigration histories of the nineteenth century are similar, although their sociocultural experiences differ. I also wanted to capture the experiences of two ethnicities with distinct cultural histories and relationships with the United States. I focused on two ethnic groups to recognize the different experiences of Asian American ethnic groups.

I used a purposeful sample of third- and fourth-year students identified through student organizations, faculty, staff, and peers. There were eight male students (five Filipin@ American and three Chinese American). All male students were included for gender balance. I randomly selected female participants (five Filipin@ American and seven Chinese American).

Interviews ranged from 40 to 120 minutes, and were audio recorded and professionally transcribed. Participants were all first- or second-generation U.S. citizens—five were born outside the United States, and most immigrated at a young age (one student emigrated from China during high school). Only two students at MU were nonresidents, and all of the CU students had grown up in the state. All students were gendered and one male student self-identified as gay. Many majors were represented, and parental educational attainment and professions were also very diverse. All interviews were conducted in English.

I applied a phenomenological perspective (Lester, 1999; Magrini, 2012; Patton, 2001; van Manen, 1990) to a quasi-traditional thematic analysis, using an emic, iterative approach, research memos, and reflections, with three rounds of coding. Exploratory coding was first conducted by hand, with written reflections following the reading of each transcript. The second layer was done by reading and coding each transcript in AtlasTI, and the third round was conducted by using AtlasTI to focus and organize participants' narratives. I contacted all participants for member checking. Seven responded (three from MU and four from CU—two Chinese American, and five Filipin@ American students). They provided feedback on my interpretations and agreed with my portrayal of their institutions and identities. I also conducted peer debriefing with two undergraduate students at another institution (a White woman and a Chinese American woman), a Korean American woman who was a student affairs practitioner and works with cultural organizations, and a White male student affairs practitioner with experience in qualitative research.

Relationships of power between researcher and participants should be considered, particularly because talking about race and identity is difficult and complex. It was important that students felt a level of safety and comfort with me. In most instances, I was afforded "insider" status because of similar racial or ethnic backgrounds. This affected our interactions and their comfort in discussing personal and sometimes difficult topics. Some students said they would not have participated in the study or been as comfortable had I not been Asian American. Interestingly, as I did not know the students before their participation, most made assumptions about my identity upon seeing my last name in an e-mail.

Beauty in the Beholder

I expected, yet was surprised by, the myriad meanings of "Asian American" that emerged. For most students, Asian American, Chinese American, and Filipin@ American were whole and holistic ways of being that were both individual/personal and collective/social. Their identities were contextual and relational; they were also imposed on their bodies, taken up by choice, and claimed with pride. I describe these as two paradoxical dialogues: one between the individual and the collective, and one between an imposed identity and a claimed identity. I found these to be constant, simultaneous, and parallel processes located at the core of racial identity construction. In some sense, identities were constructed in the interview itself because they developed by being expressed and examined. Our conversations allowed for internal processing of how students thought of their identities simultaneous with an external presentation of their sense of self. In seeking to be understood, students came to understand themselves.

Misery Loves Company: Shared Experiences of Racialization and Racism

Students recognized the diversity of ethnicities, cultures, experiences, and perspectives included in Asian America. However, because their distinct identities and histories were not generally acknowledged in dominant narratives, they experienced similar forms of direct and indirect racism. Sometimes, their right to be present seemed to be questioned, both institutionally and nationally. Often, it was the neglect they felt that had the deepest impact, in terms of not learning AAPI history or of being rendered invisible at their respective schools. While each student had different stories to share, what connected them was that they shared such stories. What united them was how others chose to define them, and their struggle to be seen as they wished. For example, Beth commented:

> I kind of realized that no matter what, it's pretty explicit because of the way I look. You know it's sort of, whether or not I want to own that identity [Asian American], [it's] the identity perceived by other people.

Leslie also felt the forceful nature of an imposed identity. She had a strong Filipin@ American identity, and more specifically as Ilokano, where her family is from, and Pinay American as a political identity. Leslie felt the experiences of Filipin@ Americans were distinct from those of other Asian American groups, but they were still raced as Asian American.

> I think it's kind of forced on us. Like, society wants us to be acclimated to this one identity, I mean, sometimes . . . you have to be part of it because it was expected of us to be a part of that already.

Nicole shared a similar perspective: "I think that the similarities we share are the result of other people lumping us together."

Many students discussed the paradox of having a monolithic and singular identity imposed on their beings and claiming agency to construct a shared identity with other Asian Americans and Pacific Islanders. The irony here is that this shared identity would not occur without the experience of being raced as a monolithic group in the United States. Integral to feeling confident in their identities was the power to define and shape what being Asian American meant. Students took up their Asian American (or AAPI) identities as a means to honor the related histories of exploitative immigration policies, racism, and discrimination that they, their families, and previous generations of Asian Americans had experienced and survived. It was a way to resist the artificially created racial categories that exclude, oppress, and marginalize communities of color. This ambivalent negotiation around owning and redefining an identity that had once been imposed through racism was challenging for many students.

Although Rosa had a strong identity as Filipin@ American, she had also experienced being seen as simply "Asian American." Rosa understood that although she might unite with other AAPI communities to form a coalition against racism, non-AAPI individuals might see them merely as one group rather than a coalition of many groups. For Rosa, it was important to come together to show the diversity within this broad community.

> I think [it's about] banding together against, combating this broader notion that Asian America, [that] we're all the same. But [what] we all have in common, the common knowledge is that we're different, [that] we're all unique in different ways.

Marc thought that although Asian Americans first came together because they were grouped together, it was important to "create" an Asian American identity that they could own. He also felt that rather than letting ethnic and cultural differences divide Asian Americans, those differences should be embraced.

> [I]t's just like we've had to create an Asian American identity. . . . I feel like what needs to be done is to . . . embrace the differences between our cultures . . . but at the same time realize we still, because of, because of the White man, we've been put together in this group, and we have to stick together.

Sam had similar experiences of being grouped with other Asian Americans. While he sought ways to express his individual identities, Sam also felt it was the struggle that brought AAPIs together.

Because when I'm walking down the street, people don't care whether or not I'm Chinese, Cantonese, Mandarin speaking, Japanese, Korean. They're gonna look at me and think I'm Asian. [AAPIs] have a shared history of discrimination and you know, like, lots of folks, a lot of White people [are] going to look at you and think you're Asian. . . . That alone is enough for us to be in common because they all, they, as in, like, the White majority or sometimes other people of color groups, treat Asian Americans a certain way and that experience of being treated a certain way is enough for us to be . . . that alone is grounds for us having commonality. . . . So I think there is kind of a value maybe in, like, how do we struggle together and how do we overcome struggle.

For Daniel, struggle was also a marker of being Asian American. Daniel's family had a Chinese restaurant in a predominantly Black neighborhood near MU, and he felt that racism connected all communities of color. "Asian American culture struggles in the USA. So struggles. . . . I mean, that's a culture."

Sherry, a Chinese American student at CU, talked about the connection she felt with other communities of color around struggle. She talked about growing up in a strong Asian/Asian American community, so her Chinese American identity was never threatened or questioned. Sherry framed the struggles of Chinese Americans (and Asian Americans) more broadly within the experiences of other communities of color.

Well, I think I also represent myself in, like, a people of color community and so then being Chinese American is being able to relate to a lot of the other experiences that other people of color have faced and working together for a cause. [I]t's just what I've learned, and it pretty much defined a lot of my experiences.

Angela, a junior at MU who was born in Taiwan, also considered struggle as a common experience among Asian Americans: "The way we felt like, the struggles that we had to go through to construct our own identity." Angela had not really thought about her racial identity until, while writing for the school newspaper, a hate incident occurred. She talked about how much this affected her personally, and that she had several arguments with her peers on the newspaper staff who did not see it as an act of racism. It was this experience that caused her to join the Asian American student group and become more involved with Asian American social issues.

Not all students expressed their Asian American identities by joining political or antiracist struggles. Some found that homogenizing discourse overwhelming and limiting, choosing to distance themselves from their Asian American peers and communities. This was not a denial of their identities as Asian American, but rather part of their struggle against a racism that doesn't allow for individual agency. Tamara chose not to participate actively or associate with the AAPI student community, partly because of negative experiences she had encountered being grouped together with other Asian Americans as she was growing up.

> I think, like, a lot of times people just group Asians as Asians, and they all do the same things, and they're all, like, really smart. Or, like, they're all really great at tennis. So I felt like I didn't want to be part of that little group. So I didn't, I guess I liked feeling unique, and it was like a way for me to feel unique by doing stuff that isn't typically Asian.

For Dedric, a senior Filipin@ American student at MU, taking a Filipin@ American studies class that had a community engagement component was the first time he had really explored his heritage, despite living in a large Filipin@ community. He volunteered at a Filipin@ cultural center and continued to do so after the class ended. Dedric felt empowered in talking with Filipin@ American youth about not letting stereotypes limit their identities and experiences. Prior to this course, Dedric did not identify strongly with Filipin@ American identity because he had not wanted to be "lumped together" with other Asian Americans. Through this class and volunteering, he realized that there were multiple ways of being Filipin@/Asian American, one of which was to work against racist stereotypes and empower youth in the community.

Not all students felt connected to other Asian Americans through shared experiences of racism. Christopher, a senior Filipin@ American student at CU, understood how Asian Americans had been put together in a broad group and that Asian Americans had some shared experiences, but he did not identify as or feel part of an Asian American identity. He had a very strong Filipin@ American identity.

> I've learned that there [have] been solidarity movements. I feel that our struggles are similar, but I characterize Asian American more by its diversity than its unity. I think that our experience in discrimination in terms of being discriminated against has been very similar in the States. But then again, this is only an intellectual argument because it's not something that I personally feel or have known.

Tanya was particularly focused on her academics and career in medicine. She was involved with the Chinese American Student Organization and used it as a way to explore her culture. Tanya's Chinese American identity was made of two parts, though not distinguishable or equal halves. Her friends in high school and college were mostly Asian Americans. She was thoughtful, but admitted that she had not reflected much on her own identity or explored issues of race or racism more deeply. Being Chinese American was simply who she was.

While Eddie recognized how Asian Americans were raced together and the discrimination that resulted, he did not approach it as a shared history of struggle. A Chinese American junior, Eddie chose CU because it had a large Asian American student population, similar to his home community. He talked at length about his fears of more racially diverse settings. His perspectives were grounded in his belief that people of different racial/ethnic groups should not mix. This fear did not come from hatred of other groups, but rather as a defense to protect and preserve his cultural identity.

Both-And: Simultaneous Identities

Students demanded space to construct their unique identities as Asian Americans, distinct from—and simultaneous to—their identities as Chinese American and Filipin@ American. Claiming these multiple identities allowed students to make meaning of their own identities and experiences. Without disregarding their cultural heritage and family histories (which students most commonly referred to as their Chinese American or Filipin@ American identities) students were able to develop an independent and dynamic identity that honored their ancestries *and* recognized their current social contexts. Their identities reflected students' individual experiences while connecting them to each other and with a broader sociopolitical history.

In all of these narratives, students located themselves and their homes in the United States. While many did explore their roots in China, Taiwan, and the Philippines, they recognized the ways that their experiences, identities, and perspectives were uniquely American. Carmen was finding new freedoms and choices in her immediate context. Her Chinese American identity, which was grounded in her perspectives and desire for a sense of belonging, was in process and, unlike some of the other students', was a very conscious process of integrating her changing views and present contexts while trying to leave behind the ideas that no longer resonated with her ways of being.

For Ruby, being Filipin@ American was a very personal experience, one that was difficult to describe. Ruby had a difficult family dynamic, and it was her mother's extended family and Filipin@ American church in Chicago that helped them through.

> When I say Filipin@ American, it's grounded more in this very personal identity. So when I think Filipin@ American, you know, I'm thinking of my family, and I'm thinking of, like, all these experiences. So, yeah,

Filipin@ American community is just like this personal cultural, it's like a glue to me. It's just very personal. I don't know if I could put words to it.

Ruby also identified as Asian American, and these identities were neither interchangeable nor separate. For Ruby, being Filipin@ American was part of her personal and family history, while her Asian American identity included her in a larger collective.

I think when I was younger and I didn't fully understand, it was very easy for me to say that's Asian. That's American. But I think ever since I started college, I don't think about that very much. . . . The focus has shifted to what does it mean for me to be Asian American. And so instead of, like, separating things into these two categories like Asian and American, I'm sort of bringing together what makes me Asian American. I feel like I'm getting a pretty good hold of, I'm very comfortable with who I am as an Asian American.

Sam identified strongly as Asian/Pacific Islander American "with a slash between the *A* and the *P*, that's really important" because he felt part of the pan-AAPI coalition and he recognized the diversity within Asian America. He also held a Chinese American identity. Like Tanya and Eddie at CU, he looked to his family's roots in China (language, cultural practices, etc.) to understand his heritage while acknowledging that his identity was greatly informed by being born and living in the United States. This was not a conflict for him, but a blending of cultures. He created a space for himself between "two worlds" as he found he did not see his experiences reflected in mainstream American or Chinese cultures. He also described them as "two identities fused into one as a Chinese American. So they are, they can be very distinct, but I think they are kind of pushed together, forced together like in second-generation folks. I think being Chinese American is one way to be an American."

Beth shared Sam's multilayered approach to understanding her identity. Beth was born in China but immigrated to the United States when she was two and a half.

[Racially], I guess I would say Asian. Ethnically, I would say Chinese. [Culturally], I say Chinese. Chinese American. I guess 'cause I kind of feel like a merging of two different worlds in my life. You know, I'm ethnically Chinese, but my upbringing has been Chinese in America, so I feel like in my life, [I'm] Chinese American.

Beth had a strong understanding of race as a social construction, and that "Asian" as a racial identity didn't exist in the same way in other places as it did in the United States. She had also talked about racial identities and dynamics through her community engagement and social justice work. This informed her thinking of race as a construction, ethnicity as heritage, and culture as common collective experiences.

Angela also understood how racial politics and constructions of "American" identities affected her. Angela immigrated from Taiwan at 14 and had a very strong identity as Chinese American. She lived with her father first in upstate New York and later in Georgia as he changed jobs. Her mother was still in Taiwan. Angela talked about her childhood and feeling pressure to assimilate to White American norms from her peers and her father.[3] Angela's Chinese American identity developed organically from her experiences.

> [Racially, I identify as] Chinese American [now]. Just being Chinese in America. It's just, like, Chinese American is part of being American. Because this is really how I am, and I feel comfortable, and I don't think anyone should have to prescribe to a certain image to be American. And that image is usually, you know, rich, White Americans.

Holding on to simultaneous identities without privileging one over the other was challenging for some participants, particularly Filipin@ American students at CU. While many of them understood how they identified with other Asian Americans, they could not always reconcile the distinctive experiences of Filipin@s and Filipin@ Americans in terms of colonization, immigration, class inequities, and ethnic hierarchies. While students claimed power to construct their own identities and cultural experiences, they did not always feel a part of that larger collective they created. They understood it, but were not in it. This complicated negotiation between their constructed realities and lived experiences added another dimension to understanding Asian American identities.

Mary commented, "Somewhere in there I want to fit in, like, that I do have an Asian American identity, as well, but I think at the forefront of my identity is me being Filipin@ American." Like Mary, Henry felt that "racially, I'm Asian American," but talked mostly about being Filipin@ American. Other Filipin@ American students at CU often felt marginalized by or excluded from Asian America; indeed, Leslie and Rosa identified themselves as "brown" while describing Asian Americans as "yellow." Although Leslie honored the importance of coalition, she felt the experiences of Filipin@ Americans were distinct from those of other ethnic groups.

> [Asian American] is more, like, an overarching, like, umbrella term, but for me, I know it doesn't apply to me. [W]hen I was growing up, like, I was, like, I'm not Asian, I'm Pacific Islander. . . . [F]or me, it's, like, . . . I felt like Asian American had this own identity. And for me, I didn't feel like I really was a part of it.

For Rosa, a senior Asian American studies major and education minor, recognizing the colonial history of the Philippines, as well as the oppression of Filipin@s and Filipin@ Americans within Asian America, was very important. She struggled to reconcile the unique experiences of Filipin@ Americans within such a generalized group. Like Rosa, Christopher did not identify as Asian American, but did understand being part of a broader coalition.

As intersectionality suggests the importance of the interplay between individuals and systems, this study highlights the dynamic and constructed nature of Asian American and racial identities. These students reclaimed Asian American identity as it had been perceived and defined previously to make sense of their racial identities as lived experiences. As discussed, not all students who might be identified as Asian American chose to own such an identity. This did not exclude them from participating in Asian American communities, however, nor did it erase their contributions to Asian American identities. It does demonstrate the multifaceted and changing meanings of being Asian American and the need for complicating understandings of race, ethnicity, and culture even further.

Intersectionality as Intervention: Antiessentialism and Antiracism in Higher Education

Chinese American and Filipin@ American students created space to construct their own identities and give voice and meaning to their own experiences, as changing and evolving ways of being, and as means for resistance. The complicated and multilayered dialogue among racial, ethnic, and cultural identities—and the various ways they are taken up, ignored, owned, defined, and changed—in simultaneous processes points to the sophisticated imaginations of today's students. Participants noted that although they were empowered to determine their racial identities, they were shaped by the racist structures around them.

In higher education research, identity development models are commonly used to study Asian American students. Although these models are intended to explain how students develop a positive sense of self, they begin with the assumption that Asian Americans are born into fixed identities. The MEIM, racial identity schema, and AAID considered racial identity as ancestry (counted as a statistical variable), participation and behaviors (based on a set of values and activities identified by the researchers), or conflict (construed as the clashing of collective Asian values and individualistic European/American values). These approaches only reify the racial categories created to divide and discriminate against different groups because they conceptualize race and culture as static, fixed, and inherent. Identity development models are predicated upon essentialist notions of identity. That they are Asian American is a foregone conclusion, so the focus is on how they come to know themselves as Asian American in positive ways. Such an approach does not give space for creating meaning around being Asian American. As McCarthy and Crichlow (1993) note,

> By essentialism, we refer to the tendency in current mainstream and radical writing on race to treat social groups as stable or homogeneous entities. Racial groups such as "Asians," "Latinos," or "blacks" are therefore discussed as though members of these groups possessed some innate and invariant set of characteristics that set them apart from each other and from "whites." . . . [C]urrent tendencies toward essentialism in the analysis of race relations significantly inhibit a dynamic understanding of the operation of race and race-based politics in education and society. (p. xviii)

Moreover, "Asian" and "Asian American" are products of White European/American imaginations, however claimed or reclaimed by individuals and communities. Traditional methods and models of racial identity development do not consider both the colonization and decolonization of bodies in the construction of racial identities. As Hall (1992) discussed, what may be of greater concern is not identity but rather identification. How one chooses—if one chooses—to identify as Asian American is grounded in the individual's construction of Asian American identities and communities. As indicated in this study, students had multiple ways of understanding, expressing, and taking up their Asian American identities, if they did so. This prismatic conceptualization of race occurred not only between individuals, but also within individuals who saw themselves and others differently, depending on relationships, contexts, and consequences. College remains an important context and time for students to explore their social identities, including race. What is needed in higher education research, as Werbner (1997) called for, is a more careful reading of how students understand and construct notions of self. Intersectionality and critical theories—such as cultural studies, queer theory, gender performance theory, critical race theory, and postcolonialism—provide innovative approaches to learning from students' lived realities and subjective experiences. Rather than adding to or combining identity models to examine multiple and simultaneous identities, scholars must find ways to incorporate intersectionality into identity studies. For example, Eddie's understanding of himself as Chinese American is predicated upon his experiences as cisgender, male, heterosexual, and middle class—including his frustrations with wanting but being unable to date a Chinese American woman. How Eddie understood being Chinese American is intimately tied to systems of racism, sexism, and patriarchy.

As student affairs practitioners, we must also consider how students are being supported and challenged in their affective growth and in cocurricular spaces. Traditional multicultural programming models also rely on essentialized concepts of culture and cultural practice.

> [M]any schools attempt to achieve multicultural education by initiating multicultural student organizations. These clubs can serve educational purposes, providing opportunities for dialogue across difference and the development of political consciousness among students. . . . Instead, these clubs tend to host dances, organize cultural festivals, or sponsor international food fairs. Although students may learn valuable lessons through the cross-cultural collaboration necessary to coordinate "cultural" events, they are concurrently helping to maintain inequity by focusing on surface-level programming instead of authentic equity concerns. Equally important, we soften multicultural education when we invest in student organizations instead of addressing the hostile climates that make them necessary. (Gorski, 2006, p. 172)

As Gorski notes, while heritage months, holiday celebrations, and similar events provide much-needed attention and visibility, they do not challenge institutionalized racism and systemic oppression. Further, when communities must compete for funding, space, and audiences, oppressed groups are pitted against each other, losing sight of their motivations for doing this work in the first place. As a practitioner myself, I choose instead to refocus programming and student organizations on relationships and community building, emphasizing *how* we do our work together and *why* we do our work. Students may still choose to plan heritage months or events to build awareness around a particular community or issue. Administrators, practitioners, and faculty must support them in their endeavors and encourage them to consider what impact they hope to have on the campus community. I also ask students to focus on what they would like to learn in the process of planning these programs to stress that in *doing*, they are *becoming* and *constructing* what it means to be.

The struggle for power and agency in defining one's own identities is an act of cultural resistance that challenges the hierarchies of current U.S. society and alters how race may be seen and understood. By centering themselves in the American landscape and demanding that their histories and experiences be included on their college campuses and in the United States, the Asian American students in this study re/claim the power to construct themselves and what it is to be Asian American.

Notes

1. Other common references include Asian American and Pacific Islander [AAPI], Asian Pacific American [APA], and Asian/Pacific Islander American [A/PIA] to be inclusive of Pacific Islanders who are often grouped together with U.S. citizens, permanent residents, and immigrants of Asian descent. I use Asian American and AAPI throughout.

2. I assigned pseudonyms to institutions and participants.

3. In the process of member checking, Angela reflected that she had actually found liberation in claiming a Chinese American identity as she had experienced emotional abuse from her father. Naming herself as Chinese American gave her space to develop her own values and sense of self, distinct from, though in relation to, her family.

References

Alexander, M. (2010). *The new Jim Crow: Mass incarceration in the age of color-blindness.* New York: New Press.

Alvarez, A. N. (2002). Racial identity and Asian Americans: Supports and challenges. In M. E. McEwen, C. J. Kodama, A. N. Alvarez, S. Lee, & C. T. H. Liang (Eds.), *New directions for student services, no. 97. Working with Asian American college students* (pp. 33–43). Danvers, MA: Wiley.

Alvarez, A. N., & Helms, J. E. (2001). Racial identity and reflected appraisals as influences on Asian Americans' racial adjustment. *Cultural Diversity and Ethnic Minority Psychology, 7*(3), 217–231.

Alvarez, A. N., & Yeh, C. T. (1999). Asian Americans in college: A racial identity perspective. In D. S. Sandhu (Ed.), *Asian and Pacific Islander Americans: Issues and concerns for counseling and psychotherapy* (pp. 105–119). Commack, NY: Nova Science Publishers.

Apple, M. (1993). Series editor's introduction to race, identity, and representation in education. In C. McCarthy & W. Crichlow (Eds.), *Race, identity, and representation in education* (pp. vii–ix). New York: Routledge.

Brah, A. (2000). Difference, diversity, differentiation: Processes of racialisation and gender. In L. Back & J. Solomos (Eds.), *Theories of race and racism: A reader* (pp. 431–446). New York: Routledge.

Dill, B. T., & Zambrana, R. E. (2009). *Emerging intersections: Race, class, and gender in theory, policy, and practice.* New Brunswick, NJ: Rutgers University Press.

Goldberg, D. (1993). *Racist culture: Philosophy and the politics of meaning.* Cambridge, MA: Blackwell.

Gorski, P. C. (2006). Complicity with conservativsm: The de-politicizing of multicultural and intercultural education. *Intercultural Education, 17*(2), 163–177. doi:10.1000/14675980600693830

Grossberg, L. (1993). Cultural studies and/in new worlds. In C. McCarthy & W. Crichlow (Eds.), *Race, identity, and representation in education* (pp. 89–105). New York: Routledge.

Hall, S. (1992). The question of cultural identity. In S. Hall, D. Held, & T. McGrew (Eds.), *Modernity and its futures* (pp. 273–316). Cambridge, UK: Polity.

Jones, S. R. (2009). Constructing identities at the intersections: An autoethnographic exploration of multiple dimensions of identity. *Journal of College Student Development, 50,* 287–304. doi:10.1353/csd.0.0070

Kim, J. (1981). *Processes of Asian American identity development: A study of Japanese American women's perceptions of their struggle to achieve positive identities as Americans of Asian ancestry.* (Unpublished doctoral dissertation). University of Massachusetts, Amherst.

Kim, J. (2001). Asian American identity development theory. In C. L. Wijeyesinghe & B. W. Jackson III (Eds.), *New perspectives on racial identity development: A theoretical and practical anthology* (pp. 67–90). New York: New York University Press.

Lester, S. (1999). *An introduction to phenomenological research.* Taunton, UK: Stan Lester Developments. Retrieved from http://www.sld.demon.co.uk/resmethy.pdf

Macey, D. (2000). *The Penguin dictionary of critical theory.* London, UK: Penguin Books.

Magrini, J. (2012). Phenomenology for educators: Max van Manen and human science research. *Philosophy Scholarship*, Paper 32. Retrieved from http://dc.cod.edu/philosophypub32

McCarthy, C., & Crichlow, W. (1993). Introduction: Theories of identity, theories of representation, theories of race. In C. McCarthy & W. Crichlow (Eds.), *Race, identity, and representation in education* (pp. xiii–xxix). New York: Routledge.

Mohanty, C. T. (1989–1990). On race and voice: Challenges for liberal education in the '90s. *Cultural Critique, 18*(14), 179–208.

Morrison, G. (2010). Two separate worlds: Students of color at a predominantly White university. *Journal of Black Studies, 40,* 987–1015. doi: 10.1177/0021934708325408

Omi, M., & Winant, H. (1994). *Racial formation in the United States: From the 1960s to the 1990s.* New York: Routledge.

Patton, M. (2001). *Qualitative research and evaluation methods.* Thousand Oaks, CA: Sage.

Phinney, J. S. (1992). The multigroup ethnic identity measure: A new scale for use with diverse groups. *Journal of Adolescent Research, 7,* 175–176.

Phinney, J. S. (1996a). Understanding ethnic diversity: The role of ethnic diversity. *The American Behavioral Scientist, 40*(2), 143–152.

Phinney, J. S. (1996b). When we talk about American ethnic groups, what do we mean? *American Psychologist, 51*, 918–927.

Phinney, J. S., & Alpuria, L. (1997). *Ethnic identity in older adolescents from four ethnic groups.* Paper presented at the biennial meeting of the Society for Research in Child Development, Baltimore, MD. (ERIC Document Reproduction Service No. ED 283058)

Roman, L. G. (1993). White is a color! White defensiveness, postmodernism, and anti-racist pedagogy. In C. McCarthy & W. Crichlow (Eds.), *Race, identity, and representation in education* (pp. 71–88). New York: Routledge.

Spade, D. (2010). *Normal life: Administrative violence, critical trans politics, and the limits of the law.* Brooklyn, NY: South End.

Torres, V., Jones, S. R., & Renn, K. A. (2009). Identity development theories in student affairs: Origins, current status, and new approaches. *Journal of College Student Development, 50*(5), 577–596.

U.S. Bureau of the Census. (2002). *Annual population estimates 2000–2002.* Retrieved from https://www.census.gov/popest/data/historical/2000s/vintage_2002/

van Manen, M. (1990). *Researching lived experience: Human science for an action sensitive pedagogy.* New York: State University of New York Press.

Weber, L. (1998). A conceptual framework for understanding race, class, gender, and sexuality. *Psychology of Women Quarterly, 22*, 13–32. Retrieved from EBSCO database

Werbner, P. (1997). Introduction: The dialects of cultural hybridity. In P. Werbner & T. Modood (Eds.), *Debating cultural hybridity: Multi-cultural identities and the politics of anti-racism* (pp. 1–28). London: Zed Books.

9

"WRITING OUR OWN RULE BOOK"

Exploring the Intersectionality of Gay College Men

Daniel Tillapaugh

> I've always tried to live by the creed that, you know, the sum of the parts don't make up for the grand total. So because I'm gay, . . . my business card doesn't say Jonathan, gay man. Jonathan, male. Jonathan, upper-class. It's not going to do anything like that. . . . Each builds up to a total. And the total could be completely different than what that little part means to me. (Jonathan)

> I guess if I were to do a day-to-day routine, if I was feeling masculine, it's just me being basically quieter, wearing certain clothing, and having less gesture . . . acting "hetero" as my [fraternity] brothers would call it. But I feel just as masculine if I'm wearing jewelry, if I'm carrying a handbag, so that's why I'm kind of like, "I juggle the concept." Yeah, it's hard. I can't really define [masculinity] for myself. (Victor)

Over the past four decades, the lesbian, gay, bisexual, and transgender (LGBT) rights movement in the United States has resulted in increased visibility for LGBT people. As universities serve as microcosms for the larger sociopolitical climate of the nation, increased attention has been paid to the development of LGBT college students (Berila, 2011; Bilodeau, 2007; Cass, 1979; D'Augelli, 1994; Dilley, 2010; Fassinger, 1998; Rhoads, 1997). However, many identity development models have focused solely on segmented aspects of one's social identities and have not explored one's multiple identities. For example, gay men as a population possess certain privileges due to their gender, yet face oppression and discrimination due to their sexual orientation. If one adds in the dimensions of race, religion, socioeconomic class, and other categories of social identities for gay men, there is increased complexity of one's holistic sense of self, given that some identities may maintain a dominant status (e.g., White, upper class, Christian), while others may be subordinated (e.g., Mexican American, working class, Jewish).

Scholars, such as R. W. Connell (2005), Michael Kimmel (2008), and Beth Berila (2011), highlight that the aggregation of "men" as a collective reinforces heteronormative and patriarchal views on men and masculinity. For gay and other nonheterosexual men, this is troublesome as their lived experiences become invisible and pushed to the margins; therefore, systems of oppression continue to privilege heterosexual men and subordinate non-heterosexual men. These complex matters affect individuals on an array of levels, from the personal (e.g., fear of others' perceptions due to one's sexual identity) to the systemic (e.g., state and federal policies restricting the rights of LGBT individuals due to their sexual and/or gender identity). With LGBT students becoming more visible on campuses, gay men in college, such as Victor and Jonathan whose quotes opened this chapter, provide an excellent opportunity to understand the negotiation and development of multiple identities, including issues of inclusion or exclusion and sense of self (Rankin, Weber, Blumenfeld, & Frazer, 2010). In this chapter, I present the stories of three gay college men—Jonathan, Mason, and Victor—to illuminate how they make meaning of their social identities through the lens of intersectionality.

Intersectionality, a concept forwarded by Kimberlé Crenshaw (2009), a critical race theory legal scholar, offers a multidimensional view of understanding the knowledge constructed at the intersection of one's identities, such as race, gender, socioeconomic class, and sexual orientation. As Tatum (2003) reminds us, "The concept of identity is a complex one, shaped by individual characteristics, family dynamics, historical factors, and social and political contexts" (p. 18). Victor's understanding of who he is as a gay man is informed by his own biracial identity as a Greek Mexican man from a middle-class family observing Greek Orthodox religious views, whereas Jonathan's identity is influenced substantially by being from a wealthy, White, Catholic, and politically conservative family. While their sexual orientation and gender identity may be the same, Victor's and Jonathan's stories are vastly different from one another. Each of the men's lived experiences and realities have shaped his overall sense of self significantly. In essence, their stories matter and give perspectives that are important to understanding the role of intersectionality among gay men in college.

As previously mentioned, I present Jonathan's, Mason's, and Victor's own words and stories to highlight how each has made meaning of his multiple identities using an intersectional lens. Critical race theory scholars have used these stories, also known as counter-stories, extensively in their research. These counter-stories are "method[s] of telling the stories of those people whose experiences are not often told" (Solórzano & Yosso, 2009, p. 138). These counter-stories serve as a reframing of the "master narrative"

(Montecinos, 1995) in which unacknowledged White privilege and racism often pervades the stories constructed about individuals from marginalized communities. Solórzano and Yosso (2009) maintain that the use of counter-stories has at least the following functions:

> (a) They can build community among those at the margins of society by putting a human and familiar face to educational theory and practice, (b) they can challenge the perceived wisdom of those at society's center by providing a context to understand and transform established belief systems, (c) they can open new windows into the reality of those at the margins of society by showing possibilities beyond the ones they live and demonstrating that they are not alone in their position, and (d) they can teach others that by combining elements from both the story and the current reality, one can construct another world that is richer than either the story or the reality alone. (p. 142)

Counter-stories serve to disrupt the majoritarian stories passed down from generation to generation through the perpetuation of "master narratives."

One must acknowledge that counter-stories were used to bring the rich dimensions of one's racial identity to the forefront. However, from an intersectional perspective, exploring the multidimensionality of one's social identities through the use of counter-stories also provides insight into how one comes to understand that fundamental question, "Who am I?" As discussed previously, the complexities of the intersectionality of gay men and their multiple identities within the college environment are fraught with challenges as well as opportunities. Yet, often, researchers and scholars focus on one dimension of identity, such as gay identity development (Cass, 1979; D'Augelli, 1994; Fassinger, 1998). As a result, these theories and models do not adequately explain how one's other dimensions of social identity influence one's gay identity. By using counter-stories, there is great potential for correcting this monovocal view.

"Identity Is Development": Their Stories

I came to know Mason, Jonathan, and Victor well as participants in a research study I conducted in southern California (Tillapaugh, 2012). Each of the men experienced both the highs and lows of coming to terms with his sexuality, especially as his sexual orientation had consequences that rippled into other aspects of his identities. However, during a conversation with Mason around understanding who he was as a gay man, he responded, "Identity is development." A simple, rudimentary answer, but it struck me as extremely authentic and honest. In this section, I let Mason, Jonathan, and Victor introduce themselves to you.

Mason

Mason, a 21-year-old Filipino, is a senior studying international security and conflict resolution. Born into a military family living on a U.S. Navy base in the Philippines, he was raised in Japan and San Juan Miguel, California.[1] Active in the Naval ROTC program, he had been selected platoon sergeant and mentor program coordinator. However, Mason does not completely fit the stereotype of being in the Navy, with his slim physical build, quiet demeanor, and self-description as "effeminate." Mason shared that being within the culture of the Navy as a closeted gay man is a challenge. He said that the Navy is "just a very macho sort of environment, and when you're put in those types of environments, things that are deemed feminine are not accepted or they're just viewed, they kind of outcast you." While out to some ROTC peers, Mason has been hesitant to do so due to homophobic comments he has heard from some of them. His perception of others within the ROTC is that "they see me as less of a person because of my perceived sexual orientation."

At the same time, Mason served as a resident assistant (RA) on campus for two years, a role he cherished because he could be open about his sexual identity with his peers, his supervisor, and even with his residents. As an RA, Mason was required to take an academic course that dealt with power and privilege. This course was transformative for him in understanding his own privilege, and he said that in his course he learned that "gender is a social construction, and I'm trying to get myself past those stupid terms of masculinity and femininity. But I know those are important social distinctions that many people in our society still hold on to." Mason experiences a significant amount of compartmentalization of his identities based on the context in which he is a part, particularly due to his ROTC experiences.

Jonathan

Born into a wealthy, conservative, Catholic, White family in northern California, Jonathan, 22, is a fifth-year political science and public law major. An athlete all of his life, he was a star baseball player growing up. However, an accident while on vacation two weeks before the start of his sophomore year left him medically ineligible to play. This was devastating for Jonathan. He states, "It would have been one thing for them to say, 'You're not good enough to play anymore,' but that it was . . . 'Your body didn't heal right.

So sorry, you're done,'. . . that was very difficult for me in terms of my identity." Jonathan's background in athletics plays a central role in how he looks at himself as a man. He describes himself as being very masculine due to his interests and his physical stature and mannerisms. However, he faced many challenges when coming out due to his sense of masculinity as well as other sociopolitical factors, especially being raised in a wealthy, Catholic, politically conservative family. After his father learned about Jonathan's sexuality, they did not speak for six months. As a result, Jonathan became clinically depressed and attempted suicide twice during college. He continues to see a therapist to assist in his feelings around his identity as well as the dynamics between him and his family. Jonathan has become involved in several student leadership positions. One of the most meaningful experiences for him was serving as the cofacilitator of the men's group sponsored by his university's LGBT Resource Center. This position helped Jonathan continue his own exploration of what it meant to be gay and a man in his world.

Victor

Identifying as half Greek and half Mexican, Victor, 22, grew up in northern San Juan Miguel County. For his first two years of college, he attended a community college in his hometown and lived at home with his family. Growing up in a conservative area of San Juan Miguel County, Victor never felt as though he fit in, especially given his early awareness of his sexual orientation. After transferring to a university in San Juan Miguel, Victor was a history major and LGBT studies minor. As an undergraduate, he was an active student leader on campus, participating on the Pride Action Committee, serving as membership chair of the Lambda Archives in San Juan Miguel, and volunteering at San Juan Miguel's LGBT community center.

One of the most significant leadership roles Victor held has been president of Delta Lambda Phi, a progressive fraternity for gay, bisexual, and straight men. In that role, he oversees the recruitment, selection, and retention of fraternity men for his chapter and has found that becoming a member was transformative in his feeling more secure in who he is as a gay man. While he feels as though his fraternity has allowed him to explore who he is authentically, he also acknowledges that, at times, some of his fraternity brothers continue to have certain expectations and socialized messages about what fraternity life should be. He states,

> I've snapped at brothers for trying to, like, imply that we weren't masculine. Like, I had one saying, "Well, shouldn't we be doing things like sports, or if we want to portray manhood and manliness, shouldn't we be doing this?" I'm like, "Well, if you want to go ahead and follow that scheme, you need

to join another fraternity because in this fraternity we talk about brother-hood and masculinity within the context of our gay, bisexual, progressive identity."

Lately, Victor has become concerned that he has focused too narrowly on his sexual identity rather than other aspects of his identity or his other personal interests.

These initial introductions to Mason, Jonathan, and Victor allow you to hear their voices, learn about some of their salient identities, and begin to understand where these men come from. In the next section, I discuss the three categories of intersectionality introduced by Crenshaw (2009): *structural*, *political*, and *representational*. Within these sections, I present and define each of the three categories, and the men's counter-stories exemplify those definitions. At their heart, the stories provide insights into how these gay men make meaning of their multiple identities within the college envi-ronment and how intersectionality helps illuminate these men's journeys of understanding who they are at their core.

Intersectionality: Framing the Narratives

Focusing on the experiences of Black women, Crenshaw (2009) introduced intersectionality as a means to illuminate how aspects of one's social identities (e.g., race, gender) shape one's lived experiences at the personal, group, and systemic levels. Crenshaw believes that the issue with "identity politics is not that it fails to transcend difference . . . but rather the opposite—that it fre-quently conflates or ignores intragroup differences" (p. 213). By aggregating all women collectively, other aspects of identity are rendered invisible. There-fore, domination and privilege are maintained without any regard for sub-ordinated or marginalized identities (Crenshaw, 2009). Crenshaw furthers this perspective by saying, "My focus on the intersections of race and gender only highlights the need to account for multiple grounds of identity when considering how the social world is constructed" (p. 214). Intersectionality offers an opportunity to closely examine knowledge constructed at the inter-sections of race, class, and gender (Collins, 2000). In the following sections, I present the three categories of intersectionality—structural, political, and representational (Crenshaw, 2009)—using the counter-stories of Jonathan, Mason, and Victor.

Structural Intersectionality

Structural intersectionality is the convergence of systems of race, gender, class, sexual orientation, and other social identities through structures (Crenshaw,

2009). Privilege is granted to certain groups whose members maintain power and dominance over others; this is implemented and maintained through structures such as policies, ideologies, and laws that play out from the societal level down to the individual level. Crenshaw (2009) points out that "intersectional subordination need not be intentionally produced; in fact, it is frequently the consequence of the imposition of one burden that interacts with preexisting vulnerabilities to create yet another dimension of disempowerment" (p. 216). Mason and Jonathan experienced some dissonance in their meaning making of their gay male identities in college when viewed from the lens of structural intersectionality.

Mason's involvement in the Naval ROTC program during his college years and its effect on his identity of being a gay man is an example of how structural intersectionality affects individuals. For the first three years of his ROTC involvement, Don't Ask, Don't Tell was still in effect. For Mason, that meant that he would have to live a compartmentalized life. He was out to close friends, but tended to avoid getting involved in LGBT organizations because he did not want his ROTC peers to find out that he was gay. As a result, he had very few gay friends and was not connected to the larger LGBT community within San Juan Miguel. The friends who did know Mason's sexual orientation had difficulty understanding why Mason would choose to be involved in the ROTC program. He states,

> Like, sometimes I'm kind of ashamed to tell them that because then they look at me funny, and they're just like, "Well, you just don't seem like you'd be in the Navy." And they don't just say that, but that's . . . that's what they're thinking. And just, like, "You just don't seem like you'd be in the Navy. You're just not masculine. Why would you want to be a part of that?" And I think, for me, it's just that I feel like it. I feel like doing this.

In Mason's story, his friends questioned not only his involvement due to his sexuality, but also his masculinity. Indeed, Mason's physicality as a slender, petite man who saw himself as more feminine did present challenges for him, especially among his ROTC peers.

For Mason, the ROTC environment was challenging, especially as he was coming out. Being in a "very macho sort of environment," Mason felt like an "outcast." He experienced harassment from a fellow cadet his first year, and that was painful for him. Since the repeal of Don't Ask, Don't Tell, Mason's perspective on the masculine culture of the military has not changed. He continues to experience structural resistance within the organization as it pertains to his sexual orientation. He shares a story about a recent request to not wear his uniform on Tuesdays due to his internship for his campus's Safe Zones program. He recalls,

I had to—I was very vague in my description. I was like, "Oh, it's for my internship." And then they asked, "What's your internship? Why can't you wear your uniform at your internship?" I was, "Because it's a gay organization." They were like, "Oh, well, yeah. Don't wear your uniform then." . . . So there's still a sort of segregation even though de facto de jure, the law has been passed.

Mason's involvement in the Naval ROTC program afforded him the opportunity to go to college, yet it came at the expense of being able to express himself openly as a gay man without the threat of discrimination. His involvement in the military as a college student presented challenges for him in making meaning of his multiple identities. However, other structural entities, such as religious beliefs and doctrines, can also influence the development of one's other identities, as Jonathan's story shows next.

Jonathan's coming out experience was complicated due to growing up in a family that was devoutly Catholic. Jonathan's parents, especially his father, accepted Catholicism's largely antigay ideology. As a result, the messages he received about what it meant to be gay were often negative. Jonathan recounts,

I mean, at 12 years old, I'm sure that you can only imagine that the only things about the gay community that I saw weren't exactly—ha!—family friendly. Let's keep it that way. But, no, you know, honestly, a lot of it had to do with Catholic home, upper class, it just wasn't even allowed in the household.

His feelings of being attracted to other men continued throughout his adolescence; yet, after coming out at 18, Jonathan's understanding of what it meant to be gay was very skewed since most of the information he had received about being gay stemmed from viewing gay pornography. He states,

Even when I came out, even with my first boyfriend, I didn't . . . I never vocalized it, but any time we were intimate, when we were done, there was that 2 to 10 minutes where I felt dirty and, like, I'd done something that I shouldn't have. Not in that "Oh, my God, I've been naughty" in a good way. No, I felt dirty in a bad way, physically.

In fact, these feelings continued for a long period of time, leading to Jonathan's diagnosis of clinical depression. A lack of support from some of his immediate family also contributed to this state of depression.

In particular, Jonathan's father had a very difficult time accepting Jonathan's sexuality when he finally disclosed that he was gay. A wealthy, Catholic

Republican, Jonathan's father struggled with the news that his son was gay and did not speak to Jonathan for six months afterward. This period was very difficult for Jonathan. Often he would act out when around his father by taking on certain stereotypical mannerisms in his conversation or demeanor just to make his father uncomfortable or angry. As a result of his emerging sexuality, Jonathan strove to be the perfect son. He states,

> I never got in trouble. I got perfect grades. I was the star athlete. Everything you could have wanted as a high school son, that was me. . . . That's one of the reasons why I was so pissed off, because I was so hurt.

This hurt intensified his depression, which ultimately resulted in Jonathan attempting suicide. In Jonathan's case, Catholic doctrine on homosexuality contributed in very significant ways to the struggles he had in coming out as gay, but so did his father's reluctance to accept Jonathan's gay identity. Structurally, these ideologies stemming from religion influenced his family's dynamics, which, in turn, influenced who Jonathan is at his core, including his sexual orientation.

Political Intersectionality

Individuals situated in two or more subordinate groups may experience the tensions of two or more conflicting social agendas; this is how Crenshaw (2009) defines *political intersectionality*. Crenshaw states, "The need to split one's political energies between two sometimes opposing groups is a dimension of intersectional disempowerment that men of color and white women seldom confront" (p. 217). However, Crenshaw's aggregation of men of color or White women omits sexual minority identities. Therefore, men of color who are also gay-identified, for example, may encounter situations in which they must decide to put their political energies toward either their gay identity or their racial identity.

Crenshaw highlights the fact that often those in power (e.g., men, Whites, heterosexuals) play a pivotal role in setting the political agendas for society at large, but also for their respective populations. However, this perpetuates the systems of oppression that continue to reify those with privilege while concurrently furthering discrimination for those who are marginalized. Discussing the antiracist and feminist movements those in privilege lead, Crenshaw (2009) argues that those in power's "specific raced *and* gendered experiences, although intersectional, often define as well as confine the interests of the entire group" (p. 217). For Mason and Victor, their lived realities as gay men of color have influenced how they make meaning of who they are as well as who they are becoming.

In conversation about the difference between White gay men and gay men of color, Mason says,

> I think part of that phenomenon is [that] White identity is not as salient to them as their gay identity. So they have more time to put into that gay identity because they're White, because I think part of privilege is being invisible and not having to acknowledge that part of yourself, because I think that when you're oppressed or marginalized, that's something that becomes important to you. . . . I think there are some cultural expectations within their race that force them to choose one or the other. I think men of color are expected to be more aggressive, more overtly masculine, and I think when you add sexuality and masculinity, that just complicates it.

Mason's statement exemplifies Crenshaw's point about those in positions of power not having to negotiate as many complexities or conflicting political agendas. From the political intersectionality standpoint, White gay men are given privilege due to their race that gay men of color are not. Additionally, the socialized messages and assumptions for White gay men are different from those for gay men of color.

Mason and Victor's experiences as gay men of color are different from their White counterparts'. Often, that exhibits itself in different ways. Mason feels as though context becomes important in how his identities show up. He reflects on this, saying,

> For some people, it's easy for them to just be themselves in any environment. But for me, myself, it just depends on the type of environment that I'm in. . . . Sometimes in one type of situation, I'll show one layer, and the other time, I'll show another layer. And it's those conflicts between the two identities or the multiple identities that make it difficult.

Mason continues,

> I have been struggling with this because they're both marginal identities, and when you talk about your identities, I feel like I have to choose one or the other. When I'm with my Filipino crew, I have to be less gay and not emphasize that as much. When I'm with my—I guess when I'm interacting in gay spaces, I have to play down my Filipino identity for the majority culture.

This feeling of having to "choose" one identity over another exemplifies Crenshaw's concept of political intersectionality.

Likewise, Victor experiences some similar difficulties in understanding how his multiple identities converge in different, and sometimes conflicting, ways. His gay identity has been a key focus for him during his college years, particularly in his extracurricular involvement, his academic studies as an LGBT minor, and his service to the greater San Juan Miguel community as an intern at two LGBT-affiliated nonprofit organizations. However, that affiliation has started to become troubling for him. He states,

> I love being a gay man, and I do enjoy all those things. But I feel that, in a way, I don't want to be determining my life based upon who I sleep with. So it's important for me to embrace who I am sexually, but if I'm interested in other things, I should be able to do that. I know a lot of gay men who are like that. Yeah, they're gay, but they're doing all these things that are involved externally, and you know, I kind of like that balanced approach; whereas, for myself, I'm so entrenched in it right now that—not that my avenue's stuck, but I want to start being more balanced about it.

Victor's statement seems to indicate that though developmentally he may have been more engaged within the LGBT community for his own personal growth in the past, he may be entering some new stages of awareness of the interconnectedness of other identity politics. Ultimately, though, his statement also highlights the inherent tensions of choice between his gay identity and other social identities or interests.

Representational Intersectionality

Representational intersectionality is when two identities converge and concerns—while presented as representing both identities—ultimately privilege one over the other (Crenshaw, 2009). Analyses of representational intersectionality must address the following main issues: (a) the construction of majoritarian stories around race, gender, and other social identities; and (b) how critiques of those stories typically marginalize those with multiple oppressed identities (Crenshaw, 2009). Addressing the subordination of Black women, Crenshaw offers a critical statement about the importance of representational intersectionality when writing,

> Aiming to bring together the different aspects of an otherwise divided sensibility, an intersectional analysis argues that racial and sexual subordination are mutually reinforcing, that Black women are commonly marginalized by a politics of race alone or gender alone, and that a political response to each form of subordination must at the same time be a political response to both. (p. 236)

For Victor, Mason, and Jonathan, their lived identities as gay men, coupled with other social identities with which they identify, clearly have an impact on how they take up their space and voice in the world. Yet, larger structures, systems, and agents of socialization have shaped them.

For Jonathan, Mason, and Victor, the media has exerted a significant influence in their socialization, especially in terms of their gender and sexual orientation. Images from popular media were important in shaping the performance of what it meant to be a gay man, especially in the college environment. Victor addresses this idea:

> That's really funny because I was thinking about this yesterday. I was like, "When did I become a gay man?" I was like, "I know that I was born with that sexual drive . . . but the actual stereotypes, I don't know." I would say I definitely learned from my peers. When I joined the fraternity especially, the terminology just started filtering in. . . . It was definitely very much a learned behavior because there's no "how to be" book, so you learn from the people around you. The people I learned from were very informative. I'll put it that way.

Victor's statement highlights the differences in how gay men are socialized compared to their straight peers. Unlike straight men, young gay men largely do not have older adults (e.g., fathers, brothers) modeling for them how to navigate important milestones in one's life, such as dating, engaging in sexual behaviors, and cultivating relationships. In fact, Jonathan, Mason, and Victor indicated a lack of significant ongoing mentorship by gay male adults in their lives. In a world where individuals are bombarded by heteronormative images in the popular media, this lack of mentorship is particularly troubling.

From a representational intersectionality perspective, media images of gay men evoked a mix of opinions among the men. In conversation with one another, Jonathan and Mason discussed the significant representations of gay men in the media that resonated with them as young gay men. Specifically, they talked about the gay characters they viewed growing up, but also the larger systemic issues of the media and how they socialize individuals. Mason said,

> The problem with *Will & Grace* is that the men were essential eunuchs. They didn't portray any sort of sexuality. It was just, "Oh, I'm in a relationship with him." But I want the details. *Queer as Folk* showed the details graphically. So we needed, the American public needed something more palatable to take in, and that was *Will & Grace*.

Jonathan replied,

> But there you run into the issue of network TV versus cable pay—for TV. So if you look at the same *Queer as Folk* from the UK, it's just as graphic,

but their TV standards are much more lax. You can show boobs and a flac-
cid penis on TV. Here if you're going to do that, your network is going off
the air.

The discussion between Mason and Jonathan exemplifies the challenges
inherent in the images of the popular media regarding gay men. However,
in both television shows, the main characters were also White, reinforcing
certain notions about what it means to be gay. While Mason and Jonathan
may not have consciously thought about those pieces, one can assume that,
on a subconscious level, this may have been internalized in their own sense
of self. Additionally, this juxtaposition of imagery also exhibits itself in how
the men often uphold and continue to replicate certain facets of hegemonic
masculinity.

From images of gay men in popular culture to socialized messages about
homosexuality and masculinity, Jonathan, Mason, and Victor each experience the phenomenon of sorting through often disparate messages about
what it means to be gay and what it means to be a man. As a result, they
tended to recognize the negative aspects of hegemonic masculinity with its
roots in patriarchy, misogyny, and heteronormativity. However, the degree to
which they subscribed to hegemonic masculinity often was directly related
to their sense of internal masculinity and their physicality. On one hand,
Mason and Victor's physical demeanor as gay men tended to be more feminine based on their own self-description. Both men also tended to be more
aware of their male privilege and actively worked to distance themselves from
hegemonic masculinity.

On the other hand, Jonathan's adherence to traditional ideals of masculinity followed very strict and normative gender roles. Through his physical
presence, mannerisms, and personal interests, Jonathan fit within traditional
male scripts. In fact, he obeyed these gender codes so well that he acknowledged he could pass as straight. At the same time, one could expect that
Jonathan would meet these traditional gender scripts given his identities.
As a White gay man from a wealthy family, Jonathan discussed his drive
to meet the expectations of others, something that was instilled in him at a
young age. Even now he understands that his race, religion, and social class
continue to play a significant role in both how he considers who he is at his
core and how others view him. He states,

> Sexual orientation, gender, culture, I think they have more to do with my
> makeup as a person. . . . They define me more as a person, whereas race,
> religion, social class more define me as how, how one of the ways I see
> things. . . . They define me more, set up my values, how I see things more
> than they define me as a person.

Jonathan's statement reflects the importance of representational intersectionality. While he understands that his sexual orientation, gender, and culture make him who he is, he may ultimately be guided more by his race, religion, and social class, which largely are privileged identities. As a result, Jonathan's meaning making of his multiple identities may be shaped to continue reifying hegemonic views, if that works to his own benefit, rather than viewing the interconnectedness of marginalized identities.

Implications for Practice

The stories of Jonathan, Mason, and Victor illuminate the importance of structural, political, and representational intersectionality in one's development within the context of higher education. Their lived experiences exemplify the realities of gay men attending colleges and universities and how they are attempting to make meaning of their multiple social identities. From their experiences, there is a set of implications for professional practice around intersectionality, which I address in this section.

Providing time and space for gay students to gather, whether in person or virtually, and discuss their own meaning making of who they are is critical. In an age when students are bombarded with socialized messages, they need to have opportunities to be critically reflective about their identities and what those identities might mean for them at the personal, group/community, and societal level. These spaces are similar to the concept of *counter-spaces for students of color*, which are defined as "sites where deficit notions of people of color can be challenged and where a positive collegiate racial climate can be established and maintained" (Solórzano, Ceja, & Yosso, 2000, p. 70). While scholars have largely discussed counter-spaces for students of color (Solórzano et al.; Tatum, 2003), it is clear that similar spaces for gay men (and their lesbian, bisexual, and transgender peers) would be helpful to continue addressing the unique experiences of these individuals.

Integrating intersectional perspectives within the academic curriculum would assist students in continuing their own journey of self-awareness through critical reflection and enable them to begin to interrogate and examine systems and structures that perpetuate power, privilege, and oppression. Mason's and Victor's academic involvement in an LGBT studies minor assisted them in gaining a deeper understanding of themselves as well as their role within the larger system. Student affairs professionals could also adapt intersectional perspectives for the curriculum they use in student leader training, whether for RAs or at multicultural student services retreats and programs. Both Mason and Jonathan benefited from programs on campus that were rooted in social justice. By taking an intersectional approach in training, these men were exposed to issues, such as heteronormativity, social construction of gender, and hegemony, in ways that their academic curriculum may not have afforded.

If we are to take an intersectional perspective, educators need to become competent at examining and questioning the status quo. As mentioned earlier in this chapter, the majoritarian stories that maintain societal hierarchies that continue to perpetuate privilege and oppression are deeply woven into the fabric of our society. However, we need to hold up these myths and stories and begin to ask the difficult questions about whom these stories empower and whom they might disadvantage. We need to educate our students to become critical consumers of media images and teach them how to engage with others in civil discourse about difficult topics. Both in the classroom and outside it, students need to be exposed to the diverse perspectives on the LGBT community beyond mainstream images that tend to veer toward those in power, such as Whites and those from the middle class or upper middle class. We need to talk with one another about issues with a variety of discordant thoughts, especially those from an intersectional lens on social identities. We also need to educate others as well as ourselves about mainstream and counter-movements within the LGBT community to explore the larger interconnections that exist among the large spectrum of individuals under the specter of the LGBT umbrella. In doing so, we move toward a holistic integration of intersectional perspectives within higher education.

Conclusion

Crenshaw (2009) concludes her article stating, "Through an awareness of intersectionality, we can better acknowledge and ground the difference among us and negotiate the means by which these differences will find expression in constructing group politics" (p. 246). An intersectional analysis of Jonathan's, Mason's, and Victor's stories provides insights into how these men are influenced by systems and structures that affect them. Within the context of the collegiate environment, these men have explored their larger sense of self through curricular and cocurricular experiences and the relationships they have developed with family and friends. Thus, they have created their own rule books about what it means to be gay men. For each, the rule book is unique—based on the construction of knowledge of one's self at the intersections of his race, gender, sexual orientation, and other social identities. At that intersection, Jonathan, Mason, and Victor continue to answer the fundamental question, "Who am I?" Intersectionality, from the structural, political, and representational perspective, continues to assist these men—and the higher education professionals working with students like them—in questioning the status quo and examining the systems of which they are a part.

Note

1. San Juan Miguel is the pseudonym for the large metropolitan city in southern California where these participants attended college.

References

Berila, B. (2011). Queer masculinities in higher education. In J. A. Laker & T. Davis (Eds.), *Masculinities in higher education: Theoretical and practical considerations* (pp. 97–110). New York: Routledge.

Bilodeau, B. L. (2007). *Genderism: Transgender students, binary systems, and higher education.* (Unpublished doctoral dissertation). Michigan State University, East Lansing.

Cass, V. C. (1979). Homosexual identity formation: A theoretical model. *Journal of Homosexuality, 4*(3), 219–235.

Collins, P. H. (2000). *Black feminist thought: Knowledge, consciousness, and the politics of empowerment* (2nd ed.). New York: Routledge.

Connell, R. W. (2005). *Masculinities* (2nd ed.). Berkeley, CA: University of California Press.

Crenshaw, K. (2009). Mapping the margins: Intersectionality, identity politics, and violence against women of color. In E. Taylor, D. Gillborn, & G. Ladson-Billings (Eds.), *Foundations of critical race theory in education* (pp. 213–246). New York: Routledge.

D'Augelli, A. R. (1994). Identity development and sexual orientation: Toward a model of lesbian, gay, and bisexual development. In E. J. Trickett, R. J. Watts, & D. Birman (Eds.), *Human diversity: Perspectives on people in context* (pp. 312–333). San Francisco: Jossey-Bass.

Dilley, P. (2010). Which way out? A typology of non-heterosexual male collegiate identities. In S. R. Harper & F. Harris III (Eds.), *College men and masculinities: Theory, research, and implications for practice* (pp. 105–135). San Francisco: Jossey-Bass.

Fassinger, R. E. (1998). Lesbian, gay, and bisexual identity and student development theory. In R. L. Sanlo (Ed.), *Working with lesbian, gay, bisexual, and transgender college students: A handbook for faculty and administrators* (pp. 13–22). Westport, CT: Greenwood.

Kimmel, M. (2008). *Guyland: The perilous world where boys become men.* New York: Harper.

Montecinos, C. (1995). Culture as an ongoing dialogue: Implications for multicultural teacher education. In C. Sleeter & P. McLaren (Eds.), *Multicultural education, critical pedagogy, and the politics of difference* (pp. 269–308). Albany, NY: State University of New York Press.

Rankin, S., Weber, G., Blumenfeld, W., & Frazer, S. (2010). *2010 State of higher education for lesbian, gay, bisexual, and transgender people*. Charlotte, NC: Campus Pride.

Rhoads, R. A. (1997). A subcultural study of gay and bisexual college males: Resisting developmental inclinations. *The Journal of Higher Education, 68*(4), 460–482.

Solórzano, D., Ceja, M., & Yosso, T. (2000). Critical race theory, racial microaggressions, and campus racial climate: The experiences of African American college students. *Journal of Negro Education, 69*(1/2), 60–73.

Solórzano, D. G., & Yosso, T. J. (2009). Critical race methodology: Counter-storytelling as an analytical framework for educational research. In E. Taylor, D. Gillborn, & G. Ladson-Billings (Eds.), *Foundations of critical race theory in education* (pp. 131–147). New York: Routledge.

Tatum, B. D. (2003). *Why are all the black kids sitting together in the cafeteria?* New York: Basic Books.

Tillapaugh, D. W. (2012). *Toward an integrated self: Making meaning of the multiple identities of gay men in college*. (Unpublished doctoral dissertation). University of San Diego.

10

SUBALTERN SUPERMEN

Intersecting Masculinities and Disabilities in Popular Culture

Karen A. Myers, Jason A. Laker, and Claire Lerchen Minneman

All the world's a stage, and all the men and women merely players; They have their exits and their entrances, and one man in his time plays many parts, his acts being seven ages.

W. Shakespeare, *As You Like It*, II.vii

Shakespeare's famous line did not represent a new idea even when he wrote it, but it holds an especially profound resonance today. Now, there are virtually unlimited stages, and their fourth walls have blurred, if not collapsed entirely. People are even more apt to be someone or something other than what they seem, whether intentionally or not, because there are more forms of communication with greater opportunities for agency over one's presentation.

In such a context, it seems especially strange that some notions about identity remain much as they were during the Bard of Avon's lifetime. For instance, gender remains perhaps the most fundamental organizing principle in societies around the world. Who or what "counts" as a "real" man or woman remains stubbornly in place, even as stigma and constraints relating to diversity of gender and sexuality may have eased in many cases and places. It is still true that physical strength, stoicism, wealth production, and overt influence are hallmarks of masculinity. Even photographs of men could be sorted into more or less "manly" categories because of the power and persistence of many ideas about gender that have magnified and proliferated— rather than diffused—in today's exploding media outlets. In this example, historical or geographic contexts might mitigate which cues inform the sorting order of such photos, but not whether such a social taxonomy exists to inform their placement on a "masculinity" continuum.

Indeed, Connolly (2002) asserts that identities are "established in relation to a series of differences that have become socially recognized. These differences are essential to the particular identity's being. If they did not coexist as differences, it would not exist in its distinctness and solidity" (p. 64).

Identity is multifaceted, and the intersection of disability and other identities such as gender and race must be considered.

> Because of the additional impact of race and gender, a White male who uses a wheelchair may differ in extraordinary ways from that of a Black female who also does. Although we may be able to conceptualize disability as occurring in the environment, the impact that it has on individuals cannot be understood without knowing the specific context of their lives. (Evans & Herriott, 2009, p. 37)

According to Warner and Brown (2011), little research has been done on the intersection of race/gender and health/related disabilities of older adults.

> An intersectionality approach posits race/ethnicity and gender are *not* separate, additive, dimensions of social stratification but are mutually defining, and reinforce one another in a myriad of ways in the production and maintenance of health across the life course. (Warner & Brown, 2011, p. 1237)

The sociologist Erving Goffman (1959) was among the first in modern times to frame identity as a performance, intended to both present and reinforce socially recognized symbols (e.g., behavior, objects, ideas). He wrote:

> When an individual plays a part, he implicitly requests his observers to take seriously the impression that is fostered before them. They are asked to believe that the character they see actually possesses the attributes he appears to possess, that the task he performs will have the consequences that are implicitly claimed for it, and that, in general, matters are what they appear to be. (p. 17)

Of course, not every part played is intentional or precise, and not every response is desired or expected. Such are the complications associated with identity politics and their effects on psychosocial development, privilege and oppression, and the contested spaces in which people perform or read identities.

Four years later, Goffman (1963) observed:

> In an important sense, there is only one complete unblushing male in America: a young, married, white, urban, northern, heterosexual Protestant father of college education, fully employed, of good complexion, weight, and height, and a recent record in sports. Every American male tends to

look upon the world from this perspective, this constituting one sense in which one can speak of a common value system in America. Any male who fails to qualify in any one of these ways is likely to view himself—during moments at least—as unworthy, incomplete, and inferior. (p. 128)

Even though this was written over 50 years ago, it could just as easily have been written today.

When it comes to identities, truth and imagination can at least feel like one and the same, with significant consequences. This is strikingly true in the case of males and the scripts of masculinity. As Kimmel and Messner (1989) note:

The important fact of men's lives is not that they are biological males, but that they become men. Our sex may be male, but our identity as men is developed through a complex process of interaction with the culture in which we both learn the gender scripts appropriate to our culture and attempt to modify those scripts to make them more palatable. (p. 10)

Of course, what is palatable to one may not be so to another. Nevertheless, the hegemonic ideal of masculinity remains quite rigid, and negotiation with it can be very difficult. What if the barrier to achieving it is not so much a question of taste or interest, but rather one of capability? To be sure, the dominant masculine script is problematic for many reasons (for many, and probably most, people), even for those who come closest to its achievement. For men with disabilities, it is structurally impossible to perform the gender script without substantial revisions. Even the stereotypes of masculinity and disability are opposites. Therefore, the co-location of these competing identities within individual men creates situations of significant tension and exceptionally rich cases for study.

Erving Goffman's (1963) work on stigma figures strongly in the analysis of the masculinity/disability intersections, discussed here by Barnhart (1994):

The pressure of idealized conduct is most clearly seen in marginalized people, whose deviance forces them into "discredited" or "discreditable" groups, based on the nature of their stigma (Goffman 1963, p. 42). The importance of impression management is most visible with these individuals, as those who are discredited must assuage the tension their stigma causes in order to successfully interact with others, while those suffering from a discrediting stigma are forced to limit the access of others to information about the stigma or assume the character of a discredited individual. The emphasis on idealized, normative identity and conduct limits the ability of the discredited individual to achieve full acceptance by the population [into which] he or she is forced to assimilate. For the discreditable individual who attempts to "pass" and employ "disidentifiers" to establish him/herself as "normal" (Goffman, p. 44), feelings of ambivalence and alienation emerge as a result of limited social intercourse. Ultimately, the existence of a stigma of any type, a part of the existence of a large segment of the population, changes the nature of impression management and, hence, interaction.

Meisner's idea of "living truthfully under imaginary circumstances" (Meisner & Longwell, 1987, p. 15) has particular resonance today because of the exponential proliferation of media environments (e.g., television, films, social networks, online channels) to which people are continuously exposed or engaged with as consumers, producers, or perhaps both. One wonders whether the imaginary circumstances also have increased in their diversity, or whether the same depictions merely are being reproduced more often and in more venues. The former could be argued to offer hopeful possibilities for legitimizing spaces for otherwise marginalized identities, whereas the latter might rigidify and reproduce hegemonic notions of status through proliferation of their articulations, colonizing newer settings as they arise.

College and university campuses are important contexts for critically examining such issues and questions of identity intersectionality, marginalization, and the impact of disability identity based on social, cultural, and economic factors. Given the perennial comings and goings of people and ideas, they represent living soundstages and experimental theaters unto themselves. As students in particular arrive on campuses, they bring with them years and volumes of experiences and messages associated with media, including those about their own and each other's identities.

Identity development is paramount for students during their college years (Chickering & Reisser, 1993), and awareness/acceptance of multiple identities can add a greater challenge to the development process (Jones & McEwen, 2000; Stewart, 2009). Body issues and the ability to form relationships may thus be magnified for individuals with disabilities (Gibson, 2006, 2011) and for college men with disabilities in particular (Gerschick & Miller, 1995).

This chapter is intended to complicate binary ideas about privilege and oppression by exploring intersections of gender and disability, particularly how male students with disabilities have seen—and continue to see—their identities depicted in the "imaginary circumstances" of the media; what they think about this; and what consequences this may have for their self-concept, development, aspirations, and success. Are the characters in film and on television accurate depictions of "real" men with disabilities? By "real," we mean both the presence of the diverse range of identity performances, and the legitimacy—or lack thereof—bestowed on the particular intersectional itera-tions of masculinities and disabilities. Thus, we address the complex inter-sections of masculinity and disability and explore implications for masculine role socialization and disability in higher education.

Historical Perspective

> What I realized was that people across this country and across the world suffer from a lack of imagination when it comes to disability. Disability lacks a frame. We get no assistance from the media, literature and popular culture, where the stories are either full of pity and sadness or impossi-ble physical feats performed by inspiring people with disabilities who run marathons using expensive prosthetic equipment. (Rapp, 2013, p. 29)

Depictions of disability began in the negative:

> A summary look at literary distortions of handicapping conditions illus-trates this point: Captain Hook (in *Peter Pan*) is intentionally an amputee with [a] prosthesis; Shakespeare links Richard III's hunchback to his evil lust. Somerset Maugham uses Philip's clubfoot (in *Of Human Bondage*) to symbolize his bitter and warped nature. (Dahl, 1993, p. 75)

Frightening and horrible associations with disability transformed into char-acters thought of as weak and pitiable, like Tiny Tim from Charles Dickens's *A Christmas Carol* and Clara from Joanna Spyri's *Heidi* (Margolis & Shapiro, 1987, p. 20). Over the course of time, characters with disabilities were no longer limited to the pages of novels, nor were they limited to one-dimen-sionality, as media have evolved to include film and television, and character development of those with disabilities has become multidimensional. No longer is disability considered a flaw or a negative; rather, the role of dis-ability in the media has changed from being a reactionary addition follow-ing World War I and World War II, to being one part, not the whole, of a character's identity.

At the start of the twentieth century, feature films introduced a new form of media to the Western world. While "in the 1910's, it was easy to detect a certain flimsy and deformed psychoanalysis of persons with dis-abilities" (Peñas, 2007, p. 3), World War I proved to be a turning point for the depiction of disability in the media. As wounded veterans returned from the battlefield, the media responded in kind, featuring many characters with disabilities. Though this certainly was an advance in representation, many films—90 of the 200 films produced in the 1920s—depicted miracles restoring sight, hearing, and mental abilities, events that rarely take place in real life, and so glaring an overrepresentation that medical associations felt compelled to caution film companies against these endings (Peñas, 2007).

World War II reignited depictions of disability in film. Most prominently, *The Best Years of Our Lives* won seven Academy Awards in 1946, including Best Motion Picture (19th Academy Awards [1947] Nominees and Winners, 2013). The film features three veterans struggling to adapt to life following their return from the war. Both the character Homer Parrish, and the actor who played him, Harold Russell, lost both hands during the war (Peñas, 2007). For his performance, Russell received the Academy Award for Best Supporting Actor (19th Academy Awards [1947] Nominees and Winners, 2013).

The 1960s further showcased disability in film and media. With a president in the White House whose sister had a developmental disability, and the founding of the Special Olympics in 1968, public attention was given to disability, and conversations surrounding disability entered the mainstream (Peñas, 2007, p. 5; *History of Special Olympics*, 2013). Similar to World War I and World War II, the end of the Vietnam War reintroduced veterans with disabilities into feature films. Notably, *Coming Home* (1978) featured Jon Voight, whose character was "multifaceted, not at all schmaltzy or pitiful. For the first time, the message was different" (Peñas, 2007, p. 5).

The 1980s introduced an era absent of major wars influencing film and media. While most films featuring disability before 1980 focused on physical, visual, and auditory disabilities, there has been a shift over the last 30 years, as films began featuring a wider variety of disabilities. Two celebrated films, *Forrest Gump* and *I Am Sam*, feature main characters with developmental disabilities. Forrest Gump is a beloved character celebrated for the fictional role he played in American culture, and Sam Dawson is a father fighting the state for custody of his young daughter, a fight many go through regardless of their abilities. Other disabilities as portrayed by men in modern films include autism, in both *Rain Man* and *What's Eating Gilbert Grape*; schizophrenia in *A Beautiful Mind*; cerebral palsy in *My Left Foot*; obsessive-compulsive disorder in *As Good as It Gets;* osteogenesis imperfecta in *Unbreakable;* and AIDS in *Philadelphia* (Timmons, 2003). These films have highlighted a shift in thinking; in historical literature, Dahl (1993) contends that Cyrano de Bergerac and Quasimodo "are remarked not for their deformity but because they are both deformed and good (as though one precludes the other). Rarely does there appear an average or ordinary person whose disability is incidental" (p. 75). In all of the aforementioned films, the plot revolves around the character with the disability, and the disability is linked to the plot. However, the disability does not wholly define the character.

While representation of disability in film has increased over the last quarter century, in terms of types of disability and frequency, the majority of the actors portraying these roles do not have disabilities. "Of fourteen actors in the category of best actor/actress won by films dealing with disability only one winner, Marlee Matlin in *Children of a Lesser God*—a film about a deaf woman's relationship with a nondisabled teacher in a school for deaf people—had experience of the impairment portrayed" (Barnes, 1992, p. 13). In *Children of a Lesser God* specifically, though "this film was about deaf people and the deaf community it was inaccessible to sign language users. The way the film was shot meant that much of the signing was not seen" and, thus, it was only accessible to hearing viewers (Barnes, p. 13). The same is true on television; neither Kevin McHale, who played Artie on *Glee*, nor Jason Ritter, who played Kevin Girardi on *Joan of Arcadia,* nor Scott Porter, who played Jason Street in *Friday Night Lights,* uses wheelchairs, leaving many with questions: Who are the role models for those with disabilities? Where are we to turn?

Actors With Disabilities

Perhaps the tides are changing. Chris Burke played Corky on *Life Goes On*, and both the character and actor have Down syndrome. In real life, Robert David Hall, who plays Dr. Al Robbins on *CSI: Crime Scene Investigation*, had both legs amputated because of a car accident. A similar story line was given to Robbins (*CSI: Crime Scene Investigation*, 2013). RJ Mitte, with mild cerebral palsy, played Walter White Jr., a character on *Breaking Bad* with cerebral palsy (Calabro, 2010). These actors have not known a professional world without their disabilities. This has not been the case for two famous actors of this generation: Christopher Reeve and Michael J. Fox. Both were famous before their disability, and both championed awareness and returned to acting.

When Christopher Reeve played Superman and other characters in the movies, it would be safe to say that most moviegoers and magazine readers saw him as a handsome, virile, "sexy" celebrity. The public saw not only the character as an amazing superhero, but also the actor as one as well. When his 1995 horse-riding accident resulted in a spinal cord injury and quadriplegia, he took on a different persona in the eyes of the public. One day we saw him posing as Superman, hands on hips, stoic strong gaze, with red cape blowing in the breeze; the next day we saw him in a hospital bed and then in a motorized wheelchair using a breathing tube. To many, he still was viewed as a superhero, though not in the physical sense with his Superman physique, but rather in the sense of his resilience, positive attitude, and perseverance while facing his own disability; his advocacy for others with disabilities; and his support for spinal cord research. In addition to raising awareness for spinal cord injuries, Reeve returned to film as both an actor and a director and branched out into literature and spoken word. Regardless of which side of the camera, Reeve's roles highlighted spinal cord injury; Reeve starred in a remake of *Rear Window*, winning a Screen Actors Guild Award for his per-formance, and directed *The Brooke Ellison Story*, the true story of one of the few Harvard University graduates with quadriplegia. In addition, his *New York Times* best-selling memoir, *Still Me*, won a Grammy for Best Spoken Word Album.

Actor Michael J. Fox is a similar celebrity. He was known for his quick wit, charming personality, and youthful appearance, and the public watched as the traits of Parkinson's disease slowly transformed his physi-cal characteristics. People continue to admire him for his courage, advo-cacy, and endless fight for Parkinson's research. His appearances on TV talk shows and as a guest star on TV comedies and dramas are welcomed by his fans. His wit and charm are alive and well. However, we do raise these questions: How does the public view him? Have people's perceptions toward the actor changed because of his disability? How do people who are not familiar with Mr. Fox's previous work perceive him now? These questions may be answered by his project *The Michael J. Fox Show*, which appeared on the Fox network (Fixmer, 2012). The show was loosely based on Fox's life, in this case depicting him as a popular news anchor who returns to television after a five-year absence precipitated by the onset of Parkinson's disease (his actual diagnosis) and a desire to spend more time with his family.

Daryl Mitchell was also a Hollywood presence before a motorcycle acci-dent that resulted in paraplegia. In his early career, he found fame in *10 Things I Hate About You* and *The Fresh Prince of Bel Air*, and he returned to acting following his accident in the role of Eli in the NBC series *Ed* ("Who Is Daryl 'Chill' Mitchell?" n.d.).

These actors bring awareness to their disabilities and turn the media's attention to disability. In addition to foundations such as the Christopher Reeve Foundation and Michael J. Fox Foundation, which raise money for research, through work with groups including the Performers with Dis-abilities Caucus for the Screen Actors Guild (SAG-AFTRA) and EQUITY, and Inclusion in the Arts and Media for Performers with Disabilities (I AM PWD), these actors are paving the way for future actors with disabilities (Calabro, 2010; *CSI, Crime Scene Investigation*, 2013).

Disability in the Media Today

Around the world, and outside of feature films, attention is being paid to the representation of disability in the media. A 2005 Special Olympics report called on the media to "emphasize the multidimensional and com-petent aspects" of the lives of those with intellectual disabilities ("Changing

Attitudes Changing the World," 2005, p. 3). In addition, the study found that "nearly three-quarters of the intellectually disabled in the media were men, while in reality the proportion between men and women is 3:2" and that men are more frequently shown as "capable of sustaining friendships and acting appropriately" ("Changing Attitudes Changing the World," 2005, p. 2).

von Krogh's 2010 report on the representation of people with disabilities in the media on Swedish television highlights the current representation as outlined by Ghersetti's 2007 study: "The time allotted to news reports that mentioned or featured disability was 0.07 percent of the total broadcast time" (as cited in von Krogh, 2010, p. 380). Ghersetti also found that "the portrayal was discriminatory, exclusionary and stereotyped" (as cited in von Krogh, 2010, p. 380). von Krogh called for an increase in representation in the media in the form of producers and commentators, and a change in attitude from treating those with disabilities as patients to treating them as human beings (p. 383).

Táboas-Pais and Rey-Cao (2012) studied physical education textbooks primarily in Spain and found that only 1.36% of the sample of 3,316 photographs showed people with disabilities and/or adapted sports, and that men were represented far more than women—57.9% of the pictures were of men, 18.4% featured men and women, and only 23.7% featured just women (Táboas-Pais & Rey-Cao, 2012, pp. 321, 322).

Hero Versus Victim

There is much to question and critique about how masculinity and heroism have been conflated in popular culture and in more intimate locations. The embodiment of masculine heroism in the heroes themselves illustrates these phenomena. We argue here that heroic figures in the media who have either congenital or acquired disabilities are in themselves what Hochschild (1994) refers to as "magnified moments." These are "episodes of heightened importance, either epiphanies, moments of intense glee or unusual insight, or moments in which things go intensely but meaningfully wrong. In either case, the moment stands out as metaphorically rich [and] unusually elaborate" (p. 4). The social historian Iain Boal (1995) defines *artifacts* as "congealed ideologies" (p. 12). Arguably, the "disabled" hero is simultaneously the magnified moment and artifact we are trying to understand here. Our interest is to envision an interpretation of these seemingly divergent identities (e.g., masculinity, disability) that resonates authentically with their lived experiences. Dominant images of masculinity and of disability are superficial, often patronizing, and in many cases disconnected from how people with these identities understand and experience them. As educators, it is critical for us to identify and pursue methods to support our colleagues' and students' agency, growth, and success. Such approaches should challenge hegemonic and oppressive norms and be rooted in principles of social justice.

To begin to construct such a framework, let us start with the following question: What constitutes a hero? According to the media, muscular physique, stamina, strength, wealth, power, good looks, and sensuality are characteristic of superheroes such as Superman, Captain America, and Thor. It is ironic that some of these extraordinary icons have disabilities. For example, Daredevil lost his vision as a child (played by Ben Affleck in the movie version); Professor Charles Xavier, the school's headmaster in *X-Men,* uses a wheelchair (played by Patrick Stewart and James McAvoy on film); and Luke Skywalker in *Star Wars* (played by Mark Hamill in the movies) lost his hand in a fight with Darth Vader, his father (who also has disabilities, but is the villain).

Some male characters in films and television shows are depicted as holding incredible intellect or other instrumental talent. These include Geordi La Forge in *Star Trek: The Next Generation,* who is blind, and Dr. Al Robbins on *CSI: Crime Scene Investigation.* Geordi was born without sight and wears a visor device that allows him to see not only visible light, but also other parts of the electromagnetic spectrum such as radio waves, infrared, and ultraviolet light. He is a Black man, though his racial identity is of limited importance in the social interactions among characters. During the years of the series, he impressed and was then recruited by Captain Picard, a White man, and worked his way up from entry level to command of a starship. Over the course of the series, he eventually transitions from the visor to working ocular implants, and then ultimately to regenerated "normal" visual capability.

The character of Dr. Robbins lost his legs at a young age in a tragic accident caused by a drunk driver and walks with the assistance of prostheses and crutches. He has a remarkable gift for analysis and serves as the chief medical examiner for the Las Vegas, Nevada, Police Department. The series also reveals that he was raised solely by his mother, a registered nurse, which explains his long-standing familiarity with hospital environments. His character has a wife and three children.

Both characters contain particularly rich thematic examples of the typical story of the "disabled" male hero. They both are portrayed as self-made male heroes who overcame almost impossible odds that were unfairly introduced into their lives, but that did not prevent them from achieving idealized personal and professional successes and eliciting the respect of those around them. One wonders then what "excuse" ordinary men (with disabilities or not) might have for not doing so as well, but one need not wonder about the sources of judgment or profound shame attached to the implicit failure of being a regular person.

Other men, who might have been considered heroes due to their daring actions in combat, experienced psychological and emotional harm in addition to physical loss or paralysis. Vietnam War veterans, including Ron Kovic (played by Tom Cruise in Kovic's biography, *Born on the Fourth of July*), Luke Martin (played by Jon Voight in *Coming Home*), and Lieutenant Dan Taylor (played by Gary Sinise in *Forrest Gump*), demonstrated anger, depression, self-pity, and addiction as coping mechanisms for living with their disabilities. At some point in each film, Kovic, Martin, and Taylor felt they had lost their virility and masculinity.

Many of the superheroes in the Marvel Universe have disabilities of some kind. In *X-Men*, created by Stan Lee and Jack Kirby in the 1960s, the superheroes are mutants. Professor Xavier, himself a mutant, intends to train young mutants to use their powers for benevolence, to help people and demonstrate that mutants can be good and can overcome evil. "Marvel writers and artists have continued to use mutants as a metaphor for groups who are disenfranchised and discriminated against in our society" (Dalton, 2011, p. 83). The mutants are hated by society because they are different. They are hated because of who they are. While it at first may seem indulgent or potentially denigrating to suggest, it is nonetheless true to state that the "mutant" metaphor often extends to the depiction of people with disabilities in popular culture and even in the language of everyday conversation. This is especially so in relation to those who identify as male.

We in higher education and student affairs have great interest in, and commitment to, understanding and promoting students' identity development and self-efficacy, and in engaging with them in intercultural dialogue and social justice education. Our oft-repeated mantra, to "meet students where they are," calls us to consider what beliefs and experiences of their own and others' identities they bring with them when arriving on our campuses. Questions about whether, how, and to what extent repeated exposures to particular media depictions affect students' self-esteem or their assumptions about and experiences of identity, privilege, and/or oppression are intractably debatable. There is likely an impact, but we argue that this is a reductionist question.

This is because popular media depictions of identity are transactional; they simultaneously influence and reflect those in social life. Popular cultural products such as Internet memes, television programs, and films are perhaps merely magnified versions of the social phenomena we contend with on campus and beyond. To be sure, this magnification can rigidify, complicate, or challenge structures of oppression and privilege, but it does not exist in a vacuum, disconnected from real life. Any critique we may have of superficial, patronizing, exploitative, or otherwise offensive portrayals in media can arguably be made about interactions we have or can observe on campus—it is the scale that is different—and so the power of its influence arguably rests in that aspect of it. Thus, just as we are often confounded by the challenge of holding two or more identities in awareness and conversation with our students, so, too, is this a problem in the media. The case of male-identified people with visible or invisible disabilities allows us to consider privileged and subordinated identities at the same time, which is potentially valuable toward troubling binary ideas shaping social life, policies, and programs on campus.

People with disabilities "are rarely depicted on television, in films, or in fiction as being in control of their own lives—in charge or actively seeking out and obtaining what they want and need" (Linton, 1998, p. 25). People with disabilities are a minority group whose members are considered marginalized because of society's perceptions (Higbee, 1998; Linton & Mitchell, 2009). This resonates with the earlier point about the media/real-life dichotomy. Indeed, Saevi (2011) notes:

> It is in part a cultural and normative experience that when facing persons with disability, the disability itself is seldom mentioned. Children are taught not to point, stare or talk aloud about the impairments of people they meet. Disability is treated as unmentionable and as something that should remain unnoticed and thus invisible, even in our society of so-called tolerance and openness.

Characters with disabilities in the media indulge and magnify the same voyeuristic dynamics of everyday life.

Disability frameworks can allow us to understand how people with disabilities are perceived, but also to engage with these identities in meaningful and transformative ways. Jones (1996) provides descriptions of disability models that continue to be used today in understanding the lives of college students with disabilities. The models include the functional limitations model, the minority group paradigm, and the social construction model. The first model, the functional limitations or medical model, focuses on the deficit of disability. It justifies the status quo, assumes something must be "fixed," and places persons with disabilities in positions of weakness. The second model, the minority group paradigm, built on the "deficit" model, emphasizes oppression and indicates a "them" and "us" mentality. Environmental factors, along with psychological and social consequences of disability, are apparent in this model, and although people can show pride and ownership of their disabilities, privilege and group status must be considered when trying to understand people with disabilities. Missing from the minority paradigm, however, is the lived experience of the individual with a disability, which is evident in the third model, originated by Asch (1984) and Asch and Fine (1988)—that is, social construction. According to Jones (1996), social construction defines *disability* "not solely on the medical condition an individual experiences but as a social construction of these phenomena that incorporate experiences living with a disability in interaction with their environment" (p. 348). It challenges the incorrect assumptions of people without disabilities, focuses on breaking down barriers constructed by society, and celebrates the individuality of people with disabilities. In the college setting, it allows the entire campus community to engage in a shared encounter, viewing the students' lived experiences through a socially constructed lens, thus considering the environment and its effects on the lives of students with disabilities.

Disability frameworks affect language used when describing or defining *disability*. Prior to the 1970s, the word *handicapped* was used when referring to a person with a disability. *Handicapped* and *impairment* appear in Section 504 of the Rehabilitation Act of 1973, a law that prohibits federally funded institutions to discriminate based on disability. "'The disabled' or 'the handicapped' was replaced in the mid-70s by 'people with disabilities'" (Linton, 1998, p. 13). The word *disability* appears in the Americans with Disabilities Act of 1990, civil rights legislation that expanded the sphere of discrimination and inclusion. Evans and Herriot (2009) explain a sequential relationship among the words *impairment, disability,* and *handicap* as follows:

> An impairment refers to the lived, bodily experience of an individual; disability [is] the way in which the impairment is perceived by the larger society; and handicap [is] the way in which the person with a disability interacts with the environment. (p. 29)

Unfortunately, even today, derogatory, antiquated language (i.e., "handicapped man" or "the handicapped") continues to appear on signage and is used by some people, including those in the media, when referring to the lived experience of people with disabilities. Replacing this verbiage with person-first language, such as "individual with a disability," places focus on the person first and the disability second. Person-first language omits labeling and shows respect for the individual. "Beginning in the early 90s, 'disabled people' has been increasingly used in disability studies and disability rights circles when referring to the constituency group" (Linton, 1998, p. 13). Choosing to "own" their disabilities, people might identify themselves by saying, for example, "I am a disabled man" or "We are disabled men." In the classroom, as in the media, it is common to use metaphors when explaining concepts or events. Phrases such as "the blind leading the blind," "falling on deaf ears," and "a lame excuse" model exclusive language and demonstrate a lack of understanding that language affects all people. "Using disability as an analogy not only offends certain individuals, but also impedes clear communication, perpetuates false beliefs about disability, and creates an environment of unease and exclusion" (Ben Moshe, 2005, p. 107). For the purposes of this chapter, which focuses on men with disabilities in the media, we have used inclusive person-first language.

So, what distinctions cast a man with a disability as a hero or a victim in the observer's perception? To be a hero, must he overcome obstacles, face adversity, and come out winning in the end? A common phrase used in the media is, "He overcame his disability." However, if disability is a part of one's character, a part of who someone is (Gibson, 2006), what is there to overcome? In her disability identity development model, Gibson (2006, 2011) describes three phases a person with a disability potentially experiences during his or her life, whether the disability's onset is from birth or acquired later in life. The three phases of development are passive awareness, realization, and acceptance. During the passive awareness phase, which can be in the early part of one's life and continue into adulthood or when the person first acquires the disability, the person has no role model of disability. The individual can be taught to deny the disability, and the disability becomes a silent member of the family in which the individual develops a codependent relationship as the "good boy" or "good girl" in the family. The individual avoids attention and does not associate with others with disabilities. In the early part of *Mr. Holland's Opus*, Cole (Mr. Holland's son, who is deaf) is in the passive awareness phase of the development model.

In the realization phase, which often occurs in adolescence or early adulthood when the disability is from birth, or occurs shortly after one acquires the disability, the individual begins to see himself or herself as having a disability, experiences self-hate, becomes angry, and asks, "Why me?" The individual is concerned with how others perceive him or her, is concerned with personal appearance, and may develop the "superman" or "superwoman" complex. When he first returns home from the war, the character of Lieutenant Dan in *Forrest Gump* is an example of a character in the realization phase.

In the acceptance phase, which often occurs in adulthood or after one has lived with a disability for a time, the focus shifts from "being different" in a negative light to embracing one's self. The individual begins to view himself or herself as relevant, no more or no less, incorporating others with disabilities into his or her life. The person might become involved in disability advocacy and activism and fully integrates himself or herself into the "majority" world—that is, into the world of people with and without disabilities.

An example of a character who is in the acceptance phase is Gerry Bertier in *Remember the Titans*. At the end of the movie, the audience learns that he is active in the Paralympics.

A "majority" world insinuates a "minority" world, one in which people with disabilities are considered "less than" and treated as second-class citizens. It intimates a dominant superior culture and a subordinate, disenfranchised one. Educator activist Simi Linton (1998) fine-tuned the 1993 *Reader's Digest Oxford Complete Wordfinder* definition of *ableism* as "discrimination in favor of the able-bodied . . . [to include] the idea that a person's abilities or characteristics are determined by disability or that people with disabilities as a group are inferior to nondisabled people" (p. 9). In *Bending Bodies: Moulding Masculinities*, the antonyms of the term *able* are addressed. "If one is able, then one is capable, apt, fit, efficient, proper, skillful and clever. The opposite is to be incompetent, incapable, silly, weak, feeble and inept. People with disabilities often have been considered grotesque creatures of disorder" (Ervø & Johansson, 2003, p. 242). Given the dichotomous nature of group status and privilege—that is, people who are "in" and people who are "out"—and in reference to ableism—that is, people who are "normal" and people who are "abnormal"—individuals without disabilities are at an advantage before they even get out of bed in the morning.

Does Type of Disability Make a Difference?

When does a given audience view characters as weak? Is it the disability that causes the weakness, or is it the others' reactions to this disability? Does the assistive aid used make a difference? If someone does not "look disabled," is he or she stronger and more attractive to the audience? For example, in *Scent of a Woman*, Al Pacino's character is wealthy, confident, successful, and attractive. He appears ruthless and cold at times. He also is blind, carries a white cane, and wears sunglasses. To most audiences, he would not appear weak even though he is vulnerable throughout the movie. Samuel L. Jackson's character in *The Avengers* and Johnny Depp's character, Jack Sparrow, in *Pirates of the Caribbean* wear eye patches, yet they are perceived as powerful. Bradley Cooper's character in *Silver Linings Playbook*, though dealing with various personal issues throughout the film, does not elicit feelings of pity or sorrow from the audience. Even in the TV animation *South Park*, the wise-cracking Jimmy, who uses crutches, and Timmy, who uses a wheelchair, are not pitied (White, 2005). On the other hand, characters such as Radio (in the movie by the same name) and Sam (in *I Am Sam*) who have developmental disabilities evoke sympathy from audiences.

Moreover, when do disabilities feminize men? In *Whose Life Is It Anyway?* Richard Dreyfuss's character, a man who is paralyzed from the neck down, bemoans he is "not a man anymore" (Longmore, 2003, p. 120). Longmore adds:

> If disablement has often been regarded as feminizing men, at other times depending on the type and extent of disability and particularly on the manner in which it was acquired, it has been perceived as a masculine "red badge of courage." That complex moral economy of disability and gender requires investigation. (2003, p. 99).

In his book *Moving Violations*, John Hockenberry (1995), American journalist and author who has paraplegia as a result of a hitchhiking accident at age 19, discusses physical sensation experienced by men with spinal cord injuries (i.e., "wheelchair crips"). When addressing paralysis, he puts men into two categories: jocks and sex gods.

> The effect of this neural ordering is to divide the wheelchair crips (males particularly) into jocks and sex gods. The lower injuries make all of the layups on the basketball courts . . . the higher injuries, the quadriplegics, get all the dates. In my case, the injury was in the middle. (1995, p. 100)

He goes on to address incontinence and the fear of losing control:

> Loss of control is a dark fear, particularly in America. . . . The notions of control and power are themes of American policy. Going with the flow. . . . The frustrations in our superpower identity, the frustrations of homelessness, bankruptcy, and incontinence are all facets of the same fear. People who lose control are deviants or failures. People who have control are heroes, role models, victors over adversity, people "with their shit together." (1995, p. 101)

Are the X-Men and their counterparts in comic books and movies the true superheroes then because they display control? On the other hand, can "everyday" men with disabilities (e.g., men in college, men in business and industry, men in the military) be heroes even though their bladders are emptied with the use of a catheter, their voices are staccato, their hands shake uncontrollably, and they speak with the use of voice synthesizers and sign language interpreters?

In *My Body Politic*, Linton (2007) addresses sexuality of men and women with disabilities and her work with sex education, which led to the National Coalition of Sexuality:

> I came to understand the linking of disability to a robust sexual life . . . is radical . . . because it debunks the myths of the long-suffering disabled

person . . . [and] challenges ideals of sexual prowess. We are saying that pleasure isn't dependent on certain standards of performance, and on intact bodies. (p. 82)

Professor Angela Smith (2012), who studies disability and deformity in horror films, developed the argument in her book that while society tells us to be healthy and perfect, horror films remind us of our bodies' vulnerability and changeability. Fear of this change leads to society's control of the body via eugenics or the treatment of people with disabilities through an ableist lens. Eugenics and euthanasia of people with disabilities, despite age, continue in parts of the world.

The intersection of disability, gender, race, and age has been studied and reported by Warner and Brown (2011). "Whereas White [m]en had the lowest disability levels at baseline, White [w]omen and racial/ethnic minority [m]en had intermediate disability levels and Black and Hispanic [w]omen had the highest disability levels" (p. 1236). How these disabilities affect actual and perceived masculinity in the media and in real life continues to be explored.

We have been interested here in surface iterations of masculine identity operating not only in conflict with disability, but also in relationship with it. Our belief was, and still is, that the structural impossibilities associated with our subjects can dislodge hidden layers of possibility. This aspiration has been challenged in some media examples presented, and reinforced in others. In the former instance, it seems plausible to realize ideal masculinities, but so far only for those living them. Such iterations begin as transgressive and counterhegemonic alternatives to a rigid dominant form that has changed very little in living memory. We wonder, must it be a postmodern idea to discard masks altogether, allowing us as actors to play ourselves, without the intrusion of a script being foisted upon us at all?

References

19th Academy Awards (1947) Nominees and winners. The Academy of Motion Picture Arts and Sciences. (2013). Retrieved from http://www.oscars.org/awards/academyawards/legacy/ceremony/19th-winners.html

Asch, A. (1984). The experience of disability: A challenge for psychology. *American Psychologist, 39,* 529–536.

Asch, A., & Fine, M. (1988). Introduction: Beyond pedestals. In M. Fine & A. Asch (Eds.), *Women with disabilities: Essays in psychology, culture, and politics* (pp. 1–37). Philadelphia: Temple University Press.

Barnes, C. (1992). *Disabling imagery and the media: An exploration of the principles for media representations of disabled people, the first in a series of reports.* Halifax, UK: Ryburn Book Production.

Barnhart, A. (1994). *Erving Goffman: The presentation of self in everyday life.* Retrieved from http://employees.cfmc.com/adamb/writings/goffman.htm

Ben-Moshe, L. (2005). Lame idea: Disabling language in the classroom. In L. Ben-Moshe, R. Cory, M. Feldbaum, & K. Sagendorf (Eds.), *Building pedagogical curb cuts: Incorporating disability in the university classroom and curriculum* (pp. 107–116). Syracuse, NY: Graduate School of Syracuse University.

Boal, I. (1995). A flow of monsters: Luddism and virtual technologies. In J. Brook, & I. Boal (Eds.), *Resisting the virtual life: The culture and politics of information.* San Francisco: City Lights.

Calabro, T. (2010, March 17). "Breaking Bad" actor RJ Mitte finds "perfect role" prepared him to become an activist. *Pittsburgh Post-Gazette.* Retrieved from http://www.post-gazette.com/stories/ae/tv-radio/breaking-bad-actor-rj-mitte-finds-perfect-role-prepared-him-to-become-an-activist-238250/

Changing attitudes changing the world: Media's portrayal of people with intellectual disabilities. (2005). Special Olympics. Retrieved from http://www.specialolympics.org/uploadedFiles/LandingPage/WhatWeDo/Research_Studies_Desciption_Pages/Policy_paper_media_portrayal.pdf

Chickering, A., & Reisser, L. (1993). *Education and identity* (2nd ed.). San Francisco: Jossey-Bass.

Connolly, W. (2002). *Identity\difference: Democratic negotiations of political paradox.* Minneapolis, MN: University of Minnesota Press.

CSI: Crime Scene Investigation. (2013). CBS. Retrieved from http://www.cbs.com/shows/csi/cast/5638/?pg=1

Dahl, M. (1993). The role of the media in promoting images of disability—Disability as metaphor: The evil crip. *Canadian Journal of Communication, 18*(1), 75–80.

Dalton, R. (2011). *Marvelous myths: Marvel superheroes and everyday faith.* Atlanta, GA: Chalice Press.

Dill, B. T., & Zambrana, R. E. (2009). *Emerging intersections: Race, class, and gender in theory, policy, and practice.* New Brunswick, NJ: Rutgers University Press.

Ervø, S., & Johansson, T. (Eds.). (2003). *Bending bodies: Moulding masculinities* (Vol. 2). Hants, UK: Ashgate Publishing Limited.

Evans, N., & Herriott, T. (2009). Philosophical and theoretical approaches to disability. In J. Higbee & A. Mitchell (Eds.), *Making good on the promise: Student affairs professionals with disabilities* (pp. 27–40). Washington, DC: American College Personnel Association and University Press of America.

Fixmer, A. (2012, August 20). Michael J. Fox returns to television in NBC comedy series. *Bloomberg.* Retrieved from http://www.bloomberg.com/news/2012-08-20/michael-j-returns-to-tv-for-comedy-series-at-comcast-s-nbc.html

Gerschick, T., & Miller, A. S. (1995). Coming to terms: Masculinity and physical disability. In D. Sabo & D. F. Gordon (Eds.), *Men's health and illness: Gender, power, and the body* (pp. 183–204). Thousand Oaks, CA: Sage.

Gibson, J. (2006). Disability and clinical competency: An introduction. *The California Psychologist, 39,* 6–10.

Gibson, J. (2011). Advancing care to clients with disabilities through clinical competency. *The California Psychologist, 44*(4), 23–26.

Goffman, E. (1959). *The presentation of self in everyday life.* Garden City, NY: Doubleday.

Goffman, E. (1963). *Stigma: Notes on the management of spoiled identity.* Englewood Cliffs, NJ: Prentice-Hall.

Higbee, J. L., & Mitchell, A. A. (Eds.). (2009). *Making good on the promise: Student affairs professionals with disabilities.* Lanham, MD: American College Personnel Association and University Press of America.

History of Special Olympics. (2013). Special Olympics. Retrieved from http://www.specialolympics.org/history.aspx

Hochschild, A. (1994). The commercial spirit of intimate life and the abduction of feminism: Signs from women's advice books. *Theory, Culture & Society, 11*, 1–24.

Hockenberry, J. (1995). *Moving violations: War zones, wheelchairs, and declaration of independence.* New York: Hyperion.

Jones, S. R. (1996). Toward inclusive theory: Disability as a social construction. *NASPA Journal, 33*(4), 347–354.

Jones, S., & McEwen, M. (2000). A conceptual model of multiple dimensions of identity. *Journal of College Student Development, 41*(4), 405–414.

Kimmel, M., & Messner, M. (1989). Introduction. In M. S. Kimmel & M. Messner (Eds.), *Men's lives* (pp. 1–14). New York: Macmillan.

Linton, S. (1998). *Claiming disability.* New York: New York University Press.

Linton, S. (2007). *My body politic: A memoir.* Ann Arbor, MI: University of Michigan Press.

Longmore, P. (2003). *Why I burned my book.* Philadelphia: Temple University Press.

Margolis, H., & Shapiro, A. (1987). Countering negative images of disability in classical literature. *The English Journal, 76*(3), 18–22.

Meisner, S., & Longwell, D. (1987). *Sanford Meisner on acting.* New York: Random House.

Peñas, E. (2007). Disability, a movie star. *Media and Disability, 1*, 3–7.

Rapp, E. (2013). *The still point of the turning world: A mother's story.* New York: Penguin.

Saevi, T. (2011). "The Experience of 'Being Seen' for Persons With Disability." *Phenomenology Online.* Max Van Manen. Retrieved from http://www.phenomenologyonline.com/sources/textorium/saevi-tone-the-experience-of-%E2%80%9Cbeing-seen%E2%80%9D-for-persons-with-disability/

Smith, A. (2012). *Hideous progeny: Disability, eugenics, and classic horror cinema.* New York: Columbia University Press.

Stewart, D. L. (2009). Perceptions of multiple identities among Black college students. *Journal of College Student Development, 50*(3), 253–270.

Táboas-Pais, M. I., & Rey-Cao, A. (2012). Disability in physical education textbooks: An analysis of image content. *Adapted Physical Activity Quarterly, 29*, 310–328.

Thorton Dill, B., & Zambrana, R. (2009). *Emerging intersections: Race, class, and gender in theory, policy, and practice.* New Brunswick, NJ: Rutgers University Press.

Timmons, J. (2003). *Movies with characters with disabilities.* Retrieved from http://www.tc.umn.edu/~rbeach/teachingmedia/student_units/module5/disabilities_timmons.pdf

von Krogh, T. (2010). From a medical to a human rights perspective: A case study of efforts to change the portrayal of persons with disabilities on Swedish television. *International Communication Gazette, 72,* 379–394. doi: 10.1177/1748048510362620

Warner, D. F., & Brown, T. H. (2011). Understanding how race/ethnicity and gender define age-trajectories of disability: An intersectionality approach. *Social Science & Medicine, 72,* 1236–1248.

White, J. (2005). Krazy kripples: Using South Park to talk about disability. In L. Ben-Moshe, R. Cory, M. Feldbaum, & K. Sagendorf (Eds.), *Building pedagogical curb cuts: Incorporating disability in the university classroom and curriculum* (pp. 67–76). Syracuse, NY: Graduate School of Syracuse University.

Who is Daryl "Chill" Mitchell? (n.d.). The Daryl Mitchell Foundation. Retrieved from http://dmmfoundation.org/index.php?option=com_content&view=article&id=102&Itemid=92

PART FOUR

INTERSECTIONALITY AND ACADEME

11

INTERLOCKING OPPRESSIONS

An Intersectional Analysis of Diversity in Diversity Action Plans at U.S. Land-Grant Universities

Susan V. Iverson

In my scholarship, critical, feminist, and poststructural theories provide a conceptual lens through which to examine sociocultural problems; to inspire different questions about educational practices, policies, and culture; and to analyze what has come to be taken for granted as "normal," everyday practice (St. Pierre & Pillow, 2000). Such approaches contest and deconstruct binaries (i.e., gender binaries of male/female) and instead provide spaces for multiple voices and various perspectives, "not only or mainly the dominant, but also and especially the marginal" (Alvesson & Sköldberg, 2000, p. 187). Poststructural approaches, in particular, are sensitive to language and the micropolitics of the text—the ways in which text "is always, in some sense, about authority and consequently about power" (Alvesson & Sköldberg, 2000, p. 194). Yet, when writing about identity and difference, challenges emerge in how to capture the complexity of difference and the interconnectedness of identities, and the ways in which interlocking discriminatory systems produce inequalities that structure the relative positions of various groups and individuals. For instance, in an analysis of diversity action plans issued at 20 U.S. land-grant universities, I (Iverson, 2005, 2008, 2012) investigated how discourses generated by these reports framed diversity in higher education. The diversity action plans typically defined *diversity* by listing multiple identity statuses—for example, race-ethnicity, gender, and sexual orientation. The plans further referred to individuals who comprise these demographic categories by using a variety of terms—for example, members of historically disadvantaged groups, targeted groups, underrepresented persons, those who have been historically marginalized and previously excluded, and diverse persons. I adopted this last term, *diverse persons*, in my own writing; however, I recognized the limitations of this signifier. We all occupy multiple dimensions of identity (Jones & McEwen, 2000) and often occupy one or more marginalized or "subordinate" identities (Purdie-Vaughns & Eibach, 2008); thus, referring to individuals with a collective term, such as *diverse persons*, renders the complexities of identity invisible to policymakers, practitioners, and researchers.

In this chapter, I argue that an intersectional approach to research can illuminate how identity differences (i.e., race, gender, sexuality), too often seen as separate spheres of experience, are systems that overlap and interlock to create complex intersections at which two or more dimensions of identity converge and that determine social, economic, and political dynamics of oppression. Following an overview of intersectionality and diversity, I illustrate the potential of an intersectional approach through my analysis of diversity action plans at U.S. land-grant universities.

Intersectionality

Researchers are increasingly aware of the limitations of particular identity dimensions as singular analytic categories (Berger & Guidroz, 2009; Montoya, 1998; Phelan, 1994; Reynolds & Pope, 1991; West & Fenstermaker, 1995). For instance, Colker (1996) critiqued the organizing of people along "bipolar lines," meaning the idea that individuals are either male or female, White or Black, disabled or able-bodied. Through an exploration of identity categorizations under the law, Colker analyzed court cases of people "living the gap"—bisexual, transgendered, multiracial individuals who defy categorization. She defended *categorization* as an organizing tool to be used for political ends, but argued for "improved" categories and mindfulness of identity "hybrids" (Colker, 1996). Fine (1994), in her "unpacking" of the bipolarity of Self-Other, called for an examination of the "hyphen that both separates and merges personal identities" (p. 131). Many feminist researchers, who have critiqued the use of a sole identity category (e.g., gender) for analysis, argue for a schema or metaphor to describe and understand the interaction of different forms of oppression and disadvantage, including race, sexuality, and gender (Andersen & Collins, 2004; Baca Zinn, Hondagneu-Sotolo, & Messner, 2000; Collins, 1998; Fine, 1994; hooks, 1984; McCall, 2005).

Various scholars have grappled with identifying an appropriate metaphor to describe the complexity of and interrelated forces acting on dimensions of identity. For instance, Ivy Ken (2007) has described the complex relations using the interlocking imagery of an octahedron puzzle, and later posited the metaphor of sugar—"the production, use, experience, and digestion of sugar as a way . . . to focus on the structural and individual forces at work in their continual and mutual constitution" (Ken, 2008, p. 154). Baca

Zinn and colleagues (2000) use the metaphor of a prism to explain how "gender is organized and experienced differently when refracted through the prism of sexual, racial/ethnic, social class, physical abilities, age, and national citizenship differences" (p. 1). Others (e.g., Andersen & Collins, 2004) deploy intersectional language to describe the "interlocking, overlapping, mutually reinforcing connections" between different dimensions of identity (Andersen, 2005, p. 444). In sum, the concept of intersectionality seems to have resonated the most with scholars (Ken, 2007).

The term *intersectionality* is credited to Kimberlé Crenshaw (1991), who critiqued the failure of "contemporary feminist and antiracist discourses" (p. 1242) to consider intersectional identities of immigrant women of color. Using male violence against women of color as her focus, Crenshaw (1991) considered how the "experiences of women of color are frequently the product of intersecting patterns of racism and sexism" (p. 1243). Using an analogy of traffic through an intersection, Crenshaw (1989) described how an individual's experience is not unidirectional. A Black woman experiencing discrimination is "harmed because she is in the intersection" (p. 149); she is navigating the "intersection" of Sexism Street with Racism Road; and if a lesbian, she would also intersect with Homophobia Boulevard. She has to "deal not only with one form of oppression but with all forms, those named as road signs, which link together to make a double, a triple, multiple, a many layered blanket of oppression" (Crenshaw, in Yuval-Davis, 2006, p. 198). Thus, using intersectionality as an analytic tool, one can explore "patriarchy within racism or heterosexism in sexism" (Cole, 2009a, p. 566).

Intersectionality as a research paradigm is based on several key assumptions. First, there is the idea that "different dimensions of social life cannot be separated into discrete or pure strands" (Brah & Phoenix, 2004, p. 76). In this way, intersectionality "resists essentializing any categories" such as treating all women as a unified group sharing the same experience (Hankivsky et al., 2010, p. 2). Second, no one dimension of identity is more important than another; as Audre Lorde noted in her poem, "There is no hierarchy of oppression" (in Gordon, 1983). Third, there are nonadditive effects of identifying with more than one social group, meaning "multiple marginalizations . . . are more than the sum of mutually exclusive parts; they create an interlocking prison from which there is little escape" (Hancock, 2007, p. 65). Finally, intersectionality, because it recognizes relational and structural dimensions of inequality, attends to "how power and power relations are maintained and reproduced" (Hankivsky et al., 2010, p. 3).

Crenshaw (1991) indicated that she was not offering a new explanatory theory of identity; rather, she offered this as a "provisional concept" (p. 1244, n9) for researchers to account for multiple categories of identity.

Many researchers (e.g., Bowleg, 2008; Cole, 2009b; Hancock, 2007; Museus & Griffin, 2011) have explored the utility of intersectionality as a methodological tool. For instance, Museus (2011) deployed an intersectional approach in his mixed-methods study of inequities in college access faced by first-generation Asian Americans, a population he describes as "situated at the intersections of multiple identities" (p. 67). Diamond and Butterworth (2008) elucidate the utility of intersectionality with their (re)analysis of data from their 10-year longitudinal study of sexual identity development. An intersectional approach, they observe, enables voice to be given to multiplicity, emphasizes the complexity of subjectivity, and captures the fluidity of identities and social locations. These studies and others (e.g., Greenwood & Christian, 2008; Harper, 2011; Hurtado & Sinha, 2008; Maramba & Museus, 2011) expand and deepen discussion of not only identity and diversity, but also research methods that typically rely on "the socially constructed and commonly used concepts of race [and other identity categories] to label students, investigate student-related problems, analyze student data, and interpret their findings" (Museus & Griffin, 2011, p. 6). Following an overview of the concept of diversity in higher education, I draw upon intersectionality to analyze diversity as framed in university diversity policies.

Diversity in Higher Education

The concept of diversity is not new to the scholarly literature of higher education; in fact, early commentary on "diversity" in higher education reaches back to the mid-nineteenth century (Orfield, 2001). However, its current use has only emerged in the last 25 years. Prior to the 1980s, concerns about access to higher education typically focused on specific identity groups—for example, women, Blacks, Native Americans. If collective references were made (e.g., minorities), they were primarily racial and typically excluded international populations. In the 1980s, assimilationist views, aptly represented in the melting pot metaphor, were eclipsed by the concept of pluralism, meaning that members of different identity groups could maintain their individuality and culture, symbolized by the tossed salad metaphor. Yet, concurrent with a growing emphasis on pluralism and multiculturalism, the "pendulum of civil rights policy" began to swing in the other direction during the Reagan-Bush era; campuses faced more legal challenges to affirmative action by Whites, experienced major cutbacks in financial aid, and increased their use of entrance exams for admission to higher education (Orfield, 2001, p. 3). Also during this time, political shifts from "territorially bound governments to [transnational] companies that can roam in the world" (Barnet & Cavanagh, in Readings, 1996, p. 203) prompted U.S. higher education to re/consider its role in educating citizens for a "diverse democracy" in an increasingly global economy (Readings, 1996).

Globalization blurred the boundaries of national and social identities, and seemingly discrete categories became more fluid and ambiguous (Readings, 1996). Attention in higher education expanded beyond the needs of individual identity groups (and beyond the geographic boundaries of states and the United States) to the delivery of multicultural education for an increasingly diverse student population (Ibarra, 2001; Readings, 1996). Pluralism and globalization—diversity—rose to the top of the agenda in the late 1980s for numerous university presidents and system chancellors who, in addition to identity-specific commissions (i.e., women's commissions), convened Commissions on Pluralism into the 1990s. Still today, senior administrators often assemble university diversity councils to document "issues" related to diversity (e.g., attrition of minority students and faculty, concerns about campus climate, exclusionary policies and practices) and to propose recommendations for change. These special committees codify their findings and recommendations in *diversity action plans*—official university policy documents that formally advance and influence policy for building diverse, inclusive campus communities.

The challenge facing universities today is coordinating the many diversity programs that have sprung up and structuring them in complementary ways (Smith, 2004). Further, consistent with the movement in higher education and government toward accountability, the emphasis in recent years has shifted from the development of diversity programs to evaluation and assessment and demonstrating the efficacy of transformative diversity initiatives (Smith, 2004; Smith & Schonfeld, 2000). Yet, largely unquestioned is how "diversity" has emerged as an all-inclusive category representing (subsuming) numerous identity groups. The diversity action plans typically define *diversity* demographically, with a reference to federally protected groups, and a list of multiple identity statuses—for example, race-ethnicity, gender, sexual orientation, disability, national origin, age, religion. However, the plans do not define these identity signifiers, suggesting that diversity means only difference. Next, I draw upon an intersectional approach to critically interrogate diversity as framed in diversity action plans; however, I first provide a brief overview of the methods.

Methods[1]

The data used in this intersectional analysis are from a study of 21 diversity action plans issued at 20 U.S. land-grant universities from 1999 to 2004. These publicly available policy documents were retrieved via a search of the website for each "1862 land-grant" institution in each of the 50 states; I used the search function on the campus website and the keywords "diversity" and "diversity plan." Of the 50 screened universities, all possessed diversity-related content (e.g., multicultural student affairs, faculty committee on diversity in the curriculum, diversity workshops). My sampling criteria included those campuses that had a diversity committee, charged by a senior administrator (president, provost), that had at least one diversity action plan[2] generated between 1999 and 2004. The search ultimately yielded a sample of 21 reports from 20 institutions.

To examine the discursive framing of diversity in diversity action plans, the following research questions served as a guide:

- What are the predominant images of diversity in diversity action plans?
- How are problems related to diversity represented in diversity action plans?
- How are solutions related to "diversity problems" represented in diversity action plans?
- What discourses are employed to shape these images, problems, and solutions?

The investigation (Iverson, 2005, 2008, 2012) used the method of *policy discourse analysis* to investigate university diversity policies to understand how these documents frame diversity and what reality these diversity action plans produce. A hybrid methodology, policy discourse analysis focuses on written documents; it is a strategy for examining policy discourses and the ways they come together to make particular perspectives more prominent than others (Allan, 2003). The use of assumptive concepts in language may limit a policy's effectiveness and actually reinscribe the very problem the policy seeks to alleviate (Allan, 2003; Bacchi, 1999; Stein, 2004). A university's diversity action plan may construct a world for underrepresented minorities that disqualifies them from participation, even as it strives to include them as full participants.

An Intersectional Analysis: Classifying and Normalizing Difference

Difference often reflects how those who are socially dominant define reality for themselves and others, and this perspective makes invisible the standard against which others are measured. An intersectional analysis can illuminate these comparisons, sometimes framed as "them" and "us," respectively; these comparisons invoke or require conformity to a standard (that which is "normal").

Nearly every diversity action plan in the sample defined *diversity* early in the document by sorting individual identities into component parts: race, gender, sexual orientation, age, and disability, among other identity statuses. Some examples of this classification in diversity action plans include the following:

> Women are still not well represented in some colleges that have been traditionally dominated by men, and a significant disparity in graduation rates persists between undergraduate students of color and white students. (Pennsylvania State University, 2004, p. 8)

> For African American and Latino/Chicano students, the Berkeley freshman class of 1999 was less representative of the California high school graduate population than the freshman class of 1997. . . . The African American work force declined from 17.1% to 14.9%. . . . Latinos and American Indians made only modest gains. (University of California at Berkeley, 2000, p. 5)

> An optional Franco American designation . . . has now been added to the UMS application. Beginning with the Class of 2004, we will have an indication of the number of Franco American students, in addition to the numbers of federally designated minority students, on campus. (University of Maine, 2003)

> The one flaw I can point out about A&M is that people of minorities— whether a religious minority, a racial minority, or a minority based on sexual orientation—are not necessarily encouraged to come here by what they see. Honestly, we are a school of white, heterosexual, Christian students. (Frank, Meltzer, Opochinski, Owens, & Bray, 1996, p. 488, as cited in Texas A&M University, 2002, p. 18)

The classification of individuals and groups reinforces an us-them binary. It also arranges, separates, and ranks diverse groups from each other. The diverse individual who achieves insider status is described in exceptional terms, and is thus ranked as different from other diverse individuals (Iverson, 2010). Some diverse individuals, whom the policies describe as having achieved insider status (e.g., Asian Americans), are also classified as different. Further, the attention to identity statuses occupied by diverse individuals implies that the majority are without race, gender, or sexual orientation, enabling those who occupy privileged identity categories (e.g., straight White males) to remain oblivious to their complicity in the systems and structures that produce and maintain (dis)advantage (Johnson, 2005).

In addition to classifying groups and marking difference, the policies delineate norms, using a "majority" in diversity action plans as the standard for success, progress, and quality. Numerous plans, for instance, use retention and graduation rates for Whites as the benchmark of achievement by which to measure the progress of "minority students." Diverse individuals, "them," are compared with and measured against a standard, "us," that is implicitly defined as normal. This "normalizing judgment" that "hierarchizes qualities, skills and aptitudes" (Foucault, 1977/1995, p. 181) is most prominent in characterizations made visible by discourses of access and disadvantage, which produce the at-risk outsider and enable comparisons to be made between "us" and "them" (Iverson, 2012). The use of training (e.g., professional development) and correction (e.g., programs designed to compensate for deficiencies)—predominant solutions to problems of disadvantage—ensure conformity to a standard "that is at once a field of comparison, a space of differentiation and the principle of a rule to be followed" (Foucault, 1977/1995, p. 182).

Throughout the diversity action plans, diverse individuals (them) are discursively constructed in binary opposition to a majority (us). One report observes: "Diversity is the recognition, value, and acceptance of . . . how we are similar to or different from others" (University of Arizona, 2003). Another document states, "The campus community [must] learn how best to interact with and support LGBT people" (University of Illinois, 2002). The implicit solution to disrupting this us-them divide is through inclusion and integration, while affirming and celebrating difference. The diverse individual must shed "otherness" to conform to the norm, "so that they might all be like one another" (Foucault, 1977/1995, p. 182). This is exemplified by one policy that recommends facilitating "learning opportunities available through interaction with international students," adding that "through these efforts, U.S. students will begin to understand the importance of having international students on campus and why they [U.S. students] should be part of the welcoming process for incoming international students" (Texas A&M University, 2002). However, a seemingly paradoxical conclusion is that while diverse individuals must be the same as the majority to be included and achieve insider status, they must also sustain their difference, an exotic otherness that enables the majority and the institution to benefit from their presence (Iverson, 2010). Next, I explore an alternative way of framing diversity.

Un/Doing the Images of Diversity: Theorizing Intersectionality

Problems arise with the broad use of identity signifiers, such as race-ethnicity, gender, and even my use of diverse individuals as a collective referent. These "identity pools" (Ibarra, 2001, p. 40) collect differences like rain barrels collecting rainwater. The streams, estuaries, and tributaries of identity flow into the larger body: diversity. While the use of a single referent (diversity) for multiple identity groups is convenient for oral and written communication, problems emerge from its use. Diversity signifies that which is not; diversity becomes the one, true difference (Phelan, 1994). Here I discuss how diversity action plans, through their use of discrete identity categories, situate individuals as one-dimensional and further reinforce an outsider/insider binary.

As introduced previously, the diversity action plans purport to define *diversity* by delineating the numerous identity categories to which the term refers: race, gender, sexual orientation, disability, and so on. This reification of categories fails to contest the fixity of diversity or give attention to how groups are constituted (Bacchi, 1999; Ken, 2007); it fails to examine the mechanisms of language that position us as different and produce our identities and experiences (Baez, 2000; Ken, 2008). Further, the reports fail to challenge homogeneity in the framing of identity.

I view identity as socially constructed. Identity is "not simply an individual characteristic or trait but something that is accomplished in interaction with others" (West & Fenstermaker, 1995, p. 23). Further, individuals are held accountable to "prevailing normative conceptions" of identity through institutions (e.g., education) that contribute to "the reproduction of social structure" (West & Fenstermaker, 1995, p. 21). These "prevailing normative conceptions" of identity that are predominant in diversity action plans are narrow and limiting. They fail to illuminate "the plurality in each of us" (Lugones, 1987, p. 3), the "interlocking categories of experience" (Andersen, 1999, p. 18), and the multidimensionality of identity (Reynolds & Pope, 1991). Further, the collective use of the term *diversity* to represent a "laundry list of 'differences' that need to be managed" (Hu-DeHart, 2000, p. 42) renders invisible how systems of domination (e.g., sexism, racism, classism) converge to construct unique experiences of oppression for individuals at the intersection of identity. Finally, clumping all diverse individuals into one category (diversity) maintains a focus on individual needs, rather than on systems, and likely (consequently) yields greater bureaucratization: better management of diversity.

A change in language, then, is necessary as are "gestures to that in each of us which is irreducible to categories" (Phelan, 1994, p. 11). Rather than more identity categories or an "additive" approach to identity (Bowleg, 2008), we need an intersectional approach. Such an approach recognizes the individual's social and historical position and understands the interlocking oppression and hierarchies individuals experience as members of multiple groups (Andersen, 2005; Phelan, 1994). From this perspective, difference is not an individual experience to be remedied, but, instead, involves a structural analysis of particular differences (Ken, 2008; Phelan, 1994). Identity is not a static and essential trait, but must be understood as multiple, constructed, dispersed, and shifting (Hobbel & Chapman, 2009); this conceptualization is consistent with discourse theory's contention that subjectivity and subject positions are "neither unified or fixed," but viewed as a "site of disunity and conflict" (Weedon, 1997, p. 21).

I recognize that my proposition to disrupt identity categories, deploy an intersectional approach, and potentially achieve what Phelan calls "specificity" is abstract, and an articulation of clear alternatives is desirable. However, neat and certain directions for practice oversimplify the complexity of a disruptive proposition that involves "tearing down this categorical infrastructure" (Yanow, 2003, p. 207). What I can do is suggest that, from growing awareness, scholars may interrogate the construction, existence, and use of identity categories. As Yanow (2003) notes, the use of identity labels creates "artificial boundaries" that may serve more as a "proxy for economic and behavioral problems . . . [and] continue to perpetuate inequality" (p. 211). Rather than accepting identity labels or tags without question, or giving a cursory nod to their limitations, scholars can commit time and energy to determine who and what are served by these classifications and categorizations (Harper, 2011).

Born out of this curiosity, scholars (and practitioners) can ask new questions about identity and difference. Yanow (2003) suggests a set of questions that turns attention to "geographic specificity" (p. 211), and other questions that push educators, scholars, and policymakers to interrogate the existing use of categories as a "system for managing difference" (p. 228). Maramba and Museus (2011) argue that researchers should ask different questions of their data through disaggregation "to generate the most accurate picture of the individuals, groups, processes, organizations, or phenomena they are studying" (p. 99). Further, some scholars (Cole, 2009a; Hobbel & Chapman, 2009) suggest narrative methodologies and (counter)storytelling to couple with an intersectional analysis, for narratives are open to different readings and interpretations and can illuminate the "cracks" in everyday lived experiences (Cole, 2009a, p. 572).

Re/Thinking Communities: Disrupting Inclusion

In addition to the potential for an intersectional approach to shift thinking and interpretations of "diversity," I posit that such an analysis complicates dominant notions of community. The diversity action plans emphasize "common ground," "shared values," "integration," and "inclusion." A commitment to an "inclusive campus community" pervades the policies. Through training and education—to "build a more tolerant community"—and facilitation of intergroup dialogue—to "develop close ties and an increased comfort level" (University of Maryland, 2000)—and many other efforts to create a "diversity-friendly environment," diversity action plans proclaim to do better by including (adding) others to "a dominant cultural frame of reference" (Tierney, 1992, p. 50). Exemplified by one plan's commitment to move "from diversity to community" (University of Maryland, 2000), the emphasis on integration and inclusion throughout the policy documents erases individuality and homogenizes difference. Further, the aspiration to integrate "diverse groups" into one community will likely fall short, since, as Clifford (1994) notes, groups that maintain important cultural allegiances and practical connections cannot be assimilated. Thus, I argue, scholars, educators, and policymakers must resist and contest dominant conceptions of communities as inclusive, welcoming, and friendly environments. I propose re/thinking about community in higher education.

An intersectional approach has utility for re/thinking about the "communities of difference" (Tierney, 1993) that are "fashionable" today (Platt, 2002). Problematic are the additive (Andersen, 2005; Bowleg, 2008) or multiplicative (Hancock, 2007) formulas for describing diversity and identity that reduce dimensions of identity into explanatory constructs (Ken, 2007) or view communities as fixed spaces into which "others" are added (Phelan, 1994). An intersectional approach contests the dominant conception in the diversity action plans of communities as welcoming, affirming, and inclusive (Iverson, 2012). The conceptualization of a community of inclusion "pays attention to that old adage that we must learn to live together" and emphasizes democratic ideals of equality constructed through "that politics of polarity" (Rutherford, 1990, p. 26)—sameness/difference, majority/minority, insider/outsider—that unwittingly reinforce practices that support exclusion and inequity. An intersectional approach disrupts the center/margin dichotomy that sustains the insider/outsider binary in dominant views of community.

Thus, an intersectional analysis invites re/thinking about diversity, difference, and community as a process; it opens "free spaces" (Phelan, 1994, p. 88) in which people may turn their attention to acts of relationships, rather than pregiven forms (and formulas) of identities, to share individual histories and expectations and connect multiple communities. It is from this "liminal" space (Heilbrun, 1999)—the borders and the intersection of our individual and collective identities—that dialogue and storytelling may occur—not the tolerant, sensitive, affirming, homogenizing dialogue described as important for communities of inclusion, but coming together for the purpose of understanding each other and our stories, to share counter-stories, to make visible the "traffic patterns" (Hobbel & Chapman, 2009).

For diversity councils, this demands a move away "from the certainty and arrogance of knowing to the uncertainty and humbleness of not knowing" (Huber, Murphy, & Clandinin, 2003, p. 353). Specifically, for the work of policy-making groups, individuals can engage in rich dialogue to explore the ambiguities, contradictions, and tensions inherent in identities and communities. This involves negotiation of understanding and attention to silences and will likely generate "moments of discomfort, feelings experienced as we hover on the threshold between certainty and uncertainty, knowing and unknowing as we step out of familiar and into unfamiliar story lines" (Huber et al., 2003, p. 359). One diversity policy in my sample hinted at this in its description of the diversity council's formation: "We were not only able to learn from each other, but perhaps even more important, we were never permitted to delude ourselves that we instinctively knew what others, situated differently, had experienced on our campus" (University of Maryland, 2000). This may provide opportunities to stay with the story of our experience and demands that we suspend the rush to knowing the other. Further, this posits that we "acknowledge our own participation in the meanings of the differences we assign to others" and challenge the communal space that is consequently generated (Yanow, 2003, p. 228).

While I intimate steps that diversity councils and other educational practitioners can employ, disrupting communities of inclusion and conceptualizing liminal communities are, in many ways, only imagined, theoretical notions about community. However, viewing communities through this conceptual lens invites scholars and practitioners to re/consider and interrogate the dominant ideology that undergirds prevailing conceptions of community and produces fixed, essential cultural realities with which "others" must conform. This theoretical proposition is challenging to enact, for few higher education practitioners and policymakers, especially senior administrators, charged with (or delivering the charge of) increasing diversity, will find comfort in liminality. Yet, it is the potential and possibilities of liminal communities that provide spaces for the multiplicity of individuals' lives and are the places of tension and uncertainty from which we may negotiate new ways of living together.

Conclusion

In this chapter, I have illuminated the utility of an intersectional approach to complicate, disrupt, and reconstruct notions of diversity as framed in diversity action plans. First, this approach reveals how different dimensions of identity cannot be separated into discrete categories. Diversity, like identity, is not fixed or static. It is not a category into which "'others' are now being added"; rather, it is always already a process into which "its 'others' are now modifying" (Ellsworth, 1999, p. 35). Further, through attention to singular identity dimensions, the diversity action plans erase those with intersecting identities. As Purdie-Vaughns and Eibach (2008) observe, "Because people with multiple subordinate identities (e.g., African American women) do not usually fit the prototypes of their respective subordinate groups (e.g., African Americans, women), they will experience . . . intersectional invisibility" (p. 378).

Crenshaw (1991) argues that we must "summon the courage to challenge groups that are after all, in one sense, 'home' to us" and wonders how we might "dare to speak" and "call attention to how the identity of 'the group' has been centered on the intersectional identities of a few" (p. 1299). By example, diversity, in university policies, is typically described through references to demographic categories; however, these broad, "lumpy" categories classify racial identity on a "highly aggregated, continental level" that erases the cultural variation within each category (Yanow, 2003, p. 187). For example, Asian American encompasses persons having origins in "the Far East, Southeast Asia, or the Indian subcontinent . . . including, for example, Cambodia, China, India, . . . and Pakistan" (Yanow, 2003, p. 39). Yet, as we recognize the limits of language and contest "identity-as-category" (Hobbel & Chapman, 2009), we open "an unspecified number of possibilities" for categorizing race-ethnicity (Yanow, 2003).

Second, an intersectional approach invites researchers to read data in different ways and ask other questions. Matsuda (1990), in her efforts to "understand the interconnection of all forms of subordination," deployed a method she called "ask the other question."

> When I see something that looks racist, I ask, "Where is the patriarchy in this?" When I see something that looks sexist, I ask, "Where is the heterosexism in this?" When I see something that looks homophobic, I ask, "Where are the class interests in this?" (p. 1187)

However, we are not bound by only "the other question" and are cautioned not to pursue (only) binaries. Nash (2008) notes that Matsuda's questioning illuminates

> the ways in which patriarchy, racism, and heterosexism buttress each other, but ignores the ways in which subjects might be both victimized by patriarchy and privileged by race (it also ignores the ways in which subjects might take pleasure in some of the trappings of patriarchal power). (p. 12)

Thus, an intersectional approach invites questions, such as, What has produced this problem? What has given rise to this issue and leads us to view it in this way? and What contributes to the maintenance of this problem and may (unintentionally) undermine efforts to solve the problem (i.e., of chilly climate for LGBT students, attrition of underrepresented minorities, and slow-to-no advancement of women, among other concerns)? It demands that scholars and practitioners "ground their work historically in the production of the dynamics of oppression" (Ken, 2008, p. 171).

Finally, with its attention to power, intersectional theorizing can expand questions of difference to investigate who benefits and who loses from existing structures (Singer, 1990). Social dimensions of identity through this lens are visible within and among people and groups and as represented in organizations and institutions (Yuval-Davis, 2006). The use of intersectionality as a tool to analyze the production of power can trace "how certain people seem to get positioned as not only different but also troublesome and, in some instances, marginalized" (Staunæs, 2003, p. 101). Bowleg (2008) argues that it is "virtually impossible to escape" reductive categories and "the additive assumption implicit in the questions we use" (p. 322). Further, one cannot "substitute [one oppression] for the others—as if oppressions were equivalent or the same" (Andersen, 2005, p. 446). "Ironically," Andersen and Collins (2004) wrote, "this form of recognizing differences can erase the workings of power" (p. 5).

Policy, a site of power (Foucault, 1977/1995), is a place where the construction of identity and difference are produced, and where agendas can be furthered. I believe policy holds potential as a tool for change. As Gilmore (2002) argues, "The problem is not the 'master's tools' as objects, but the effective control of those 'tools'" (p. 22, n3). Thus, rather than abandon the "tool" of policy, we must consider the power of language (discourse) carried in these policy documents and endeavor to rewrite them. McCall's use of "anticategorical complexity" affords conceptual possibilities as it "rejects" or destabilizes categories of identity (i.e., gender, race, sexuality). Further, intersectionality deconstructs normalization and classification, evident in policies.

Shields (2008) asserts that intersectionality is "an urgent issue" for researchers committed to promoting positive social change. Others argue that the methodological implications of this theoretical perspective are underexplored, posing challenges for "translating intersectionality theory into methodological practice" (Hancock, 2007; Hankivsky et al., 2010, p. 3; Nash, 2008). Yet, not to deploy an intersectionality approach until research designs and methods are developed or until scholars have certainty as to how, when, and where intersectionality theory can be applied would have "significant human costs" (Hankivsky et al., 2010, p. 3). Researchers and practitioners are invited to embrace "intersectionality's conceptual imperfections" (Davis, 2008, p. 77) in analyses of how multiple social identities shape the lives of marginalized individuals and groups.

Notes

1. For more detail about methods, see Iverson (2005, 2008, 2012).

2. While committees and reports have various titles, I was seeking plans that addressed diversity in the broadest sense. This parameter excluded reports generated by other committees charged by senior administrators—for example, commissions on women, disabilities, race.

References

Allan, E. J. (2003). Constructing women's status: Policy discourses of university women's commission policy reports. *Harvard Educational Review, 73*(1), 44–72.

Alvesson, M., & Sköldberg, K. (2000). *Reflexive methodology: New vistas for qualitative research*. Thousand Oaks, CA: Sage.

Andersen, M. L. (1999). The fiction of "diversity without oppression": Race, ethnicity, identity, and power. In R. H. Tai & M. L. Kenyatta (Eds.), *Critical ethnicity: Countering the waves of identity politics* (pp. 5–20). New York: Rowman & Littlefield.

Andersen, M. L. (2005). Thinking about women: A quarter century's view. *Gender & Society, 19*(4), 437–455.

Andersen, M. L., & Collins, P. H. (Eds.). (2004). *Race, class, and gender: An anthology* (5th ed.). Belmont, CA: Wadsworth.

Baca Zinn, M., Hondagneu-Sotolo, P., & Messner, M. (Eds.). (2000). *Gender through the prism of difference* (2nd ed.). Boston: Allyn & Bacon.

Bacchi, C. L. (1999). *Women, policy and politics: The construction of policy problems*. Thousand Oaks, CA: Sage.

Baez, B. (2000). Diversity and its contradictions: How support for diversity in higher education can undermine social justice. *Academe, 86*(5), 43–47.

Berger, M. T., & Guidroz, K. (Eds.). (2009). *The intersectional approach: Transforming the academy through race, class, and gender*. Chapel Hill, NC: University of North Carolina Press.

Bowleg, L. (2008). When Black + lesbian + woman ≠ Black lesbian woman: The methodological challenges of qualitative and quantitative intersectionality research. *Sex Roles, 59*(5–6), 312–325.

Brah, A., & Phoenix, A. (2004). Ain't I a woman? Revisiting intersectionality. *Journal of International Women's Studies, 5*(3), 75–86.

Clifford, J. (1994). Diasporas. *Cultural Anthropology, 9*(3), 302–338.

Cole, E. R. (2009a). Gender, narratives and intersectionality: Can personal experience approaches to research contribute to "undoing gender"? *International Review of Education, 55*(5–6), 561–578.

Cole, E. R. (2009b). Intersectionality and research in psychology. *American Psychologist, 64*(3), 170–180.

Colker, R. (1996). *Hybrid: Bisexuals, multiracials, and other misfits under American law.* New York: New York University Press.

Collins, P. H. (1998). It's all in the family: Intersections of gender, race, and nation. *Hypatia, 13*(3), 62–82.

Crenshaw, K. (1989). Demarginalizing the intersection of race and sex: A Black feminist critique of antidiscrimination, feminist theory, and antiracist politics. *The University of Chicago Legal Forum 1989,* 139–167.

Crenshaw, K. (1991). Mapping the margins: Intersectionality, identity politics, and violence against women of color. *Stanford Law Review, 43*(6), 1241–1299.

Davis, K. (2008). Intersectionality as buzzword: A sociology of science perspective on what makes a feminist theory successful. *Feminist Theory, 9*(1), 67–85. doi: 10.1177/1464700108086364

Diamond, L. M., & Butterworth, M. (2008). Questioning gender and sexual identity: Dynamic links over time. *Sex Roles, 59*(5–6), 365–376.

Ellsworth, E. (1999). Multiculture in the making. In C. A. Grant (Ed.), *Multicultural research: A reflective engagement with race, class, gender and sexual orientation* (pp. 24–36). London, UK: Falmer Press.

Fine, M. (1994). Working the hyphens: Reinventing self and other in qualitative research. In N. Denzin & Y. Lincoln (Eds.), *Handbook of qualitative research* (pp. 130–155). Thousand Oaks, CA: Sage.

Foucault, M. (1977/1995). *Discipline and punish: The birth of the prison* (2nd ed.) (A. Sheridan, Trans.). New York: Vintage Books.

Frank, R., Meltzer, T., Opochinski, R., Owens, E., & Bray, T. (2002) The best colleges. In *The Princeton Review 2002 Edition.* Natick, MA: Princeton Review Publishing.

Gilmore, R. W. (2002). Fatal couplings of power and difference: Notes on racism and geography. *The Professional Geographer, 54*(1), 15–24.

Gordon, L. (Ed.). (1983). *Homophobia and education: How to deal with name calling.* New York: Council on Interracial Books for Children.

Greenwood, R. M., & Christian, A. (2008). What happens when we unpack the invisible knapsack? Intersectional political consciousness and inter-group appraisals. *Sex Roles, 59*(5–6), 404–417.

Hancock, A. (2007). When multiplication doesn't equal quick addition: Examining intersectionality as a research paradigm. *Perspectives on Politics, 5*(1), 63–79.

Hankivsky, O., Reid, C., Cormier, R., Varcoe, C., Clark, N., Benoit, C., & Brotman, S. (2010). Exploring the promises of intersectionality for advancing women's health research. *International Journal for Equity in Health, 9*(5), 1–15.

Harper, C. E. (2011). Identity, intersectionality, and mixed-methods approaches. *New Directions for Institutional Research, 151,* 103–115. doi:10.1002/ir.402

Heilbrun, C. (1999). *Women's lives: A view from the threshold.* Toronto, ON: University of Toronto Press.

Hobbel, N., & Chapman, T. A. (2009). Beyond the sole category of race: Using a CRT intersectional framework to map identity politics. *Journal of Curriculum Theorizing, 25*(2), 76–89.

hooks, b. (1984). *Feminist theory: From margin to center.* Boston: South End Press.

Huber, J., Murphy, M. S., & Clandinin, D. J. (2003). Creating communities of cultural imagination: Negotiating a curriculum of diversity. *Curriculum Inquiry, 33*(4), 343–362.

Hu-DeHart, E. (2000). The diversity project: Institutionalizing multiculturalism or managing differences? *Academe, 86*(5), 39–42.

Hurtado, A., & Sinha, M. (2008). More than men: Latino feminist masculinities and intersectionality. *Sex Roles, 59*(5–6), 337–349.

Ibarra, R. A. (2001). *Beyond affirmative action: Reframing the context of higher education.* Madison, WI: University of Wisconsin Press.

Iverson, S. V. (2005). *A policy discourse analysis of U.S. land-grant university diversity action plans* (Unpublished doctoral dissertation). University of Maine, Orono.

Iverson, S. V. (2008). Capitalizing on change: The discursive framing of diversity in U.S. land-grant universities. *Equity and Excellence in Education, 41*(2), 1–18.

Iverson, S. V. (2010). Producing diversity: A policy discourse analysis of diversity action plans. In E. Allan, S. Iverson, & R. Ropers-Huilman (Eds.), *Reconstructing policy analysis in higher education: Feminist poststructural perspectives* (pp. 193–213). New York: Routledge.

Iverson, S. V. (2012). Constructing outsiders: The discursive framing of access in university diversity policies. *The Review of Higher Education, 35*(2), 149–177.

Johnson, A. (2005). *Privilege, power and difference* (2nd ed.). Boston: McGraw-Hill.

Jones, S. R., & McEwen, M. K. (2000). A conceptual model of multiple dimensions of identity. *Journal of College Student Development, 41*(4), 405–414.

Ken, I. (2007). Race-class-gender theory: An image(ry) problem. *Gender Issues, 24*(2), 1–20.

Ken, I. (2008). Beyond the intersection: A new culinary metaphor for race-class-gender studies. *Sociological Theory, 26*(2), 152–172.

Lugones, M. (1987). Playfulness, "world"-travelling, and loving perception. *Hypatia, 2*(2), 3–19.

Maramba, D. C., & Museus, S. D. (2011). The utility of using mixed-methods and intersectionality approaches in conducting research on Filipino American students' experiences with the campus climate and on sense of belonging. *New Directions for Institutional Research, 151,* 93–101. doi:10.1002/ir.401

Matsuda, M. (1990). Beside my sister, facing the enemy: Legal theory out of coalition. *Stanford Law Review, 43,* 1183–1192.

McCall, L. (2005). The complexity of intersectionality. *Signs: Journal of Women in Culture and Society, 30*(3), 1771–1800.

Montoya, M. E. (1998). Border/ed identities: Narrative and the social construction of legal and personal identities. In A. Sarat, M. Constable, D. Engel, V. Hans,

& S. Lawrence (Eds.), *Crossing boundaries: Traditions and transformations in law and society research* (pp. 129–159). Evanston, IL: Northwestern University Press.

Museus, S. D. (2011). An introductory mixed-methods intersectionality analysis of college access and equity: An examination of first-generation Asian Americans and Pacific Islanders. *New Directions for Institutional Research, 151,* 63–75. doi:10.1002/ir.399

Museus, S. D., & Griffin, K. A. (2011). Mapping the margins in higher education: On the promise of intersectionality frameworks in research and discourse. *New Directions for Institutional Research, 151,* 5–13. doi:10.1002/ir.395

Nash, J. C. (2008). Re-thinking intersectionality. *Feminist Review, 89,* 1–15.

North Carolina State University. (1999). *Diversity initiative.* Raleigh, NC: North Carolina State University Office of the Provost.

Ohio State University. (2000). *Diversity action plan.* Columbus, OH: Ohio State University Office of University Relations.

Oklahoma State University. (2004). *Institutional diversity strategic plan.* Stillwater, OK: Oklahoma State University Office of Institutional Diversity.

Orfield, G. (Ed.). (2001). *Diversity challenged: Evidence of the impact of affirmative action.* Cambridge, MA: Harvard Education Publishing Group.

Pennsylvania State University. (2004). *Framework to foster diversity, 2004–09.* University Park, PA: Pennsylvania State University Office of the Vice Provost for Educational Equity.

Phelan, S. (1994). *Getting specific: Postmodern lesbian politics.* Minneapolis, MN: University of Minnesota Press.

Platt, T. (2002). Desegregating multiculturalism: Problems in the theory and pedagogy of diversity education. *Social Justice, 29*(4), 41–46.

Purdie-Vaughns, V., & Eibach, R. P. (2008). Intersectional invisibility: The distinctive advantages and disadvantages of multiple subordinate-group identities. *Sex Roles, 59*(5–6), 377–391.

Readings, B. (1996). *The university in ruins.* Cambridge, MA: Harvard University Press.

Reynolds, A. L., & Pope, R. L. (1991). The complexities of diversity: Exploring multiple oppressions. *Journal of Counseling and Development, 70,* 174–180.

Rutherford, J. (Ed.). (1990). *Identity: Community, culture, difference.* London: Lawrence & Wishart.

Shields, S. A. (2008). Gender: An intersectionality perspective. *Sex Roles, 59*(5–6): 301–311.

Singer, J. W. (1990). Property and coercion in federal Indian law: The conflict between critical and complacent pragmatism. *Southern California Law Review, 63,* 1821–1841.

Smith, D. G. (2004). *The campus diversity initiative: Current status, anticipating the future.* Washington, DC: Association of American Colleges and Universities. Retrieved from http://www.irvine.org/assets/pdf/pubs/education/CDIStatusand-Future2004.pdf

Smith, D. G., & Schonfeld, N. B. (2000). The benefits of diversity: What the research tells us. *About Campus, 5*(5), 16–23.

Staunæs, D. (2003). Where have all the subjects gone? Bringing together the concepts of intersectionality and subjectification. *NORA, The Nordic Journal of Feminist and Gender Research, 11*(2), 101–110.

Stein, S. J. (2004). *The culture of education policy.* New York: Teachers College Press.

St. Pierre, E. A., & Pillow, W. S. (Eds.). (2000). *Working the ruins: Feminist poststructural theory and methods in education.* New York: Routledge.

Texas A&M University. (2002). *Report by the President's Ad Hoc Committee on Diversity and Globalization.* College Station, TX: Texas A&M University Office of the President.

Tierney, W. G. (1992). *Official encouragement, institutional discouragement: Minorities in academe—the Native American experience.* Norwood, NJ: Ablex Publishing.

Tierney, W. G. (1993). *Building communities of difference: Higher education in the twenty-first century.* Westport, CT: Bergin & Garvey.

University of Arizona. (2003). *Diversity action plan, 2003–04.* Tucson, AZ: University of Arizona Office of the President.

University of Arkansas. (2002). *Diversity plan, 2002–05.* Fayetteville, AR: University of Arkansas Office of the Provost and Vice Chancellor for Academic Affairs.

University of California at Berkeley. (2000). *Report of the Chancellor's Advisory Committee on Diversity.* Berkeley, CA: University of California Office of the Vice Chancellor for Diversity and Equity.

University of Connecticut. (2002). *The report of the Diversity Action Committee to the University of Connecticut Board of Trustees.* Storrs, CT: University of Connecticut Office of the Vice Provost for Multicultural and International Affairs.

University of Georgia. (2002). *Institutional diversity strategic plan, 2002–05.* Athens, GA: University of Georgia Office of Institutional Diversity.

University of Idaho. (2004). *Diversity and human rights at the University of Idaho: Comprehensive plan for action and accountability.* Moscow, ID: University of Idaho Office of the President.

University of Illinois. (2002). *Final report of the Diversity Initiatives Planning Committee.* Urbana, IL: University of Illinois Office of the Provost.

University of Maine. (1999). *Diversity action plan.* Orono, ME: University of Maine Office of Equal Opportunity and Diversity.

University of Maine. (2003). *Diversity action plan, 2003–05.* Orono, ME: University of Maine Office of Equal Opportunity and Diversity.

University of Maryland. (2000). *Report and recommendations of the President's Diversity Panel.* College Park, MD: University of Maryland Office of the President.

University of Nebraska. (1999). *Comprehensive diversity plan.* Lincoln, NE: University of Nebraska–Lincoln Office of the Chancellor.

University of Nevada. (2002). *Strategic plan for diversity initiatives.* Reno, NV: University of Nevada Office of the President.

University of Wisconsin. (1999). *Plan 2008: The campus diversity plan.* Madison, WI: University of Wisconsin Office of the Provost.

Virginia Tech University. (2000). *Diversity strategic plan, 2000–05.* Blacksburg, VA: Virginia Polytechnic Institute and State University Office of Multicultural Affairs.

Weedon, C. (1997). *Feminist practice and poststructuralist theory* (2nd ed.). Oxford, UK: Blackwell.

West, C., & Fenstermaker, S. (1995). Doing difference. *Gender & Society, 9*(1), 8–37.

Yanow, D. (2003). *Constructing "race" and "ethnicity" in America: Category-making in public policy and administration.* Armonk, NY: M.E. Sharpe.

Yuval-Davis, N. (2006). Intersectionality and feminist politics. *European Journal of Women's Studies, 13*(3), 193–209.

12

IN THE "WEB" OF THE TWENTY-FIRST-CENTURY AMERICAN ACADEMY

Reflections of a Black and an Indian Female Faculty

Namita N. Manohar and Pauline E. Bullen

Van Maanen (1997) observes that reflection is a part of developing "pedagogical tact," the ability to "see what goes on . . . to understand [the other's experience], to sense the pedagogical significance of a situation, to know how and what to do, and to actually do something right" (p. 44). Reflexive practitioners like us, therefore, need to see ourselves as subject rather than object, and in the process question and confront our own and our students' life experiences. In this reflective chapter, we undertake an intersectional analysis of our experiences as Black and Asian Indian (hereafter Indian) women faculty at our public university. We focus on how our race/ethnicity, class, nationality, gender, and other categories of difference constitute our bodies as (in)appropriate members of our academic community, determine our access to professional mobility, and structure the privileges and disadvantages we face. Following a brief review of the scholarship on minority women faculty in the American academy, we speak to our experiences of being simultaneously called in(to) and called out of the academy, efforts to stay on track for tenure, and the friendships and collaborations that allow us to nevertheless survive and thrive in the academy.

The "Web" of the Academy: Minority Women Faculty in the American Academy

There is a growing emphasis in the twenty-first-century American academy on "education that is multicultural and globalized . . . , [that values] different perspectival epistemologies and interdisciplinary methodologies" (Lim, 2006, p. xiv), resulting in the appreciating employment of faculty from more diverse backgrounds, such that minority faculty constituted 17% of full-time faculty positions in 2007 (Boyd, Cintrón, & Alexander-Snow, 2010). At the same time, however, these positions continue to be dominated by men, so even as women now represent 44% of faculty in higher education, there is limited racial diversity among them (Lee, 2002). Minority women faculty accounted for 16,733 (20.98%) of the 79,767 (47.3%) of women at the assistant professor (tenure-earning) rank in fall 2007 (Boyd et al., 2010), with the bulk at junior ranks, with much lower retention and promotion rates compared to their white[1] counterparts (see Hune, 2006; Li & Beckett, 2006; Turner, 2002).

Intersectionality theory argues that race and gender (and other axes of difference such as class, sexuality, nationality, religion, etc.) are not merely individual identities but structures of domination that constitute "mutually constructing systems of oppression" (Collins, 2000, pp. 227–228) to position groups differently within society and social institutions (e.g., the academy). Power emerges from these intersecting oppressions, and human agency fashions viable lives within these structures (Collins, 2000; Zinn & Dill, 1996). For minority women faculty, being positioned as having the "wrong" race, class, and/or gender directly affects their equitable participation and progression in academe. They are treated as multicultural ambassadors for the university—expected to perform substantial minority/gender-related service (Boyd et al., 2010; Kuykendell, Johnson, Nelson Laird, Ingram & Niskodé, 2006; Thompson, 2008) and to teach the multicultural/diversity courses that nonminority faculty are able to avoid (Lin, Kubota, Motha, Wang, & Wong, 2006; Marbley, Wong, Santos-Hatchet, Pratt, & Jaddo, 2011). This results in heavier workloads than those of their white, male counterparts. With very little institutional support, and in institutional climates that construct minority peoples as "inferior" vis-à-vis the Euroamerican, masculine standard, valorized as the norm, minority women faculty often experience alternatively hostile or isolating work environments. They are stigmatized for being "affirmative action hires" (Boyd et al., 2010, p. 10); perceived as less qualified and competent than white faculty (Hune, 2006); rendered invisible and outside of support and mentoring networks by gendered-racialized stereotypes (Knight, 2007; Li & Beckett, 2006; Thompson, 2008); and discredited as serious scholars because of the perception that their feminist/culturally informed/diversity-based research is "illegitimate," or "unscientific," compared to the hegemony of rationalist research paradigms within the academy (Hune, 2006; Johnsrud & Sadao, 1998; Mayuzumi, 2008; Turner, 2003). Promotion and tenure is thus a problematic process for minority female faculty, threatening their "meritocratic" progress in the academy.

Much of this theorizing has focused on comparing minority with majority experiences, notably those of African American women. Also, the scant literature on Asian faculty homogenizes this group by focusing largely on East Asians, making invisible those from South Asia. In this chapter, then, we attempt to extend this scholarship by (a) drawing attention to Indian women, and (b) comparing two minority groups on the same campus, whose members, despite other demographic differences (age, family status), are similarly positioned as tenure-earning, junior faculty at our public university, thereby enabling us to think "relationally" about our experiences (Museus & Griffin, 2011). Namita functions in an institutionally recognized department (sociology), and while under a "social science umbrella," Pauline's department (SEEK [Search for Education, Excellence and Knowledge]) has no clear disciplinary affiliation, but was established to facilitate the academic success of historically underrepresented students and appears to be marginal on campus due to its "minority" status.

Called In(to) and Called Out: Outsiders Within Our Academic Positions

It is not happenstance that both of us find ourselves teaching at a public, liberal arts college located in a northeastern immigrant gateway metropolis. Our university not only has a reputation for attracting experienced practitioners to its faculty, but also prides itself on being one of the more diverse higher education institutions, advertising an international and inclusive student and faculty body. Despite this, both of us confront an insider/outsider dilemma in our school: simultaneously "called in(to) and called out," depending on the interplay of our intersectional locations and the situation at hand, resulting in the paradoxical experience of support and critique from our colleagues.

Namita's Story: Becoming an Immigrant, Indian Woman of Color in America

Well-meaning colleagues have often assured me of the "ease" of my job prospects in that by "fill[ing] multiple categories as a woman, person of color and an immigrant," I am "the kind of candidate schools want these days." Far from being a neat checking of boxes, my identity in America is, rather, a product of my engagement with American society. I came to the United States in 2004 to pursue graduate studies in sociology and gender studies. Coupled with my racialization as a South Asian—imageries of being hardworking, docile, and the model minority (see Hune, 2006)—and the gradual resolution of where my home is, I have come to self-identify as an immigrant, Indian woman in the United States both personally and professionally. In turn, I accepted my position because it offered me the opportunity to work with a diverse and immigrant study body, and on women's and gender issues, both aligned with my personal politics.

Straddling Tenure-Earning and Director Positions

I have held the tenure-earning position of assistant professor in sociology (hereafter also referred to as department), *and* director of the Women's and Gender Studies program (hereafter also referred to as program). Part of the incongruity of this appointment involved being housed in sociology, which is responsible for my evaluation and tenure, and essentially "loaned out" to the program for a negotiable period (three years), an arrangement that is personally advantageous in that I am not held hostage to disparate progress criteria, as is often the case in joint appointments (Boyd et al., 2010). Nonetheless, it makes sociology keen to protect its own, and my, interests by ensuring that I am tenured. To this effect, I have learned that as an immigrant, Indian woman, I am the ideal candidate for the position because of expectations that I am capable of hard work, of being strong enough to lead and "stand up to" senior faculty without alienating them, and of maintaining the delicate balance between department/program—all of which subtly allude to cultural imagery of Asians as the model minority (Asher, 2006; Hune, 2006). Needless to say, the institution also benefits from my pay grade, which is lower than that of a tenured faculty member, and from procuring my essentially "free" labor (my only reward as director was limited teaching release time) for heavy service work no one else was willing to perform.

Almost from the first, I struggled with the lack of a clear job description. While graduate school in many ways had prepared me for being an assistant professor, I was conscious that as junior faculty and a relative newcomer to both academia and work worlds in the United States,[2] I lacked the extensive service experience that is the only preparation for heading a program. I was hesitant to ask for mentoring in program management because I did not want to appear incompetent or to undermine my position as director, which could risk reinforcing cultural biases that South Asian women are better technicians and researchers rather than leaders (Asher, 2006). In addition, as a newcomer to our school, I was excluded from institutional networks (Boyd et al., 2010; Turner, 2002), premised on long-term personal and professional affiliations, that dispense information and opportunities. Together, these created huge impediments as I grappled with learning the program and strategizing its growth, all the while maintaining an active scholarship record and the contractually agreed-upon teaching load.

My first year, in retrospect, was both isolating and frenetic as I attempted to situate myself, build networks, establish my credentials, and run the program successfully. Integral to this was managing the dissonance between being the authority in one context (program) and a subordinate in the other (department). This necessitated continuous and often stressful mental transitions to be recognized as director while consciously avoiding alienating senior faculty who might have a role in determining my tenure (Pyke, 2011). In this, my age, (lack of) seniority, and ethnicity colluded to disenfranchise me, most evinced in the discrediting of my position as program director. This was especially apparent in my early interactions with administrative bodies, where in a particularly memorable encounter, being a new, junior faculty member attempting program change, I was viewed with blatant skepticism. Despite days of back-and-forth e-mails with the chair of the school's curriculum committee—an older, senior, white man—to finalize new cross-listed sociology/women's and gender studies courses, at the monthly college-wide faculty governance meeting, he approached my chair in sociology, sitting beside me, to exclaim, "There's someone new in women's studies who's making all sorts of curricular changes with sociology. I don't know what she's doing. Do you agree with them?" His tone conveyed his deep annoyance, and his words alluded to my incompetence in curricular matters. Further, his demand that sociology endorse my work as legitimate discredited my authority to make curricular revisions in the program.

Additionally, women's studies was not always a safe space (see Li & Beckett, 2006) for me. In fact, the mentoring I was receiving from senior, feminist, women faculty appeared to give some the license to subtly and/or overtly undermine me. In one instance, an older, senior, fellow South Asian woman accused me of assigning "sweatshop work"[3] to a student assistant in the program. She sent me an e-mail explaining: "Namita, I just made an executive decision which was not my business. [Student] was sitting here doing your work. It looked like unfair work—like a sweatshop—so I had her stop." While I admit accepting correction for assigning a mindless task to the student, I was livid at its characterization. More important was this woman's ease in overriding my authority as director to make an "executive decision" beyond her jurisdiction without consulting with me because she believed that as the more senior faculty member she knew best. I realized that considering our shared ethnicity she had asserted her privilege as an older, senior South Asian woman to infantilize me rather than treat me as a colleague worthy of a professional conversation. This situation left me helpless to assert my position—I was new, junior, as yet lacking strong support networks, and needing to establish my competence. I chose, whether correctly or not, not to confront her, but to reassert my authority in my own way: apologizing to the office staffer caught in the melee and thereafter very determinedly owning and defending the authority inherent to the position.

Both incidents, however, were reminders that although I had been vetted and welcomed as the director and charged with an enormous task, I am marginal—my legitimacy as director continuously questioned and subjected to endorsement by senior faculty, and my leadership skills discredited to position me as an outsider. In turn, I have had to prove my competence to both the largely white, male-dominated administration and fellow minority women—by quickly learning organizational procedures, making few mistakes, developing the confidence to tackle challenges head-on, and being decisive. At this writing, after having served for three years, I decided against renewing my term as director—a move supported by all of my colleagues who worry about my ability to achieve tenure, as I outline later.

Pauline's Story: From the North to the South, How Far Have I Come?

I am a Canadian citizen born in Guyana, and I identify as African Caribbean—a Black woman. Black is given an initial capital "to stress a common heritage, a cultural and personal identity proudly claimed by Black people who assert their African origins" (Bhaggiyadatta & Brand, 1986, p. iii), and I assert mine. I am an educator and have been working as a teacher and counselor for over 25 years. I am also a writer and a researcher primarily on the subject of race and sociopolitical thought in Canada and the United States. Much of my writing has shared the voices of Black youth and teaching and administrative personnel who spoke about the impact of racism on their academic and professional lives (see Bullen, 2000, pp. 80–81). I have been engaged in the struggle against forced silence and enforced invisibility that allows me only "a shadowless participation in the dominant cultural body" (Morrison, 1993, pp. 9–10). I approach my work from a radical Black feminist stance—a stance that has empowered me to confront authority, face intolerance, and do work that disrupts the status quo. It is a "counter-stance" of a Black, working-class woman, developed as a result of having confronted and coped with a life of need arising from poor socioeconomic circumstances in an exploitative capitalist system, and of repeatedly struggling against the expectation that I must continually justify my very existence in classist, racist, and patriarchal societies. I am the last of nine children, and to date I am also the first and only member of my family to have earned master's and doctorate degrees. As a result of my quest for an education and my eventual entrance through doors that some no doubt would have preferred remain shut, I learned that "outside-within locations can foster new angles of vision on oppression" (Collins, 2000, p. 11) and assist in the ability to question and respond to the contradictions within and between "dominant" ideologies.

I began my career with the Toronto Board of Education as a half-time social science teacher in an inner-city school from where I would begin to write and publish about racism in the public education system. It had taken me over two years following my bachelor's degree in education to get a foothold in a system that was described as an "enigma" for its contradiction of school board representatives who claimed there were few minority teachers available for hire, and the minority teachers' complaints about their inability to get any positions other than that of "supply" or "adjunct" (Lewis, 1992, p. 22). Upon nearing completion of my doctorate in equity studies in education, and formed by these experiences, I accepted my current position as a tenure-earning professor in a department expressly created to redress the racism in the United States that has historically denied minority groups access to education.

Assistant Professor in Search for Education, Excellence, and Knowledge (SEEK)

My position in the SEEK Department involved, according to my initial appointment, "teaching freshman orientation courses, conducting individual and group counseling, [and] researching topics related to the diverse population of students" in addition to committee and community outreach work. I believe that the chair responsible for my hire felt that she had accomplished a coup for our school by recruiting a senior Black educator with 20 years of teaching, counseling, and inclusive equity leadership at the salary of lecturer until such time as I completed the doctorate. Moreover, I believe that my hire might have been viewed as a proactive response to calls for a "revitalization" of supposed affirmative action programs to reverse the "slow and halting" pace of building an inclusive faculty body at our school[4] (Abbas & Hogness, 2009).

I regarded my position as an opportunity to do the work that I was passionate about at a "higher" level, in a city I found to be culturally rich and vibrant. I could teach and advise students who, like me, were primarily the first in their families to enter academe. I imagined that despite the extensive literature on the sabotaging of minority scholars in academia, I would be granted the space to write, research, and collaborate, supported by an institution that professes to encourage such efforts. However, my location as marginal or illegitimate was made quickly apparent. I quickly realized I was not being regarded as a "real scholar," evidenced in the following comment of a female professor at a prestigious American private research institution, who was then one of my best friends:

> I know real scholars at [your institution] and could not understand why you elected to be in the basement—you don't make a decent wage, the people you work with are not your intellectual equals, you don't even have the basics of a faculty member in one of the worst HBCUs, which tend to be the poorest schools in the academy in this country. The reality is that the longer you stay there, the harder it will be to move.

I felt that her statement was a reflection of a deep-seated prejudice toward not only access programs but also individuals minoritized and racialized as outsiders and viewed as lacking potential and power. Nevertheless, it was an attitude that was reinforced by the toxic (blatant race and religious discrimination and bullying) environment and then hostile (exclusionary, reactive rather than proactive) leadership practices that I encountered. As the number of tenured and tenure-track PhDs in my department decreased, leaving only me and one other Black female tenure-track scholar, the toxicity increased with the desire to change the status of the department to that of a program, with, I believe, the ultimate aim of replacing the two remaining PhDs (institutional "misfits") with lower-credentialed individuals at much lower salary levels.[5] In this, it appears to me to be an ideological resistance to the fact that a group of students perceived as "inferior" with a few professors labeled as "misfits" should benefit from the status given to departments within the academy, some of which include greater representation and governance and relatively competitive remuneration associated with full-time, tenure-track/tenured positions. These actions reflect "high turnover quotients," institutional "revolving door" hiring practices (Abbas & Hogness, 2009), and hypocritical claims to access and equity. A formal complaint with our school union about persistent discrimination and the hostile and untenable working environment that threatened the quality of my productivity (Johnson-Bailey & Cervero, 2008; Johnsrud & Sado, 1998; Knight, 2007; Marbley et al., 2011) resulted in considerable backlash from individuals who, it appears, were given license to misuse their voting powers to influence reappointment and promotion decisions. Several of these individuals (credentialed with master's degrees) had voiced their feelings that their years of "suffering" at the institution trumped my PhD, and that I expected special treatment in requesting office space that afforded some privacy for the counseling and research work expected of me. It was these individuals who were assigned to observe my classroom teaching and given voice at promotion and tenure meetings.

As a "minority" scholar, I fully understand that I am expected to function well, even excel, in the "crooked room" of my institution. I am expected to believe that the room is straight, and that I am the one who is "off-kilter" because I am supposedly not one of the "acceptable others" or "good white folks who play by the rules, and never avoid their responsibilities" (Harris-Perry, 2011, p. 44). I have come to realize that I am expected to internalize the crooked room and to see myself as someone who is undeserving, a cheat—not necessarily the "welfare cheat" that many Black women are deemed to be, but definitely of that group willing to abuse the system. I am not expected to be someone who continues "to act beyond the cultural confines" (Johnson-Bailey & Cervero, 2008, p. 312) imposed by the fears of others.

Tenure: Staying on Track

As junior faculty, for both of us, tenure and promotion are the holy grail of the academy. Our ability to become tenured is determined not merely by our own labor, but, more important, by institutional criteria for such labor. We have observed that as minority women faculty, we receive unrealistic and often contradictory directives about tenure (see Beckett & Zhang, 2006; Boyd et al., 2010; Hune, 2006), which are subjectively interpreted and judged by different departments for individual faculty. Thus, even while accounting for our disciplinary differences, which generate their own scholarly demands, each of us has been given different milestones to achieve tenure at the same school. We have also become aware of the unwritten norm that despite our identity as a liberal arts college, reflected in a very heavy teaching load, research drives the promotion and tenure process, with teaching being secondary and service not being sufficiently rewarded (Thompson, 2008). In our cases, this is particularly unsustainable, because our appointments, by design, are service- and teaching-heavy (in that order), creating challenges in different ways and demanding strategizing to stay on track for tenure.

Namita's Experience: "Your Work (Director) Should Not Infringe On Your Writing!"

From the outset, I was told that there would be no change in teaching and research demands for my tenuring in consideration of my very heavy administrative responsibilities. The latter involves intellectual and emotional labor that, coupled with the stresses inherent to my incongruous position and my attentiveness to teaching, makes writing a very slow and sometimes marginal activity that I have to consciously make an effort to undertake. Additionally, throughout my time as director, well-intentioned senior colleagues have continually admonished me with, "You are doing a great job, BUT . . . focus on the writing, writing, writing. Don't let this infringe on your writing!" In so doing, I argue that they not only reinforce the salience of research in the tenure process, but also in many ways devalue my service (Lin et al., 2006; Turner, 2002) by the implication that the quality and efficacy of my service would count just as much in my tenuring as if I had been ineffective at it—as long as I am getting the requisite amount published. In many ways, then, undeclared was the expectation that I would not (and frankly should not!) achieve much in the program as a junior faculty member, resulting in my colleagues' sheer surprise at the programmatic growth I oversaw. Therefore, as a minority woman faculty member, I faced what Turner (2002) calls a "double whammy": "little opportunity and support for work that is valued and rewarded [i.e., research], and too much demand for work that is not rewarded [i.e., service]" (p. 82).

My resultant apprehension about my retention at our school was the impetus for me to strategize *how* to stay on track for tenure. To this effect, I very consciously used my annual evaluations—the most salient professional record in tenure decisions at our school—to create detailed written documentation about the breadth of my service, listing not only my accomplishments in the program, but also the labor involved. In this way, I am able to reconstitute my administrative service work as not merely "volunteer work," as perceived by the institution, but, rather, as skilled labor vital to the functioning of the university and to my activism (Pyke, 2011; Turner, 2003). Additionally, just like other faculty with heavy service loads, I worked to create "writing time," especially following a difficult second-year annual review during which I was reprimanded for my inadequate publishing, even as my teaching and service were evaluated highly. As a result, I had to develop realistic publishing goals such as deciding against a book (especially valorized in tenure decisions) in favor of a series of peer-reviewed articles, the writing of which I am better able to fit into my schedule. I also developed a workable writing schedule around my teaching/service responsibilities such that I set up organizational practices to routinize the daily work of the program to free up some blocks of writing time interspersed between numerous meetings. Far from being simple, these efforts were incredibly stressful and exacted an emotional toll that negatively affected my personal life.

The efficacy of these individual strategies is critically buttressed by the academic mentoring of my department chair, a senior, white male who became a key ally in navigating my appointment (Rong & Preissle, 2006). As a proactive advocate for junior faculty in the department, he has been instrumental in creating support mechanisms to mitigate the potential unsustainability of my appointment to afford me a smoother path to tenure. This involved facilitating a slightly reduced teaching load, including my preference to teach the same courses while serving as director, thereby allowing me to displace some teaching preparation time onto writing; encouraging my successful applications for writing fellowships; shielding me from additional service work in the department; and endorsing my previously mentioned publishing goals as a workable strategy in my unusual position. In addition, considering our departmental emphases on critical sociology that interrogate inequality and power, my culturally oriented research, like that of my colleagues', is valued rather than discredited, as is often the case with minority women faculty (see Lin et al., 2006; Thompson, 2008; Turner, 2003), not merely as contributing to the knowledge, but also as enhancing the departments' character. Thus, for instance, I am encouraged to frame my scholarship within feminist theories and methodologies, and target my work to specialty (gender, immigration, families, etc.), interdisciplinary (Asian/South Asian/women's and gender studies) journals rather than more traditional, quantitatively oriented sociology journals, which aligns with my politics of making my research accessible. As a result, I have been formally assured at the time of this writing that I am well placed to earn tenure in the next two years.

Pauline's Story: "Your Writing Should Not Infringe on Your Work (Academic Counseling)!"

Differential, discriminatory, and racist treatment are key factors in the inability of Black women to climb the ranks of academe despite the fact that as a group we "have shown much success in doctoral attainment and overall representation in the professorate relative to other faculty of color" (Edwards, Beverly, & Alexander-Snow, 2011, p. 15). In fact, their inability to break the glass ceiling stems from "questions about their place within the academy, cultural affronts to their personhoods, alienation, severe marginalization, pressure to prove continually that they deserve positions, lack of mentoring, devaluing professional interests, rare access to resources for research that lead to greater prestige . . . and job mobility . . . and their invisibility" (p. 16), all of which are emblematic of my case.

My biggest challenge has been that despite the heavy service intrinsic to my appointment, research is the primary criterion in determining my tenure. Unlike other faculty on campus, including Namita, who have some freedom in determining their schedules, for four years, I was confined to a nine-to-five, four-day-a-week schedule with a half-hour lunch, during which I taught and counseled. This then evolved into a required five-day office presence (atypical at our school), with a newly instituted electronic system to track the number of students who are called in or drop by for advisement. Coupled with scheduling changes that have curtailed the summer hiatus integral to research and professional development, these factors posed significant challenges to my staying on track for tenure. I have had no support from my chairs in trying to build my students' understanding that I am expected to publish, and do additional service, and have received no support in developing my scholarship. In fact, supposed suggestions for "improvement" have often been made in a blatantly condescending and threatening manner as I have been told that I must curtail the collaboration with the women's studies program that allowed me to teach courses in the summer and plan various workshops for faculty, staff, and students.

The departmental climate I encounter is detrimental to my ability to stay on track for tenure. Unlike Namita, I have never been mentored in any meaningful, informed, and consistent manner about publishing goals for tenure. Rather, my work has been routinely discredited. In one instance, noting I had chapters in two books (publications acceptable in Namita's case), it was observed that this might be considered writings done with and approved by "friends." There appeared to be an assumption that the writers were all like me, Black individuals—supposed affirmative action hires trying to "get over" in the system and, thus, insufficient. Such experiences have brought to my mind descriptions of nonwhites as "savage," only "partially capable of being brought into society as subordinate citizens, by white men" (Mills, 1997, p. 13) and white women who have earned their "rightful" place by white men. I have had to "strategize" to produce a body of work within the limitations of my position. Taken together, my challenges in staying on track in the absence of institutional support mechanisms are perhaps best illustrated by the denial of a petition for (early) promotion that I filed two years ago. The petition was filed with my chair's approval, based largely on her claims that I had met the criteria for early promotion (before filing a grievance against her), but resulted in three subsequent nonreappointment letters that eventually led to my leaving the institution despite a list of publications that rival those of a number of tenured individuals, a signed contract for a book that has been accepted for publication by an "A" press, numerous research presentations at national and international conferences, service on college-wide committees, and community affiliations that have helped to advance the leadership and scholarship potential (in teacher education, math, and science) of the students I counseled and taught.

Being Activist Scholars and Reflective Practitioners

hooks (1990) observes that "marginality [is] much more than a site of deprivation; . . . it is also the site of radical possibility . . . for the production of counter-hegemonic discourse that is not just found in worlds but in habits of being and the way one lives" (p. 149). As minority women faculty, for both of us, this radical possibility is realized by our love of and commitment to teaching and mentoring, from which we derive great satisfaction and sense of accomplishment. We construct our teaching and mentoring as "sites of resistance" to forces of "othering," wherein we are able to translate our structural marginalization into an (academic and lived) expertise in interrogating the "dynamic, context specific intersections of race-class-gender-culture-language-history-and-geography" (Asher, 2006, p. 170) to become activist scholars and reflective practitioners with the goal of empowering students.

Namita's Critical, Feminist Pedagogy

Over my time at our school, I have routinely taught undergraduate courses on sociology of gender and of work. My teaching draws upon critical feminist pedagogical insights centered on three principles: deconstructing the social world as organized around intersecting axes of domination; uncovering the simultaneous relational experience of power, privilege, and disadvantage; and the salience of individual agency (as determined by different social locations) in the reproduction and transformation of social reality (Asher, 2006; Collins, 2000; hooks, 1990). As a feminist teacher, then, my focus is to afford my students the tools to theorize—that is, to look at the social world from the "margins within," and thereby examine their taken-for-granted assumptions about themselves and of society—and in this way enable them to critically engage with the world.

In my curriculum development, then, not only are issues of difference, power, and inequality central, but also issues that students are grappling with in their communities, thereby making coursework relevant to their lives. In particular, I am attentive to the nexus of immigration-ethnicity-class that defines our students' experiences, designing coursework to discuss their ethnic/immigrant communities of origin, their daily experiences of racializing and gendering (police profiling, job barriers, partnering commodification/objectification), and those on constructing possible alternatives and transformations.

Because I am an immigrant, Indian woman, a key component of my teaching activism is to deconstruct and correct hegemonic cultural imagery about South Asians of "the" community being a "model minority" (Asher, 2006; Lim, 2006), and of the culture being, as some of my students query, "More patriarchal and backward than Western societies, yes?" In my corrective teaching, I focus attention on the underlying colonial and neoliberal historicopolitical contexts that generate these discourses; the cultural essentialism inherent to them; and how they continue to retain white, male, and Western hegemony.

While my students value my critical feminist pedagogy (as reflected in my teaching evaluations), it also leaves me open to critique, challenge, and discrediting (see Beckett & Zhang, 2006; Boyd et al., 2010; Turner, 2003) from both white and minority women and men students. The first either interpret my pedagogy as an attack on whiteness (and masculinity) as the "norm"; and the other, who, on the presumption of our shared marginality, are expecting me to give them an easy ride. In both cases, these students draw upon the social construction of Asian/South Asian women as "passive and permissive" (Mayuzumi, 2008, p. 176) educators, so they become belligerent, confrontational, and aggressive with me. In one incident, when in sheer anger over what he phrased "the excessive amount of work in your course," a white, male student ambushed me in the corridor after class. In the presence of other students, he got into my personal space, loudly demanding to know whether or not I had any sense of the work I had assigned, that he had run my syllabus past a friend of his who had deemed it to be graduate (rather than undergraduate) level, and whether or not I had any previous teaching experience. I was angered at his attempts to strip me of my legitimacy as an instructor (see Boyd et al., 2010; Thompson, 2008) based on the presumption that because I was a young-looking, South Asian woman, my course would be sociology-lite, that he could slide by without being prepared for class or properly completing assignments, and his disbelief that that was not the case. This incident placed me in the position of not only reasserting my professional authority, but also having a difficult conversation with him, drawing attention to his disrespectfulness and to whether he would have similarly approached a white male professor, in addition to needing to reinforce the value of the assignments and course material to the class at the next meeting. Every such incident is personally painful and demoralizing—reminding me that I continue to be an "outsider" in the academy, identified first in racial terms rather than in professional terms (i.e., a competent and qualified professor). Moreover, it demands my response: to work extra hard to establish my credibility (e.g., I make it clear that students should address me as Dr. or Professor while in the course, thereby establishing and reinforcing my credentials; I remind them of the tested efficacy of assignment methodology etc.); and to create, retain, and maintain control of the classroom environment (Knight, 2007; Lin et al., 2006).

Despite this, my critical teaching, areas of scholarly expertise, and overt self-identification also afford me opportunities to mentor women and/or minority students. In addition to academic mentoring, I have had deeply emotional conversations with students about the ongoing struggles in their personal lives while they are completing their academics; struggles with overt racism and sexism and, in one case, a student's mental health emergency. In all these cases, students—both men and women—have approached me by citing their valuing of my courses and classroom interactions, coupled with their sense that I could understand them because of our shared status along several intersecting differences. My mentoring not only focuses on their academic growth, but also on holistic life development—building and bolstering their self-esteem and pointing them toward concrete resources and persons to help realize their future plans (Boyd et al., 2010). While deeply personally fulfilling, needless to say, serving as "mentor, mother, counselor, in addition to educator" (Turner, 2002, p. 83) takes an emotional toll on me and, in addition to my personal struggles to establish my place in the academy, has the potential to sap time away from the publishing I need to gain tenure.

Pauline's Work as a Teacher-Counselor-Pedagogue of the Oppressed

Although I have taught the introductory course in the women's and gender studies program, most of my teaching at our school has been connected to a counseling workshop course designed to orient incoming SEEK students to college life and encourage completion of a set of "benchmarks"—academic, college life, and personal—itemized for the students in pamphlet form. In this, I emphasize the salience of advancing students' thinking to a higher level through multiple perspectives. I thus created an inclusive program of study that encourages the development of critical consciousness, combined with social awareness and decisiveness, and promotes questioning, especially important among students who are first-generation college attendees and/or are from groups historically excluded from institutions of higher learning. Thus, although Namita articulated it differently, my ultimate goal is similar: to assist my students in developing abilities not only to "read the word, but also read the world."

My teaching, therefore, focuses on facilitating the academic success of my students, especially considering that, due to their disadvantaged social location, many lack the dominant cultural capital for success, are not aware of or underestimate the skills needed to succeed in a primarily research and writing academic environment, and are challenged in visualizing long-term goals in the face of their struggles to meet immediate short-term needs (food; clothing; safe, clean housing). Accordingly, my pedagogy involves critical inquiry techniques in reading and answering questions on reflection pieces, such as "The First in Your Family to Go to College" and "Limbo," which explore the anxieties attached to being the first to leave one's home, one's neighborhood, and one's friends, and the possible feeling of being caught between two worlds—working class and middle class—each with its own cultural demands and values. My classroom lessons include exercises that assist students in developing a strong approach to learning, such as one examining their "typical schedules" versus a "proposed schedule"; completing a poem with four stanzas that begin with "I Am From"; and an activity entitled "Bloom of the Whole Self," which allows them to share different aspects of their identities in class. They also complete work that allows them to report on a library or museum exhibit, attend career or "major selection" workshops, or even requires them to host individuals willing to facilitate an information session tailored specifically to their needs.

Although some of my students complain about their workload and/or are culturally unaccustomed to mutual sharing of the self in building professional and personal friendships, they all participate and work diligently at all of the tasks assigned. Many find the work fun and the exposure to campus and community presentations and cultural events enlightening. Even more importantly, echoing Namita's claims, through their coursework, my students gain new perspectives on their lives as they develop a critical, sociological perspective to describe their race, culture, ethnicity, gender, class, and more. Unlike Namita, and perhaps because their disadvantaged social location precludes any sense of entitlement on their part, I have not had students challenge or discredit my teaching skills. Neither have I experienced in the classroom any race/gender power struggles. I have had to work hard at making the course one that is not simply based on rote learning of college "facts." As a result, my students have appeared to value being introduced to new ways of thinking, evaluating, and expressing themselves as global citizens. In my counseling relationships, I strive to make my students feel that I take a personal interest in helping them to become academically successful. I build trust and confidence in following my advice by carefully listening to various student concerns; showing a willingness to research for answers to any questions they may have for which I do not have an immediate response; highlighting student strengths; and offering my own services as mentor, tutor, editor, and coach (Kuykendall et al., 2006; Marbley et al., 2011; Turner, 2003). In my helping relationships, I take the front line as an advocate and as a buffer, not a "savior"; am hypervigilant, not hyperarrogant, in naming institutional barriers to students' success; respect the fact that students are the experts of their own experiences; and teach and counsel that making mistakes is part of becoming an effective learner.

Surviving and Thriving as Minority Faculty

In contradiction to Edwards et al. (2011), we are not "leery" of labeling ourselves as professionally successful. In addition to our academic accomplishments, teaching accolades, and scholarly work, we are proud of the support systems that we have developed over time within the institution and within the larger local and global communities. Developing these support networks has become especially salient given our institutional marginalization, in that the inequities we face are not random acts of vindictiveness that can be attributed to "ignorance" but symptoms of an inequitable system in which those with striking, still numerous privileges seek to retain them through their actions—even while appearing to be liberal and progressive about the politics of inequality (Memmi, 2000). For those of us who do not enjoy such an elevated status, our strategies for surviving and thriving take several creative forms as we attempt to collaborate and forge friendships with like-minded individuals from varied departments and cultural and ethnic groups, including white individuals who recognize white privilege and are committed to "unpacking their invisible knapsacks" (McIntosh, 1988, pp. 1–2) both personally and professionally. We build our friendship networks through shared experiences and based on culture and interests in and outside of the academy, and in this way carve out "safe" spaces where we are able to express our frustrations and are celebrated instead of "tolerated."

For Namita, these friendships support the cohering of her professional identity as a critical, feminist teacher and scholar whose work deconstructs the gendered racialization of Indians in the United States. Drawing upon the collegiality and diversity of her department, she has developed professional networks with sociologists there, who afford her peer mentoring, which enables her to consolidate her position in the academy. In her unique position as director, she reached out to integrate diverse faculty into the functioning of the program, thereby building professional and personal friendships across campus. While this does not automatically mitigate her marginalization, these friendships have provided opportunities for collaborative work— an important example of which is writing this chapter—and for integrating her into bureaucracies integral to running the program successfully. These friendships have become an advocacy group for both the program and her accomplishments on campus (Rong & Preissle, 2006). Through national academic conferences, she has maintained a network of South Asian faculty from across the United States who have become an important source of "ethnic mentoring" in strategizing how to thrive as South Asian faculty. At similar events, she has also forged cross-cultural connections (see Rong & Preissle, 2006) with scholars doing like research, resulting in coauthored projects. Perhaps most important to her are the kinship ties—both chosen and biological—outside the academy, which include family, close friends in America and India, her volunteer work in her neighborhood, her interest groups in the city, and her spiritual community, that provide her unconditional love, a place to "just be," and the strong determination and strength to stay true to herself despite the odds.

Similarly, Pauline has used several proactive strategies to continue the writing that she started as a secondary school teacher in Canada and develop her research on race and sociopolitical thought in Canada and the United States into areas that include gender issues and feminist theories, which are evinced in her most recent publication. She has maintained relationships with Black professional and business organizations in Toronto and continues to write articles on the education of Black children for local newspapers. She has collaborated with professors from one of our sister colleges to build literacy-training programs for teachers in Jamaica and other parts of the Caribbean. She also accepted the invitation to become an affiliate faculty in the Women's and Gender Studies program, collaborating to organize programs, speakers, and artists to visit campus. Following a meeting with the vice-chancellor of the Women's University in Africa, Zimbabwe, she networked to secure an invitation to be a visiting scholar there, and she has done all of this despite the oppressive and hostile conditions in her department. Thus, she continues to grow as a "strong-willed" resister of oppression (Collins, 2000, p. 98).

For both of us, then, our varied relationships sustain us by bringing joy, laughter, the sharing of resources, spiritual guidance, and the provision of strategies crucial to navigating the academy. In so doing, we continue to learn to trust our own cognitive powers; think against the grain; and develop our own concepts, insights, modes of explanation, and overarching theories that "oppose the epistemic hegemony of conceptual frameworks designed in part to thwart and suppress the exploration of such matters" (Mills, 1997, p. 119) that we share in this chapter and, thereby, reclaim our personhood.

Conclusion

It has been painful to relive and then write about our experiences in the academy. However, this work has been a necessary part of alleviating the psychological effects of the violence of the multiple intersectional marginalities that permeate the culture of our everyday lives. It is also our way of speaking truth to power. In writing this chapter, we also contribute to the body of work by providing our unique, comparative, intersectional analyses of higher education, which, as Museus and Griffin (2011) argue, are still sorely lacking. When viewed from an intersectional perspective, our relational experiences as Black and Indian women in the twenty-first-century American academy provide two main insights.

First, far from being a neutral workplace, the academy is a "highly contested and politicized space" (Hune, 2006, p. 16), tightly enmeshed with and organized by the structures of domination of the larger American society, a society that differentially locates groups within its opportunity structure, resulting in their different accesses to opportunities, privileges, and disadvantages (Zinn & Dill, 1996). For us, this is manifested in the interplay of our intersecting differences (race/ethnicity, class, gender, nationality) with an institutional system designed in many ways to reconstitute the disparities of the larger society, such that, as Black and Indian women, we are positioned at the margins of our school. Despite the institution's apparent prizing of diversity, the absence of institutional mechanisms to support the unique needs of minority faculty has resulted in our shared experience of multiple marginalities at our school, such as the heavy service loads built into our appointments; vulnerability to critique, bullying, and discrediting by our colleagues; risky tenuring; and exclusion from mentoring networks. We argue that far from being personal obstacles to be overcome by "hardworking" faculty as part of their meritocratic rise in the academy, these marginalities are structural impediments—structurally rather than culturally or individually produced—that have the potential to slow our successful professional progression at our school. For us, then, the academy continues to function as an ivory tower—an instrument to reproduce white, male entitlement (Mayuzumi, 2008).

Second, even in the face of these marginalities, strategies that give us voice and enable us to thrive at our school illustrate the dynamicity of our agency in creating viable lives within constraining structures, an area not sufficiently theorized in the research on minority women faculty in the academy. Our agency involves using our intersectional social location as a springboard to construct our teaching as a site of our activism and our research as a means of critiquing and analyzing not only our racialization, but also the politics of inequality. We are agents who exercise agency as we work to build community and a sense of belonging, not just "visibility" within our institution. We acknowledge not only the conflict-ridden nature of our lives, but also the richness of our lives as scholars who persist in doing what we do best.

Notes

1. In not capitalizing "white" in this chapter, we draw upon Bhaggiyadatta and Brand's (1986) argument that "white" without an initial capital letter reflects the expressed belief that whites in our society do not claim their color as a distinctive heritage, and as the so-called dominant race it is not necessary. For most white people in Canada (and the United States) their heritage lies in being "Canadian" ("American"), Italian, English, Polish, and so on (p. iii).

2. At the time of my appointment, I had been in the United States for five years, and, apart from working as a teaching assistant in graduate school, this was my first engagement with work in the United States. My previous "service" experience included leading nonprofit projects in India and chairing a graduate student social science conference in school.

3. I had been laboriously correcting the misspelled e-mail address on my business cards without asking for or expecting any assistance. Our student assistant, who at the time had no program work to complete and was aware of my busy schedule for the day, volunteered to complete a few more cards for me, so I would have enough for an upcoming conference. I agreed after ascertaining her willingness and agreement to prioritize any emergent program work.

4. In fact, the percentage of assistant professors hired who are Black had fallen between 1997 and 2007 from 16.5% to 13.8% (Abbas & Hogness, 2009).

5. In fact, a tenure-track PhD who had been hired and placed in the position of supervising a tutoring center specifically for SEEK students was replaced by a former student, who had been assisting in the center and had recently completed a bachelor's degree.

References

Abbas, S., & Hogness, P. A. (2009). A look at race and employment at CUNY: Slow and halting change. *Clarion Newsletter*, 6–7.

Asher, N. (2006). Brown in black and white: On being a South Asian woman academic. In G. Li & G. H. Beckett (Eds.), *"Strangers" of the academy: Asian women scholars in higher education* (pp. 163–177). Sterling, VA: Stylus.

Beckett, G. H., & Zhang, J. (2006). Moderation, modesty, creativity and criticalness: A Chinese American medical professor speaks. In G. Li & G. H. Beckett (Eds.), *"Strangers" of the academy: Asian women scholars in higher education* (pp. 233–248). Sterling, VA: Stylus.

Bhaggiyadatta, K. S., & Brand, D. (1986). *Rivers have sources, trees have roots: Speaking of racism.* Toronto, ON: Cross Cultural Communications Center.

Boyd, T., Cintrón, R., & Alexander-Snow, M. (2010). The experience of being a junior minority female faculty member. *The Forum on Public Policy*, 2, 1–23.

Bullen P. E. (2000). *A multifaceted study of institutional racism in the Toronto public educational system: Perspectives of a Black educator* (Unpublished MEd thesis). Brock University, St. Catherine's, Ontario.

Collins, P. H. (2000). *Black feminist thought: Knowledge, consciousness, and the politics of empowerment* (2nd ed.). New York: Routledge.

Edwards, N. N., Beverly, M. G., & Alexander-Snow, M. (2011). Troubling success: Interviews with Black female faculty. *Florida Journal of Educational Administration & Policy*, 5(1), 14–27.

Harris-Perry, M. V. (2011). *Sister citizen: Shame, stereotypes and Black women in America.* New Haven, CT: Yale University Press.

hooks, b. (1990). *Yearning: Race, gender, and cultural politics.* Boston: South End.

Hune, S. (2006). Asian Pacific American women and men in higher education: The contested spaces of their participation, persistence, and challenges as students, faculty, and administrators. In G. Li & G. H. Beckett (Eds.), *"Strangers" of the academy: Asian women scholars in higher education* (pp. 15–36). Sterling, VA: Stylus.

Johnson-Bailey, J., & Cervero, R. (2008). Differing worlds and divergent paths: Academic careers defined by race and gender. *Harvard Educational Review*, 78(2), 311–332.

Johnsrud, L. K., & Sadao, K. C. (1998). The common experience of "otherness": Ethnic and racial minority faculty. *The Review of Higher Education*, 21(4), 315–342.

Knight, W. B. (2007). Entangled social realities: Race, class, and gender a triple threat to the academic achievement of Black females. *Visual Culture & Gender*, 2, 22–38.

Kuykendall, J. A., Johnson, S. D., Nelson Laird T. F., Ingram, T. N., & Niskodé, A. S. (2006, November). *Finding time: An examination of faculty of color workload and non-instructional activities by rank.* Paper presented at the Association for the Study of Higher Education, Anaheim, CA.

Lee, S. M. (2002). Do Asian American faculty face a glass ceiling in higher education? *American Educational Research Journal*, 39(3), 695–724.

Lewis, S. (1992, June 9). *Stephen Lewis report on race relations in Ontario: Letter to the Premiere.* Toronto, ON: Government of Ontario.

Li, G., & Beckett, G. H. (2006). Reconstructing culture and identity in the academy: Asian female scholars theorizing their experiences. In G. Li & G. H. Beckett (Eds.), *"Strangers" of the academy: Asian women scholars in higher education* (pp. 1–11). Sterling, VA: Stylus.

Lim, S. G. (2006). Identities, Asian, female, scholar: Critiques and celebrations of the North American Academy. In G. Li & G. H. Beckett (Eds.), *"Strangers" of the academy: Asian women scholars in higher education* (pp. xiii–xviii). Sterling, VA: Stylus.

Lin, A., Kubota, R., Motha S., Wang, W., & Wong, S. (2006). Theorizing experiences of Asian women faculty in second- and foreign-language teacher education. In G. Li & G. H. Beckett (Eds.), *"Strangers" of the academy: Asian women scholars in higher education* (pp. 56–82). Sterling, VA: Stylus.

Marbley, A. F., Wong, A., Santos-Hatchet, S. L., Pratt, C., & Jaddo, L. (2011). Women faculty of color: Voices, gender, and the expression of our multiple identities. *Advancing Women's Leadership, 31,* 166–174.

Mayuzumi, K. (2008). "In-between" Asia and the West: Asian women faculty in the transnational context. *Race Ethnicity and Education, 11*(2), 167–182.

McIntosh, P. (1988). *White privilege and male privilege: A personal account of coming to see correspondences through work in women's studies.* Working Paper #189. Wellesley, MA: Wellesley College Center for Research on Women.

Memmi, A. (2000). *Racism.* Minneapolis, MN: University of Minnesota Press.

Mills, C. W. (1997). *The racial contract.* Ithaca, NY: Cornell University Press.

Morrison, T. (1993). *Playing in the dark: Whiteness and the literary imagination.* New York: Vintage.

Museus, S. D., & Griffin, K. A. (2011). Mapping the margins in higher education: On the promise of intersectionality frameworks in research and discourse. *New Directions in Institutional Research, 151,* 5–13.

Pyke, K. (2011, January). Service and gender inequity among faculty. *The Profession, 44*(1), 85-87.

Rong, X. L., & Preissle, J. (2006). From mentorship to friendship, collaboration and collegiality. In G. Li & G. H. Beckett (Eds.), *"Strangers" of the academy: Asian women scholars in higher education* (pp. 266–288). Sterling, VA: Stylus.

Thompson, C. Q. (2008). Recruitment, retention and mentoring faculty of color: The chronicle continues. *New Directions for Higher Education, 143,* 47–54.

Turner, C. S. (2002). Women of color in academe: Living with multiple marginality. *The Journal of Higher Education, 73*(1), 74–93.

Turner, C. S. (2003). Incorporation and marginalization in the academy: From border toward center for faculty of color? *Journal of Black Studies, 34*(1), 112–125.

van Maanen, M. (1997). *Researching lived experience: Human science for an action sensitive pedagogy.* London, ON: Althouse Press.

Zinn, M. B., & Dill, B. T. (1996). Theorizing difference from multiracial feminism. *Feminist Studies, 22,* 321–331.

13

ME-SEARCH IS RESEARCH

My Socialization as an Academic

Tamara Bertrand Jones

My Blackness, woman-ness, and educated status all converge to create a sometimes unique perspective on the world that in some instances, and at some institutions, is not valued or welcomed. . . . One of my colleagues calls research on populations like yourself "navel gazing." Why is this? I'm not sure because I feel that all research comes from our lived experiences. Our lives inform our questions, our methods, our populations of study, as well as colors our interpretation. There is no such thing as objective research. As long as humans are involved at any stage, there is no such thing as objectivity. I think if we go deep enough we will find a connection to one's self in all research. (Bertrand Jones, journal entry, January 2012)

Systems of privilege and oppression often converge for those without privilege. This convergence can shape how individuals view themselves and their world in ways that those in privilege cannot understand. The work of Kimberlé Crenshaw (1989) and Patricia Hill Collins (2000) brought to light the ways that this convergence, manifested through intersecting identities like race, class, and gender (among others), can influence the experiences and challenges of Black women. Intersectionality as a research paradigm encourages multiple levels of analysis to understand the role that several categories of difference play in an individual's experience (Davis, 2008). This notion not only advances my scholarship, but also contributes to understanding my own life and the lives of the women I research. How individuals choose to identify themselves is important to "understanding our worldviews, values, and beliefs. It is difficult to separate our individual identities from the group memberships we hold and grasp how our identities are constructed in relation to others and the cultures in which we are implanted" (Stanley, 2006, p. 716).

In this chapter, I use entries from my personal journal to introduce a discussion of how my own intersecting racial and gender identities have influenced my socialization as an academic. This type of "me-search" is influenced by scholarly personal narrative (SPN). Developed by Robert Nash, SPN writing focuses the writer's experiences and voice, allowing the writer to use his or her personal story to test suppositions and explore personal issues of interest (Nash & Bradley, 2012). SPN emphasizes that an individual's personal narrative is valuable and deserves to be told. The writer uses the personal story to develop generalizable themes that connect to a broader audience.

My personal journal has become a tool I use to process and document my experiences in academia. Through journaling, I have been able to talk with myself. As a result, reading previous entries allows me to gain clarity, answer questions, and raise questions I would not usually raise aloud with others. The journal entries also have become data that can be analyzed and used to illuminate my experience and the experiences of others. Additionally, these data point to future questions to explore in research, especially research on Black female faculty and doctoral students.

In academia, where researchers use explicit statement of paradigms to support a study, SPN and intersectionality provide a framework from which to view my experience as a Black female in the academy. In this way, discussions of how both race and gender as interlocking oppressions influence my experience and shape my worldview are encouraged. Consequently, my experiences as a formally educated Black female in America have an effect on who I am, shaping what I see and how I see it. Along the same lines, my identities ultimately shape how what I see and understand is then articulated to others through my work.

What Is Socialization? Defining My Research Agenda

> Research is not value or judgment free. We investigate people, phenomena, and situations that are inherently messy, involving multiple perspectives, layers, and even truths. However, as researchers our goal is to employ all of the skills we've been taught to dig deeper until we reach the center. We dig until our shovels can go no further; and once there, we continue to try to uncover something that often has no beginning or ending. (journal entry, January 2012)

Definitions of *socialization* in the literature usually describe a process whereby the values, norms, knowledge, and beliefs of a group are conveyed to a new member (Clark & Corcoran, 1986; Johnson, 2001; LaRocco & Bruns, 2006; Reynolds, 1992). The traditional socialization process into academia fails to provide adequate preparation for a faculty career, regardless of race or gender (Ortlieb, Biddix, & Doepker, 2010).

I propose that the socialization process includes three main elements— academic preparation, mentoring, and professional development (Bertrand Jones & Osborne-Lampkin, 2013). Together these three components contribute to how a new faculty member adapts to his or her professional environment (Austin & McDaniels, 2006; Weidman, Twale, & Stein, 2001). Academic preparation includes formal school experiences from undergraduate, graduate, and/or postgraduate academic study. These academic experiences serve as the foundation for the remainder of the socialization process, as academic departments, at least at the doctoral level, are considered the primary source of socialization for the professional context (Austin & McDaniels, 2006; Girves & Wimmerus, 1988; Tinto, 1993; Weidman et al., 2001). Mentoring is described as the relationships between individuals within or outside of the professional context, whether among peers or with junior and senior colleagues. Many mentoring relationships develop as a result of academic experiences and interactions with departmental faculty and peers. Professional development involves formal and informal experiences—professional or paraprofessional daily work and additional training and development in a particular professional context. New scholars often learn of these activities through professional organizations or mentors. The focus of many socialization activities includes discipline-based knowledge and skills; however, often missing is consideration of race and gender.

Evidence suggests that scholars of color often enter the academy for different reasons from majority faculty, value teaching and service (Gregory, 2001), enjoy working with and advising students (Thomas & Hollenshead, 2001), receive inspiration and strength from communal working environments, experience racism and sexism (Thompson & Louque, 2005), and often are not perceived as equals in academe (Stanley, 2006; Thompson & Louque, 2005). In view of these issues, it should be no surprise that many Black female faculty members experience challenges in some academic environments.

Academic Preparation: The Start of My Journey to Academia

As a Black female I was always taught that I had to be better. It was something my parents instilled in me early on. I always had to earn As in school, treat others kindly and respectfully, and be my best at all times. I have learned that those values have not only informed who I am, but also how I think. All of these aspects of me influence my research lens. I dig deeper, trying to get at what others may not see, understand, or even be aware of. I dig deeper to try to understand people who may be misunderstood, advocate for people who may not speak the academic language, and try to understand people and systems that "don't make no sense." (journal entry, February 2012)

Education was thought to be the great equalizer, and for generations, Black parents have instilled in Black boys and girls the importance of education. This reliance on education served to uplift the race. From my reading of other Black female intellectuals, I have found that a commonality of academic excellence runs throughout our narratives (Evans, 2007; Reed, 2011; Tillman, 2001). Many Black women scholars recount stories of being required to perform at above A level. Those requirements came from family and were cultivated at young ages. This behavior, which we internalized, continued as we entered college and graduate school.

Because of my hard work, I expect the same effort from others. I assumed that because I gave my best, others expected my best. This has not always been the case in my experience. I wrote my second dissertation proposal in one week, at the prompting of two friends who were recently minted PhDs. I had sent a draft of my proposal to the two of them; my proposal was due in less than two weeks and I needed their feedback. When they requested a face-to-face meeting, I was not surprised and was ready to accept their pats on the back for my good work. What I received was shocking, to say the least.

Those two poked holes in my research questions, questioned my theoretical underpinnings, and told me that I needed to reconceptualize my whole study. I was floored. Why had others not caught these issues? What would have happened if I had gone to my defense with this proposal? For four hours, that first night, my friends helped me to reframe my study, which morphed into a completely different idea. I will never forget feeling as though something was missing from my relationships with my advisers that they would allow me to get to the proposal stage and not expect my best. In this case and future instances, I would learn that my sister friends and colleagues always expected more of me than others did.

Mentoring: Collaborating in Academia

Despite the years that have passed since the first Black woman entered the academy and despite our inclusion, the space we occupy is still cramped and oftentimes dark. (journal entry, August 2012)

As my network has broadened, so have my relationships with other Black female scholars. The mentoring I have received has been invaluable in my transition from graduate student to scholar. Among the many benefits, mentoring serves both psychosocial and career development purposes, fosters faculty productivity and collegiality (Stanley & Watson, 2007), and enhances retention and job satisfaction (Ponjuan, Conley, & Trower, 2011). Mentoring has also been found to be particularly beneficial for women and faculty of color (Stanley & Watson, 2007). Unfortunately, discussions of faculty-to-faculty mentoring do not fully address the complex dynamics for Black faculty (Tillman, 2001). These dynamics become even more complex when gender and race/ethnicity are involved.

The limited number of Black female faculty makes same-race/same-gender mentoring impractical for many Black female scholars. When mentoring does occur for Black women, it is more often the result of a peer relationship (Thomas & Hollenshead, 2001). Mentoring is one way that Black women counter the dark and cramped spaces that can be found in academia. These developmental relationships with others help to create networks that Black females, specifically Black female faculty members, use to position ourselves in our chosen arenas.

Creating a Network: Sisters of the Academy Institute

Why is the work I do called advocating, while the work others do scholarship? Why is it when a White woman does work on Black women, it's ground-breaking scholarship, and when a Black woman does work on Black women it's called navel gazing? Is my training as a researcher so limited that I cannot separate my own personal experience from another Black woman's experience? According to Patricia Hill Collins sometimes I don't have to. Collins says that Black women possess a commonality of experience. These commonalities provide not only more understanding for other Black women, but they also serve to unite us in our journey through the world. (journal entry, October 2011)

During my doctoral program, the Black women in my network ensured that I had publication, presentation, and other professional development opportunities. These women read and critiqued my writing and served as role models of professional behavior. Largely because of this support, six other women and I founded Sisters of the Academy (SOTA) Institute, an organization for Black women in higher education. All of the SOTA founders were either doctoral students or recent PhD graduates, so the academic experience was fresh in our minds. As we reflected on our common experiences in academia, and what we all wanted or felt we needed during our doctoral programs, access to Black female role models, as well as assistance with research and publication, was at the top of our list. Thus, SOTA was developed to provide a support network for Black women in higher education, while SOTA's motto—scholarship through collaboration—defined one of the strategies we'd identified in academia and sought to perpetuate through our membership. In the "publish or perish" atmosphere of academia, the quality and, especially, quantity of publications matters. As such, we wanted to improve the chances of professional success by seeking opportunities for SOTA members to conduct research, write, and ultimately publish with each other.

Because of the SOTA network, many Black females have contributed to my socialization as a scholar. Through their mentoring and guidance, I have been able to receive honest and critical critique and support for my personal and professional endeavors. When I entered my role as a faculty member, the work of one sister in the network, Dr. Linda Tillman, provided the framework for my career. In her work, Tillman (2001) identifies the following main barriers to tenure for Black faculty: lack of (a) a well-defined research agenda, (b) socialization, and (c) mentoring. With this in mind, I set out to develop a research agenda that I thought would put me on the right path to tenure. I considered work that interested me, inspired me, and generated many possible research questions. For me, ironically, that included new faculty socialization, with a specific focus on Black women.

Professional Development: Preparation for Success in the Academy

> I have often asked myself, "Do I conduct research that does not speak to my soul to get tenure? Or do I conduct research that contributes not only to my understanding but that of others regarding the issues and complexities of the system that other Black women face? Research that will equip others not only with the master's tools, but tools I've created to help chip away at the foundation of the house in which I reside?" (journal entry, February 2012)

Professional development for many faculty members includes regional and national conferences, trainings or workshops related to various aspects of teaching, research, and service to professional organizations and the campus community. These activities help participants learn new skills, gain confidence regarding existing skills through further development, and provide access to individuals and networks on and off campus. Professional development, also categorized as faculty development, is an essential component of a new scholar's career success. Recently, many professional development opportunities have targeted underrepresented scholars, including Black women (Davis, Chaney, Edwards, Thompson-Rogers,& Gines, 2012).

Through SOTA and the addition of several professional development programs, we sought to equip Black women with the knowledge and skills associated with personal and professional success in academia. For many members, success included securing tenure at a Research I institution; for others, success meant promotion to a position in upper administration. With either chosen path, scholarly activity and writing are important. Given this reality, our professional development programs sought to build the research and writing capacity of participants.

Professional development programs in SOTA include the Research Boot-Camp, the Writing Retreat, and an Intensive Grants Workshop. These programs were designed to impart specific knowledge and skills related to success in the academy. What differentiates these events from similar professional development is that race and gender are at the center of the events. Much like the idea behind the clothing line, FUBU (For Us By Us), the presenters, participants, and planning committee members are majority Black and female. The focus of these SOTA events is on equipping Black female scholars with the tools necessary for success. The information shared at these events has also been tailored to the issues and challenges that Black females face in academia.

Participation in SOTA events (i.e., Research BootCamp, Writing Retreat, Intensive Grants Workshop) has led me to understand the nuances of being an educated Black female from a research perspective. For example, in SOTA, I learned how to design and conduct research, develop and articulate a viable research agenda, and create a professional network that met my mentoring needs. After 10 years as an administrator, when a faculty position became available at my institution, I was excited about the opportunity to put into practice all that I'd learned through SOTA. What I hadn't realized is that, despite my knowledge, there would be certain challenges for which my own professional and SOTA experiences had not prepared me.

Me-Search Is Valid Research: Gaining Voice in the Academy

A recent reading of hooks and West's *Breaking Bread* gave me pause. Would I be considered an intellectual or just an academic? I'd like to think I was an intellectual, but I haven't lived the life of the mind so long, despite having spent most of my life in school. It saddened me for a while to think that I was not a part of those counted in the number of Black intellectuals who contribute to a better understanding of issues those in the Black community face. However, I had to remember that my voice as an academic was just as strong and relevant. The stories of Black women faculty need to be heard and retold. Academic environments need to change the way business is done to account for the needs of those who make up the environment. (journal entry, September 2012)

Linda Tillman (2011) argues that the academy is not going to change, so Black faculty need to prepare to operate within a system that devalues and fails to acknowledge our meaningful contributions. She suggests that Black female scholars take ownership of their careers and develop a strategic plan for their success (Tillman, 2012). Audre Lorde (2007) contends that the master's tools will never dismantle the master's house. This same notion can be applied to the socialization of Black females in higher education. Enhancing new Black female scholars' success in academia requires developing new socialization models that address the intersectionality of race, gender, and other social identities. Doing so allows the development of voice and validation of perspective that is often missing in academia.

References

Austin, A. E., & McDaniels, M. (2006). Preparing the professoriate of the future: Graduate student socialization for faculty roles. In J. C. Smart (Ed.), *Higher education: Handbook of theory and research* (Vol. 21, pp. 397–456) The Netherlands: Springer.

Bertrand Jones, T., & Osborne-Lampkin, L. (2013). Early career professional development: Enhancing Black female faculty success. *Negro Educational Review, 64*(1–4), 59–75.

Clark, S. M., & Corcoran, M. (1986). Perspectives of the professional socialization of women faculty: A case of accumulative disadvantage? *The Journal of Higher Education, 57*(1), 20–43.

Collins, P. H. (2000). *Black feminist thought: Knowledge, consciousness, and the politics of empowerment* (2nd ed.). New York: Routledge.

Crenshaw, K. (1989). Demarginalizing the intersection of race and sex: A black feminist critique of antidiscrimination doctrine, feminist theory and antiracist politics. *The University of Chicago Legal Forum, 140*, 139–167.

Davis, D. J., Chaney, C., Edwards, L., Thompson-Rogers, G. K., & Gines, K. T. (2012). Academe as extreme sport: Black women, faculty development, and networking. *Negro Educational Review, 62/63*(1–4), 167–187.

Davis, K. (2008). Intersectionality as buzzword: A sociology of science perspective on what makes a feminist theory successful. *Feminist Theory, 9*(1), 67–85. doi: 10.1177/1464700108086364

Evans, S. Y. (2007). *Black women in the ivory tower, 1850–1954: An intellectual history.* Gainesville, FL: University of Florida Press.

Girves, J. E., & Wimmerus, V. (1988). Developing models of graduate student degree progress. *The Journal of Higher Education, 59*(2), 163–189.

Gregory, S. T. (2001). Black faculty females in the academy: History, status, and future. *The Journal of Negro Education, 70*(3), 124–138.

Johnson, B. J. (2001). Faculty socialization: Lessons learned from urban Black colleges. *Urban Education, 36*(5), 630–647. doi:10.1177/0042085901365007

LaRocco, D. J., & Bruns, D. A. (2006). Practitioner to professor: An examination of second career academics' entry into academia. *Education, 126*(4), 626–639.

Lorde, A. (2007). *Sister outsider: Essays and speeches by Audre Lorde.* Berkeley, CA: Crossing Press.

Nash, R. J., & Bradley, D. L. (2012, March–April). The writer is at the center of the scholarship: Partnering me-search and research. *About Campus, 17*(1), 2–11. doi:10.1002/abc.21067

Ortlieb, E. T., Biddix, J. P., & Doepker, G. M. (2010). A collaborative approach to higher education induction. *Active Learning in Higher Education, 11*(2), 109–118. doi:10.1177/1469787410365655

Ponjuan, L., Conley, V. M., & Trower, C. (2011). Career stage differences in pre-tenure track faculty perceptions of professional and personal relationships with colleagues. *The Journal of Higher Education, 82*(3), 319–346.

Reed, L. C. (2011). Star light, star bright: A Black female scholar seeks to find "voice" in the academy. *Diversity in Higher Education, 10*, 283–301.

Reynolds, A. (1992). Charting changes in junior faculty: Relationships among socialization, acculturation, and gender. *The Journal of Higher Education, 63*(6), 637–652.

Stanley, C. A. (2006). Coloring the academic landscape: Faculty of color breaking the silence in predominantly White colleges and universities. *American Educational Research Journal, 43*(4), 701–736.

Stanley, C. A., & Watson, K. L. (2007). Meeting the professional development needs of new faculty: A three-year evaluation study of a new faculty orientation program. *Journal of Faculty Development, 21*(3), 149–160.

Thomas, C. D., & Hollenshead, C. (2001). Resisting from the margins: The coping strategies of Black females and other females of color faculty members at a research university. *Journal of Negro Education, 70*(3), 166–175.

Thompson, G. L., & Louque, A. C. (2005). *Exposing the "culture of arrogance" in the academy: A blueprint for increasing Black faculty satisfaction in higher education.* Sterling, VA: Stylus.

Tierney, W. G., & Bensimon, E. M. (1996). *Promotion and tenure: Community and socialization in academe.* New York: State University of New York Press.

Tillman, L. C. (2001). Mentoring African American faculty in predominantly White institutions. *Research in Higher Education, 42*(3), 295–325.

Tillman, L. C. (2012). Inventing ourselves: An informed essay for Black female scholars in educational leadership. *International Journal of Qualitative Studies in Education, 25*(1), 119–126.

Tinto, V. (1993). *Leaving college: Rethinking the causes and cures of student attrition* (2nd ed.). Chicago: University of Chicago Press.

Weidman, J. C., Twale, D. J., & Stein, E. L. (2001). *Socialization of graduate and professional students in higher education: A perilous passage?* San Francisco: Jossey-Bass.

14

THE EXPERIENCES OF MARGINALIZED ACADEMICS AND UNDERSTANDING THE MAJORITY

Implications for Institutional Policy and Practice

Dannielle Joy Davis

Contrary to claims of the nation's expedited evolution into a postracial society, the gross underrepresentation and marginalization of Black faculty in predominantly White U.S. postsecondary institutions persists. Culprits in marginalization include the behaviors and attitudes of not only White faculty and administrators, but also students (Thompson & Louque, 2005). Thompson and Louque's (2005) *Exposing the "Culture of Arrogance" in the Academy: A Blueprint for Increasing Black Faculty Satisfaction in Higher Education* found that 82% of study participants experienced direct and indirect cultural insensitivity from students, and 74% perceived these student insensitivities as racist. Cultural insensitivities included rude, disrespectful behavior; prejudiced perceptions based on bigoted stereotypes; and addressing Black faculty more informally than non-Black peers. Forty-five percent of respondents also agreed that "African American faculty [were] less respected than other faculty" (p. 61). Picca and Feagin's (2007) analysis of 626 White college students' journals revealed that 75% of racist commentary centered upon African Americans. This illustrates the gravity of the issue as it pertains to student perception of and interaction with Black faculty. Research also suggests that students evaluate minority professors less favorably than White ones in academe (Carle, 2009).

Yet, what would these research results show if responses reflected differences based on gender between Black female and Black male faculty? Including gender adds an additional element of complexity to consider when

Adapted from Davis (2010)

understanding others' beliefs or judgments of intersectional identity. The double minority status of Black women illustrates how the intersection of these marginalized identities may contribute to Whites' perceptions of Black women and subsequent experiences of this population. As Bertrand Jones's chapter, "Me-Search IS Research" (chapter 13, this volume) exemplifies, the double minority status of Black women prompts enriching, deep introspection for those at both the margins and centers of research, institutions, and society. This chapter explores the author's experiences of race within higher education as a person holding these specific intersecting identities.

Review of Literature

In terms of race, Leonardo (2009) argues that Whites who "consistently evad[e] a racial analysis of education should not be represented as [not participating] in a racialized order, [but that they showcase] precisely how they . . . perpetuate the racial order by turning the other cheek to it or pretending that it does not exist" (Ayers, Quinn, & Stovall, 2009, p. 231). The evasion of racial analysis, particularly regarding challenges African Americans teaching in predominantly White institutions face, also emerges upon review of racial minority faculty members' student evaluations by White European colleagues. One Black female member of the professoriate describes this challenge:

> During my first year of teaching, an African American man . . . at another institution received some negative student evaluations. A senior White male professor . . . gave him some advice on how to maintain discipline in this classroom. [The African American professor] responded: "With all due respect, Sir, when you try to take control of your class, the students accept it. Maybe they're grateful for it. When I try to take control of my classes, I get student evaluations that say 'I'm mean,' 'I'm intimidating,' 'I make them uncomfortable,' 'I force my opinions on them,' or 'I'm racist.'" With this type of resistance, many students avoid all challenges to some of their core values and assumptions. Consequently, African American faculty are marginalized by both their colleagues and by students resistant to having racist views challenged in the classroom. (King & Watts, 2004, p. 117)

Even minority faculty who receive positive evaluations report that students initially don't give them "the benefit of the doubt," compared to their White peers, whose credentials were not questioned and were deemed respectable (Sekayi, 2004). In essence, a double standard exists for Black and White faculty. While discussing her strategy to address students' negative perceptions of her Black race, gender, and youth, one faculty member shared:

> At some point I began to realize that there was very little I could do about students' negative perceptions of me based on that combination of race,

gender, and age. I was not willing or even interested in "proving myself" to people, students included. That was a new discovery for me. After tirelessly seeking the approval of students to "make up for" being younger than the average professor, I decided that this was an exercise in futility. I will teach. I will tell them what I know, I will tell them what I think, I will encourage them to express their knowledge and thoughts, and I will attempt to create an environment where we can all be learners and feel comfortable in that role. I came to this philosophy as I moved further into my own personal process of transformation and away from my lifetime of miseducation [Woodson, 1933]. (Sekayi, 2004)

Racist and sexist microaggressions from students, members of the professoriate, or administration; racial battle fatigue; and lacking a "protective network of sympathetic senior faculty" (Davis, 2004, p. 136) can result in toxic work environments for Black academics. Such inequities suggest an unequal playing field between Black faculty and their more supported White peers that remains overlooked. In her work "The Slippery Slope of Student Evaluations for Black Women Faculty," Beverly Davis notes how the intersectionality of race and gender contributes to fewer genuine relationships with senior faculty and fewer opportunities for research collaboration and professional development for Black female academics (2004). White racial identity development and subsequent student processing of both race-related course material and having a racial minority instructor counters the perception of student evaluations as "authoritative and unappealable" (Coren, 1998, p. 203). It further questions that students perceive faculty as equals (Davis, 2004; Thompson & Louque, 2005). A faculty member in Krenzin's (1995) study held: "Some of my students have never had a Black professor, never even knew a Black adult that did anything. So they look at me like, "How'd you do this?" (p. 124).

For a surprising number of undergraduate and graduate students, not studying under a Black professor continues to be the norm throughout the nation due to the group's low numbers in academe. Blacks comprise only 5.5% of the professoriate (Cataldi, Bradburn, Fahimi, & Zimbler, 2005). The challenge of insufficient diversity in the professoriate reflects research suggesting that course material taught by White men "was perceived as more controversial when taught by women and Black faculty" (Ludwig & Meacham, 1997, in Davis 2004, p. 134). Students' double standards in their perceptions of faculty suggests the importance of addressing the lack of racial parity within academe.

While the election of Barack Obama as the 44th president of the United States indicates a degree of racial progress, this is only the beginning of the end for what Cornell West calls the "Ice Age," or the age of indifference to the marginalized and suffering in our society (West, 2009). The long history of this country's use of race to exploit and dehumanize (as with the institution of slavery), coupled with the lower frequencies of spirit that promote such actions, cannot be erased by the election of one man. Such racism is not unique to the United States; it poses a problem throughout the Western world (Chakraborti, 2010; Stevens, 2009; Velisek, 2010). Janet Helms (1990) suggests that racism, or the lack thereof, may be understood through examining specific psychological stages of White racial identity development. Her work inspired me to view some of the racial micro- and macroaggressions of White students and colleagues I have encountered along my academic journey in a new light.

Why is understanding White racial identity development important? How does the model assist in moving us beyond merely illustrating the known: that racism exists and that people are racist to varying degrees? This work seeks to address these questions as they pertain to teaching and working in postsecondary settings.

As a new scholar, I had the opportunity of coteaching two courses in different sociopolitical, predominantly White contexts. The first course was on race, class, and gender at a northern institution. The second was an educational policy course taught at a southern university. As the United States continues to struggle with overt and covert racism, the history of America's enslavement of Africans and legal segregation makes the South particularly interesting in the study of prevailing racist attitudes and their influence on teaching and learning. This study focuses on my interactions with White students and female colleagues from these two regions. Because society tends to portray Whiteness as "normal" and thus invisible, White majority students and faculty rarely reflect on their experiences as Whites or these experiences in regard to racial minorities (Brion-Meisels, 2009). Helms's Racial Identity Model for Whites (Helms, 1990) provides a framework to understand classroom and workplace dynamics between diverse groups. The intent of this work is to understand White racial identity development and how it manifests in the postsecondary learning environment, while considering the intersecting identities of featured individuals. While Helms's work helped me interpret interactions with White students and faculty as a Black woman, the experiences herein might reflect those of non-Black minority peers in other academic settings as well.

Methods

Using an autoethnographic approach, with myself as the "autobiographical subject" (Reed-Danahay, 1997, p. 6), this research features two classrooms or units of study that individually represent bounded systems (Merriam, 2009;

Yin, 2009) within the general context of American higher education, particularly predominantly White institutions. As coinstructor for the featured courses, I used journaling to record my experiences and reflections following each class session. Journaling allows researchers to be more reflexive (Janesick, 1999; Mertens, 2009) and facilitates "deepening knowledge of whatever subject matter the researcher takes part in," while serving as a member check for one's thoughts (Janesick, 1999, p. 522). Through journal writing, "individuals become connoisseurs of their own thinking and reflection patterns, and indeed their own understanding of their work" (p. 506). Triangulation of data through location and time (Denzin, 1978) took place via study of two regions and settings at different points of my career. Triangulation also occurred in regard to demographics of students in terms of age, as one class comprised traditional-aged students (18 to 21 years old) and the other graduate students. This work employs Helms's White Racial Identity Model to analyze and understand the journal data. Specifically, journal entries were sorted based on their applicability to Helms's stages.

Limitations

Limitations of this work include truncated variation in data collection, differing subject matter of the courses taught, and student age differences between classes. Also, the study yields little generalizability. However, the experiences described herein may mirror those of others and inform academics of similar backgrounds or White allies, therefore yielding transferability. It likely will spark subsequent work on the topic. Future work in this area may triangulate the data further by incorporating interviewing and content analysis of student evaluations as additional data sources. Applying Helms's model to multiple cases promises to enhance transferability and contribute further to this new direction of inquiry.

Conceptual Model: White Racial Identity Statuses and Mental Processing Strategies

Janet Helms's White Racial Identity Model offers a framework to view the featured study. The first segment of the model, Contact Stage, comprises realization of the existence of Black individuals as those holding phenotypically African features. One lives with "either naïve curiosity or timidity and trepidation" (Helms, 1990, p. 55) regarding Blacks. While Contact Stage individuals may benefit from institutional racism, they may not be aware of their advantages, reflect on their experiences in terms of race, or have faced moral issues embedded within racist paradigms. Someone in Contact Stage approaches issues "with a color-blind or cultureless perspective and general naiveté about how race and racism impact herself and himself as well as other people" (p. 68). They have limited occupational and social interaction with Blacks unless that interaction is with Blacks who "seem" White to them, regardless of whether the individual has traditional African features. Generally, anxiety emerges when Contact Stage individuals relate with Blacks. Should the Contact person begin to interact with Blacks and maintain that interaction, Whites may move on to the Disintegration Stage (Helms, 1990). The Disintegration Stage marks one's conscious, yet conflict-laden acknowledgment of his or her Whiteness, yielding moral challenges related to the White experience. Here, the individual questions racist ideas previously taught and recognizes the social inequities between Blacks and Whites. Helms (1990) describes this as being caught between the acknowledgment of humanity and conflict of continued oppression.

Following Disintegration, Whites move into the Reintegration Stage, where Whiteness is idealized and Blackness denigrated. Overt or covert anger characterizes the dominant emotion at this point. In addition, Whites in this stage tend to distort information to favor their own racial group (Helms, 1990). Reintegration may evolve into Pseudo-independence. At the Pseudo-independence Stage, Whites have the capacity to understand their individual roles in ameliorating the outcomes of racism. Whites at this juncture possess an intellectual understanding of the culture of Blacks and acknowledge their own White privilege in the U.S. context. Those dwelling in this phase tend to make life choices to "help" marginalized races (Helms, 1990).

At the Immersion-Emersion Stage, individuals honestly acknowledge racism and the significance of their own Whiteness. Understanding the benefits of Whiteness may spur racial activism (Helms, 1990). Reeducation at this step involves a redefinition of Whiteness and acquiring more informed racial views. In the final stage, Autonomy, Whites "internaliz[e] a positive, nonracist White identity, value cultural similarities and differences, feel a kinship with people regardless of race, and seek to acknowledge and abolish racial oppression" (p. 68). At this stage, individuals exhibit flexible analyses of race-related material, and they are willing to relinquish the privileges of racism via various life choices (Helms, 1990). In Helms's Racial Identity Model for Whites, both the statuses and the mental processes used when responding to racial stimuli serve as the framework for data analysis of the study. The next section illustrates examples of these stages in relation to the data.

Findings

The following briefly reviews Helms's stages as they relate to the journal data. Examples from my experiences exemplify components of Helms's model in the classroom and academic work setting. The work seeks to demonstrate how Helms's model may help us understand interactions between racial minority and majority groups in both the classroom and the academic workplace.

Contact status is indicated by satisfaction with the racial status quo as well as one's obliviousness to racism and participation in it. Racial factors may influence life decisions only in a simplistic fashion (Helms, 1990). The Mental Processing Strategies used include denial, obliviousness, or avoidance of anxiety-evoking racial information (Helms, 1990). This was demonstrated in a southern graduate classroom through the incivilities of two White students, one who left the room loudly multiple times and another who talked throughout a film on Black men in education, despite disapproval from me and criticism from classmates. Their behavior may have served as forms of denial, avoidance, or resistance for these students.

Disintegration status involves "conscious, though conflicted, acknowledgement of one's Whiteness" (Helms, 1990, p. 58). In other words, the person feels disintegrated or caught between two conflicting worlds of Black and White. Confusion, dissonance, and avoidance of information that counter emerging realties on race inequities include the processing strategies employed (Helms, 1990). Disintegration occurred in the North with White undergraduate students' expressions of discomfort when learning about the past and present injustices racial minorities suffered in the United States.

Reintegration status refers to idealization of one's socioracial group, yet expressing denigration and intolerance for other groups. At this stage, racial factors may strongly affect life decisions (Helms, 1990). Reintegration behavior took place in the North when one undergraduate student likened the Black Panther Party to the Ku Klux Klan. In response, I noted the historical genesis of both groups, the former rooted in self-defense against a racist social system (resistance to oppression) and the latter as terror and oppression toward the marginalized. An additional example includes a southern colleague's reluctance to discuss students' disrespect of me as an instructor, stating that she didn't see the offense and insinuating that the occurrence did not happen. Another was when a southern White male (graduate student) discussed a connection among Black males, baggy pants, and the style's prison origins. When I asked whether this was a function of race or class, he suggested it was a function of race. This was the same male who was disruptive during the documentary on African American males. Hence, individuals may use more than one processing strategy when taking in race-related material.

Immersion-Emersion status entails the search for understanding personal meanings of racism, ways by which individuals benefit, and the redefinition of Whiteness (Helms, 1990). Life choices may include racial activism, and reeducation and searching for internally defined racial standards aid in processing information (Helms, 1990). An example of this is a northern colleague's openness to discussing and confronting White students' differential treatment of us as instructors during a specific class session. For instance, when I posed questions to students, some would look only at my White colleague when answering, rather than at me. She was the first to bring this up following the class and prompted our dialogue on the issue. This differed from the southern colleague's response to students' disrespect toward me, which was abruptly claiming not to see the occurrence and avoiding the topic, rather than discussing it further.

Those demonstrating Autonomy Status hold informed, positive socioracial group commitments, use internal standards for self-definition, and are able to relinquish the privileges of racism (Helms, 1990). These individuals hold flexible, less stringent responses and analyses to racial material (Helms, 1990). A northern colleague's willingness to split her salary with me as a coteacher, even though this was not required or asked of her, illustrates Autonomy. She said that this was her effort to actively counter economic exploitation of me as a new instructor.

Summary

The majority of White students at the southern university did not move beyond Reintegration status. However, the northern White students shared thoughts and demonstrated behaviors at almost every stage, including the final, most advanced stage, Autonomy. This contrasts with findings of Brion-Meisels (2009), who notes how despite having a diverse educational environment, her students dwelled at the initial Contact Stage of Helms's model (Ayers et al., 2009). The northern colleague held strong communication and collaboration skills and respectfully worked through challenges as an instructional partner. The southern coteacher at the less advanced Reintegration level was less willing to confront race issues directly and collaborated less in terms of teaching. The quality of experiences with White colleagues and students often reflected specific developmental stages. Examples of the Pseudo-independence Stage were not identified in the data.

Figure 14.1 illustrates highlights from this journal-centered work as it relates to White racial identity development. Others' perceptions of and responses to me as a Black professor, coupled with race-based material and the students' or colleagues' developmental stages, merged to influence interpersonal interactions and classroom experiences.

Figure 14.1   White Racial Identity Development in the Postsecondary Setting

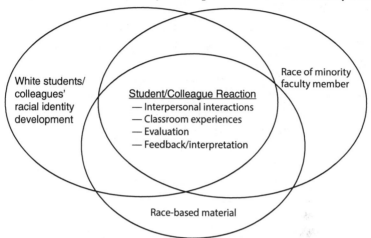

The figure shows how racial identity development, the race of the professor, and race-based material can help us understand classroom and workplace dynamics, regardless of national context. Understanding these dynamics may educate White colleagues who review the teaching evaluations and practices of minority peers. Unearthing the complexity of White perceptions of and responses to minority professors promises to lead to more egalitarian evaluation, tenure, and promotion policies in postsecondary settings.

Conclusion: Implications for Institutional Policy

This chapter contributes to the field by illustrating continued challenges faced by female faculty of color face at predominantly White institutions, how we might understand racism in academic communities, and the interactions between people from different racial backgrounds. Understanding the intersecting identities of Black women and other women of color, as well as White perspectives of these identities, proves significant, as others' erroneous beliefs of their "having the 'wrong' race, class, and/or gender directly affects their equitable participation and progression in academe" (this volume, p. 232). Acknowledging intersecting identities such as race, gender, and class of those featured within this chapter prompts us to consider the complexity of prejudice and its amelioration via fostering positive communication across racial, gender, and class lines.

Minority challenges often take root in the failure of postsecondary institutions to address both structural and curricular diversity. As Fred Bonner (2006) notes in his comparison of racism exhibited in the Bush administration's poor response to Hurricane Katrina survivors with racism in the ivory tower, "merely occupying the same space does not constitute [an academic] community" (p. 3). The August 2014 race riot in Ferguson, Missouri, illustrates our nation's continued need to foster cross-race, cross-cultural, cross-class, and cross-gender understanding. Intersectionality offers a framework for facilitating healthy boundary crossing required for such understanding to occur (Renn, 2004).

Via sharing my experience and applying Helms's model, I illustrate the need for improving campus climate for diverse populations by unveiling challenges the White majority faculty and students face that hinder their capacity to understand and engage minority groups, their histories, and worldviews. Helms's model and the work herein suggest that education can play a key role in the development of an autonomous, healthy White racial identity. It further exemplifies the importance of continued inclusion of race- and gender-based diversity-related material throughout university studies that explore intersecting identities in moving toward Autonomy.

The work presented in this chapter also informs academic promotion and tenure policies, in which faculty are evaluated on their teaching via student evaluations and collegiality. Women and racial minority faculty tend to be rated more harshly than their White male peers (Carle, 2009; Davis, 2004). This, coupled with the likelihood of women and minorities teaching race- and gender-based material, which may cause some White learners discomfort, contributes to the possibility of students' expressing resistance to these difficult classroom topics. Consideration of how students' individual racial identities influence the ratings of underrepresented faculty should be a component of both annual evaluations and promotion and tenure decisions. Such acknowledgment promises to increase levels of fairness in review processes and facilitate retention of minority faculty. The information would also be valuable for helping hiring committees understand the past teaching performances of minority candidates. Implications of such considerations in the review process are far-reaching, as postsecondary institutions continue to lack democratic parity in terms of faculty representation. Though they account for more than one fourth of the U.S. population, underrepresented minorities comprise merely 9% of the professoriate, with Blacks comprising 5.5% and Hispanics representing 3.5% in tenure-track, tenured, and nontenure lines. (These groups represented 12.3% and 12.5%, respectively, of the population during the 2000 U.S. Census [Cataldi et al., 2005; Grieco & Cassidy, 2001].) In terms of gender, Black women make up 3.6% of all faculty across rank (NCES, 2009). Sparse numbers within the population for marginalized academics, coupled with the need to retain these members of our academic community for the depth and excellence offered by their intersecting diverse perspectives, suggests the importance of understanding White racial identity development as it affects their work.

Application of Helms's White Racial Identity Model promises to counter the effects of racial battle fatigue or the "response to the distressing mental/ emotional conditions that result from facing racism daily (e.g., racial slights, recurrent indignities and irritations, unfair treatments, [and] . . . contentious classrooms" (2004, p. 180). By informing the pedagogy and evaluation of minority academics with courses containing high numbers of White students, the model offers a fuller understanding of teaching and learning in racialized contexts.

Understanding that White students operate at varied developmental levels facilitates efforts to design curricula that meet students where they are, while not compromising course content. For instance, students at lower stages may require substantially more background or history pertaining to marginalized groups. Application of Helms's work in the classroom may serve as a tool, therefore, to understand and address racism in educational settings. While this work features a U.S. context, application of the framework may transfer to global educational arenas in understanding race. Hence, employing Helms's work may be useful regardless of context, holding utility internationally as well.

References

Ayers, W., Quinn, T., & Stovall, D. (2009). *Handbook of social justice in education.* New York: Routledge.

Bonner, F. (2006, February 3). Wade in the water: Lessons learned from Katrina by one African American academic. *Teachers College Record.* Retrieved from http://www.tcrecord.org. ID Number: 12318

Brion-Meisels, G. (2009). Playing in the light: Experiential learning and White identity development. In W. Ayers, T. Quinn, & D. Stovall (Eds.), *Handbook of social justice in education* (pp. 661–667). New York: Routledge.

Carle, A. C. (2009). Evaluating college students' evaluations of a professor's teaching effectiveness across teaching and instruction mode (online vs. face-to-face) using a multilevel growth modeling application. *Computers and Education, 53*(2), 429–435.

Cataldi, E. F., Bradburn, E. M., Fahimi, M., & Zimbler, L. (2005). *2004 National study of postsecondary faculty (NSOPF: 04): Background characteristics, work activities, and compensation of instructional faculty and staff: Fall 2003 (NCES 2005-176).* Washington, DC: U.S. Department of Education, Institute of Education Sciences.

Chakraborti, N. (2010). Beyond "passive apartheid"? Developing policy and research agendas on rural racism in Britain. *Journal of Ethnic and Migration Studies, 36*(3), 501–517.

Coren, S. (1998). Student evaluations of an instructor's racism and sexism: Truth or expedience? *Ethics and Behavior, 8,* 201–213.

Davis, B. A. (2004). The slippery slope of student evaluations for Black women faculty. In C. Y. Battle & C. M. Doswell (Eds.), *Building bridges for women of color in higher education: A practical guide for success.* Lanham, MD: University Press of America.

Davis, D. J. (2010). The experiences of marginalized academics and understanding the majority: Implications for institutional policy and practice. *The International Journal of Learning, 17*(6), 355–364.

Denzin, N. K. (1978). *Sociological methods: A source book* (2nd ed.). New York: McGraw-Hill.

Grieco, E. M., & Cassidy, R. C. (2001). *Overview of race and Hispanic origin: Census 2000 brief. United States Census 2000.* Washington, DC: U.S. Bureau of the Census.

Helms, J. (1990). Towards a model of White racial identity development. In J. Helms (Ed.), *Black and White racial identity: Theory, research, and practice* (pp. 49–66). New York: Greenwood.

Janesick, V. J. (1999). A journal about journal writing as a qualitative research technique: History, issues and reflections. *Qualitative Inquiry, 5*(4), 505–524.

King, K. L., & Watts, I. E. (2004). Assertiveness or the drive to succeed? Surviving at a predominantly White university. In D. Cleveland (Ed.), *A long way to go: Conversations about race by African American faculty and graduate students* (pp. 110–119). New York: Peter Lang.

Krenzin, J. (1995). Factors influencing the retention of Black faculty on predominantly White campuses. *Research in Race and Ethnic Relations, 8,* 115–138.

Leonardo, Z. (2009). Reading whiteness: Antiracist pedagogy against White racial knowledge. In W. Ayers, T. Quinn, & D. Stovall (Eds.), *Handbook of social justice in education* (pp. 231–248). New York: Routledge.

Ludwig, J., & Meacham, J. (1997). Teaching controversial courses: Student evaluations of instructors and content. *Educational Research Quarterly, 21,* 27–38.

Merriam, S. B. (2009). *Qualitative research: A guide to design and implementation.* San Francisco: Jossey-Bass.

Mertens, D. M. (2009). *Transformative research and evaluation.* New York: Guilford Press.

National Center for Education Statistics (2009). *Digest of education statistics: 2009.* Retrieved from http://nces.ed.gov/pubsearch/pubsinfo.asp?pubid=2010013

Picca, L. H., & Feagin, J. R. (2007). *Two-faced racism: Whites in the backstage and frontstage.* New York: Routledge.

Reed-Danahay, D. E. (Ed.). (1997). *Auto/ethnography: Rewriting the self and the social.* Oxford, UK: Berg.

Renn, K. A. (2004). *Mixed race students in college: The ecology of race, identity, and community on campus.* Albany: State University of New York Press.

Sekayi, D. (2004). From disbelief, presumption, and disrespect to membership in the legacy of competence: Teaching experiences at the HBCU and the PWI. In D. Cleveland (Ed.), *A long way to go: Conversations about race by African American faculty and graduate students* (pp. 110–119). New York: Peter Lang.

Stevens, P. A. (2009). Pupils' perspectives on racism and differential treatment by teachers: On "stragglers," the "ill" and being "deviant." *British Educational Research Journal, 35*(3), 413–430.

Thompson, G. L., & Louque, A. C. (2005). *Exposing the "culture of arrogance" in the academy: A blueprint for increasing Black faculty satisfaction in higher education.* Sterling, VA: Stylus.

Velisek, Z. (2010). Different times in a different Europe. *New Presence: The Prague Journal of Central European Affairs, 13*(1), 12–14.

West, C. (2009). *State of the Black union.* CSPAN Archives DVD Media Recording.

Woodson, C. G. (1933). *The miseducation of the Negro.* Trenton, NJ: Africa World Press.

Yin, R. K. (2009). *Case study research design and methods.* Thousand Oaks, CA: Sage.

CONCLUSION

James L. Olive

The chapters in this volume speak to the multifaceted nature of intersectionality and its applicability to a diverse range of contexts and issues within education. Whether applied in quantitative, qualitative, or mixed-methods lines of inquiry, when used as a lens, intersectional theory provides a tool through which the interactions among power, politics, identity, and social structures can be analyzed critically. This conclusion summarizes the contributions of each section to the larger, ongoing discussion surrounding intersectionality and its use in education. Endeavoring to further such dialogue, I conclude by posing additional thoughts and questions related to the future of intersectionality and its function within the broader educational context.

The three chapters that comprise the first part, "Intersectionality and Methodologies," illustrated how intersectionality can be used in tandem with other theoretical frameworks of critical analyses and emphasized its relevance to quantitative and qualitative lines of inquiry. As discussed in chapter 1, the fundamental nature of intersectionality and its focus on the interplay of multiple identities naturally lends itself to working in conjunction with other theoretical frameworks that may have a better-defined focus. Similarly, Vaccaro's use of intersectionality in qualitative inquiry and Ruiz Alvarado and Hurtado's application of intersectional theory within a quantitative paradigm exemplify the theory's malleability and applicability to a wide range of methodological approaches.

The second part, "Intersectionality and K–12 Education," highlighted uses of intersectionality within K–12 education. Whether exploring the nuances of privilege through a "multiple identity advantage," as Stoll's chapter explains, or deepening our understanding of how individuals "do" certain identities depending on social context, as Prior shows through her research, intersectionality supplies a new level of complexity in the investigation of the experiences of K–12 teachers, staff, and students. This is critical given that many in this segment of education may feel vulnerable and less likely to raise their voices in opposition to exclusion due to fears of losing their job or simply because of their young age.

The works presented in part three, "Intersectionality and Postsecondary Education," demonstrated how the lens of intersectionality problematizes unidimensional views across all margins of identity. A core argument put forth in the chapters crafted by Fujimoto; Guillermo-Wann; Wong; Tilla-paugh; and Myers, Laker, and Minneman is that current research practices related to race, gender, sexual orientation, and ability still tend toward over-simplification and generalization due to their narrow focus on one facet of identity. In and of themselves, such practices are insufficient to capture and explore fully the inherent complexity that exists within each group or sub-population.

The fourth and final part of the text, "Intersectionality and Academe," examined the uses of intersectionality as an instrument of exploration and analysis within higher education. Iverson's chapter on how multiple identities can converge to play a significant role in forms of oppression underscored the importance of intersectional work to college and university diversity action plans. Along those same lines, the chapters authored by Manohar and Bul-len, Bertrand Jones, and Davis served as exemplars of how intersectionality can be used to deepen our understanding of experiences that occur at the intersections of identity categories and inform policies and practices.

Where Do We Go From Here?

Historical movements toward equality and social justice have shown that while positive progress is made, it can at times come at the expense of those within the group (i.e., feminism's earlier treatment of non-White and non-heterosexual women). The underlying logic in this practice is that recogniz-ing the subtle differences within a marginalized group is divisive and works against the "larger" common goals of said group. Research conducted through the lens of intersectionality, however, has unearthed the fallacies inherent in this line of thought and has shown that true social justice means justice for *all*—not simply the majority of those being marginalized.

What began as a recognition of exclusionary practices against poor and non-White women within the establishment of feminism has subsequently evolved into a comprehensive theory that addresses exclusion along any and all margins of difference. That is to say, the boundaries of intersectionality's use are drawn only by the sheer number of identity categories that have been recognized thus far and the types of intersections that exist among those myriad combinations of identities. As is often the case with quality research, more questions and potential lines of inquiry are presented in this volume than are answers to specific questions. At the forefront of these debates is the acknowledgment that human experience cannot be captured through an analysis along one, singular frame of reference. Rather, any examination that seeks to address social and educational inequities requires a higher theoretical and methodological complexity that takes into account the interplay of all identity structures as well as their corresponding inequities and privileges.

Since its conceptual introduction by the Combahee River Collective (1978) and subsequent literal codification by Crenshaw (1989, 1991, 1993), academe is beginning to recognize the potential of intersectionality. However, the totality of its scholarly implications has yet to be determined—thus, much work still remains to be done. As educators and researchers, it falls upon us to highlight the experiences and perspectives of those whose voices may not be heard. To that end, what follows are concluding thoughts and questions related to the future of intersectionality, its function within the larger contexts of theory and social justice, and its salience to research methodologies.

Theoretical Implications

Statistician George Box once wrote, "Essentially, all models are wrong, but some are useful" (Box & Draper, 1987, p. 424). Though at the time his quote was in reference to empirically based research designs, the same can be said for models of social identity and behavior. When viewed through an intersectional lens, such models and their corresponding theoretical frameworks have proven insufficient in capturing the totality of the concept(s) for which they were originally created. This is due to the fact that many structured models and frameworks currently in use are historically based on a finite (and in some cases normative) portion of a larger group and, thus, are incapable of encapsulating the full range of diversity that exists within said category or subpopulation. For example, earlier models of sexual identity development were based primarily on college-age White males, since that group constituted the most convenient sample at the time. However, subsequent research on sexual identity development has recognized certain limitations related to the earlier models, which has resulted in more comprehensive models that better speak to the "coming out" process.

An intersectional approach to social justice issues is multidimensional and founded on a belief that the systems of oppression are interconnected and, as such, cannot be analyzed on an individual basis. As a number of the chapters in this text have posited, my own included, intersectionality possesses the potential to augment and, in some cases, deepen the analytical strength of social identity models and their related frameworks. Intersectionality's rejection of a unidimensional view on any identity category brings with it a reexamination of how identity-based models and their related frameworks are applied and forces a deeper consideration of whether instances of exclusion that are still occurring are based on the nuances within each category. Future intersectional research should continue in this vein to ensure that all voices are heard within any given identity category.

Methodological Implications

As a theoretical approach to inquiry, intersectionality introduces a number of methodological implications. Intersectional analyses function across multiple planes—at both the micro (individual) and macro (societal) levels. As privilege and oppression can occur simultaneously, depending on one's context, work conducted through an intersectional lens focuses on the points at which multiple identities intersect—enabling a deeper and more comprehensive understanding of the relationships and external factors that are in play.

Given the complex nature of human identity, as well as the historical foundations on which privilege and oppression are based, it is not surprising that doing intersectional work can be extremely challenging. Even when the context in which an analysis is being conducted limits the number of identity categories that must be addressed, the integration of multiple categorical frameworks can be a herculean task. So much so that some have raised a question about whether the current methodological tools of social science are even capable of handling an analysis on the interrelatedness of all pertinent categories as intersectionality calls for. However, to sustain the forward momentum that has been achieved in just the last few decades, new methods must be fashioned that are able to simultaneously account not only for the diversity *of* identity categories, but also for the diversity *within* identity categories. That is to say, future intersectional analyses necessitate methodological approaches that address a wide range of social phenomena that are not limited to a single subjugated group of individuals.

Conclusion

The enduring disparities and inequities in society and education clearly necessitate an ongoing critical dialogue that centers on the components that facilitate exclusion, and intersectionality serves as a powerful means of facilitating that process. Academe bears a responsibility to identify and, whenever possible, address such areas of deficiency and thus should avail itself of intersectional theory. I, and the other authors of this volume, hope that future intersectional works will continue this line of inquiry and work toward a truly equal and equitable future.

References

Box, G. E. P., & Draper, N. R. (1987). *Empirical model-building and response surfaces.* New York: Wiley.

Combahee River Collective. (1978). A Black feminist statement. In Z. Guy-Eisenstein (Ed.), *Capitalist patriarchy and the case for socialist feminism* (pp. 210–218). New York: Monthly Review Press.

Crenshaw, K. (1989). Demarginalizing the intersection of race and sex: A Black feminist critique of antidiscrimination, feminist theory, and antiracist politics. *The University of Chicago Legal Forum 1989, 140,* 139–167.

Crenshaw, K. (1991). Mapping the margins: Intersectionality, identity politics, and violence against women of color. *Stanford Law Review, 43*(6), 1241–1299.

Crenshaw, K. (1993). Beyond racism and misogyny: Black feminism and 2 Live Crew. In M. J. Matsuda, C. R. Lawrence III, R. Delgado, & K. W. Crenshaw (Eds.), *Words that wound: Critical race theory, assaultive speech, and the First Amendment* (pp. 111–132). Boulder, CO: Westview.

CHAPTER REFLECTIVE QUESTIONS

Chapter 1: Queering the Intersectional Lens (James L. Olive)

1. Exclusion took place along many lines in Raven's example. Can you think of any other facets of her identity that were excluded?
2. Why are some facets of identity given more prominence in our society?
3. Given the increased recognition of nonheterosexuals within society, what are some possible reasons for the continued absence of unisex restrooms in modern public buildings?
4. If one were to create a conceptual model for the use of critical race theory in intersectional research, would it look the same? How might it differ from the QIA?
5. How would a queer intersectional qualitative research study that used personal characteristics as its unit of analysis differ from a study in which the units of analysis were historic processes or structures?
6. Qualitative research consists of myriad approaches to inquiry and exploration of the human experience. Are certain approaches better suited to intersectional research than others? If so, why?

Chapter 2: A Case for Using Qualitative Inquiry to Study Intersectionality in College Students (Annemarie Vaccaro)

1. Have you emphasized any of these key elements in your own research projects? If yes, what was the outcome? If not, why?
2. Of the key elements described in this chapter, which do you think are the most difficult to honor in your work? Why?
3. The notion of emergent and flexible design can be unsettling for some scholars. How comfortable would you be altering your research design? What implications might a flexible design have for your scholarship?
4. What are your reactions to the intersectionality journeys presented in this chapter?
5. What did you learn from the student narratives about intersectionality? What would you still like to know?

6. Compare and contrast the concepts, arguments, and narratives in this chapter to others in this volume. Discuss their similarities and differences.

Chapter 3: Salience at the Intersection (Adriana Ruiz Alvarado and Sylvia Hurtado)

1. Why might the salience of subordinated or less privileged identities transcend contexts?
2. Consider your own intersecting identities. Has your awareness of those identities changed in different environments?
3. Why is it difficult to look at overlapping identities and contextual domains of power? What are the advantages and limitations of using quantitative research to study intersectionality?
4. What do the results of the study reveal about the complexities, not only of individual identity, but also of group identity?
5. How does using salient identities differ from using the traditional social categories in quantitative research? Can we use identity salience in educational practice?
6. This chapter highlights the heterogeneity within the Latina/o population. How does exploring such heterogeneity within an underrepresented group help to further the understanding of power?

Chapter 4: Teachers' Perspectives on Race and Racial Inequality (Laurie Cooper Stoll)

1. The author argues that an increase in the number of antiracist teachers in the classroom would be more beneficial to alleviating racism in schooling than current forms of multiculturalism. In what ways do you think antiracist teachers might have a more significant impact on addressing racial inequality in schooling than simply adding multicultural curricula to the standard curriculum?
2. The author points out that empirical evidence suggests that young, working-class women compared to other demographic groups are perhaps the most likely to be racially progressive. How might race, class, and gender intersect in the lives of these women to produce a greater understanding of racial inequality?

3. The author argues that in the United States race is pervasive yet "invisible," and invisible yet "obvious." In what ways is race pervasive, invisible, and obvious at the same time?

4. In her research, the author found that multiculturalism in District 21 did not include any systematic critique of White privilege and inequality. Other race scholars have found the same in their studies. If multiculturalism does not include a systematic critique of White privilege and inequality, can it alleviate institutional discrimination?

5. Consistent with the premises of strategic intersectionality, the teachers of color in this study, as well as White teachers who were themselves part of marginalized groups or who were intimately connected to marginalized groups, were the most likely to acknowledge the existence of institutional and individual racism. How might these teachers' social locations explain their greater awareness of racial inequality?

6. The author claims that three types of privilege work against teachers' addressing contemporary racial inequality in schooling: privilege associated with individual teachers' social location, privilege associated with White students and their families, and privilege associated with affluent communities. How can antiracist educators work to overcome these obstacles to equality?

Chapter 5: Gender in Schools (Sarah Prior)

1. In what ways can teachers and administrators challenge the often hidden curriculum of normativity and instead prioritize curriculum that reflects students' multiple intersecting identities?

2. Lilly Jade spoke frequently about the influence of her family and culture on her ideas about what it means to be a man and what it means to be a woman. How can policies and curriculum be created that take into consideration the strong familial influence on how young people understand identity?

3. The students in this project frequently talked about their identities as overlapping and often conflicting. How can/should policymakers, school personnel, advocates, and so on take these overlapping identities into consideration when designing policy?

4. When discussing multiple identities, many people often use additive language rather than discuss the complexity of identities. How did the young people in this project challenge additive notions of identity to promote their agency in identity construction?

5. These students spoke specifically about sexuality, race, and religion. What other identities can influence how young people understand gender identity construction?
6. How can policymakers, advocates, school personnel, researchers, and so on learn from intersectionality, particularly as it relates to issues of agency, youth culture, and citizenship?

Chapter 6: Understanding the Academic Achievement of Latina College Graduates (María Oropeza Fujimoto)

1. Think about an underrepresented group on your campus that you work with: How is this particular group talked about? How do the social identity labels we place on these students assist us in our work? How do the labels limit our understanding and/or effectiveness? How can intersectionality help to define the experiences of this group more accurately in terms of their social identities?
2. How might the concept of "intersectionality" enhance what we do as practitioners?
3. How does intersectionality help us to see the limitations of comparison studies that may be overly simplistic in how they categorize students?
4. How can intersectionality influence the way you think about your research purpose, questions, and study design?
5. How does intersectionality help us to understand, in the broadest possible terms, not the outcomes of scientific inquiry, but the process itself?
6. How does understanding our students' intersecting social identities contribute to our comprehension of the systemic nature of educational inequality?

Chapter 7: Intersectionality of Multiple Racisms (Chelsea Guillermo-Wann)

1. How do these three case studies prompt your thinking about issues mixed race people may face in college and throughout their lives?
2. What are some examples of racial language that tends to be normative in higher education and society?
3. How have you seen these monoracially constructed norms intersect with other social identities?
4. How have these multiracially identifying students been marginalized in college contexts? How might a change in racial context (e.g., a

minority-serving institution [MSI], or a predominantly white institution [PWI]) potentially produce different experiences?

5. What institutional or organizational actions might help improve a campus climate for multiraciality?

6. How might future intersectionality research and practice approach mixed race identity with additional socially constructed categories?

Chapter 8: Intersectionality in and of Race (Alina S. Wong)

1. How can multicultural centers create dynamic subaltern spaces that allow students of color to explore, express, and construct fluid identities? How can practitioners best support students in the process of knowing and understanding themselves?

2. What is the responsibility of predominantly White institutions to challenge normative culture and behaviors? What does an antiracist climate entail?

3. How can faculty, staff, and students create liberatory moments and experiences for students of color to interrogate imposed identities and claim agency of one's own identities?

4. How can faculty and staff support all students to understand how systems of power and social categorization inform and influence identities and experiences? What educational programs, opportunities, and resources are necessary?

5. Recognizing that understanding the experiences of students of color in colleges and universities is valuable, what research methods and paradigms do not homogenize or essentialize their experiences further? How can scholars shift the focus to interrogate the impact of racism on students' experiences, rather than the impact of race?

6. This study focuses on the intersectionality of systems of power in the context of understanding racial identity construction. How can future work also examine multiple and simultaneous identities?

Chapter 9: "Writing Our Own Rule Book" (Daniel Tillapaugh)

1. Consider your own social identities (e.g., race, socioeconomic class, gender, sexuality). In what ways do these social identities interplay with one another to make up your holistic identity?

2. From a structural intersectionality perspective, in what ways have structures either privileged or subordinated you? In particular, how

have structures within the context of higher education played out in such ways?

3. Political intersectionality is when individuals of two or more subordinated identity groups experience the tensions of two or more conflicting social agendas. How might colleges and universities as systems force individuals to experience political intersectionality?

4. In this chapter, Jonathan, Mason, and Victor are each affected by representational intersectionality in distinct ways. Considering your own identity, have you experienced the privileging of one of your social identities over another? If so, what consequences did that have on your holistic sense of self?

5. When scanning your own institutions, what programs and/or services exist to assist individuals, particularly those within the LGBT population, to make meaning of their own individual intersectionality as well as the systems in which they are a part? What might you be able to do to create those opportunities or spaces for these students?

6. In what ways are you "interrogating the status quo" at your institution? How might you work to actively advocate for positive social change within your sphere of influence?

Chapter 10: Subaltern Supermen (Karen A. Myers, Jason A. Laker, and Claire Lerchen Minneman)

1. In what ways do depictions of disabilities manifesting as extraordinary abilities (e.g., supernatural powers, superhuman physical strength) influence perceptions of disabilities? For example, do such images mitigate or reinforce stereotypical assumptions of helplessness or weakness?

2. Does Sanford Meisner's description of the dramatic arts—"living truthfully under imaginary circumstances"—give directors a "pass" in casting, allowing them to cast actors without disabilities, when they could have cast actors with the disabilities portrayed (Longwell & Meisner, 1987, p. 34)?

3. To what extent have media images of masculinity changed over the past decade? What impact is this having, if any, on portrayals of disabilities in movies, television, and other media?

4. Dahl argued in 1993 that disability is rarely incidental to a character. Twenty years later is that still the case?

5. Students on college and university campuses are more diverse than ever before, particularly as diversity relates to disability. Does this

bring greater awareness to how diversity is portrayed in the media, or greater demand that it be portrayed accurately?

6. The proliferation of social media has made it very easy for people to portray themselves in ways that might be very different from how they are perceived in person. In what ways might this challenge or reinforce Goffman's concept of impression management for people with disabilities?

Chapter 11: Interlocking Oppressions (Susan V. Iverson)

1. What are limitations of adopting collective referents (such as targeted groups, underrepresented persons, at-risk populations, and diverse persons) when describing diversity efforts in higher education?

2. How might a policy author adopt an intersectional approach in writing about diversity? What concepts, terms, or signifiers might one adopt when writing a diversity action plan?

3. Iverson reviewed several metaphors to describe the complexity of and interrelated forces acting on dimensions of identity, ultimately adopting Crenshaw's (1989, 1991) analogy of traffic through an intersection. How does this analogy help practitioners and researchers rethink diversity efforts? What are limitations to this analogy, and what alternatives might be more useful?

4. Contemporary use of "diversity" as a collective signifier, inclusive of multiple demographic groups, emerged from historical efforts focused on specific identity groups—for example, women, Blacks, persons with disabilities. Might diversity planning efforts in the future revert to identity-specific language? What would be the benefits and/or shortcomings of this? What new concepts and terms might eclipse our current language for diversity?

5. An intersectional approach illuminates how categories may create "artificial boundaries" that may serve more as a "proxy for economic and behavioral problems . . . [and] continue to perpetuate inequality" (Yanow, 2003, p. 211). Using your campus as a point of analysis, how might current conceptualizations of and categories for diversity serve as a "proxy" for other problems? Who or what is being served by existing classifications and categorizations?

6. Does Iverson offer little more than theorizing in this chapter? Is the possibility of a common language reflective of an intersectional understanding of diversity a dream?

Chapter 12: In the "Web" of the Twenty-First-Century American Academy (Namita N. Manohar and Pauline E. Bullen)

1. How did Namita, as an Indian woman, and Pauline, as a Black woman, relationally experience privilege and disadvantage in their academic careers? How are these experiences organized by the structure of academe?
2. Why are "situated" feminist practices that are not neutral, but contextualized and historical, important to the development of feminist theory?
3. Explain how Namita's and Pauline's experiences in academe reflect a key tenet of intersectional praxis that is framed by one's social location: One experiences privilege and disadvantage simultaneously.
4. What are some of the vested interests involved in reflection as feminist practice?
5. How does reflexive feminist praxis as described in this chapter facilitate resistance to marginality? How can women of color be agents with academe?
6. What is the unique Black feminist standpoint expressed in this chapter?

Chapter 13: Me-Search IS Research (Tamara Bertrand Jones)

1. Researchers have many labels for the method used in this chapter, scholarly personal narrative, including autoethnography, ethnobiography, personal narrative, among others. How can this method be incorporated into curricula for qualitative methodology courses?
2. Writing is both a craft and an art. What steps can be taken to ensure that both craft and art are recognized as valuable in academic writing?
3. Intersectional analysis and scholarly personal narrative both privilege the relevant experiences of the researcher and/or participant. What role does self-definition play in how a new scholar or researcher enters academic conversations?
4. Tierney and Bensimon (1996) argue that the individual is not only socialized into an organization, but also influences the organization. If this is true, can you identify ways that your department or organization has been changed by the diverse individuals who are members of your group?
5. My racial and gender identities have been most salient for me and thus used to frame my personal experiences in academia. What identities

have the most meaning for you when interpreting your experience in academia (or the academy)?

6. What parts of your personal story help to make meaning of larger ideas in your discipline? What ideas in your discipline could benefit from an intersectional or scholarly personal analysis?

Chapter 14: The Experiences of Marginalized Academics and Understanding the Majority (Dannielle Joy Davis)

1. How might intersectionality, in terms of faculty and student interactions, inform further practice in higher education?

2. Have you experienced or witnessed an incidence of racism in higher education? If so, in what ways can the Helms model assist you in understanding the experience?

3. In what ways can the Helms model assist you in deconstructing the experience of racism?

4. What implications does understanding of the Helms model have in your future practice in higher education?

5. Review the presented Helms phases for racial identity development. Where do you think you fall in your own racial identity development?

6. How might the Helms model inform your personal cross race interactions?

EDITORS AND CONTRIBUTORS

Editors

Rachelle J. Brunn-Bevel is an assistant professor of sociology and anthropology at Fairfield University. Her research examines how students' race, ethnicity, class, gender, and immigrant status intersect to influence their educational experiences and outcomes. Her work has focused primarily on students attending elite postsecondary institutions, but she is also interested in bullying victimization among K–12 students and the unique experiences of female faculty members. She received a bachelor of arts, with distinction, in sociology and political science from the University of Delaware and an MA and a PhD in sociology with a graduate certificate in urban studies from the University of Pennsylvania. Her previous academic appointments include a postdoctoral fellowship at the Robert F. Wagner Graduate School of Public Service at New York University and assistant professor of sociology and Africana studies at Virginia Tech. In 2014, Dr. Brunn-Bevel (in collaboration with Byrd and Sexton) published an article in the *Du Bois Review: Social Science Research on Race*, titled, "'We Don't All Look Alike': The Academic Performance of Black Student Populations at Elite Colleges." Her current work includes research projects examining First Lady Michelle Obama's Let's Move! campaign and racial-ethnic disparities in standardized test scores among K–12 students in Virginia.

Dannielle Joy Davis is an associate professor of higher education at Saint Louis University. A graduate of the University of Illinois at Urbana–Champaign, she has studied and conducted research in Ghana, South Africa, Senegal, Egypt, Germany, the Netherlands, and Belgium. Her interdisciplinary research examines the experiences of marginalized groups in educational settings, the role of organizational policy and practice in the promotion or inhibition of egalitarian academic and occupational outcomes, and spirituality in the workplace and other learning environments. She has published more than 40 refereed journal articles, book chapters, academic commentaries, volumes, and reviews. She also coedited the books *Black Women in Leadership:*

Their Historical and Contemporary Contributions (Peter Lang, 2012) and *Social Justice Issues and Race in the College Classroom: Learning From Different Voices* (Emerald Group Publishing, 2013). Dr. Davis has served as an associate editor for *Learning for Democracy: An International Journal of Thought and Practice* and *The International Journal of Religion and Spirituality in Society*.

James L. Olive is an associate professor in the Department of Leadership Studies at Ashland University in Ashland, Ohio. Prior to joining Ashland's faculty, Dr. Olive served on the University of Dayton's Steering Committee for its successful reaccreditation by the Higher Learning Commission in 2007 and as curriculum, assessment, and technology coordinator for the School of Education and Allied Professions. His research focuses include LGBT issues in higher education; exploring the ways in which social class, gender, race, sexuality, and ability shape the human experience; and the intellectual and identity development of postsecondary students. He currently serves on the editorial board of the *American Secondary Education Journal*. Dr. Olive earned a PhD in educational leadership and an MS in educational administration from the University of Dayton and a BS in education from The Ohio State University.

Contributors

Adriana Ruiz Alvarado is a postdoctoral scholar with the Higher Education Research Institute at UCLA. Her research examines student mobility patterns, campus climate and intergroup relations, and college contexts that influence the persistence of underrepresented students. She received her BA from UC Berkeley and her MEd and PhD from UCLA.

Tamara Bertrand Jones is an assistant professor of higher education at Florida State University. Her research examines the sociocultural contexts that influence the graduate education and professional experiences of underrepresented populations, particularly Black women, in academia. Her previous work as an administrator and program evaluator also influences her other research interests in culturally responsive assessment and evaluation. She is a founder and past president of Sisters of the Academy Institute, an international organization that promotes collaborative scholarship and networking among Black women in the academy. She collaborated with fellow scholars to write *Pathways to Higher Education Administration for African American Women* (Stylus, 2012) and *Cultivating Leader Identity and Capacity in Students From Diverse Backgrounds: ASHE Higher Education Report, 39:4* (Jossey-Bass, 2013).

Pauline E. Bullen is an activist scholar with research interests in sociology and equity studies in education and African women and gender development. A former equity instructional leader with the Toronto Board of Education and assistant professor with the SEEK Department at Brooklyn College, CUNY, Dr. Bullen currently is a senior lecturer in gender development studies at the Women's University in Africa, Zimbabwe. Her most recent chapter, "Mother Love, My Mother: Pages From a Feminist Diary," was published in the *Journal of the Motherhood Initiative for Research and Community Involvement* in 2014. She has published several articles on counseling and educating Black youth in urban environments and is currently working with the University of Toronto Press to complete her book, *Black Academics Speak Out on Racism, Genocide, Race and Microagressions.*

María Oropeza Fujimoto has taught in the Educational Leadership Program at California State University Fullerton since 2011. Prior to that, she taught in Educational Leadership and Policy Studies at the University of Washington. Dr. Oropeza Fujimoto completed her doctoral studies at the University of Washington. Her most recent administrative position was assistant dean of students, and she has worked in leadership development, academic advising, and multicultural affairs and at a women's center. In addition, she has worked in both public and private institutional settings as a student affairs administrator and academic support services counselor.

Chelsea Guillermo-Wann leads research and evaluation for the Santa Barbara Unified School District. A graduate of the University of California, Los Angeles, she earned a doctorate in higher education and organizational change. Her research and practice focus on diversity and equity in educational pathways and success, campus climate for diversity, intergroup dialogue and relations, college access and completion, and developing organizational cultures for data-based decision making to leverage collaborative change across educational sectors at the local level. Her work has included Title V grant research for Hispanic-Serving Institutions; curriculum development for gender-in-STEM high school student dialogues; and contributions to national research projects developing frameworks and survey instruments integrating campus climate for diversity, educational practice, and student outcomes for the twenty-first century. She has published several articles and given more than 30 presentations at national associations.

Sylvia Hurtado is a professor at the Graduate School of Education and Information Studies at UCLA, in the Division of Higher Education and Organizational Change. She is currently director of the Higher Education

Research Institute, which houses the Cooperative Institutional Research Program (CIRP). CIRP is the longest-running empirical study of higher education involving data collection on students and faculty. Her numerous publications focus on undergraduate education, student development in college, and diversity in higher education.

Susan V. Iverson is an associate professor of higher education administration and student personnel at Kent State University, where she is also an affiliated faculty member with both the women's studies and LGBT studies programs. Her scholarly interests include women and leadership, multicultural competence, feminist pedagogy, and the use of feminist poststructural research. In addition to numerous journal articles and book chapters, she coedited *Reconstructing Policy Analysis in Higher Education: Feminist Poststructural Perspectives* (Routledge, 2010) and *Feminist Community Engagement: Achieving Praxis* (Palgrave, 2015). Prior to becoming a faculty member, she worked in student affairs administration for more than 10 years.

Susan R. Jones is a professor in the Higher Education and Student Affairs program at The Ohio State University. Her research interests include psychosocial perspectives on identity, intersectionality and multiple social identities, service learning, and qualitative research methodologies. She is the coauthor (with Dr. Elisa S. Abes) of *Identity Development of College Students* (Jossey-Bass, 2013) and *Negotiating the Complexities of Qualitative Research: Fundamental Elements and Issues* (with Drs. Vasti Torres and Jan Arminio) (Routledge, 2006, 2nd edition published in 2014).

Jason A. Laker is a professor of counselor education (and former vice president for student affairs) at San Jose State University in California. He previously served as a fellow at the Centre for the Study of Democracy and on the gender studies faculty at Queen's University in Canada. He holds a PhD from the University of Arizona's Center for the study of higher education and an MA in community counseling. His international activities include engagements as board member, visiting faculty, consultant, or speaker, particularly in Europe. His scholarly work includes two edited texts regarding gender and men's development and two texts coedited with colleagues in Spain and Croatia focused on the role of postsecondary institutions in fostering citizenship and democratic education, comparing the contexts of Eastern and Western Europe with those of North America.

Namita N. Manohar is an assistant professor of sociology at Brooklyn College, City University of New York and served as director of the Women's and

Gender Studies program at Brooklyn College from 2009 to 2012. She specializes in international migration, gender, and families with a focus on Indian immigrants in the United States. Her research examining Indian immigrant women's gendered subjectivities around work and mothering in the United States has been published in *Journal of the Motherhood Initiative for Research and Community Involvement, Advances in Gender Research, AAPI Nexus Journal,* and *International Journal of Multiple Research Approaches.* She has also published several articles on dating and marriage among second-generation Indians in the United States and on innovative pedagogical practices for sociology classrooms.

Claire Lerchen Minneman, EdM, is associate director of college counseling at Miss Porter's School in Farmington, Connecticut. She received her master's in education, with a focus on higher education, from Harvard's Graduate School of Education.

Karen A. Myers is an associate professor and director of the Higher Education Administration graduate program at Saint Louis University and cofounder and director of the award-winning international disability education project, *Allies for Inclusion: The Ability Exhibit,* the Ability Ally Initiative, and the Saint Louis University Ability Institute. She has been a college teacher and administrator at nine institutions since 1979; is a national disability consultant and trainer, as well as author of numerous journal articles, book chapters, and books; and teaches her self-designed graduate course, Disability in Higher Education and Society. She has received the ACPA College Student Educators International Voice of Inclusion Medallion, Annuit Coeptis Senior Professional Award, Standing Committees Advocate Award, and the ACPA Foundation Diamond Honoree award. In addition, she is a cofounder of the ACPA Standing Committee on Disability and coauthor of the recently published ASHE monograph *Allies for Inclusion: Disability and Equity in Higher Education* (Jossey-Bass, 2013).

Penny A. Pasque is an associate professor of educational leadership and policy studies and women's and gender studies at the Center for Social Justice, University of Oklahoma.

Sarah Prior is a lecturer in criminology and criminal justice at Northern Arizona University, is a graduate of Arizona State University's Justice Studies program. Her interdisciplinary research examines the intersectional experiences of marginalized youth in a variety of school settings from a critical youth studies standpoint. Her most recent refereed journal article, which appeared in the *International Journal of Multiple Research Approaches*, examines the ethical and methodological dilemmas of a youth-centered research agenda.

Laurie Cooper Stoll is an assistant professor in the Department of Sociology and the founding director of the Institute for Social Justice at the University of Wisconsin–La Crosse. Her research explores inequalities related to race, class, gender, and sexuality in the context of social institutions, particularly education. In her first book, *Race and Gender in the Classroom* (Lexington Books, 2015), from which the data in her chapter in this volume are drawn, she follows 18 teachers carrying out their roles as educators in an era of "postracial" and "postgender" politics. She has also published her research in several academic journals, including *Violence Against Women* (forthcoming), *Journal of Latinos and Education* (forthcoming), *Race Ethnicity & Education*, and *Qualitative Sociology*, among others.

Daniel Tillapaugh is an assistant professor in the Counseling and College Student Personnel program at California Lutheran University. A graduate of the University of San Diego's PhD in Leadership Studies program, Dr. Tillapaugh focuses broadly on intersectionality in higher education contexts, particularly intersections of sexuality and gender on student development as well as college student leadership development. He currently chairs the Standing Committee on Men and Masculinities for ACPA-College Student Educators International.

Annemarie Vaccaro strives to be an engaged educator whose teaching, research, and service are connected by a commitment to social justice and passion for inclusive praxis. She is also committed to active engagement in both the field of student affairs and the University of Rhode Island (URI) community. At URI, she is involved in a variety of social justice programs (LGBT Fellows), events (Women's Leadership Initiative), and committees (e.g., Equity Council, President's LGBTQ Commission, Academic Affairs Diversity Task Force). Over the past decade, she has volunteered for numerous professional leadership and committee roles in her professional organizations. She currently serves as an editorial board member for NASPA's *Journal of Student Affairs Research and Practice*.

Alina S. Wong, associate dean for student life at Barnard College, specializes in community building, identity exploration, and inclusive leadership. Her research, which examines the processes of racial identity construction using critical theory and intersectionality to understand racial identity construction as one part of decolonization projects, is included in *The Misrepresented Minority: New Insights on Asian Americans and Pacific Islanders, and the Implications for Higher Education* (Stylus Publishing, 2013).

Black women's oppression and, 213
categories of, 177–87
characteristics and tensions of, xi
characterized by theoretical interventions, 155
communities of difference approach to, 221–22
context as key component in, 143–45
defining, ix–x, 3–6
disabilities and masculinity, 189–210
in educational research, 9
embracing conceptual imperfections in, 224–25
exploration, 172–87
gay college men's exploration of, 172–87
as guiding framework, 120
higher education and importance of, 185–87
identities and complexity of, 12, 33
of identities in gender research, 99–112
identity studies incorporated by, 167–68
in interlocking oppressions, 212–14
invisibility in, 223
K–12 education and, 9–10, 275
key assumptions in research of, 213
Latina/o informed analysis and, 123–24
Latinas/os and, 48–50, 105, 120–29
Latinas/os provided understanding by, 125–27
learning objectives of, 2
methodologies and, 9, 117–29, 214, 224
multifaceted nature of, 275
of multiple racism, 133–48
paradigms of, 19–20
political, 180–82, 186–87
postsecondary education and, 10–11, 276
power and, 224

as problematizing privilege, 72–73, 87–89
purposes of, 97–98
qualitative inquiry and LGBTQ, 33–46
qualitative inquiry studies and, 31–46
in and of race, 153–69
representational, 182–87
research and, 5–7, 50
social inequalities and, 72–73, 224
structural, 177–80, 186–87
theories disputes in, xi
theorizing and diversity images in, 218–20
for training of helping professions, 12
types of, 3
understanding theories in, 2
variables in salience research, 54
youth and, 97–98
Intersectionality and "race" in education
(Bhopal and Preston), 6
intersectional language, 213
intersectional perspectives, 185–87
intersectional research. *See also* analysis;
Asian American study; educational research; gender expression research; Latina College Graduate Survey; "me-search"; qualitative research; racial analysis; research; salience research
approaches for, 50, 94
future of, 11, 276–78
limiting identity dimensions in, 50
in queer theory, 29
sets of engagements in, 4–5
intersections, 48–50, 105, 205. *See also* masculinity/disability intersections
interventions, theoretical, 155
interviews
Chinese Americans', 154–69
Filipinos', 154–69

Additional titles available in the **Engaged Research and Practice for Social Justice in Education** series (Series editors: Edward P. St. John, Penny A. Pasque, Estela Mara Bensimon and Shaun R. Harper)

Research, Actionable Knowledge, and Social Change

Reclaiming Social Responsibility Through Research Partnerships
Written by Edward P. St. John
Foreword by Penny A. Pasque

"St. John has spent his career studying the intersections of policy, practice, and research. He has struggled with how those of us concerned with social justice might move away from entrenched notions of research and measurement and instead infuse our work in more direct ways to achieve ends aimed at improving the public good. This book summarizes his ideas and suggests that actionable research has the potential of promoting social justice and fairness in education and social systems. The book will appeal to educational and social researchers interested in collaborating with practitioners committed to improving equity."

—*William G. Tierney, Wilbur-Kieffer, Professor of Higher Education, University of Southern California*

Reflection in Action

A Handbook for Student Affairs Faculty and Staff
Kimberly A. Kline
Foreword by Edward P. St. John
Kline and her colleagues deftly examine the art of reflection in pursuit of effectively addressing multicultural and social justice issues on campus. This book details the most contemporary principles and techniques that can assist emerging and seasoned professionals alike bring theory, research, and reflection to bear on their practice.

—*John A. Mueller, EdD, Professor, Department of Student Affairs in Higher Education, Indiana University of Pennsylvania*

22883 Quicksilver Drive
Sterling, VA 20166-2102

Subscribe to our e-mail alerts: www.Styluspub.com